Physical Health of Adults with Intellectual Disabilities

Physical Health of Adults with Intellectual Disabilities

Edited by

Vee P. Prasher

Monyhull Hospital, Kings Norton, Birmingham

and

Matthew P. Janicki

University of Illinois at Chicago

Blackwell
Publishing

© 2002 by Blackwell Publishing Ltd
Editorial Offices:
Osney Mead, Oxford OX2 0EL, UK
  Tel: +44 (0)1865 206206
108 Cowley Road, Oxford OX4 1JF, UK
  Tel: +44 (0)1865 791100
Blackwell Publishing USA, 350 Main Street,
Malden, MA 02148-5018, USA
Tel: +1 781 388 8250
Iowa State Press, a Blackwell Publishing Company,
2121 State Avenue, Ames, Iowa 50014-8300, USA
  Tel: +1 515 292 0140
Blackwell Munksgaard, Nørre Søgade 35, PO Box
2148, Copenhagen, DK-1016, Denmark
  Tel: +45 77 33 33 33
Blackwell Publishing Asia, 550 Swanston Street,
Carlton, Victoria 3053, Australia
  Tel: +61 (0)3 9347 0300
Blackwell Verlag, Kurfürstendamm 57,
10707 Berlin, Germany
  Tel: +49 (0)30 32 79 060
Blackwell Publishing, 10 rue Casimir Delavigne,
75006 Paris, France
  Tel: +33 1 53 10 33 10

First published 2002

A catalogue record for this title is available from the
British Library

ISBN 1-4051-0219-5

Library of Congress
Cataloging-in-Publication Data
Is available

Set in 10/13pt Palatino
by DP Photosetting
Printed and bound in Great Britain by
MPG Books, Bodmin, Cornwall

For further information on
Blackwell Publishing, visit our website:
www.blackwellpublishing.com

To
Dr Trevor Parmenter who, through his leadership of the IASSID and thoughtful
guidance to those of us with the World Health Organization, provided the impetus
for the development of this book
and
Suman, Monisha and Aaran, whose support and patience were very
much appreciated

Contents

Contributors

Louise Barnard BSc (Hons) Psychology
Research and Development Co-ordinator, Developmental Psychiatry Research Unit, School of Neurosciences and Psychiatry, University of Newcastle, Newcastle upon Tyne, UK

Helen Baxter MA, MSc
Research Fellow, Welsh Centre for Learning Disabilities, Meridian Court, Cardiff, Wales, UK

Helen Beange MB, BS, MPH, FAFPHM
Clinical Lecturer, Centre for Developmental Disability Studies, University of Sydney, NSW, Australia

Stephen Brown MA, MB, BChir, FRCPsych
Professor of Developmental Neuropsychiatry, Plymouth Postgraduate Medical School, Cornwall, UK

Matthew Janicki PhD
Associate Research Professor and Director for Technical Assistance, Department of Disability and Human Development, College of Health and Human Development Sciences, University of Illinois at Chicago, Illinois, USA

Gerard, J. Kerins MD, FACP
Assistant Professor of Medicine and Geriatrics, University of Connecticut Health Center on Aging, Farmington, Connecticut, USA

Michael Kerr MBChB, MSc, MRCGP, MRCPsych
Senior Lecturer in Neuropsychiatry, Welsh Centre for Learning Disabilities, Meridian Court, Cardiff, Wales, UK

Nicholas Lennox MBBS, BMedSc, DipObst, FRACGP
Associate Professor of Developmental Disability, Developmental Disability Unit, The University of Queensland, South Brisbane, Australia

Hans Malmstrom DDS
Associate Professor, Eastman Dental Center, University of Rochester, Rochester, New York, USA

Aidan McElduff MB, BS, PhD, FRACP
Clinical Associate Professor of Medicine, University of Sydney, Sydney, Australia

Dawna Torres Mughal PhD, RD, FADA
Director, Dietetics Program, Gannon University, Erie, Pennsylvania, USA

Gregory O'Brien MB, CLB, MA (Cantab), FRCPsych, FRCPCH, MD
Professor of Developmental Psychiatry, University of Northumbria, Northumberland, UK

Joanne Pearson BSc (Hons) Psychology
Research Assistant, Developmental Psychiatry Research Unit, School of Neurosciences and Psychiatry, University of Newcastle, Newcastle upon Tyne, UK

Vee Prasher MBChB, MMedSc, MRCPsych, MD, PhD
Associate Professor of Neuro-developmental Psychiatry, Monyhull Hospital, Kings Norton, Birmingham, UK

Clyde E. Rapp MD
Director of the Center for Adults with Developmental Disabilities, Albert Einstein Medical Center, Department of Pediatrics, Philadelphia, PA, USA

Yan-Fang Ren DDS, PhD
Instructor, Division of General Dentistry, Eastman Dental Center, University of Rochester, Rochester, New York, USA

Lisa Rippon MB, BS, MRCPsych
Consultant in Child and Adolescent Psychiatry and Learning Disability, Prudhoe Hospital, Northumberland, UK

Rosemeire R. Santos-Teachout DDS, MS
Assistant Professor, Developmentally Disabled Dental Clinic Coordinator, Eastman Department of Dentistry, University of Rochester, Rochester, New York, USA

Margarita Torres MD
Director, Eastern Regional Center for Adults with Spina Bifida, Moss Rehab, Albert Einstein Healthcare Network, Philadelphia, USA

Mette Warburg DMed Sci
Emer Adj. Professor of Genetic Ophthalmology, Centre for Handicaps, Glostrup Hospital, Copenhagen, Denmark

Sybil Yeates MRCS, LRCP, MBBS (Lon), FRCPCH
Retired Honorary Consultant in Paediatric Audiology, 185 Lawrie Park Gardens, London, UK

Series Foreword

Physical Health of Adults with Intellectual Disabilities is the second book in a series of publications associated with the International Association for the Scientific Study of Intellectual Disabilities (IASSID). These publications are designed to address the issue of health, adult development and aging among persons with intellectual disabilities. Originally, a foundational health policy initiative undertaken by the IASSID at the behest of the World Health Organization, this continuing inquiry into health issues undertaken by the members of IASSID, has grown into an international effort to explore a number of topics related to health and aging. It has also evolved into worldwide effort to promote research and practice designed to improve longevity and promote healthy aging of people with lifelong disabilities among the world's nations.

In this second book, the chapters have been contributed by a wide range of practitioners and researchers in the area of adult physical health and disability. Following a meeting and the development of a series of health policy reports for the World Health Organization (WHO), it was decided to pursue a text composed of in-depth explorations of a range of conditions affecting adults with intellectual disabilities as they mature and age. The editors have included a number of topics of most significance to understanding health problems and health promotion strategies. Using the information gathered in this book, it is anticipated that health practitioners, administrators and providers will become more aware of the developmental health issues faced by adults with disabilities and thus will be in a position to provide more effective and targeted services.

It is anticipated that as the IASSID, an international organization dedicated to research, continues to contribute to the worldwide interest and better understanding of the circumstances of people with intellectual disabilities and their conditions, this series will, in part, serve as a catalyst and contributor to the improvement of life conditions and our understanding of adult development and aging as related to lifelong disability.

Matthew P. Janicki, PhD
Series Editor
University of Illinois at Chicago
Department of Disability and Human Development
College of Health and Human Development Sciences
Chicago, Illinois, USA

Foreword

The publication of this book would have spurred no interest 30 or 40 years ago. Then, adults with moderate or severe intellectual disabilities were largely residents in government operated or supported institutions that provided medical care of varying quality. But times have changed. With the movement of such people into the community and with a larger percentage living in group homes, or with aging parents, or in independent housing, their lives have improved dramatically. But access to, and the quality of, health care are problematic.

Several factors are responsible for the current medical neglect of persons with intellectual disabilities in the community. The training of physicians, physician assistants and nurses as to the special needs of persons with intellectual disabilities is inadequate. Internists, surgeons, and to a lesser degree, family physicians have no exposure to this population's health needs during residency training. Time for examination is high and reimbursement is low, especially by government payment schemes. In many countries, local health authorities do not welcome such patients. The increased life span of adults with intellectual disabilities also increases the need for more medical services at a time when compliance with medical directions may be limited. In summary, there is more demand, less service.

Studies of longevity confirm the higher vulnerability of adults with intellectual disabilities, particularly those among the lower economic strata and those disengaged from formal services. There are also differences in risk linked to cultural or racial groupings. The need for continuity of care is great. The challenge is to balance the right for autonomy whilst living in the community with sound medical supervision when a life-threatening condition is present. Arguments abound for maintaining facilities for adults who are severely medically fragile, with community care for those with lesser degrees of disability.

In more structural systems of medical care such as those in the UK, Germany, Canada and elsewhere, quality care is more likely, providing there is adequate government interest.

However, all is not gloom and doom. As a result of the efforts of President John F. Kennedy and his sister, Eunice Shriver, in the US, a network has been established of university centers for research, technical assistance to states, model clinical care, and training programs for health care personnel – doctors, psychologists, nurses, social workers, physical and occupational therapists, and communication specialists and special education teachers.

Both editors of this book have labored successfully to increase professional and lay interest in adults with intellectual disabilities. This text is a culmination of their efforts. It describes in detail the physical complications which may coexist with mental disabilities. It is timely since in the US, the Surgeon General convened a conference concentrating on the gap in medical care for persons with intellectual disabilities as compared with the general population. The National Institutes of Health have also sponsored workshops in mental illness complicating intellectual disability (commonly referred to as 'dual diagnosis'). Although this volume does not address psychiatric disorders (this is covered in the companion volume, *Mental Health, Intellectual Disabilities, and the Aging Process* by Davidson, Prasher and Janicki), it is worth remembering that physical illness may appear in this population as a severe disturbance in behavior.

The format of this text moves the student from general problems that exist in persons with intellectual disabilities to specific conditions such as Prader Willi, cri-du-chat, fragile-X syndromes and many more. Physical complications are carefully documented in association with specific diagnoses.

The most recent attitudinal change in the care of persons with intellectual disabilities is described in the section on health promotion and prevention of secondary disabilities. Governments in a number of countries have instigated studies of these conditions. Obesity complicating intellectual disability is common, and problems in speech, hearing and vision abound. Dental care is abysmal. Yet, there are some bright spots; for example, the Healthy Athlete Program of Special Olympics, under the leadership of Timothy Shriver, is pioneering in health promotion in persons with intellectual disabilities.

This text will complement these efforts, with the final product a healthier, more fulfilling life for persons with intellectual disabilities.

Robert E. Cooke, MD
Scientific Advisor
Joseph P. Kennedy Jr, Foundation
Washington, DC
Former Pediatrician in Chief
Johns Hopkins Hospital

Preface

The area of intellectual disabilities has often been described as the Cinderella discipline of medicine. It would now appear that, as in the fairy tale, Cinderella has come to the ball, with politicians, professionals, carers, academics and indeed the general public taking notice of the conditions and needs of people with intellectual disabilities. However, although Cinderella is at the ball it remains to be determined whether Prince Charming will take her hand and lead her to the center of the dance floor. This book aims to enable Cinderella to take a few steps onto the dance floor by highlighting some of the more prevalent health conditions which affect, and identifying some of the effective health promotion strategies which can help, people with intellectual disabilities.

A number of books have been published focusing on the conditions affecting people with intellectual disabilities, but many have either focused specifically on psychiatric and psychological problems, or been focused generally on subgroups, such as individuals with Down syndrome, cerebral palsy or autism. This text specifically focuses on a wide range of physical health conditions which occur in adults with intellectual disabilities, and on their prevention or amelioration. Many other aspects affecting adults with intellectual disabilities, such as the developmental, educational, behavioral, psychological and social are not specifically discussed unless they are specifically associated with one or more of the physical disorders covered. In addition, because of limited space, discussions on recent advances, such as molecular genetics, are excluded. What is included are the conditions and diseases that may present to a practitioner or diagnostician as part of routine care.

This book is part of a series developed by the International Association on the Scientific Study of Intellectual Disabilities (IASSID) to give professionals and carers working with people with intellectual disabilities a more detailed and focused text on particular areas of concern that they may experience as part of their day-to-day work. A number of internationally recognized experts, from a wide variety of medical specialties and allied health disciplines, have come together to give the latest view on the commonest physical health conditions that occur in people with intellectual disabilities. Particular emphasis is given to the early diagnosis and management of such problems with a view to promoting good health in this population.

The editors are extremely grateful to our colleagues, made up of a group of internationally renowned physicians, researchers and scientists, who have contributed to this book with clarity and scholarly knowledge. The contributors to the book have been actively involved in academic and clinical work in the field of intellectual disabilities and have all published and/or conducted research in their respective areas. They provide an insight and personal experience and understanding of conditions that occur in people with intellectual disabilities that are not readily encountered by generic professionals. We acknowledge the breadth of information, knowledge and experience of the many countries that are represented in this text.

A comment on terminology adopted for this text. We have decided to use the term 'intellectual disabilities' throughout the text, while recognizing that the use of the term has not yet gained universal acceptance. Other terms are still being used in the world to connote what we (and IASSID) refer to as an intellectual disability. For example, although the term 'mental retardation' (while having gained a pejorative connotation) is still used in parts of the United States, 'learning disabilities' is in use in the United Kingdom (although it has a completely different meaning outside of the UK), and 'mental handicap' or 'intellectual handicap' (or variants) are in use in other nations, it is our belief that these terms are synonymous and generally understood to reflect the same condition. We also recognize that the term 'developmental disability' reflects a category of conditions, only one of which is an intellectual disability. Therefore, where our authors have specifically implied a broader application or usage, we have left this term in place.

Thus, with this book, we hope that with Cinderella having arrived at the ball, with tentative steps towards the dance floor, Prince Charming will take notice and enable Cinderella to experience the full ambience of the evening.

Vee Prasher
Matthew Janicki

Acknowledgement

Thanks to Dr Graham Martin from the UK who brought to our attention the paradigm of Cinderella.

1 Epidemiological Issues

Helen Beange

Introduction

Adults with intellectual disabilities are now more frequent consumers of health care because they are living longer and fewer are living in institutions. In most western societies institutions are closing and the former residents have become members of their community, sharing health services with other people. For instance, research in Australia in 1997 showed that only 7.9% of people with intellectual disabilities lived in establishments, the other 92% were in households (Wen, 1997). These people are no longer the responsibility of institutional staff, but are the responsibility of general health care providers. This has made their illnesses more visible and more of a worry: we do not know whether they are sicker or whether their ill-health was previously taken for granted. The gross inequality in health status between people with and without disabilities is now more obvious than in the past, and like inequality between the health of national groups, it is politically, socially and economically unacceptable (Cohen, 2001). This chapter discusses a number of issues relating to health morbidity and mortality in people with intellectual disabilities. Further areas of interest are highlighted.

Definition of intellectual disability (mental retardation)

In the tenth revision of the International Classification of Diseases (ICD-10; World Health Organization, 1992) intellectual disability (or mental retardation; F70-F79) is defined as 'a condition of arrested and incomplete development of the mind,' which is especially characterized by impairment of skills manifested during the development period, which contribute to the overall level of intelligence (i.e. cognitive, language, motor and social abilities). Intelligence tests and scales assessing social adaptation estimate degrees of intellectual disability. The codings are: mild (IQ 50–69), moderate (IQ 35–49), severe (IQ 20–34), profound (IQ less than 20), other and unspecified. Unfortunately, at present researchers use different definitions of intellectual disability; use of the above standardized classification would enhance the validity of future epidemiological studies.

Age-specific prevalence of intellectual disability

The overall prevalence of intellectual disabilities varies from country to country, and varies according to the prevailing definition. In developed countries it is usually accepted to be somewhere in the vicinity of 1%. A review of many international estimates found that whole population studies gave a prevalence rate of 1.25%, while agency records yielded prevalence rates of 0.3–0.4% (Mclaren & Bryson, 1987). Agency records are always likely to give lower prevalence rates than epidemiological surveys, as not all persons with disabilities receive services. In 1991, the estimated rate in the US was 1.1% (Fujiura & Yamaki, 1997). In 1993 the overall prevalence in Australia was estimated to be 0.99% (Wen, 1997). The prevalence of intellectual disabilities in China, which is a rapidly developing country, is said to be 1% (Sonnander & Claesson, 1997). Surveys in undeveloped countries usually find higher rates (Miles, 1997; Yacob *et al.*, 1995). Age specific prevalence will alter with time and place; as described by Fryers (1997), the highest prevalence was among the age group 25–29 years.

In early childhood the prevalence of severe intellectual disability is low, due to difficulties of recognition. During school age, recognition is at a high level and rates increase. In later life the prevalence of severe intellectual disabilities decreases due to the earlier death of those with the most profound problems and because the gap between administrative and real prevalence widens. In New Zealand in 1990 the prevalence of intellectual disabilities among all people aged 55 years and over was 0.14%, with wide regional variations (Hand, 1993). In Australia in 1993 the overall prevalence rate at 55 years and over was estimated to be 0.13%, similar to the estimate in New Zealand (Wen, 1997). In New York in 1982 the prevalence rate of those aged 53 years and over was 0.16% (Janicki & MacEachron, 1984). This was about 16% of the intellectual disabilities population, whereas 28% of the overall population was 53 and over. This reflects the relatively small proportion of aged people in the disabilities population.

Risk factors for ill-health

Genetic make-up and lifestyle are the major determinants of health risks. Risks vary according to residential environments, and according to the capacity of individuals to choose their own way of life. Residents of community homes will have more choice about food and sleep than residents of institutions. Individuals with a mild degree of intellectual disability are as able as the rest of us to eat junk food, smoke tobacco, drink alcohol and take no exercise. Individuals who are more dependent on the support of others may be unable to take these risks with their health but have their own problems due to relative inactivity, swallowing disorders and multiple medication. Three of the significant risk factors for ill-health are highlighted here: nutrition, lack of exercise and medication.

Nutrition

Nutrition is an outstanding risk for adults with intellectual disabilities. Numerous studies have reported a high prevalence of overweight and obesity, especially for community dwellers. In an Australian survey, 25% of community residents were obese compared to 8.5% of the local community (Stewart et al., 1994). Others have reported 56% of men and 73% of women to be obese or overweight (Bell & Bate, 1992). In the US, 27.5% of men and 58.5% of women were found to be obese compared to 19% and 28% respectively in the general community (Rimmer et al., 1994). Obesity is a special risk for adults with Down syndrome (Prasher, 1995) and Prader-Willi syndrome. Undernutrition is also prevalent (Simila & Niskanen, 1991) especially in institutions, and may be a cause of mortality unless artificial feeding is instituted. Dysphagia, or difficulty in swallowing, can result in choking which is a leading cause of death (Dupont & Mortenson, 1990). The use of percutaneous endoscopic gastrostomies (PEGS) is increasing and may decrease the prevalence of malnutrition. Pica, or the ingestion of non-food substances, occurs with reported prevalence between 9% and 25% in institutionalized populations, 0.3% to 14% in the community (Ali, 2001). The significance of pica is still largely unknown although it is theorized that it may be associated with mineral deficiencies. See Chapter 10 for further nutritional issues.

Lack of exercise

Inactivity is common, ranging from the immobility of adults with spastic quadriplegia to adults who are mobile but are either unable or disinclined to exercise. Adults with intellectual disabilities are often prevented from exercising because of staffing, financial and transport barriers to the practice of exercise (Pitetti et al., 1993). The resulting inactivity is a risk for cardiovascular and other diseases, and prevents the attainment of well-being. There is evidence that exercise has beneficial effects on mental health, including reduction of hostility, anger and depression. When lack of exercise is combined with unemployment there is likely to be apathy and boredom, also contributing to mental ill-health and behavioral disorder. There has been great neglect of exercise provision in programs for community residents, but there are a few published studies of successful programs and these models could be replicated (Pitetti & Tan, 1991). Rehabilitation therapy for adults with cerebral palsy and other movement disorders is effective in reducing immobility and dependence and for increasing well-being.

Medication

Polypharmacy is common both in institutional and community care (Beange *et al.*, 1995; Reiss & Aman, 1997). People with disabilities have been referred to as 'helpless drug receivers'. However, many individuals need daily medications because of the high prevalence of epilepsy, psychiatric disorders and other serious disease. Movement disorders such as akathisia and dystonia and the potentially fatal condition, neuroleptic malignant syndrome, are occasional consequences of psychotropic medications which are frequently prescribed inappropriately to control behavior (Stone *et al.*, 1989). There is an increased risk of side effects because of inadequate medication review and the need to rely on third party reports. Authors have urged that structured mechanisms should be used to monitor efficacy and recognize adverse effects, such as a tendency to fall (Einfeld, 1990).

Prevalence of health problems

Studies have found a high prevalence of health problems in this population, whether in institutional or community care (Kapell *et al.*, 2000; Maaskant & Haveman, 1990; Minihan, 1990; Nelson & Crocker, 1978; Wilson & Haire, 1990; Van Schrojenstein Lantman-de Valk *et al.*, 2000). An Australian epidemiological population study in Northern Sydney found significantly increased risk factors, increased rates of medical consultation, and hospitalization greater than in the general population. The 202 randomly selected individuals had an average of 5.4 medical disorders, only half of which had previously been detected (Beange *et al.*, 1995). In New Zealand a population health screen found that of 1311 people screened, 72% required health-related actions (Webb & Rogers, 1999). The wide range of health needs in people with intellectual disabilities suggest that professional training and access to health services need to be increased (Turner & Moss, 1996). The increased prevalence and unmet health needs suggest that health care screening is necessary. In spite of this evidence, systematic health screening is rarely instituted as a national health policy.

Age distribution of health problems

The health problems of young and middle-aged persons with intellectual disabilities differ from those of the aged. The health problems of older individuals are similar to those of the general population, whereas those of the younger cohorts are dissimilar. The reason for this anomaly lies in the differential mortality among groups of individuals with intellectual disabilities, according to the case mix and the degree of intellectual disability, with the more severely affected and those with Down syndrome tending to die at a younger age. Many surveys have demonstrated that older groups function at a higher level than younger groups (Bigby, 1994; Janicki & Dalton, 2000; Moss, 1991). As individuals with severe intellectual disabilities have a diminished life expectancy compared to those with mild intellectual disabilities, there will be a healthy survivor effect. In addition, Down syndrome is more prevalent in older groups due to a lower life expectancy (Janicki & Dalton, 2000).

In younger populations the mix of health problems is unlike that in the general population, with an increased risk of epilepsy, sensory disorders, nutrition problems and gastrointestinal disease. The prevalence of epilepsy and cerebral palsy is higher in the young than the old, while the youngest age groups are more likely to have cardiac disorders, including congenital heart disease (Van Schrojenstein Lantman-de Valk et al., 2000). In a further study, younger people with intellectual disabilities were found to have significantly more dermatological disorders, neurological problems, ear nose and throat disorders and congenital heart disease than older individuals (Cooper, 1998).

Among older adults with intellectual disabilities, the range of medical disorders is the same as in the general population but the disorders differ in relative frequency (Evenhuis, 1997; Janicki et al., 2002; Van Schrojenstein Lantman-de Valk et al., 1997). Impaired mobility, respiratory problems, arthritis and heart disease are common. Dementia increases with age. A study in the UK found that older people with intellectual disabilities had significant health needs, with higher rates of urinary incontinence, immobility, deafness, arthritis, hypertension and cardiovascular disease found among the older groups (Cooper, 1998). In New York Kapell et al. (2000) found by screening 278 older adults with and without Down syndrome that compared to the general population there was an increased frequency of thyroid disorders, non-ischemic heart disorders and sensory impairment.

Sex distribution of health problems

Males die younger than females, although the differential manifests itself 25 years later than in the general population (Patja *et al.*, 2000). Adult males in Denmark had an excess mortality of malignant neoplasms, diseases of respiratory system, congenital malformations and accidents (Dupont & Mortenson, 1990). Male fertility is almost certainly limited, especially in Down syndrome where only one case of paternity has been verified (Zuhlke *et al.*, 1994). Cryptorchidism is common in males who have Down syndrome and other chromosomal abnormalities (Cortes *et al.*, 1999) and this gives a fourfold risk of testicular cancer. Hypogonadism, which is increased in males, is a cause of osteoporosis (Center *et al.*, 1998). Males are sometimes the victims of sexual abuse (Sullivan *et al.*, 1991).

Females need help with gynecological care, especially menstrual disorders (Wingfield *et al.*, 1994). They are less likely to reproduce than the general population and therefore have fewer medical disorders of the reproductive tract (Beange *et al.*, 1995; Trumble, 1999). Primary and secondary amenorrhoea are increased in frequency and need treatment. Prolactin elevation associated with the use of phenothiazines is one cause of amenorrhea and should lead to investigation to exclude pituitary adenomas. Fertility control is an issue for females, and many have been victims of sexual abuse (Chamberlain *et al.*, 1984). Menstrual suppression by the use of continuous or injectable progestogens, or oral contraceptives, is frequently practiced, but should only be used 'when less restrictive options have been tried and failed' (Palmer 1999). Endocrinological issues are further discussed in Chapter 8.

Distribution of health problems according to level of intelligence

Studies have consistently found a relationship between degree of intellectual disability and ill-health. In the Australian study, the more severely disabled had significantly more medical disorders than the mildly disabled (Beange *et al.*, 1995). In a survey of general practices in Holland, 318 persons were compared to those in the general population. People with severe intellectual disabilities had 2.7 times more health problems than people without intellectual disabilities. People with mild intellectual disabilities had 2.2 times more problems. People with severe intellectual disabilities had more congenital disorders, epilepsy and visual problems, and persons with mild intellectual disabilities had a higher prevalence of deafness, obesity, fractures and skin problems than the general population (Van Schrojenstein Lantman-de Valk, *et al.* 1997).

Mortality

Improvement in public health has resulted in improved life expectancy for people with intellectual disabilities, but it is still less than that of the general population. A California study showed that the life expectancy at one year of age for people with mild to moderate intellectual disabilities is about 65 years, while for those with Down syndrome it is about 55 years (Strauss & Eyman, 1996). A Finnish study of life expectancy among people with intellectual disabilities showed that those persons with mild intellectual disabilities shared a similar life expectancy with the general population, while few of the people with profound intellectual disabilities reached old age. Severe and moderate intellectual disabilities also had increased mortality (Patja *et al.*, 2000). A London study showed that age and sex-adjusted mortality rates were from 9.6 to 18 times higher than in the general population (Hollins *et al.*, 1998). An analysis in Northern Sydney found similar results, with standardized mortality rates almost five times that of the local population (Durvasula *et al.*, in press). Respiratory disease, often associated with dysphagia and aspiration, is the commonest cause of death (Richards & Siddiqui, 1980). Other common causes are cardiovascular disease, external causes and cancer (Durvasula *et al.*, in press; Janicki *et al.*, 1999). Predictors of mortality are non-ambulation, lack of feeding skills, regression in toilet training, severe ID and major medical problems (Hayden, 1998). Another California study found increased mortality in 2000 persons moved from institutional to community care (Shavelle & Strauss, 1999).

Morbidity

Morbidity is defined as the ratio of sick to well persons in a community. This is an important element in staffing ratios, manpower planning and cost-benefit analysis. However, there is surprisingly little research available. The Sydney population study found that of 200 randomly selected adults, almost twice as many had been hospitalized in the previous twelve months as in the local population (Beange *et al.*, 1995). Compared to the local population almost twice as many (30% v. 17%) had consulted a doctor in the previous two weeks. In the US, health care expenditure and hospitalization rates are increased among those adults with severe intellectual disabilities (Birenbaum *et al.*, 1990).

In the late 1990s, the Health Issues Special Interest Research Group (Health SIRG) of the International Association for the Scientific Study of Intellectual Disability (IASSID) prepared a list of health guidelines for adults with intellectual disabilities, and these have been incorporated by the World Health Organization (see Appendix at the end of this book). The guidelines, written by experts in a variety of fields, were adopted by the IASSID after an extensive process of consultation and were originally published as a series of health targets (Beange *et al.*, 1999). The guidelines were developed because reliable surveys had shown that certain conditions were prevalent, easily detected and amenable to readily available treatments. The epidemiology of these (and several other) conditions will be described below. Specific detailed information on these conditions is also provided in several other chapters in this book.

Individual health problems

Dental health

Oral health problems were the most frequent health problem cited in the Australian survey, occurring in 86% of the 202 subjects. Scott *et al.* (1989) found that various types of dental disease were up to seven times as frequent as in the comparable general population. Dentists providing community dental care have often documented an operating loss (i.e. lack of full payment for time spent providing dental services), and have noted that one of the barriers to good dental care is the lack of subsidized clinics (Gotowka *et al.*, 1982). Oral health in people with intellectual disabilities is further discussed in Chapter 9.

Sensory problems

A screening of hearing and visual function in 672 Dutch institutionalized people found an 'alarmingly high' prevalence of combined sensory impairment and considerably increased prevalence as compared with the general population (Evenhuis *et al.*, 2001). Many studies have shown the high frequency of visual impairment among adults with disabilities (Cathels & Reddihough, 1993; McCulloch *et al.*, 1996; Wilson & Haire, 1990). Warburg (2001) described the prevalence of visual impairment and blindness in adults with intellectual disabilities as alarming. She estimated that 50% of people with severe intellectual disabilities (intelligence quotient below 50) have visual impairment, and found that noncorrectable visual impairment was present in 10% of adults, seven times more frequent than the general population (Warburg, 1994). Visual disorder increases with age and may not be detected. An international consensus statement has recommended routine screening for age-related visual loss (Evenhuis & Nagtzaam, 1998). Chapter 5 reviews visual impairment in detail.

Hearing loss is prevalent in all age groups but increases with aging. Hearing impairment was present in 25% of the Sydney sample compared to 2% of the local population. It is often unrecognized and if recognized poorly managed (Wilson & Haire, 1990). In the Netherlands, people with mild intellectual disabilities had an almost four times higher risk of deafness than the general population (Van Schrojenstein Lantman-de Valk et al., 2000). See Chapter 6 for a full review of hearing impairment.

Epilepsy

Epilepsy is experienced by many people with intellectual disabilities, with prevalence between 20% and 30% (Coulter, 1993; Wilson & Haire, 1990). Significant mortality and morbidity risks are associated with epilepsy. The standardized mortality ratio (ratio of observed deaths to expected deaths) is increased as high as five for adults with intellectual disabilities with epilepsy (Bowley & Kerr, 2000), and epilepsy is associated with increased risk for sudden unexpected death (McKee & Bodfish, 2000). Morbidity is increased due to fractures and soft tissue injury, hospital admissions and the impact on learning, which may increase intellectual disability. Additional strain and burden have been documented in carers of epileptics (Wilson, 1998). Epilepsy and its association with intellectual disabilities is discussed further in Chapter 7.

Thyroid disease

Thyroid disease is important both as a cause and a complication of intellectual disability. In the population study in Sydney, thyroid disease occurred with a frequency of 12% compared to the self-reported rate in the population of 0.1% (Beange et al., 1995). Hyperthyroidism may be a cause of behavior disorder. Hypothyroidism is difficult to diagnose and should be screened for on any unusual presentation. Regular screenings should be conducted with adults with Down syndrome and other syndromes at risk (such as Turner's syndrome and congenital rubella). For further information see Chapter 8.

Gastroesophageal reflux disease

Gastroesophageal reflux disease (GERD) is increased in prevalence among adults with intellectual disabilities and is a possible cause of challenging behavior. Unfortunately diagnosis is difficult, because it usually depends upon the patient presenting with typical symptoms such as heartburn, epigastric pain, regurgitation and painful swallowing. Most adults with intellectual disabilities find it difficult to articulate these complaints. As pain may be so severe as to resemble angina, it is not surprising that challenging behavior occurs. A large survey in the Netherlands found that reflux disease was present in 50% of institutionalized individuals (Bohmer *et al.*, 2000). Possible predisposing factors included scoliosis, cerebral palsy, use of anticonvulsant drugs and an intelligence quotient below 35. Symptoms indicating reflux in individuals with intellectual disabilities are vomiting, hematemesis and rumination. Alarm symptoms are dysphagia, nocturnal cough or choking. Complications include ulcerative esophagitis leading to bleeding and anemia, stricture of the esophagus and Barret's esophagus. Barrett's esophagus is a consequence of longstanding and severe reflux, and has the potential to develop into esophageal cancer. Treatment of gastroesophageal reflux disease should be the same as for the general population and usually involves long-term use of proton pump inhibitors.

Helicobacter pylori

Helicobacter pylori infection is often prevalent in institutionalized populations of adults with intellectual disabilities (Harris *et al.*, 1995; Proujansky *et al.*, 1994). Studies have reported much higher rates of infection (60–90%) compared to matched groups in the general population (30–40%). H. pylori causes gastritis in 100%, peptic ulcer in 6–20%, and gastric cancer in about 1% of those adults who are chronically infected (Howden, 1996). H. pylori may be instrumental in increased institutional mortality rates from stomach cancer and perforated ulcers (Duff *et al.*, 2001). It is not known to what extent community dwelling adults are infected but it is likely that those discharged from institutions are at risk. It has been shown in the Netherlands that institutional employees in close physical contact with residents, and those who have worked longer than five years at an institution, are at increased risk of infection (Bohmer *et al.*, 1997). This important public health problem needs further evaluation. In the meantime individuals infected should have eradication therapy with the same indications as for the general population.

Constipation

Constipation has always been common in institutions. A recent Dutch survey found that 69% of 215 cases showed constipation. This was significantly associated with cerebral palsy, medication usage, food refusal and an intelligence quotient below 35 (Bohmer *et al.*, 2001). Constipation causes physical and behavioral difficulties and may be a cause of death (Jancar & Speller, 1994). Because of risk factors, it merits vigorous treatment.

Osteoporosis and fractures

Osteoporosis and osteomalacia are both increased in the population with intellectual disabilities. An unselected population study in Australia demonstrated that 94 community living adults had a lower bone mineral density than an age-matched reference population. Factors associated were small body size, hypogonadism and Down syndrome (Center *et al.*, 1998). Osteomalacia is the result of vitamin D deficiency. It is common where there is inadequate exposure to sunlight and prolonged use of anticonvulsant medication (Tohill, 1997; Wagermans *et al.*, 1998). There is a significant relationship with age, epilepsy and the occurrence of fractures (Jancar & Jancar, 1998; Lee *et al.*, 1989; Spreat & Baker Potts, 1983). Subgroups of people are at increased risk of fracture and should be screened for osteoporosis (Tohill, 1997). For more information, see Chapter 8.

Genetic disease

It is generally agreed that 40–50% of cases of intellectual disability are due to genetic disease, 15–20% are due to environmental factors and 30–45% are unknown (Raynham *et al.*, 1996). A significant proportion of the latter are also suspected to be genetic (Partington *et al.*, 2000). New genetic knowledge is constantly becoming available, therefore every effort should be made to reach diagnosis, even in adults (Van Gelderen, 1992). It is recommended that every patient without an etiological diagnosis be referred to a genetic clinic regardless of age. This will enable the prognosis and complications of the condition to be known, and will allow informed management (Beange *et al.*, 1999).

Cerebral palsy

Cerebral palsy is associated with intellectual disability in about 50% of cases. There is no reliable data to quote about the prevalence of cerebral palsy in intellectual disability, but experienced clinicians are aware that it is very frequent. Cerebral palsy occurs in about two per 1000 live births, while severe intellectual disability is present in about four per 1000 children, according to most surveys (Mclaren & Bryson, 1987). A survey in Victoria found that of 66 young adults with cerebral palsy, 14 had intellectual disabilities and almost all (97%) had ongoing health problems (Cathels & Reddihough, 1993). See Chapter 4.

Cancer

A recent Finnish review found cancer incidence comparable to the general population in spite of low smoking levels (Patja *et al.*, 2001). The distribution of cancer is different to that in the general population with a high proportion of cancers which affect the intestinal tract, and fewer which affect the lungs, breast and prostate (Cooke, 1997; Jancar, 1990). Jancar (1990) pointed out that 13% of the deaths over a 10-year period were caused by breast cancer, while there were no deaths from cancer of the cervix. Breast cancer screening is more important in this population than screening for cervical cancer, but is often neglected (Davies & Duff, 2001). Cancer of the male reproductive organs has been found to be frequent, especially among men with Down syndrome (Braun *et al.*, 1985; Dexeus *et al.*, 1988). Leukemia is increased in the Down syndrome population (Scholl *et al.*, 1982).

Accidents, falls and fractures

Dupont & Mortenson (1990) in a Danish study reported an excess mortality from accidents with a standardized mortality ratio of 3.73 among persons with severe intellectual disabilities. Drowning had a standardized mortality ratio of 29, falls six. In a Chicago (US) study, Hsieh *et al.* (2001) noted that 11% of nursing home residents with intellectual disabilities had injuries, 50% of which were caused by falls. Significant risk factors were seizures, age above 70 years and destructive behavior. Tannenbaum *et al.* (1989) found a higher rate of fracture among intellectual disability residents of intermediate care facilities than in the general population. A survey of fractures in an institution for persons with intellectual disabilities found that the majority of fractures occurred in the colder months, and that impaired mobility and use of three anti-convulsants (phenytoin, carbamazepine and phenobarbitone) were significant associations (Tohill, 1997). Movement disorders, which sometimes result from neuroleptic medications, and oversedation, increased the propensity to fall. An Australian population study of injury in young people found high annual injury rates, with age standardized mortality ratio of eight and morbidity ratio of two (Sherrard *et al.*, 2001). From this evidence there is a case for injury prevention programs in populations with disabilities.

Infectious diseases

Hepatitis B and hepatitis A are known to be increased in institutions (Devuyst & Maesen-Collard, 1991; Vellinga *et al.*, 1999). Helicobacter pylori is increased in institutions (see above). In the past, parasite infestation was common in institutions. The likelihood of transmission of infectious disease is increased by overcrowding and insanitary conditions.

Behavior

The extent to which behavior disorder functions as a surrogate for symptoms of ill-health in adults with intellectual disabilities is unknown, although some studies are beginning to show an association between these factors (e.g., Davidson *et al.*, in press). We do know that this population is distinguished above all populations by the frequency of behavior disorder (often termed 'challenging behavior'). There is no doubt that some of this behavior is due to constitutional factors and may represent a nervous system not robust enough to adapt to life changes. Much behavior can be attributable to environmental stresses and the result of poor living conditions, lack of occupation and lack of intimacy. However, given the poor communication skills of people with intellectual disabilities, and the fact that medical diagnosis depends heavily on an accurate history of events, it is probable that many illnesses and causes of pain go undetected. Physical complaints should always be considered as a cause of change in behavior.

Conclusion

People with intellectual disabilities have increased death rates, they are hospitalized more frequently and they consult doctors more often. They are more likely to be blind, deaf, malnourished, in wheelchairs, having fits and suffering untreated pain than others in society. Although these facts have been known for some time, adults with intellectual disabilities still generally have less access to health care than adults in the general population. This situation has not been affected for the better when caring professionals who might have been expected to demand better health care for their charges have instead focused their attention on altering community medical care delivery practices through minimizing a focus on the 'the medical model', and insisting that generic health services are sufficient. Given what we are now learning about the health status of adults with intellectual disabilities and their often minimal health care, it is obvious that there is a need for improvement in planning and organizing health services for this group. If we are successfully to cope with the growing numbers of older adults with lifelong disabilities, then better and more equitable health service delivery is needed. At minimum, the following should be part of any community's health services delivery structure:

- More surveillance and early intervention
- Well person checklists
- Mental health screening
- Screening for the most common physical disorders
- Regular physical examination
- Local generalists supported by regional specialists
- Multidisciplinary teams
- Improved training of health workforce
- Collaboration between health and accommodation service providers.

References

Ali, Z. (2001) Pica in people with intellectual disability: a literature review of etiology epidemiology and complications. *Journal of Intellectual & Developmental Disability*, **26**, 205–217.

Beange, H., McElduff, M.B. & Baker, W. (1995) Medical disorders in adults with intellectual disability: a population study. *American Journal on Mental Retardation*, **99**, 595–604.

Beange, H., Lennox, N. & Parmenter, T.R. (1999) Health targets for people with an intellectual disability. *Journal of Intellectual & Developmental Disability*, **24**, 283–297.

Bell, B. & Bate, M. (1992) Prevalence of overweight and obesity in Downs syndrome and other mentally handicapped adults living in the community. *Journal of Intellectual Disability Research,* **36**, 359–364.

Bigby, C. (1994) A demographic analysis of older people with intellectual disability registered with community services Victoria. *Australia and New Zealand Journal of Developmental Disabilities*, **19**, 1–10.

Birenbaum, A., Guyot, D., Cohen, H.J. (1990) Health care financing for severe developmental disabilities. *Monograph of the American Association on Mental Retardation*, **14**, 1–150.

Bohmer, C.J.M., Klinkenberg-Knoll, E.C., Niezen de Boer, M.C., Schreuder, H., Schucink-Kool, F. & Meuwissen, S.G.M. (1997) The prevalence of Helicobacter Pylori infection among inhabitants and healthy employees of institutes for the intellectually disabled. *American Journal of Gastroenterology*, **92**, 1000–1004.

Bohmer, C.J., Klinkenberg-Knol, E.C., Niezen-de-Boer, M.C. & Meuwissen, S.G. (2000) Gastroesophageal reflux disease in intellectually disabled individuals: how often, how serious, how manageable? *American Journal of Gastroenterology*, **95**, 1868–1872.

Bohmer, C.J., Taminidu, J.A., Klinkenberg-Knol, E.C. & Meuwissen, S.G.M. (2001) The prevalence of constipation in institutionalized people with intellectual disability. *Journal of Intellectual Disability Research*, **45**, 212–218.

Bowley, C. & Kerr, M. (2000) Epilepsy and intellectual disability. *Journal of Intellectual Disability Research*, **44**, 529–543.

Braun, D., Green, M., Rausen, A., David, R., Wolman, S., Alba Greco, M. & Muggie F (1985) Downs syndrome and testicular cancer: a possible association. *American Journal of Paediatric Haematology and Oncology*, **7**, 208–211.

Cathels, B.A. & Reddihough, D.S. (1993) The health care of young adults with cerebral palsy. *The Medical Journal of Australia*, **15**, 444–446.

Center, J., Beange, H. & McElduff, A. (1998) People with mental retardation have an increased prevalence of osteoporosis: a population study. *American Journal of Mental Retardation*, **103**, 19–28.

Chamberlain, A., Rauh, J., Passer, A., McGrath, M. & Burket, R. (1984) Issues in fertility control for mentally retarded female adolescents: I. Sexual activity, sexual abuse, and contraception. *Pediatrics*, **73**, 445–450.

Cohen, J. (2001) Countries' health performance. *The Lancet*, **358**, 929.

Cooke, L.B. (1997) Cancer and learning disability. *Journal of Intellectual Disability Research*, **41**, 312–316.

Cooper, S.A. (1998) Clinical study of the effects of age on the physical health of adults with mental retardation. *American Journal on Mental Retardation*, **102**, 582–589.

Cortes, D.V.J., Moller, H. & Thorup, J. (1999) Testicular neoplasia in cryptorchid boys at primary surgery: case series. *British Medical Journal*, **319**, 889.

Coulter, D.L. (1993) Epilepsy and mental retardation: An overview. *American Journal of Mental Retardation*, (Supplement), **98**, 1–11.

Davidson, P.W., Janicki, M.P., Ladrigan, P., Houser, K., Henderson, C.M. & Cain, N.N. (in press) Associations between behavior problems and health status in older adults with intellectual disability. *Aging and Mental Health.*

Davies, N. & Duff, M. (2001) Breast cancer screening for older women with intellectual disability living in community group homes. *Journal of Intellectual Disability Research*, **45**, 253–257.

Devuyst, O. & Maesen-Collard, Y. (1991) Hepatitis B in a Belgian institution for mentally retarded patients: an epidemiological study. *Acta Gastroenterologica*, **54**, 12–18.

Dexeus, F., Logothetis, C., Chong, C., Sella, A. & Ogden, S. (1988) Genetic abnormalities in men with germ cell tumours. *Journal of Urology*, **140**, 80–84.

Duff, M., Scheepers, M., Cooper, M. & Hoghton, M. & Baddeley, P. (2001) Helicobacter pylori: Has the killer escaped from the institution? A possible cause of increased stomach cancer in a population with intellectual disability. *Journal of Intellectual Disability Research*, **45**, 219–225.

Dupont, A. & Mortenson, P.B. (1990) Avoidable death in a cohort of severely mentally retarded. In: *Key Issues in Mental Retardation Research* (ed. W.I. Fraser) 1st edn., pp. 28–34. Routledge, London.

Durvasula, S., Beange, H. & Baker, W. (in press) Mortality of people with intellectual disability in Northern Sydney. *Journal of Intellectual and Developmental Disability*.

Einfeld, S.L. (1990) Guidelines for use of psychotropic medication in individuals with developmental disability. *Australia and New Zealand Journal of Developmental Disability*, **16**, 1.

Evenhuis, H. M. (1997) Medical aspects of ageing in a population with intellectual disability: III. Mobility, internal conditions and cancer. *Journal of Intellectual Disability Research*, **41**, 8–18.

Evenhuis, H. & Nagtzaam L.M.D. (eds) (1998) IASSID International Consensus Statement. *Early identification of hearing and visual impairment in children and adults with an intellectual disability*. IASSID, Special Interest Research Group on Health Issues. Available at www.iassid.org

Evenhuis, H.M., Theunissen, M., Denkers, I., Verschuure, H. & Kemme, H. (2001) Prevalence of visual and hearing impairment in a Dutch institutionalized population with intellectual disability. *Journal of Intellectual Deficiency Research*, **45**, 457–464.

Fryers, T. (1997) Epidemiology in relation to community and residential services. *Current Opinion in Psychiatry*, **10**, 349–353.

Fujiura, G.T. & Yamaki, K. (1997) Analysis of ethnic variations in developmental disability prevalence and household economic status. *Mental Retardation*, **35**, 286–294.

Gotowka, T.D., Johnson, E.S. & Gotowka, C.J. (1982) Costs of providing dental services to adult mentally retarded: a preliminary report. *American Journal of Public Health*, **72**, 1246–1250.

Hand, J.E. (1993) Summary of national survey of older people with mental retardation in New Zealand. *Mental Retardation*, **31**, 424–428.

Harris, A., Douds, A., Meurisse, A., Dennis, M., Chambers, S. & Gould, S. (1995) Seroprevalence of Helicobacter pylori in residents of a hospital for people with severe learning difficulties. *European Journal of Gastroenterology & Hepatology*, **7**, 21–23.

Hayden, M.F. (1998) Mortality among people with mental retardation living in the United States: Research review and policy application. *Mental Retardation*, **36**, 345–349.

Hollins, S., Attard, M.T., von Fraunhofer, N., McGuigan, S. & Sedgwick, P.

(1998) Mortality in people with learning disability: risks, causes and death certification findings in London. *Developmental Medicine and Child Neurology*, **40**, 50–56.

Howden, C.W. (1996) Clinical expressions of Helicobacter pylori infection. *American Journal of Medicine*, **100**, 27S–32S.

Hsieh, K., Heller, T. & Miller, A.B. (2001) Risk factors for injuries and falls among adults with developmental disabilities. *Journal of Intellectual Disability Research*, **45**, 76–82.

Jancar, J. (1990) Cancer and mental handicap. A further study. *British Journal Psychiatry*, **156**, 531–533.

Jancar, J. & Jancar M.P (1998). Age-related fractures in people with intellectual disability and epilepsy. *Journal of Intellectual Disability Research,* **42**, 439–433.

Jancar, J. & Speller, C.J. (1994). Fatal intestinal obstruction in the mentally handicapped. *Journal of Intellectual Disability Research*, **38**, 413–422.

Janicki, M.P. & MacEachron A.E (1984) Residential, health and social service needs of elderly developmentally disabled persons. *The Gerontologist*, **24**, 128–137.

Janicki, M.P. & Dalton A.J. (2000) Prevalence of dementia and impact on intellectual disability services. *Mental Retardation*, **38**, 276–288.

Janicki, M.P., Dalton, A.J., Henderson, C.M. & Davidson, P.W. (1999) Mortality and morbidity among older adults with intellectual disability: Health services considerations. Disability and Rehabilitation, **21**, 284–294.

Janicki, M.P., Henderson, C.M., Davidson, P.W., McCallion, P., Taets, J.D., Force, L., Sulkes, S.B., Frangenberg, E. & Ladrigan, P.M. (2002) Health characteristics and health services utilization in older adults with intellectual disabilities living in community residences. *Journal of Intellectual Disabilities Research*, **46**, 287–298.

Kapell, D., Nightingale B, Rodriguez A., Lee, J.H., Zigman, W.B. & Schupf, N. (2000) Prevalence of chronic medical conditions in adults with mental retardation: comparison with the general population. *Mental Retardation*, **36**, 269–279.

Lee, J., Lyne, D., Kleerekoper, M., Logan, M. & Belfi, R.A. (1989) Disorders of bone metabolism in severely handicapped children and adults. *Clinical Orthopaedics and Related Research*, **245**, 297–302.

Maaskant, M.A. & Haveman, M.J. (1990) Elderly residents in Dutch mental deficiency institutions. *Journal of Mental Deficiency Research*, **34**, 475–482.

McCulloch, D.L., Sludden, P.A., McKeon, K. & Kerr, A. (1996) Vision care requirements among intellectually disabled adults. *Journal of Intellectual Disability Research*, **40**, 140–150.

McKee, J.R. & Bodfish, J.W. (2000) Sudden unexpected death in epilepsy in adults with mental retardation. *American Journal on Mental Retardation*, **105**, 229–235.

Mclaren, J. & Bryson, S.E. (1987) Review of recent epidemiological studies of mental retardation: prevalence, associated disorders, and etiology. *American Journal on Mental Retardation*, **92**, 243–254.

Miles, M. (1997) Mental retardation and service development. *Behinderung und Dritte Welt*, **8**, 25–32.

Minihan, P.M. (1990) Meeting the needs for health services of persons with mental retardation living in the community. *American Journal of Public Health*, **80**, 1043–1048.

Moss, S. (1991) Age and functional abilities of people with a mental handicap: evidence from the Wessex Mental Handicap Register. *Journal of Mental Deficiency Research*, **35**, 430–445.

Nelson, R.P. & Crocker, A.C. (1978) The medical care of mentally retarded persons in public residential facilities. *The New England Journal of Medicine*, **299**, 1039–1044.

Palmer, D. (1999) Women's Health Issues. In: *Management guidelines: people with developmental and intellectual disabilities* (eds N. Lennox & J. Diggens) 1st edn, pp. 151–165. Therapeutic Guidelines Ltd, Melbourne.

Partington, M.W., Mowat, D., Einfeld, S., Tonge, B. & Turner, G. (2000) Genes on the X chromosome are important in undiagnosed mental retardation. *American Journal of Medical Genetics*, **14**, 9–14.

Patja, K., Ivanainen, M., Vesala, H., Oksanen, H. & Ruoppila, I. (2000) Life expectancy of people with intellectual disability: a 35-year follow-up study. *Journal of Intellectual Disability Research*, **44**, 591–599.

Patja, K., Eero, P. & Iivanainen, M. (2001) Cancer incidence among people with intellectual disability. *Journal of Intellectual Disability Research*, **45**, 300–307.

Pitetti, K.H. & Tan, D. (1991) Effects of a minimally supervised exercise program for mentally retarded adults. *Medicine and Science in Sports and Exercise*, **23**, 594–601.

Pitetti, K.H., Rimmer, J.H. & Fernhall, B. (1993) Physical fitness and adults with mental retardation. An overview of current research and future directions. *Sports Medicine*, **16**, 23–56.

Prasher, V.P. (1995) Overweight and obesity amongst Down syndrome adults. *Journal of Intellectual Disability Research*, **39**, 437–441.

Proujansky, R., Shaffer, S., Vinton, N. & Buchrach, S. (1994) Helicobacter pylori infection in young patients with severe neurological impairment. *Journal of Paediatrics*, **125**, 750–752.

Raynham, H., Gibbons, R., Flint, J. & Higgs, D. (1996) The genetic basis of mental retardation. *QJM: Monthly Journal of the Association of Physicians*, **89**, 169–173.

Reiss, S. & Aman, M.G. (1997) The international consensus process on psychopharmacology and intellectual disability. *Journal of Intellectual Disability Research*, **41**, 445–448.

Richards, B.W. & Siddiqui, A.Q. (1980) Age and mortality trends in residents of an institution for the mentally handicapped. *Journal of Mental Deficiency Research*, **24**, 99–105.

Rimmer, J.H., Braddock, D. & Fujiura, G. (1994) Cardiovascular risk factor levels in adults with mental retardation. *American Journal on Mental Retardation*, **98**, 510–518.

Scholl, T., Stein, Z. & Hansen, H. (1982) Leukaemia and other cancers, anomalies and infections as causes of death in Down syndrome in the United States in 1976. *Developmental Medicine and Child Neurology*, **24**, 817–829.

Scott, A., Marsh, L. & Stokes, M.L. (1989) A survey of oral health in a population of adults with developmental disability: comparison with a national oral health survey of the general population. *Australian Dental Journal*, **43**, 257–261.

Shavelle, R. & Strauss, D. (1999) Mortality of persons with developmental disabilities after transfer into community care:a 1996 update. *American Journal on Mental Retardation*, **104**, 143–147.

Sherrard, J., Tonge, B.J. & Ozanne-Smith, J. (2001) Injury in young people with intellectual disability: descriptive epidemiology. *Injury Prevention*, **7**, 56–61.

Simila, S. & Niskanen, P. (1991) Underweight and overweight cases among the mentally retarded. *Journal of Mental Deficiency Research*, **35**, 160–164.

Sonnander, K. & Claesson, M. (1997) Classification, prevalence, prevention and rehabilitation of intellectual disability: an overview of research in the People's Republic of China. *Journal of Intellectual & Developmental Disability*, **41**, 180–192.

Spreat, S. & Baker-Potts, J.C. (1983) Patterns of injury in institutionalized mentally retarded residents. *Mental Retardation*, **21**, 23–29.

Stewart, L., Beange, H. & McKerras, D. (1994) A survey of dietary problems of adults with learning disabilities in the community. *Mental Handicap Research*, **7**, 41–50.

Stone, R.K., May, J.E., Alvarez, W.F. & Ellman, G. (1989) Prevalence of dyskinesia and related movement disorders in a developmentally disabled population. *Journal of Mental Deficiency Research*, **33**, 41–53.

Strauss, D., & Eyman, R.K. (1996) Mortality of people with mental retardation in California with and without Down syndrome, 1986–1991. *American Journal on Mental Retardation*, **100**, 643–653.

Sullivan, P.M., Brookhouser, P.E., Scanlan, J.M., Knutson, J.F. & Schulte, L.E. (1991) Patterns of physical and sexual abuse of communicatively handicapped children. *Annuals of Otolology, Rhinology and Laryngology*, **100**, 188–194.

Tannenbaum, T.N., Lipworth, L. & Baker, S. (1989) Risk of fractures in an intermediate care facility for persons with mental retardation. *Journal of Intellectual Disability Research*, **45**, 83–87.

Tohill, C. (1997) A study into the possible link between anti-epileptic drugs and the risk of fractures in Muckamore Abbey Hospital. *Journal of Intellectual & Developmental Disability*, **22**, 281–292.

Trumble, S.C. (1999) Developmental disability medicine. PhD thesis. *Monash University*, Victoria, Australia.

Turner, S. & Moss, S. (1996) The health needs of adults with learning disabilities and the Health of the Nation Strategy. *Journal of Intellectual Disability Research*, **40**, 438–450.

Van Gelderen, I.G. (1992) Benefits of a second look at the causes of mental handicap in an institution. In: *Mental Retardation and Medical Care* (ed. J.J. Roosendahl) pp. 120–126. Uitgeverij Kerkebosch, Zeist.

Van Schrojenstein Lantman-de Valk, H.M.J., Akker, M.V.D., Maaskant M.A, Haveman, M. J. & Urlings, H. (1997) Prevalence and incidence of health problems in people with intellectual disability. *Journal of Intellectual & Developmental Disability*, **41**, 42–51.

Van Schrojenstein Lantman-de Valk, H.M.J., Metsemakers, J.F.M., Haveman, M.J. & Crebolder, H.F.J.M. (2000) Health problems in people with intellectual disability in general practice: a comparative study. *Family Practice*, **17**, 405–407.

Vellinga, A., Van Damme, P. & Meheus, A. (1999) Hepatitis B and C in institutions for individuals with intellectual disability. *Journal of Intellectual Disability Research*, **43**, 453–453.

Wagermans, A.M.A., Fiolet, J.F.B.M., van der Linden, E.S. & Menheere P.P.C.A. (1998) Osteoporosis and intellectual disability: is there any relation? *Journal of Intellectual Disability Research*, **42**, 370–374.

Warburg, M. (1994) Visual impairment among people with developmental delay. *Journal of Intellectual Disability Research*, **38**, 423–432.

Warburg, M. (2001) Visual impairment in adult people with intellectual disability: Literature review. *Journal of Intellectual Disability Research*, **45**, 424–438.

Webb, O.J. & Rogers, L. (1999) Health screening for people with intellectual disability: the New Zealand Experience. *Journal of Intellectual Disability Research*, **43**, 497–503.

Wen, X. (1997) The definition and prevalence of intellectual disability in Australia. *Australian Institute of Health and Welfare*. Catalogue no. DIS 2, Australian Institute of Health and Welfare, Canberra.

Wilson, R. (1998) Carer burden in learning disability with co-existent epilepsy. MSc thesis. *University of Wales College of Medicine*, Cardiff.

Wilson, D.N. & Haire, A. (1990) Health care screening for people with mental handicap living in the community. *British Medical Journal*, **301**, 1379–1381.

Wingfield, M., Healy, D. L. & Nicholson, A. (1994) Gynaecological care for women with intellectual disability. *Medical Journal of Australia*, **160**, 536–538.

World Health Organization (1992) The ICD-10 Classification of Mental and Behavioural Disorders. Clinical Descriptions and Diagnostic Guidelines. WHO, Geneva.

Yacob, M., Bashira, K., Tareen, K.H., Gustarson, R., Nazir, F., Jalil, U., VonDoben & Ferngren, H. (1995) Severe mental retardation in 2 to 24-months-old children in Lahore, Pakistan: a prospective cohort study. *Acta Paediatrica*, **84**, 267–272.

Zuhlke C., Thies V., Braulke I., Reis A. & Schirren C. (1994) Down syndrome and male fertility: PCR-derived fingerprinting, serological and andrological investigations. *Clinical Genetics*, **46**, 324–326.

2 Assessing Physical Health

Gerard J. Kerins

Introduction

The assessment of physical health in adults with intellectual disabilities is both extremely rewarding and challenging. Real opportunities exist to improve the physical health of this group through early identification of health problems to reduce future morbidity and mortality. The clinical care of this group is provided by a variety of professionals; thus, standards of care must be developed and disseminated in order to ensure that minimum levels of care are applied to all groups. The appropriate history taking, physical examination and assessment of health in adults with intellectual disabilities will continue to become more important as this group ages, and with increasing age the disease burden also increases, making the assessment all the more crucial.

One important aspect of the care of those with intellectual disabilities is the notion that they may not desire or may not benefit from the same diagnostic or therapeutic approaches as in the general population. Nothing is further from the truth, and those who care for this population must always ensure that those with intellectual disabilities receive the most appropriate care. As more data concerning the care of this group emerges, clearly those adults with intellectual disabilities may respond no less optimally in terms of morbidity and mortality, as do adults in the general population to standard and accepted treatments. In addition, there may be certain modifications in terms of diagnostic testing and treatment that would be most appropriate for adults with intellectual disabilities.

This chapter reviews appropriate history-taking mechanisms as well as physical examination approaches with adults with intellectual disabilities. Emphasis is placed on those common conditions which affect adults with intellectual disabilities, and the relevant ways to make such diagnoses in an early and appropriate manner.

First, a summary of history taking will be reviewed with attention being paid to how such a process can be completed using surrogate informants and functional status to compile an appropriate and relevant history. In addition, focusing on certain historical factors for specific conditions that may affect this group more commonly should foster early diagnosis and treatment. The history, especially in this population, may be the most appropriate and accurate way to assess current health status and enable appropriate decisions to be made regarding diagnostic testing and treatment strategies.

Second, the physical assessment and evaluation of this population will be reviewed, realizing that modification of the typical physical examination procedure may at times be needed in order to obtain the most relevant clinical information. The logical use of lab data and other ancillary testing can serve to further improve the diagnostic accuracy and foster early identification of potentially serious health problems. Certainly the efficient and effective use of diagnostic testing, such as blood tests, X-rays examination and scans, for example, in this population may be difficult because of certain physical and intellectual limitations which may impact on the ability to complete certain diagnostic testing. At times, for instance, conscious or general sedation may be required to complete routine tests and screening procedures. One should be assured that if such tests are indicated, they are completed even if additional measures are required to help during the diagnostic process.

History taking

The process of obtaining a detailed history from adults with intellectual disabilities often depends on the availability of surrogate informants. How such persons with intellectual disabilities and their surrogates perceive wellness or healthiness obviously can impact on this history-taking process. In the general population it has been observed that the older the person, the more likely the person is to report very good health status (Ebly *et al.*, 1996). Little data exists, however, on self-perceptions of health status among adults with intellectual disabilities. Certainly, because of baseline communication difficulties – whether it is inability to speak, see, hear or communicate – adults with such disabilities may not be able to express even in simple terms what might be their main health complaint. Inability to communicate should not be mistaken for lack of health concerns, pain, disability or illness.

Particular attention must be paid to alternative expression of a chief medical problem or complaint that has prompted an adult with an intellectual disability to seek medical attention. Surrogates may be the other means of eliciting such information as it relates to an individual with an intellectual disability. The traditional format should be followed when completing the history-taking process. The chief complaint, which is in the adult's own words as to why he or she is seeking medical care, should be the first step in this process. Obviously, this information may have to be obtained by a surrogate or by a non-verbal means depending on the baseline communication capabilities and deficits of the individual presenting for care.

History taking should always be completed in a quiet, well-lit environment with appropriate surrogates present and interviewed as needed using a standard format (Table 2.1). Health care providers should always respect the autonomy of those with intellectual disabilities, and should never by appearance alone assume that anyone is unable or unwilling to provide an accurate or detailed history. Many times, however, carers or other informants are crucial to this data-gathering process, in particular with reference to type of medication prescribed and information regarding any previous hospital admissions. Asking the patient about his health, even if the patient may not fully understand, should precede any attempt to obtain history from carers. Written information and records may also serve to augment verbal history; in the case of emergency treatment and evaluation they may be the only source of information. Cooperation, or lack of it, by an adult during the history and physical examination should never be a barrier to appropriate care and treatment, but data does suggest that patient behavior in adults with intellectual disabilities can and does impact on health care outcomes for certain types of conditions and treatments (Pulcini et al., 1999).

Table 2.1 Elements of a comprehensive history.

 (1) Principal informant
 (2) Chief complaint
 (3) History of present illness
 (4) Review of systems
 (5) Current and recent medication use (prescription and non-prescription)
 (6) Past medical history
 (7) Family history
 (8) Allergies
 (9) Alcohol and tobacco use
(10) Current living arrangement and residential history
(11) Social support and family support

Adults with intellectual disabilities, like the population in general, may have non-specific presentation of specific illnesses or may have atypical presentation of common diseases where certain symptoms may be altered or absent. In addition, acute diseases in many adults with intellectual disabilities are often manifested by changes in activities of daily living (i.e. changes in ability to bathe oneself, dress and eat). Functional change from baseline status may be the only indicator of an underlying emerging disease (Levy & Hyman, 1993). A keen knowledge of baseline function is crucial in assessing any functional change.

Even those adults with marked physical and functional deficits at baseline may exhibit further, more accelerated decline as the only sign of a new or progressing illness. Focusing on functional change in obtaining a history will then be an effective manner to enhance early identification of developing morbidity in this group. Although a variety of functional assessment tools have been validated and are widely used in adults in general, these tools may be relevant and useful to a lesser extent in measuring functional status in this population. Just asking directly about any change or alteration from baseline regarding self-care (i.e. dressing, feeding, washing or sleeping) may be an adequate way to assess functional change. Although such adults or their carers may be able to report a chief complaint at the onset of the history-taking process, lack of such specific history is often common. Functional assessment can be completed using any available tool or process. Asking the patient or carer in an open-ended manner to describe daily routine is one practical method to accomplish this questioning. Looking for any change manifested by altered daily routine may be another way to help identify a developing illness or disease.

Review of systems

A typical review of systems should be completed, with particular attention being paid to those conditions which may occur more commonly in this group; for instance, Alzheimer's dementia, thyroid disease, seizure disorder, cataracts, congenital heart disease, sleep apnea, fungal and nail infections and osteoporosis (Kerins, 1999). Each patient should be asked on a routine basis about the following areas with regard to review of systems. The skin history should specifically include questions about any nail or related fungal infections or atopic dermatitis (Schepsis, 1997). Although such skin conditions may at times appear to be trivial, they may significantly impact on functioning as well as create significant carer need among adults with intellectual disabilities. Therefore dismissing such concern is inappropriate, and trying to find the best treatments for skin conditions may be best accomplished by first elaborating a detailed history, whether it relates to recurrent fungal nail infections, atopic dermatitis, pruritus, rashes or such similar complaints. In addition, it is important to ask specifically about any new or changing skin patterns or moles, recognizing that many adults with intellectual disabilities are at the same risk as age-peers in the general population for the development of skin cancers.

History taking as it relates to the head and related structures should specifically focus on any recent, new or different character or nature to existing seizure disorders. Any abnormal movements should not be dismissed, for they may be atypical seizures. An examiner should specifically ask about any new tics, neurological changes or repetitive motions which may, in fact, represent atypical seizures in this population. The eye review must include any information concerning changes in vision or visual status, particularly any evidence of cataracts, which might be impacting on function but might not be readily apparent. One should not be discouraged from asking about such visual changes, even if there has been a full ophthalmologic evaluation within the past year, recognizing that among some adults with intellectual disabilities cataracts and visual disturbance may progress very rapidly and present even at an earlier age. Therefore, established standards of care for screening for visual changes in normal adults may have to be modified as they relate to this population. One should always ask about any evidence of visual changes. For an elaboration of visual pathology in adults with intellectual disabilities see Chapter 5.

Any evidence of recent or recurrent ear infections or tendency toward impacted cerumen should be asked about specifically in the review of systems. (For a detailed discussion on audiological disorders and intellectual disabilities see Chapter 6). The mouth and throat examination is important with regard to any changes or new difficulty in swallowing, any recent or prior history of aspiration, or any tendency to choke while eating certain types of foods. Extensive dental caries or related dental diseases should always be reviewed, as well as any previous indication for prophylaxis with antibiotics prior to dental procedures (see Chapter 9). The review of systems of the neck in general, and the thyroid in particular, is especially important in this population, given the high rate of thyroid disease observed in adults with Down syndrome. For a review of thyroid disorders in Down syndrome, see Prasher (1999). The review of systems related to thyroid should involve questioning about any of the classic symptoms of either underactive or overactive thyroid, whether it is constipation, cold intolerance, weight-loss or gain, palpitations, or related such complaints. However, often such traditional symptoms may be lacking or may not be reportable and, therefore, the examiner must be careful to elicit detailed evidence of such thyroid disease.

With regard to the history of breast disease, the review of systems among female patients should include asking specifically about any prior history of lumps or masses; asking such history of male patients is also appropriate. Prior history or routine use of mammography should also be reviewed at this time. There is no evidence to suggest that the use of screening mammography is any less effective among women with intellectual disabilities (when compared at any specific age to the general population) but may be more problematic – particularly among adults with aversion to screening devices. The respiratory review of systems should particularly focus on any evidence of recurrent infections, atypical pneumonia, or any new or changing character to breathing pattern including new or worsening exertional dyspnea.

The heart review of systems should focus on hypertension, elevated cholesterol and specifically on any prior history or treatment of congenital heart disease, coronary artery disease or chest pain. It is important to note that congenital heart disease (which may be present at a higher rate among adults with Down syndrome) which may be present from birth, may be only first diagnosed with the development of obvious symptoms as these adults age (Murdoch, 1984). In addition, Down syndrome itself has not been shown to be a risk factor for poor outcome after repair of congenital heart defects; thus, uncovering heart disease, congenital or otherwise, may lead to appropriate surgical intervention among these adults (Reller & Morris, 1998).

The gastrointestinal review of systems should focus on any history or signs and symptoms of hepatitis, especially with the known association of adults with Down syndrome who have thyroiditis and the high coincident rates of being tested positive for hepatitis B surface antigen. Asking about malabsorption syndromes in general, and celiac disease in particular, is strongly recommended (George, 1996). Any change in character or nature of bowel habits should be fully explored when asking about the gastrointestinal review of systems. The urological review should be specific and include any new incontinence or any new symptoms of dysuria, polyuria or inability to complete normal toileting procedures by oneself. Incontinence may be a particular urological issue among certain adults with intellectual disabilities; thus, as detailed a history as possible should be obtained in an attempt to uncover the type, nature and character of the incontinence. Often such a detailed history can reveal environmental and behavioral factors which can be modified to reduce incontinence or at least improve episodes so as to decrease carer burden.

A detailed sexual history is extremely important, with particular attention being paid to any signs or symptoms by history of sexual abuse or mistreatment, or any evidence of sexually transmitted diseases. In women, presence of menstruation and related history and menopausal symptoms should be asked about, especially since women with Down syndrome generally experience an early menopause and may be predisposed to early osteoporosis (Schupf et al., 1997). Any history of such osteoporosis and bone loss should be reviewed, as well as any history of bone density testing and use of supplemental vitamin D, calcium, estrogen replacement or other treatments for osteoporosis (Center *et al.*, 1998). For a detailed review of osteoporosis see Chapter 8.

Neurological review of systems should include any history of seizures, particularly any abnormal movements that may indicate atypical seizures. Most important, however, is a detailed review of baseline cognitive status or any change in such function. How cognitive decline is affecting daily activities and work performance should also be reviewed in detail (Zigman *et al.*, 1996). Although various tools are available to assess cognitive status in adults with intellectual disabilities, none has been fully validated. A history of declining function, memory loss, or related changes in daily activities may provide the first clue to declining cognition. The examiner should ask specifically about changes in mood or other signs or symptoms of depression. Many times, as in the general older population, depression may be misdiagnosed as early dementia or some other behavioral disorder. Depression in this population may be present, only presenting as cognitive deficit and changing behavior and related functional decline without the presence of the more traditional somatic complaints of decreased appetite, constipation and sleep disturbance. Detailed questioning about sleep should also include any evidence of snoring, respiratory difficulties during sleep, or any other signs or symptoms of sleep apnea.

A comprehensive review of drug use should include both prescription and non-prescription (over the counter) medications, supplements and vitamins. One helpful approach is the 'brown-bag' method where carers are instructed to place all current medications being used in a bag and to physically bring them to the appointment. One other tact to consider is the increasing use in the general population of alternative and herbal therapies and medicines. One should, therefore, elicit information about the use of medications, asking directly about any use of supplemental vitamins, herbs or alternative therapies, realizing that patients, or more importantly carers, may not readily include this information in a traditional pharmacological review of systems. A nutritional history is also important, recognizing that a change in eating habits may be a marker for a developing illness or disease. Particularly important may be the relationship between nutritional status and obesity in adults with intellectual disabilities (Golden, 1997).

The review of systems should use information derived from a variety of written and oral sources. Many times such a process will require additional data-gathering steps in that the patients themselves may not be able to provide any or all important information. It is important to realize that for adults with intellectual disabilities, a detailed history may be the most crucial step to the early identification of morbidity and, therefore, the examiner should strive to be as comprehensive as possible in obtaining this data. As with all aspects of caring for adults with intellectual disabilities, one must be flexible in how and when one obtains all relevant information, recognizing that even when something appears to be, at first glance, trivial or insignificant, it may have greater significance as one proceeds to uncover the nature of the underlying disease and functional change.

Finally, one must be sensitive to the whole issue of cultural diversity and how such factors may affect history, perception of disease, and reporting of illness in various cultural groups. Cultural differences can impact not only on direct care but also on carer roles, expectations and related perceptions. It is, therefore, important whether obtaining a history or caring for adults with intellectual disabilities, to be sensitive to the possible impact of cultural variation and differences as they relate to such factors.

Physical examination

In completing the physical examination (Table 2.2) with adults with intellectual disabilities, the examiner should realize that it is important to be flexible on how to conduct the examination. Although standardized approaches should be used in general, the individual needs and capabilities of each adult require that the examiner be able to modify the

Table 2.2 Important aspects of the physical examination.

(1) General appearance
(2) Mood
(3) Behavior
(4) Consciousness level
(5) Skin (all areas for stigmata associated with genetic conditions)
(6) Head (evidence of trauma)
(7) Ears (cerumen, hearing deficits)
(8) Eyes (visual impairment, cataracts)
(9) Mouth (including dentition)
(10) Neck (lymph nodes, thyroid)
(11) Respiratory system
(12) Heart (rate, rhythm, murmurs, with particular attention to any evidence of congenital heart disease)
(13) Abdomen (in particular, organomegaly and hepatomegaly)
(14) Genitourinary (including breast examination)
(15) Skeletal system (particular attention to any signs of osteoarthritis, musculoskeletal deformities, atlantoaxial syndrome)
(16) Neurological system (limb movement and tone, gait)
(17) Extremities
(18) Cognition

general approach at any moment. All relevant symptoms and systems should be examined, but particular attention should be paid to completing as detailed an examination as possible on those specific organs and systems that may yield early diagnosis of common conditions in this group. The associated history may be non-specific and may not point to a particular organ system as the sole source of morbidity. Any change in function, however, which may be the only presenting symptom or sign of a disease process, should prompt a thorough review and physical examination. Functional loss may be the final common pathway for most clinical problems in adults with intellectual disabilities, especially in adults over the age of 75 years (Besdine, 1983).

Before starting the physical examination the patient should be made to feel as comfortable as possible in the examination room; however, if circumstances dictate, the patient should be examined where he or she would be most comfortable (remembering that flexibility is the key to a successful examination). Allowing the carer, who may have accompanied the adult, to stay with him or her during the examination may make the patient feel more relaxed and comfortable and may enhance the examination process. The examiner should follow an organized systematic format in conducting the physical examination, recognizing that modification and adaptation may be necessary depending on patient cooperation and related circumstances.

In general, observe the patient's overall appearance and presentation. Vital signs should be completed with blood pressure and pulse taken both lying and standing to check for evidence of orthostatic hypotension (which is common among adults with intellectual disabilities, but on many occasions may be underdiagnosed or underappreciated as the cause of falls, gait disturbance, or functional change in general). The skin examination should focus on close examination of nails to check for fungal infection, which commonly occurs in persons with Down syndrome. In addition, any evidence of moles or related skin changes deserves as full and aggressive an evaluation as would occur in the general population. Lack of patient cooperation and limited ability to follow certain directions may at times impact on the ability to complete a detailed skin examination. However, the face, neck, arms and legs, chest and back should always be examined for any new rash or moles, or changing character and nature of previously identified lesions.

Examination of the head should include close inspection for any evidence of trauma. Ears should be checked for cerumen impaction, and hearing should be screened as completely and routinely as possible. Many times traditional audioscopic evaluation may not be possible in some adults with intellectual disabilities. Therefore, the examiner may wish to rely on alternative methods to assess hearing. Rubbing the hands together or speaking softly to see if there is any change from either ear may be one way to pick-up hearing changes in a less invasive manner. For further details on assessment of hearing see Chapter 6.

Detailed examination of the eyes may be best left to an ophthalmologist, but the primary care provider should complete routine screening for cataracts, which occur more commonly and progress more quickly in adults with Down syndrome. Every patient should have routine oral and dental examinations, to look not only for dental caries but for any evidence of gingival hyperplasia or underlying gum disease (which may be the result of taking certain medications which are prescribed to people with intellectual disabilities). In addition, the need for endocarditis prophylaxis prior to routine dental examinations or treatment should be explored and reviewed at every relevant opportunity. For further details see Chapter 9.

The examination of the thyroid gland is extremely important when the high rate of thyroid disease is considered among people with Down syndrome. Both poles of the thyroid should be inspected and palpated to evaluate for any nodules, enlargement or goitres. Observing how the patient swallows a glass of water may be an additional maneuver which can be completed at the time of the thyroid examination. This may not only enhance the evaluation of the thyroid but it may also reveal any underlying previously undetermined swallowing disorder or propensity toward aspiration. Even having the patient attempt to swallow various types of fluids may help, in a crude way, to complete a baseline swallowing assessment which may uncover underlying dysphagia or odynophagia not previously appreciated.

A complete respiratory system examination is extremely important, recognizing that certain adults with an intellectual disability have a propensity for recurrent pneumonias and related types of infections. Auscultation should include all lung fields and assess for any evidence of wheezing, rhonchi or rales, or changing character and nature of breath sounds. The cardiac examination should include a comprehensive auscultatory examination with particular attention to evaluate for any rubs, murmurs, gallops or extra heartbeats. Realizing that congenital heart disease in general, and valvular heart disease in particular, occurs more commonly among certain persons with intellectual disabilities, the examiner should pay particular attention to this aspect of the cardiac examination. In addition, the cardiac examination may reveal underlying disease which warrants further, more invasive diagnostic testing.

The abdominal, genitalia and rectal examination may best be completed together. A high degree of sensitivity and flexibility will be required. If, for instance, a pelvic examination is absolutely clinically indicated because of vaginal bleeding, general sedation may be required (the use of sedation also may be the safest and most comfortable way to complete a detailed examination). All extremities should be checked for edema and cyanosis, and for any evidence of underlying musculoskeletal disorders. In addition, particular attention must be paid for any evidence of atlantoaxial subluxation syndrome or osteoporosis, which affects selected adults with intellectual disabilities at earlier ages than it does age-peers in the general population. Direct observation of the patient rising from a chair and walking a certain distance may also provide valuable information regarding gait and related functional disability (Podsiado & Richardson, 1991). Having the patient place both hands behind his or her head, or the lack of ability to complete this simple maneuver, may also help uncover underlying significant musculoskeletal disease which has a functional impact. The utility of a neurological examination may be limited although any specific neurological deficits may require further detailed examination or additional diagnostic testing, (i.e. an electroencephalogram or head scan). Such additional testing may be necessary in particular if a vascular event or seizure may be a diagnostic consideration.

Finally, all adults with intellectual disabilities, especially as they age, should have a routine evaluation for cognitive changes. Although no standardized tool may be applicable to all populations, various screening tools, i.e. the Down's Syndrome Mental Status Examination (DS MSE; Haxby, 1989) the Psychiatric Assessment Schedule for Adults with a Developmental Disability (PASS-ADD; Moss *et al.*, 1993) or the Multi-dimensional Observational Scale for Elderly Subjects (MOSES; Dalton & Fedor, 1997) may be useful. Obviously, the utility of such tools will be impacted by the patient's baseline cognitive status and related comorbidity. One important factor is that whatever baseline cognitive assessment is completed, it should be reapplied at various set intervals to pick up any slight changes which might not otherwise be appreciated in the course of daily functioning. It is becoming increasingly clear that early identification, modification and possible treatment of cognitive changes in adults with intellectual disabilities may, as with the general population, be the best way to delay related morbidity and functional change as it relates to such cognitive decline.

Investigations

Laboratory testing and related investigatory tools (see Table 2.3) are important components of the history and physical examination. They can be adjuncts to information uncovered during the course of a comprehensive history and physical examination. Such tests should be aimed at

Table 2.3 Ancillary investigations which can be undertaken.

Blood examination (haematology, biochemistry, vitamin levels, blood sugar, cholesterol, hormones)
Urine examination (sugar, albumin, evidence of infection)
X-ray examination (chest, skull)
Electroencephalography
Echoencephalography
Brain imaging (computerized tomography, magnetic resonance imaging, positron emission tomography)

---

early identification of those common conditions affecting this population. Clearly, routine screening procedures and preventive medicine practices should be applied with the same rigor as in the general population, but particular attention should be paid to screening for those conditions which occur more commonly in this group.

Blood examinations, including biochemical, cholesterol, blood sugar and thyroid function tests, should be administered at routine intervals (often at more frequent intervals than in the general population). Thyroid function testing, for example, should be conducted at least every two years among adults with Down syndrome. In addition, even subtle biochemical changes in thyroid function may result in more marked behavioral changes, which may be out of proportion to the slight biochemical change. It is for this reason that frequent testing of thyroid function has been recommended among adults with Down syndrome. Full hepatitis screening should be completed for any evidence of chronic hepatitis state or evidence of hepatitis A, B or C. If available, other routine screening procedures, as they are applied to the general population, should also be adhered to. Monitoring and preventive screening for hypertension, breast disease and osteoporosis, and an application of routine immunizations (including pneumococcal, influenza and tetanus) should be conducted with the same rigor as in the general population.

Although specific data on the value of disease prevention for these screening tools does not exist for adults with intellectual disabilities, there is no reason to believe that they are any less useful than when applied to the general population. In certain situations the availability of certain screening modalities may limit their usefulness, but in general, as stated, they should be applied with the same rigor as has been recommended for the general population. Certain procedures (i.e. electrocardiograms, electroencephalograms, brain scans) should not be used as screening tools and should only be completed when there is a specific clinical indication. As with all such screening procedures, certain precautions may have to be followed. Adapting available personnel or modifying protocols may be indicated for such specialized tests. Sometimes the use of conscious sedation or even general anesthesia may be required if the tests are to be completed effectively.

Conclusion

The physical assessment of adults with intellectual disabilities may be, at the same time, extremely rewarding and challenging. By following routine and timely practices, many common conditions can be identified at early stages, such that real opportunities exist to minimize morbidity and ultimately mortality. The history-obtaining process may at times rely on surrogates, and thus the examiner may need to adapt the standardized comprehensive approach in completing this aspect of the evaluation. Seeking-out additional sources of information is crucial as an adjunct to that which may be provided by the adult and primary carer, or can be found in accompanying medical records. The physical examination should be comprehensive and complete, with the realization that on many occasions, because of a variety of factors, the examination may have to be modified or curtailed. Ensuring that the person being examined is comfortable should be a high priority, even if it may mean omitting certain aspects of the examination. By combining a detailed history with a focused examination, the clinical care of adults with intellectual disabilities can be optimized in such a way as to ensure the early identification of medical conditions and prompt appropriate treatment.

References

Besdine, R. (1983) The educational utility of comprehensive functional assessment in the elderly. *Journal of The American Geriatric Society*, **31**, 651–656.

Center, J., Beange, H. & McElduff, A. (1998) People with mental retardation have an increased prevalence of osteoporosis: A population study. *American Journal on Mental Retardation*, **103**, 19–28.

Dalton, A. & Fedor, B. (1997) The Multidimensional Observational Scale for Elderly Subjects (MOSES): Longitudinal changes in adults with Down's syndrome. The National Association for The Dually Diagnosed. *Proceedings of the International Congress III on the Dually Diagnosed*, 176–181.

Ebly, E.M., Hogan, D.B. & Fung, J.S (1996) Correlates of self-related health in persons age 85 and older; results from the Canadian study of health and aging. *Canadian Journal of Public Health*, **87**, 28–31.

George, E. (1996) High frequency of celiac disease in Down's syndrome. *Journal of Pediatrics*, **128**, 555–557.

Golden, E. (1997) Nutritional knowledge and obesity of adults in community residences. *Mental Retardation*, **35**,177–84.

Haxby, J.V. (1989) Neuropsychological evaluation of adults with Down's syndrome: Patterns of selective impairment in non-demented old adults. *Journal of Mental Deficiency Research*, **33**, 193–210.

Kerins, G. (1999) Clinical conditions affecting older adults with Down's syndrome. *The Gerontologist*, **39**, 471.

Levy, S.E., & Hyman, S.T (1993) Pediatric assessment of the child with developmental disability. *Pediatric Clinics of North America*, **40**, 465–477.

Moss, S.C., Patel, P., Prosser, H., Golberg, D.P., Simpson, N., Rowe, S. & Lucchino, R. (1993) Psychiatric morbidity in older people with moderate and severe learning disability (mental retardation). Part I. Development and reliability of the patient interview (the PAS-ADD). *British Journal of Psychiatry*, **163**, 471–480.

Murdoch, J. (1984) Congenital heart disease as a significant factor in the morbidity of children with Down's syndrome. *Journal of Mental Deficiency Research*, **29**, 147–151.

Podsiado, D. & Richardson, S. (1991) The timed up and go: a test of basic functional mobility in frail elder persons. *Journal of the American Geriatric Society*, **39**, 142–148.

Prasher, V.P. (1999) Down syndrome and thyroid disorders: A review. *Down Syndrome Research and Practice*, **6**, 105–110.

Pulcini, J., Taylor, M.O. & Patelis, T. (1999) The relationship between characteristics of women with mental retardation and outcomes of the gynecological examination. *Clinical Excellence for Nursing Practitioners*, **3**, 221–229.

Reller, M.D., & Morris, C.D. (1998) Is Down's syndrome a risk factor for poor outcome after repair of congenital heart defects? *General Pediatrics*, **132**, 738–741.

Schepsis, C. (1997) Prevalence of atopic dermatitis in patients with Down's syndrome. A clinical survey. *Journal of the American Academy of Dermatology*, **6**, 1019–1021.

Schupf, N., Zigman, W., Kadell, D. & Lee, J.H. (1997) Early menopause in women with Down's syndrome. *Journal of Intellectual Disability Research*, **41**, 264–267.

Zigman, W., Schupf, N., Sersen, E. & Silverman, W. (1996) Prevalence of dementia in adults with and without Down's syndrome. *American Journal of Mental Retardation*, **100**, 403–412.

# **3** Physical Health and Clinical Phenotypes

Gregory O'Brien, Louise Barnard, Joanne Pearson and Lisa Rippon

Introduction

When we consider the relationship between physical health and intellectual disability the causal syndrome is of clinical importance. This chapter discusses the critical health issues that can affect people with specific syndromes associated with intellectual disabilities. This is followed by a brief synopsis of the major characteristics of 45 of the most common and/or most important clinical phenotypes.

Although discussed independently here, the medical complications associated with intellectual disabilities interact with one another and rarely appear in isolation within the same syndrome. For example, people who are immobile, incontinent and who have poor nutritional status are more susceptible to infections. Obesity can be secondary to immobility and this can result in hypertension and subsequently cardiovascular and cerebrovascular disease. Fractures are also more common in the immobile person with intellectual disability because of an increased risk of osteoporosis, even when calcium intake is adequate. Some of the consequences of medical complications can be ameliorated by adequate preventative measures such as good diet, appropriate continence aids, physiotherapy and regular screening (breast, cervical, testicular, etc.) for secondary complications. As such, it is vitally important that practitioners are able to anticipate, recognize and treat medical complications at an early stage, in order to increase quality of life and life expectancy.

Aging individuals with intellectual disabilities pose a number of health challenges. These are best understood if the cause of the intellectual disability – the syndrome – is considered. Opportunities for intervention can be explored through the study of the mechanisms by which syndromes associated with intellectual disabilities result in health problems for the ageing individual. This is complemented by a review of the health challenges posed by individual syndromes that commonly cause intellectual disability. The importance of holistic and multidisciplinary programs of assessment and intervention are stressed throughout.

Life expectancy

In general, the more severe the level of intellectual disability, the more common and more severe are the respective associated medical conditions and abnormalities (O'Brien, 2001a; Barnard *et al.*, in press) and the consequent associated impaired quality of life and reduced life expectancy. A number of factors appear to operate here as intervening variables. These include: feeding difficulties; obesity; respiratory problems; cardio-vascular problems; epilepsy; premature aging and other abnormalities. The role of these factors is reviewed in the following section.

Morbidity and mortality

Feeding difficulties

Feeding disorders are particularly common among individuals with severe intellectual disabilities, and have been reported to occur in 33–80% of cases. Feeding and gastrointestinal disorders include vomiting, regurgitation, hyperphagia, anorexia, constipation, abdominal distension and chewing, sucking and swallowing difficulties. These all contribute to failure to thrive and other feeding disorders, which in some syndromes can be life threatening (e.g. Cornelia de Lange syndrome; O'Brien & Yule, 1995). Poor nutritional status lowers the body's immune responses, leaving it open to infection. There is a lack of knowledge about the etiology of feeding problems associated with some clinical phenotypes. It has been suggested that there is a high prevalence of undiagnosed gastroesophageal reflux in this population, and that many feeding problems may be partially attributed to this. Severe feeding abnormalities are common in Noonan syndrome, but the cause of these remains poorly understood and they are often not detected until the patient becomes clinically malnourished. In one study of 25 patients with Noonan syndrome, 16 had severe gastrointestinal symptoms, all requiring nasogastric feeding (Shah *et al.*, 1999).

Hypotonia is also a frequent cause of feeding difficulties among people with severe intellectual disabilities. Diminished skeletal muscle-tone makes chewing and swallowing problematic in syndromes such as cri-du-chat, fragile-X, Lesch-Nyhan and Prader-Willi. The necessary intervention of tube-feeding, and also the swallowing difficulties associated with hypotonia, can lead to aspiration. If this is not successfully managed, a secondary complication can be aspiration pneumonia; however, this can be successfully treated with antibiotics.

Specific clinical phenotypes, such as phenylketonuria and galactosemia, have dietary implications. Phenylalanine and lactose, respectively, require restricting from the diets of patients with these conditions, in order to prevent severe medical and adaptive deterioration. In both syndromes, regular dietary monitoring is crucial to ensure that essential nutrients, other than those that are being restricted, are not deficient. Diet can be supplemented to prevent secondary complications developing, such as osteoporosis.

In phenylketonuria, the degree of the enzyme deficiency is to some extent relative to the individual, therefore highly individual dietary programs are necessary. Cessation of the phenylalanine-free diet is associated with a decline in neuropsychological abilities, an increase in behavioral problems and an increased incidence of psychiatric disorders. There is controversy as to whether the restriction diet should be life-long, and if not, at what age it should be relaxed. Although dietary restriction is initially highly effective for individuals with galactosemia, this syndrome is associated with a secondary deterioration, which is characterized by speech deficits and cognitive decline.

Obesity

Obesity is a common problem in Angelman, Prader-Willi, Turner, Rubinstein-Taybi and 48 XXYY syndromes. Obesity can lead to serious medical problems, such as non-insulin dependent diabetes, hypertension and cardiovascular disease. In the cases of Angelman and Rubinstein-Taybi syndromes, although both are associated with failure to thrive in infancy, subsequent obesity in adulthood – particularly in females – is common. Prader-Willi syndrome is characterized by an insatiable appetite, reduced and delayed satiety response, reduced calorific requirement and inability to vomit. The resulting obesity is potentially life threatening. Intervention techniques, such as restricting sources of food (locking the refrigerator) and managing calorific intake, are effective. Behavioral modification strategies that have an emphasis on self-monitoring and reinforcement, in combination with exercise programs, can be effective at maintaining a healthy weight. Dietary management and healthy eating should be encouraged in any individual with intellectual disability, particularly where the causal syndrome is associated with obesity.

Respiratory problems

Respiratory disorders, including aspiration pneumonia, congenital defects and recurrent respiratory infections are frequent complications in a number of clinical phenotypes and are a major cause of mortality in persons with organic etiologies of intellectual disabilities (Barnard *et al.*, in press). Their incidence is elevated when compared to the normal population. In a sample of 2000 people with intellectual disabilities, respiratory complications accounted for 52% of deaths, compared with 15–17% in the general population (Hollins *et al.*, 1998).

Aspiration and respiratory tract infections can be caused by congenital defects, vomiting, epilepsy, coughing, feeding, breathing and swallowing difficulties, regurgitation and gastroesophageal reflux (Shah *et al.*, 1999). Otolaryngologic congenital abnormalities, such as thickened vocal cords and a narrowed trachea, can contribute to upper obstructive airway disease and are commonly observed in certain mucopolysaccharidoses, notably Morquio, Maroteaux-Lamy, Sly and Hurler-Scheie syndromes. In some cases, these complications necessitate tracheostomies or tonsillectomies. Respiratory complications impact on all aspects of functioning, for example, by disturbing sleep. In a syndrome already characterized by an atypical sleep pattern, such as Sanfilippo syndrome, this can be extremely distressing and can contribute to behavioral disturbances.

Cardiovascular problems

The cardiovascular system is often implicated in syndromes associated with intellectual disabilities. Williams syndrome is associated with abnormalities of the cardiovascular system, including supraventricular aortic stenosis and peripheral pulmonary artery stenosis. As a result, adults with Williams syndrome are at risk of subacute bacterial endocarditis and hypertension. Up to one third of people who suffer from the fragile-X syndrome also have congenital heart defects, in particular dilatation of the aortic root, hypoplasia of the aorta and mitral valve prolapse. All of these conditions can result in morbidity and mortality if not rectified at an early stage. Cardiovascular disease can also be secondary to obesity.

Epilepsy (seizure disorders)

Seizure disorders frequently cooccur with intellectual disabilities. Some reports indicate that up to 50% of people with severe intellectual disabilities experience seizures. Seizure disorders associated with the syndromes of intellectual disability are often difficult to manage and can lead to considerable morbidity and a lower life expectancy. The presentation of epilepsy varies according to the syndrome; for example in autism, epilepsy may not develop until after puberty. In other conditions, such as Angelman syndrome, seizures are present in infancy but become less frequent with the passage of time. For a number of syndromes, the presence of epilepsy can contribute to the clinical diagnosis. Children with Aicardi and Angelman syndromes have diagnostically distinctive encephalographic patterns, although less markedly so after puberty.

Epilepsy can be an underlying cause of behavioral disturbance in individuals with a clinical phenotype. In many syndromes, anti-convulsants are used to manage and control epilepsy. Surgical intervention may also be considered in some instances, for example in tuberous sclerosis. The use of electrophysiological measures in addition to standard behavioral measures can help determine the impact of epilepsy on an individual's behavior. Routine screening of epilepsy should be commonly performed, particularly in the presence of deteriorating adaptive functioning. For further information see Chapter 7.

Other

A number of intellectual disability syndromes are associated with premature aging. Bloom and Cockayne syndromes are two such disorders. Congenital abnormalities of the musculoskeletal system are common among many of the intellectual disability syndrome phenotypes, notably in Rubinstein-Taybi, Williams and Hurler syndromes. Abnormalities of the genito-urinary and reproductive tracts are also common. In Williams syndrome, the genito-urinary tract and renal systems are affected. Kidney function deteriorates with age and the syndrome is often associated with nephrocalcinosis, nephrolithiasis and recurrent urinary tract infections.

Accidents are a small but not insignificant cause of morbidity and mortality in this population. In a sample of 216 deceased individuals, 14% had died from accidental death. Causes included drowning, choking, suffocation and suicide by poisoning (Raitasuo et al., 1997). People with severe intellectual disabilities are over three times more likely than the general population to sustain fractures (Beange & Lennox, 1998). Obvious causes of fractures include seizures and unstable gait. There are reported associations between the prescription of multiple anticonvulsants and the propensity to fracture, and also between decreased mobility and propensity to fracture. Other contributory factors include lower bone mineral density (Beange & Lennox, 1998). For example, individuals with Turner syndrome who are not treated with growth hormone therapy or estrogen therapy, show intrinsic bone mass deficits which are complicated by hormonal factors during and after puberty. Self-injury and mutilation are a common source of injury among some adults with intellectual disabilities. A number of syndromes are associated with these problems, including Lesch-Nyhan, Prader-Willi, Cornelia-de-Lange, Smith Magenis and fragile-X syndromes.

Chronic physical deteriorating conditions

Muscular degeneration

A number of clinical phenotypes are characterized by progressive muscular and/or skeletal degeneration (Aicardi, Cockayne, cri-du-chat, Duchenne muscular dystrophy, Lowe, congenital myotonic dystrophy, Prader-Willi, Rett, Smith-Lemli-Opitz and Wolf-Hirschhorn syndromes, the mucopolysaccharidoses and X-linked alpha-thalassaemia). These, in addition to congenital heart abnormalities (Wolf-Hirschhorn, Noonan, Rubinstein-Taybi, Smith-Magenis and velocardiofacial syndromes), contribute to respiratory weakness, pulmonary infection and premature death.

The etiology of progressive muscle deterioration varies. In the mucopolysaccharidoses, it is due to an accumulation of glycosaminoglycans (mucopolysaccharides) in the cells, tissues and organs. Duchenne muscular dystrophy is associated with a deficiency of dystrophin (Barnard *et al.*, in press). The delayed muscle maturation and subsequent myotonia seen in congenital myotonic dystrophy, are thought to be due to fiber atrophy. It has been suggested that this may partly be caused by a deficiency of protein kinase.

Muscle degeneration and progressive skeletal abnormalities can lead to hypotonia. Skeletal abnormalities, especially scoliosis, kyphoscoliosis and kyphosis, are common in intellectual disability syndromes, particularly in Wolf-Hirschhorn, Prader-Willi, Rett, cri-du-chat, Morquio, neurofibromatosis type 1 and Lowe syndromes and X-linked alpha-thalassaemia. Curvature of the spine can impair mobility and if left untreated may lead to restriction of respiratory movement and compression of the spinal cord, and can therefore ultimately be fatal. Examples of other skeletal abnormalities include the characteristic rib anomalies of Aicardi syndrome and the progressive joint swelling and arthritis that is associated with Lowe syndrome.

At present, there are no cures for many of these progressive degenerative conditions. Treatment is aimed at managing symptoms and medical complications through the use of surgery, pharmacotherapy, physiotherapy and mobility aids. For example, the myotonia of congenital myotonic dystrophy can be treated with pharmacological agents and splints. Bone marrow transplantation can slow down the progression of mucopolysaccharide disorders, and in some cases reversal of specific symptoms is possible. Physiotherapy and exercise that places low stress on muscles can be beneficial in Duchenne muscular dystrophy and Angelman syndrome (Gilbert, 1999). Corrective surgery can be effective for scoliosis/kyphosis where it is deemed appropriate. This can alleviate and/or help to prevent compression of the spinal cord.

Sensory impairments

The prevalence of sensory impairments in individuals with intellectual disabilities is higher than in the general population (Janicki & Dalton, 1998; Van Schrojenstein Lantman-de Valk *et al.*, 1994). There is progressive visual failure in many clinical phenotypes (Aicardi, Hurler-Scheie, Prader-Willi, congenital myotonic dystrophy, Rubinstein-Taybi, Turner and Hunter syndromes); premature cataract formation is one of the most common causes of visual loss. In Hurler-Scheie syndrome, corneal clouding significantly impairs vision (Keith *et al.*, 1990).

Clinical phenotypes associated with hearing loss include Sanfilippo, Turner, Hunter, Sotos, Angelman, Smith-Magenis and Wolf-Hirschhorn syndromes. In the case of Turner syndrome, premature aging of the hearing organs, which may be linked to a genetic defect, can lead to hearing loss (Hultcrantz *et al.*, 1994). Recurrent otitis media can lead to hearing loss in Wolf-Hirschhorn, Sotos, Angelman and Smith-Magenis (Battaglia *et al.*, 1999). Research highlights the need for regular and thorough monitoring of sensory abilities, particularly in individuals who have communication deficits or in cases where there is an unexplained deterioration in adaptive functioning.

Major specific disorders

The following synopses provide detailed and specific phenotypic information regarding many syndromes associated with intellectual disability that are encountered in clinical practice. For each phenotype, incidence, genetic mode(s) of transmission and typical degree of intellectual disability are listed. Incidence per live birth is reported where this data is known. Otherwise, the number of reported cases, given in brackets, is indicated, along with the date of this finding. Levels of intellectual disability vary within all of the phenotypes associated with intellectual disability. This chapter reports the most typical degree for each syndrome, based on DSM IV criteria (American Psychiatric Association, 1999): borderline (70–79 IQ points), mild (50–69), moderate (35–49), severe (20–34) and profound (less than 20).

Aicardi syndrome

Incidence   (200 cases reported by 1997)
Genetics   X-linked dominant disorder
Intellectual disability   Severe

Aicardi syndrome, found only in females, is characterized by agenesis of the corpus callosum, severe visual system defects, infantile spasms and skeletal abnormalities, particularly of the ribs and spine (O'Brien & Yule, 1995). The course of the syndrome is characterized by progressive psychomotor retardation, kyphoscoliosis and vision failure. Infantile mortality, due to pulmonary infection, is common. However, rare cases do survive into adolescence with one known case surviving to 19 years (Costa *et al.*, 1997).

Angelman syndrome

Incidence   1:30 000
Genetics   Usually sporadic, normally deletion of maternal
                             15q11–13
Intellectual disability   Severe to profound

Angelman syndrome is typically defined by characteristic facies, seizures, ataxia, hypopigmentation, severe intellectual disability, absence of speech, inappropriate laughter, microcephaly and abnormal electroencephalogram. Respiratory tract infections, otitis media and obesity are common complications in adulthood, although seizures become less prevalent with age. Life expectancy is thought to be normal (SSBP, 2000). The oldest known adult was reported to have survived beyond 75 years (Salmon, 1978). Life expectancy would seem to be unrelated to the presence of a visible deletion.

Apert syndrome

Incidence   1:100 000–160 000
Genetics   Autosomal dominant; vast majority of cases are
                             sporadic and represent new mutations
Intellectual disability   Normal to mild

Apert syndrome is an acrocephalosyndactyly syndrome characterized by craniosynostosis, severe syndactyly of the hands and feet and dysmorphic facial features (Gilbert, 1999). This syndrome is associated with numerous medical conditions, including gastrointestinal, urinary tract and cardiac malformations. Corrective surgery can be performed on the skull and may help prevent intellectual disability, and on the hands and feet to improve functionality (Gilbert, 1999). Life expectancy can be normal but is dependent on the severity of the typical malformations; there is high mortality in the first year of life (Salmon, 1978).

Cerebral palsy

Incidence   1.5–2.5:1000
Genetics   Genetic factors are not common
Intellectual disability Normal to profound

Cerebral palsy is a disorder of posture and movement caused by pathology of the immature brain. The five major types of cerebral palsy are hemiplegia, spastic and ataxic diplegia, tetraplegia, athetoid and ataxic. Depending on the type of cerebral palsy, clinical features include unilateral paresis, spasticity, increased tendon reflexes, contractures, and speech and language defect. Complications include congenital cataracts, epilepsy and feeding difficulties (Aicardi & Bax, 1992). The diagnosis is usually a clinical diagnosis but can be difficult and needs to be differentiated from other neurological disorders.

Cockayne syndrome

Incidence   Rare
Genetics   Autosomal recessive
Intellectual disability Progressive

One of the defining characteristics of Cockayne syndrome is a prematurely aged appearance (McElvanney et al., 1996). There are two accepted expressions of this phenotype: congenital (type II), which is apparent from birth, and classical (type I) which is apparent after one year of age. There may also be a third expression, which has a later onset. In this syndrome, exposure to ultraviolet radiation prevents transcription-coupled repair of DNA. Cockayne syndrome presents with growth failure, typical facies, severe sensitivity to sunlight, microcephaly, hearing and vision impairments, tremor, hydrocephalus, and delayed developmental milestones (McElvanney et al., 1996). There is progressive loss of both mental and physical abilities, which eventually necessitates full-time care

(Gilbert, 1999). Life expectancy has been correlated to the presence of cataracts in the first three years of life, with an increased expectancy if early cataracts are absent (McElvanney *et al.*, 1996). Mortality usually occurs at around 12 years of age (McElvanney *et al.*, 1996).

Coffin-Lowry syndrome

Incidence	(Over 100 reported cases by 1996)
Genetics	X-linked with diminished expression in females. Xp22.1–22.2
Intellectual disability	Severe in males, usually normal in females

Coffin-Lowry syndrome is a systemic connective tissue disorder. It affects males more severely than females. It is characterized by unusually coarse facies, seizures, small stature, generalized hypotonia, characteristic hands (plump lax, soft hands with tapered, hyperextensible fingers) and metabolic abnormalities in collagen. Scoliosis and kyphosis can emerge during adolescence (Gilbert, 1999). With age, the presentation becomes more marked. The cause of death is most commonly due to cardiac and respiratory complications, although life expectancy is typically normal (Gilbert, 1999).

Coffin-Siris syndrome

Incidence	Very rare
Genetics	Autosomal recessive
Intellectual disability	Mild to severe

The main defining feature of Coffin-Siris syndrome is a missing or underdeveloped terminal phalanx and terminal fingernails. Other features include retarded growth leading to delayed skeletal development, hypotonia, gastroesophageal abnormalities, teeth, vision and hearing problems, undescended testes, microcephaly, coarse facies and sparse scalp hair with hypertrichosis of the face and body. This syndrome may be associated with central nervous system complications, secondary to cranial malformations. Life expectancy depends on the severity of intellectual disability (Salmon, 1978).

Cornelia de Lange syndrome

Incidence	1:40 000–100 000
Genetics	Unclear cause, most cases are sporadic
Intellectual disability	Moderate to severe

Cornelia de Lange syndrome has a recognized dichotomy between a classical and mild phenotype. Both phenotypes have typical facial characteristics; however, the milder form is associated with less severe intellectual disability and less severe cardiac and limb abnormalities. The classical phenotype is characterized by small stature, limb abnormalities, frequent respiratory infections, typical facies, self-injury, autistic-like behaviors and eye abnormalities. It has been suggested that the lower the birthweight, the more severe the phenotype and the greater the risk of infection (O'Brien & Yule, 1995; Salmon, 1978). Early mortality can be due to failure to thrive, aspiration pneumonia and feeding difficulties. However, increasingly more infants with Cornelia de Lange syndrome survive into childhood and even adulthood as a result of better medical intervention (O'Brien & Yule, 1995).

Cri-du-chat syndrome

Incidence   1:50 000
Genetics   Partial deletion of 5p15.2
Intellectual disability   Mild to severe
Clinical characteristics of cri-du-chat syndrome include low birthweight, typical facial appearance, microcephaly, a strange high-pitched cry during infancy, prematurely graying hair, and gastrointestinal, cardiac and respiratory problems/infections. Cri-du-chat syndrome is more common in females. Progression from childhood to adulthood is marked by failure to thrive, growth retardation and poor muscular development. These problems previously resulted in mortality in the early years of life; however, this is increasingly less common due to medical advances. There is recent evidence for a milder phenotype of cri-du-chat syndrome, where deletions of chromosome 5 do not fall into the critical region; these persons have a better prognosis.

Duchenne muscular dystrophy

Incidence   1:3500 male births (decreasing due to genetic counseling)
Genetics   X-linked (short arm) recessive disorder, or spontaneous mutations
Intellectual disability   Mild (in 20–30% of cases)
Duchenne muscular dystrophy is a severe degenerative disorder, only affecting males. It is characterized by progressive wasting of the muscles, which eventually leads to respiratory muscle weakness and increasing

respiratory insufficiency. Affected individuals experience difficulty in walking prior to the age of 3 years and are unable to walk by 11 years. There is no progressive deterioration of cognitive skills in affected individuals regardless of whether they have intellectual disability. Respiratory or cardiac failure lead to death in the late teens to mid twenties and survival beyond the second decade is rare.

Fragile-X syndrome

Incidence	1:2000–4000
Genetics	Distal arm Xq27.3; associated with the FMR 1 gene
Intellectual disability	Mild to moderate

Fragile-X syndrome is caused by a large expansion of a sequence of trinucleotide repeats in the first exon of the FMR-1 gene. It is the most commonly inherited cause of neurodevelopmental disability. The phenotypic expression of fragile-X syndrome is characterized by typical facies, macro-orchidism (onset at puberty), autistic-like behavior, macrocephaly, and connective tissue disorder, which can contribute to heart defects and infections. Affected females often have a milder expression of the phenotype, having less severe intellectual disability and clinical features (fragile-XE). Life expectancy is typically normal, but this depends on the severity of cardiovascular involvement.

Galactosemia (classical)

Incidence	1:45 000
Genetics	Autosomal recessive
Intellectual disability	Borderline

Galactosemia is caused by a deficiency of the enzyme galactose-1-phosphate uridyl transferase (GALT), which results in an intolerance to galactose. Long-term dietary restriction of lactose is essential; failure to do this results in feeding difficulties, vomiting, jaundice and renal-tubular damage. Mortality is high if the condition is left untreated; complications include septicemia, coagulopathy, liver disease and encephalopathy (O'Brien & Yule, 1995). Despite dietary control, a secondary deterioration can develop, characterized by intellectual disability, speech difficulties, cerebellar ataxia, intention tremor, apraxia and extra-pyramidal dysfunction. This is thought to be due to endogenous galactose production (Berry et al., 1995). Galactosemia usually results in infertility/reduced fertility in women (Berry et al., 1995), although some galactosemic women can have natural pregnancies. This syndrome is associated with a normal life expectancy.

Joubert syndrome

Incidence   (Over 100 reported cases by 1996)
Genetics   Autosomal recessive
Intellectual disability   Mild to moderate

Joubert syndrome is characterized by congenital ataxia, hypotonia, characteristic breathing patterns, agenesis of the corpus callosum and defects of the visual and renal systems (O'Brien & Yule, 1995). 30–50% of affected individuals die before the age of two years (SSBP, 1996).

Lesch-Nyhan syndrome

Incidence   1:380 000
Genetics   X-linked recessive
Intellectual disability   Mild to moderate

Lesch-Nyhan syndrome is caused by a deficiency in the enzyme hypoxanthineguanine phosphoribosyl transferase (Saito & Takashima, 2000). Affected boys appear normal at birth; however before 12 months they show prominent signs of motor dysfunction such as involuntary movements and hyponia. These are in addition to small stature, seizures, visual defects, microcephaly, feeding difficulties and hyperuricaemia (Harris *et al.*, 1998; O'Brien & Yule, 1995). Uric acid build-up can result in aggression and severe self-mutilation, especially to the fingers and mouth. Pharmacological interventions can be useful to reduce self-injury (Saito & Takashima, 2000). Infection, renal failure and respiration difficulties typically result in death in early adulthood (O'Brien & Yule, 1995). Unexpected and sudden death is frequently noted (Saito & Takashima, 2000). There would seem to be a correlation between the degree of deficiency of the HPRT enzyme, intellectual disability and self-mutilation (greater deficiency is associated with both lower IQ and more pronounced self-injury) (Saito & Takashima, 2000).

Lowe syndrome

Incidence   1:200 000
Genetics   X-linked recessive disorder
Intellectual disability   75% have intellectual disability, usually moderate to severe

Lowe syndrome is characterized by congenital eye abnormalities, infantile hypotonia, renal tubular dysfunction, typical facies, serum enzyme and muscular-skeletal abnormalities, self-injury and juvenile stereotypes. No known survivors have been reported beyond the age of 40 years; death is usually due to renal failure, dehydration or pneumonia (O'Brien & Yule, 1995).

Myotonic dystrophy (congenital)

Incidence	1:18 000–43 000
Genetics	Non-coding region of chromosome 19. Autosomal dominant, almost always maternal transmission
Intellectual disability	Mild to moderate in 75% of cases

Congenital myotonic dystrophy is characterized by muscle weakness, feeding difficulties, skeletal abnormalities, hypotonia, respiratory problems and facial diplegia (Tanabe & Nonaka, 1987). Myotonia develops around 10 years of age (Thornton, 1999). Patients surviving into adulthood present with the same symptoms as patients with late onset myotonic dystrophy (Tanabe & Nonaka, 1987). Mortality is often attributed to feeding and respiratory difficulties that result from muscle atrophy. There is considerable neonatal mortality, however babies who do survive show an improvement in muscle tone.

Neurofibromatosis type 1

Incidence	1:2500-3500
Genetics	Autosomal dominant 17q11.2, 50% of cases are sporadic
Intellectual disability	Borderline

Neurofibromatosis type 1 is the most common form of neurofibromatosis. It is characterized by the formation of tumors, café au lait spots, neurofibromas and lesch nodules, of the central nervous system. It is also associated with microcephaly, short stature, and endocrinological and thorax disorders. Potentially life-threatening complications develop in one third of affected individuals, including plexiform neurofibromas, skeletal abnormalities and hypertension. The risk of malignancy is 3–15%. Treatment is aimed at managing medical complications and removing neurofibromas where appropriate. The presentation of cutaneous neurofibromas is correlated with increasing age; these are seldom reported before mid-adolescence. The occurrence of café au lait decreases after middle age.

Noonan syndrome

Incidence   1:1000–2500
Genetics   Autosomal dominant or sporadic
Intellectual disability   Mild

Noonan syndrome is a multimalformation disorder, comprising of characteristic facies, short stature, delayed puberty, undescended testes (males), and skeletal and congenital cardio-respiratory abnormalities (Bader-Meunier *et al.*, 1997; Noonan, 1999). In addition, there are often abnormalities in the lymphatic, visual and hearing systems (Bader-Meunier *et al.*, 1997). Early feeding difficulties can result in a failure to thrive (Shah *et al.*, 1999) and muscle hypotonia can result in mild motor delay, although hypotonia improves over time (Noonan, 1994). Facial characteristics become less dysmorphic with age. Life expectancy is thought to be normal, unless cardiac complications are serious (O'Brien & Yule, 1995).

Phenylketonuria

Incidence   1:5000–14 000
Genetics   Autosomal recessive
Intellectual disability   Moderate to severe (if untreated)

Individuals with phenylketonuria (PKU) are unable to metabolize the amino acid phenylalanine due to the absence of the enzyme phenylalanine hydroxylase. Treatment consists of a phenylalanine-low diet. The initiation, quality and duration of blood phenylalanine control are the three main parameters of PKU management. Discontinuation/non-initiation of the diet prior to the age of 10 years causes intellectual disability. It is important that the diet should be implemented within the first few weeks of life. If the diet is started early in life and is carefully maintained, a normal life expectancy can be expected.

Prader-Willi syndrome

Incidence   1:10 000
Genetics   Abnormality in paternal 15q11–13 is observed in
                                 60–70% of cases; most of the remaining cases
                                 have maternal uniparental dysomy
Intellectual disability   Borderline to moderate

Prader-Willi syndrome is characterized by marked hypotonia, failure to thrive, delayed sexual development, scoliosis, acromicria, small stature, typical facies and persistent skin picking (Clarke *et al.*, 1995; Holland, 1998). Between 1 and 6 years of age, hyperphagia develops as a result of hypothalamic abnormalities. Strict behavioral and dietary controls are necessary, as the resulting obesity and its complications (hypertension, cardiovascular symptoms, respiratory difficulties and diabetes) can be fatal. Growth hormone treatment increases growth and decreases fat formation. Life expectancy is dependent on weight control.

Rett syndrome

Incidence   1:10 000–15 000
Genetics   Distal arm of Xq28
Intellectual disability   Profound

Rett syndrome usually affects females, but rarely occurs in males. Infants with this neuro-degenerative disorder often appear normal until 18 months old, when they begin to regress, physically (scoliosis and leg deformities), socially, linguistically and adaptively. A four-stage pathway of the disorder is observed: early stagnation in development after initial progress, rapid regression, plateau, and late motor deterioration characterized by truncal apraxia/ataxia and gait apraxia. Rett syndrome is associated with breathing abnormalities, specifically hyperventilation and breath holding, and stereotypic hand movements (hand wringing, clapping). Two-thirds of patients survive beyond the second decade (Ellaway & Christodoulou, 1999). Those who do not survive tend to be poorly nourished and have chest deformities; these patients often die during sleep (O'Brien &Yule, 1995). Mortality in older patients is often due to respiratory infections, or accidents (Ellaway & Christodoulou, 1999). Earlier mortality is associated with more severe intellectual disability (Ellaway & Christodoulou, 1999).

Rubinstein-taybi

Incidence   1:125 000
Genetics   Autosomal dominant. Microdeletion at 16p13.3
Intellectual disability   Mild to severe

Facial characteristics that are typical of Rubinstein-Taybi change predictably with age. Skeletal abnormalities, short stature, stereotypic and self-stimulatory behaviors (rocking and hand-flapping), and cardiac and renal defects are all typical of the syndrome, as are feeding problems, poor weight gain in infancy and frequent infections. Some cases exhibit self-injurious behaviors and there is a tendency to become overweight.

There is no information on life expectancy although patients can survive into their seventh decade. Medical complications, such as congenital heart, renal and urinary tract abnormalities affect mortality.

Smith-Lemli-Opitz

Incidence   1:20 000–40 000
Genetics   Autosomal recessive
Intellectual disability Borderline to severe

Smith-Lemli-Opitz syndrome is a metabolic disorder in which there is abnormal metabolism of cholesterol, due to lower levels of 7-dehydrocholesterol reductase (7DHC) (cholesterol precursor). Consequently, there is impaired growth and development. It would appear to be three times more common in males. However, this may reflect the fact that it is more easily detectable in males. Characteristics include typical facies, hypertonia (although initially hypotonia), growth deficiency, psychomotor delay, recurrent infections, microcephaly, and congenital abnormalities of most major organs including the rectal and urinary tracts and the external genitalia (de Die-Smulders & Fryns, 1992). Longevity is determined by severity of malformations and the treatment received. Some persons die during childhood, but the milder expression of the phenotype is associated with a near-normal life expectancy.

Smith Magenis

Incidence   1:50 000
Genetics   Partial/complete deletion of band 17p11.2
Intellectual disability Moderate

The typical presentation of Smith Magenis syndrome includes multiple congenital abnormalities, characteristic facies, hearing and vision difficulties, scoliosis, self-injurious behavior, aggression and sleep disturbance (Allanson et al., 1999). Melatonin is of reported efficacy in the treatment of sleep disturbances. Medical complications seen in a quarter of these patients include hypothyroidism, immunoglobin deficiency and congenital heart defects (Allanson et al., 1999). Life expectancy is normal, with one severely affected patient reaching 72 years (O'Brien & Yule, 1995).

Sotos syndrome

Incidence   (200 reported cases by 2001)
Genetics   Probably autosomal dominant
Intellectual disability Borderline to mild

Sotos syndrome is characterized by accelerated growth during the first five years of life. Infants often present with jaundice, early feeding problems and hypotonia. Advanced bone age, connective tissue anomalies, abnormal electroencephalograms, asthma and allergies are all typical of this syndrome. Frequent ear infections can often lead to hearing loss and there are frequent upper respiratory infections.

Tuberous sclerosis

Incidence	1:7000
Genetics	Autosomal dominant either chromosome 9q34.3 or 16p13.3
Intellectual disability	50% have intellectual disability, usually severe–profound

Tuberous sclerosis is a non-degenerative multisystem condition. Its typical presentation includes hamartias, hamartomas, true neoplasms, skin lesions, intellectual disability, autism, other behavioral abnormalities and seizures. Recent findings suggest that pulmonary lymphangioleiomyomatosis is common in females with this condition (Costello *et al.*, 2000). Life expectancy is dependent on the severity and location of cerebral and peripheral lesions. Renal and brain lesions are the most common causes of mortality.

Turner syndrome

Incidence	1:2000–2500 female births
Genetics	Sex aneuploidy: total or partial absence of the second X-chromosome
Intellectual disability	Normal

Turner syndrome is associated with an increased incidence of osteoporosis, diabetes mellitus, premature aging of the hearing organs, obesity, cardiovascular disease, hypertension, thyroid dysfunction and strokes (Garden *et al.*, 1996; Hultcrantz *et al.*, 1994). Growth failure and failure of normal pubertal development respond to growth hormone therapy. Approximately 50% of deaths in Turner syndrome are due to cardiovascular disease, and death occurs 6–13 years earlier than in the general population.

Velocardiofacial

Incidence   Estimated at 1·4000
Genetics   Autosomal dominant; sub-microscopic deletion
                             22q11.2 (85% of cases)
Intellectual disability   Borderline

There is wide variability in the expression of velocardiofacial syndrome but typical presentation is that of congenital heart disease, typical facial characteristics, intellectual disability, cerebellar ataxia, generalized hypotonia and immune disorders. Recurrent respiratory infections are common and there is a high coincidence of schizophrenia (Murphy *et al.*, 1999). Life expectancy is determined by the severity of heart abnormalities.

Williams syndrome

Incidence   1:25 000
Genetics   Usually sporadic; microdeletion on chromosome
                             7
Intellectual disability   Moderate to severe

Williams syndrome is a neuro-developmental disorder presenting in infancy with severe feeding difficulties, failure to thrive and typical facies. The cardiovascular, connective tissue, skeletal, gastrointestinal, urogenital and renal systems are also implicated and hypercalcemia and menstrual difficulties are common. These complications, particularly cardiovascular problems, may result in premature death. There is an age-related decrease in renal function; however, gastrointestinal and bowel-related complications improve with age (Howlin *et al.*, 1998).

Wolf-Hirschhorn

Incidence   1:50 000
Genetics   Partial deletion 4p16.3
Intellectual disability   Severe to profound

Wolf-Hirschhorn syndrome is characterized by a number of congenital physical and neuromuscular abnormalities such as renal defects, heart defects, hypotonia and frequent respiratory tract abnormalities. Other features include microcephaly, characteristic facial features, seizures and growth retardation (Battaglia *et al.*, 1999). These abnormalities increase susceptibility to respiratory infections, and life expectancy is dependent on the number and severity of these malformations. There is a high prevalence of aspiration pneumonia, which often necessitates continuous maintenance antibiotic therapy. Approximately one third of infants die before two years of age (SSBP, 2000) as a result of cardiac failure or broncho-pneumonia. However, there are reported adults who have survived into their third decade. The condition is twice as common in females as in males.

X-linked alpha-thalassemia

Incidence	(44 reported cases by 1994)
Genetics	X-linked recessive. Locus on proximal long arm of X chromosome Xq12-q21.31; disorder of hemoglobin synthesis
Intellectual disability	Severe

All known cases of X-linked alpha-thalassemia have been male. This phenotype is characterized by dysmorphic facial features, genital abnormalities, gastrointestinal anomalies, growth deficiency, mild HbH disease, feeding difficulties, seizures, kyphoscoliosis, hypotonia and microcephaly (Logie *et al.*, 1994). Life expectancy is severely reduced with 90% of cases dying in infancy (O'Brien & Yule, 1995).

X-linked hydrocephalus

Incidence	1:30 000
Genetics	Mutations in gene Xq28 encoding for L1 – a neural cell adhesion molecule
Intellectual disability	Severe

X-linked hydrocephalus is the most common form of hydrocephalus, accounting for 2–15% of cases in new-born males (Kenwrick *et al.*, 1996). The course of the syndrome is dependent on the medical complications (Schrander-Stumpel & Fryns, 1998). This syndrome is typically characterized by adducted thumbs, typical facies, scoliosis, seizures, congenital ataxia, hydrocephalus, abnormalities of the nervous system, paraplegia and intellectual disability. Cases where hydrocephalus is diagnosed prenatally potentially have a worse prognosis (Schrander-Stumpel & Fryns, 1998). There is an accumulation of cerebrospinal fluid, which increases intracranial pressure and can lead to early mortality (Kenwrick *et al.*, 1996). However, intracranial pressure can be reduced by inserting surgical shunts, thus increasing life expectancy (Kenwrick *et al.*, 1996).

Mucopolysaccharidoses (MPS)

The mucopolysaccharidoses are lysosomal storage diseases, caused by deficiencies of lysosomal enzymes which catalyse glycosaminoglycans.

Hunter (MPS II)

Incidence	1:132 000 male births
Genetics	X-linked recessive
Intellectual disability	Mild to severe

Hunter syndrome typically presents before 4 years of age. Its defining features are physical, mental and central nervous system deterioration/ wasting. Chronic diarrhea, recurrent ear infections, progressive hearing and visual impairment are reported in most cases. This syndrome is characterized by two phenotypes: mild (MPS IIB) and severe (MPS IIA). MPS IIA results in mortality in the first or second decade due to obstructive airway disease and cardiac failure. MPS IIB has a later age of onset and the progression of the syndrome is slower (O'Brien & Yule, 1995); patients with this phenotype usually survive into their fifth or sixth decade.

Hurler (MPS IH)

Incidence	1:100 000
Genetics	Autosomal recessive chromosome 4
Intellectual disability	Moderate to severe

Hurler syndrome is a progressive condition, characterized by increasing medical complications, including heart, liver and spleen abnormalities, obstructive hydrocephalus, severe skeletal deformities, respiratory infection, stiffening joints, cognitive deterioration, carpal tunnel syndrome, weight loss and muscle wasting (O'Brien & Yule, 1995). Death usually occurs within the first decade of life and is often due to cardio-respiratory and neurological complications. Bone-marrow transplantation improves prognosis by decelerating the progression of the disorder and has been reported to extend survival by many decades.

Hurler-Scheie (MPS IH/S)

Incidence	Less than 1:100 000 births
Genetics	Autosomal recessive chromosome 4
Intellectual disability	Mild

Hurler-Scheie syndrome is an intermediate phenotype of Hurler syndrome and Scheie syndrome. It typically presents between 3 and 8 years of age and survival into adulthood is common. Progressive visual impairments can severely impair sight by the fourth decade (Keith *et al.*, 1990).

Maroteaux-Lamy (MPS VI)

Incidence	Less than 1:100 000 births
Genetics	Autosomal recessive chromosome 5
Intellectual disability	Normal to mild

Maroteaux-lamy syndrome is similar to Hurler syndrome, but life expectancy extends into the second or third decade of life or beyond (O'Brien & Yule, 1995). Spinal cord compression, carpal tunnel syndrome and hydrocephalus are common neurological complications of this syndrome. Complications of the cardio-pulmonary system are a frequent cause of death (O'Brien & Yule, 1995).

Morquio (MPS IV)

Incidence	1:100 000
Genetics	Autosomal recessive chromosomes 3, 16
Intellectual disability	Normal to mild

Typical medical complications of Morquio syndrome include growth retardation, heart complications, joint hypermobility and quadriplegia/ myelopathy (due to compression of the cervical cord). Skeletal abnormalities can result in heart failure in the second or third decade of life; however, providing these are dealt with, survival beyond the third decade is possible (O'Brien & Yule, 1995).

Sanfilippo (MPS III)

Incidence	1:25 000–200 000
Genetics	Autosomal recessive chromosomes 7, 12, 14
Intellectual disability	Moderate to severe

Sanfilippo syndrome is a progressive, multisystem disorder, primarily affecting the central nervous system and skeleton. By the age of 10 years neurological degeneration is severe. This is often paralleled by a progressive deterioration of acquired skills (O'Brien & Yule, 1995). Balance disturbance causes frequent falls, difficulties with swallowing usually necessitate tube feeding, and connective tissue deterioration and joint stiffness require wheelchair use before the age of 20 years. Mortality usually occurs around the second or third decade of life, due to respiratory infections, but adults with milder instances typically survive beyond the fourth decade.

Scheie (MPS is formerly MPS V)

Incidence   1:500 000
Genetics   Autosomal recessive chromosome 4
Intellectual disability   Normal to mild
Scheie syndrome has a milder expression than Hurler syndrome. It is associated with late childhood onset, typical facies, and skeletal and cardiac abnormalities (Keith et al., 1990). Life expectancy is normal.

Sly (MPS VII)

Incidence   (20 cases world-wide 1994)
Genetics   Autosomal recessive chromosome 7
Intellectual disability   Moderate
The clinical picture of Sly syndrome involves moderate skeletal abnormalities, recurrent respiratory infections, visual and auditory deterioration, typical facies, hepatosplenomegaly and inguinale and umbilical hernias. There is a huge variability in the expression of the phenotype. Those persons with more severe situations die in the first few years of life; however, those with milder situations have a normal life expectancy.

Sex chromosome aneuploidies

Klinefelter syndrome

47 XXY
Incidence   1:750 male births
Genetics   Sex aneuploidy
Intellectual disability   Normal to mild
47 XXY syndrome is not normally diagnosed before adolescence and it is thought that 64% of cases are never diagnosed (Ratcliffe, 1999). Symptoms vary in severity, but generally the disorder is characterized by hypogo-

nadism, microcephaly, growth retardation, obesity, transient gyneco-mastia, androgen deficiency, impaired spermatogenesis and decreased fertility (Smyth & Bremner, 1998). Research suggests that patients have an increased risk of developing breast carcinoma, autoimmune diseases, osteoporosis and psychiatric disorders (Smyth & Bremner, 1998). Osteoporosis responds to testosterone replacement therapy (Smyth & Bremner, 1998). Life expectancy is thought to be normal.

48 XXYY

Incidence   (60 published cases by 1995)
Genetics   Sex aneuploidy
Intellectual disability   Mild to moderate

48 XXYY syndrome is similar to 47 XXY and 47 XYY. However, patients tend to be even taller. It is characterized by mild dysmorphic facial features, intellectual disability and behavioral problems. Sexual development is similar to 47 XXY (O'Brien & Yule, 1995).

49 XXXXY

Incidence   1:85 000 male births
Genetics   Sex aneuploidy: probably maternal non-dis-junction (meiosis I and II)
Intellectual disability   Borderline

Typical characteristics of 49 XXXXY syndrome include typical facies, typical habitus, congenital heart defects, hypogonadism and other genital abnormalities, multiple skeletal abnormalities (i.e. radioulnar synostosis, delayed bone age) and language difficulties.

Other aneuploidies

47 XXX

Incidence   1:1000 female births
Genetics   Sex aneuploidy: non-disjunction of the X chromosome
Intellectual disability   Normal to borderline

Clinical symptoms of 47 XXX include low birthweight, delayed pubertal development (by 6 months), developmental delay, microcephaly, social immaturity and problems with fine motor coordination and balance (Harmon *et al.*, 1998). There is a high representation of this phenotype in the forensic (offender) population (Harmon *et al.*, 1998). Life expectancy is thought to be normal, and fertility does not appear to be affected.

47 XYY

Incidence	1:1000 male births
Genetics	Sex aneuploidy: non-disjunction of Y chromosome
Intellectual disability	Borderline

In 47 XYY, there is accelerated leg and body growth, an increased pubertal growth spurt, behavioral problems and delayed puberty (by approximately 6 months). Sexual development and fertility are normal. There is a four-fold increase in the prevalence of criminal conviction and it would appear that there is a correlation between low IQ and criminal activity (O'Brien, 2001b). Life expectancy is thought to be normal.

Conclusion

The characteristics of persons with intellectual disabilities are changing as many are living longer. This is due to a greater understanding of the syndromes that contribute to intellectual disability and consequently greater knowledge of how to manage these syndromes. This chapter has discussed the factors with primary impact on physical health, but it should also be emphasized that factors which affect quality of life in the general population also exert an influence on the situation of people with intellectual disabilities. Currently, tobacco, alcohol and non-medical use of drugs are used less commonly by individuals with intellectual disability than by the normal population. However, given the increasing availability of these substances to this population, we can expect them to be increasingly implicated.

The incidence of cancer among persons with intellectual disabilities is also increasing (Raitasuo *et al.*, 1997) due to the increasing life expectancies. The high use of prescribed medication must also be considered (for example anticonvulsants and antipsychotics may be associated with gastroesophageal diseases and extra pyramidal events respectively; Beange & Lennox, 1998). For these various reasons, the health care of people with intellectual disabilities is changing. The challenge for the future lies in combining a detailed knowledge of the health challenges of individual syndromes with the changing social context and resultant health problems of the aging individual with an intellectual disability.

References

Aicardi, J. & Bax, M. (1992) Cerebral palsy. In: *Diseases of the Nervous System in Childhood* (ed. J. Aicardi), pp. 330–374. MacKeith Press, London.

Allanson, J.E., Greenberg, F. & Smith, A.C. (1999) The face of Smith-Magenis syndrome: a subjective and objective study. *Journal of Medical Genetics*, **36**, 394–397.

American Psychiatric Association (1999) *Diagnostic and Statistical Manual of Mental Disorders*. APA, Washington DC, USA.

Bader-Meunier, B., Tchernia, G., Mielot, F., Fontaine, J.L., Thomas, C., Lyonnet, S., Lavergne, J. M. & Dommergues, J.P. (1997) Occurrence of myeloproliferative disorder in patients with Noonan syndrome. *Journal of Pediatrics*, **130**, 885–889.

Barnard, L., Pearson, J., Rippon, L. & O'Brien, G. (in press) Behavioural phenotypes of genetic syndromes: Summaries. In: *Behavioural Phenotypes in Clinical Practice* (ed. G. O'Brien). MacKeith Press, London.

Battaglia, A., Carey, J.C., Cederholm, P., Viskochil, D.H., Brothman, A.R. & Galasso, C. (1999) Natural history of Wolf-Hirschhorn syndrome: Experience with 15 cases. *Pediatrics*, **103**, 830–836.

Beange, H. & Lennox, N. (1998) Physical aspects of health in the learning disabled. *Current Opinion in Psychiatry*, **11**, 531–534.

Berry, G.T., Nissim, I., Lin, Z., Mazur, A.T., Gibson, J.B. & Segal, S. (1995) Endogenous synthesis of galactose in normal men and patients with hereditary galactosaemia. *Lancet*, **346**, 1073–1074.

Clarke, D.J., Boer, H. & Webb, T. (1995) Genetic and behavioural aspects of Prader-Willi syndrome: A review with a translation of the original paper. *Mental Handicap Research*, **8**, 38–53.

Costa, T., Greer, W., Rysiecki, G., Buncic, J.R. & Ray, P.N. (1997) Monozygotic twins discordant for Aicardi syndrome. *Journal of Medical Genetics*, **34**, 688–691.

Costello, L.C., Hartman, T.E. & Ryu, J.H. (2000) High frequency of pulmonary lymphangioleiomyomatosis in women with tuberous sclerosis complex. *Mayo Clinic Proceedings*, **75**, 591–594.

de Die-Smulders, C. & Fryns, J.P. (1992) Smith-Lemli-Opitz syndrome: the changing phenotype with age. *Genetic Counseling*, **3**, 77–82.

Ellaway, C. & Christodoulou, J. (1999) Rett syndrome: Clinical update and review of recent genetic advances. *Journal of Paediatric Child Health*, **35**, 419–426.

Garden, A.S., Diver, M.J. & Fraser, W.D. (1996) Undiagnosed morbidity in adult women with Turner syndrome. *Clinical Endocrinology*, **45**, 589–593.

Gilbert, P.C. (1999) *A-Z of Syndromes and Inherited Disorders*. Stanely Thorpe Ltd, Gloucestershire, UK.

Harmon, R.J., Bender, B.G., Linden, M.G. & Robinson, A. (1998) Transition from adolescence to early adulthood: adaptation and psychiatric status of women with 47 XXX. *Journal of the American Academy of Child & Adolescent Psychiatry*, **37**, 286–291.

Harris, J.C., Lee, R.R., Jinnah, H.A., Wong, D.F., Yaster, M. & Bryan, R.N. (1998) Craniocerebral magnetic resonance imaging measurement and findings in Lesch-Nyhan syndrome. *Archives of Neurology*, **55**, 547–553.

Holland, A.J. (1998) Understanding the eating disorder affecting people with Prader-Willi syndrome. *Journal of Applied Research in Intellectual Disabilities*, **11**, 192–206.

Hollins, S., Attard, M.T., von Fraunhofer, N., McGuigan, S. & Sedgwick, P. (1998) Mortality in people with learning disability: Risks, causes, and death certification findings in London. *Developmental Medicine and Child Neurology*, **40**, 50–56.

Howlin, P., Davies, M. & Udwin, O. (1998) Syndrome specific characteristics in Williams syndrome: To what extent do early behavioural patterns persist into adult life? *Journal of Applied Research in Intellectual Disabilities*, **11**, 207–226.

Hultcrantz, M., Sylven, L. & Borg, E. (1994) Ear and hearing problems in 44 middle-aged women with Turner's syndrome. *Hearing Research*, **76**, 127–132.

Janicki, M.P. & Dalton, A.J. (1998) Sensory impairments among older adults with intellectual disability. *Journal of Intellectual and Developmental Disabilities*, **23**, 3–11.

Keith, O., Scully, C. & Weidmann, G.M. (1990) Orofacial features of Scheie (Hurler-Scheie) syndrome (alpha-L-iduronidase space deficiency). *Oral Surgery, Oral Medicine and Oral Pathology*, **70**, 70–74.

Kenwrick, S., Jouet, M. & Donnai, D. (1996) X-linked hydrocephalus and MASA syndrome. *The Journal of Medical Genetics*, **33**, 59–65.

Logie, L.J., Gibbons, R.J., Higgs, D.R., Brown, J.K. & Porteous, M.E.M. (1994) Alpha thalassaemia mental retardation (ATR-X): an atypical family. *Archives of Disease in Childhood*, **70**, 439–440.

McElvanney, A.M., Wooldridge, W.J., Khan, A.A. & Ansons, A.M. (1996) Ophthalmic management of Cockayne's syndrome. *Eye*, **10**, 61–64.

Murphy, K.C., Jones, L.A. & Owen, M.J. (1999) High rates of schizophrenia in adults with velo-cardio-facial syndrome. *Archives of General Psychiatry*, **56**, 940–945.

Noonan, J.A. (1994) Noonan syndrome: An update and review for the primary pediatrician. *Clinical Pediatrics*, **33**, 548–555.

Noonan, J.A. (1999) Noonan syndrome revisited. *Journal of Pediatrics*, **135**, 667–668.

O'Brien, G. (2001a) Defining learning disability: what place does intelligence testing have now? *Developmental Medicine & Child Neurology*, **43**, 570–573.

O'Brien, G. (2001b) Adult outcome of childhood learning disability. *Developmental Medicine & Child Neurology*, **43**, 634–638.

O'Brien, G. & Yule, W. (eds) (1995) Behavioural Phenotypes. *Clinics in Developmental Medicine*, no. 138, MacKeith Press, London.

Raitasuo, J., Molsa, P., Raitasuo, S. & Mattila, K. (1997) Deaths among the intellectually disabled: A retrospective study. *Journal of Applied Research in Intellectual Disabilities*, **10**, 280–288.

Ratcliffe, S. (1999) Long term outcome in children of sex chromosome abnormalities. *Archives of Disease in Childhood*, **80**, 192–195.

Saito, Y. & Takashima, S. (2000) Neurotransmitter changes in the pathophysiology of Lesch-Nyhan syndrome. *Brain and Development*, **22**, S122–S131.

Salmon, M.A. (1978) *Developmental Defects and Syndromes*. HMM Publishers, London.

Schrander-Stumpel, C. & Fryns, J.P. (1998) Congenital hydrocephalus: nosology and guidelines for clinical approach and genetic counselling. *European Journal of Pediatrics*, **157**, 355–362.

Shah, N., Rodriguez, M., Louis, D.S., Lindley, K. & Milla, P.J. (1999) Feeding difficulties and foregut dysmotility in Noonan's syndrome. *Archives of Disease in Childhood*, **81**, 28–31.

Smyth, C.M. & Bremner, W.J. (1998) Klinefelter syndrome. *Archives of Internal Medicine*, **158**, 1309–1314.

SSBP (1996) *Proceedings of the 4th international symposium of the Society for the Study of Behavioural Phenotypes*. Marino Institute of Education, Dublin, Ireland.

SSBP (2000) *Proceedings of the 6th International Symposium of the Society for the Study of Behavioural Phenotypes*. Venice International University, San Servolo, Italy.

Tanabe, Y. & Nonaka, I. (1987) Congenital myotonic dystrophy: Changes in muscle pathology with ageing. *Journal of the Neurological Sciences*, **77**, 59–68.

Thornton, C. (1999) The myotonic dystrophies. *Seminars in Neurology*, **19**, 25–33.

Van Schrojenstein Lantman-de Valk, H.M., Haveman, M.J., Maaskant, M.A., Kessels, A.G.H., Urlings, H.F.J. & Sturmans, F. (1994) The need for assessment of sensory functioning in ageing people with mental handicap. *Journal of Intellectual Disability Research*, **38**, 289–298.

4 Cerebral Palsy

Clyde E. Rapp and Margarita Torres

Introduction

The usual definition of cerebral palsy is that of a non-progressive disorder of motor function in young children which has its onset in the prenatal or perinatal period (Ingram, 1964). Frequently included in the definition are paresis and incoordination and the occurrence of involuntary movements (Scoles, 1982). Although the definition usually requires a lack of neurologic progression, some observers have noted the appearance of extrapyramidal symptoms, including dystonia, with age (Burke *et al.*, 1980). In another report, dystonia and spastic paraparesis became progressively worse in individuals aged between 14 and 40 years of age (Treves & Korczyn, 1986).

In our clinic, where we follow over 300 adults with cerebral palsy, we have noted an increase in the frequency of seizures, decreasing cognitive ability and increasing frequency and severity of pulmonary aspiration as the patients age. Other observers (Jahnsen & Holm, 2001) have noted a deterioration in the ability of adults to walk before age 45 in 87.9% of the cohort that was studied. They postulated that the cause of the deterioration was pain and fatigue. A second group of authors have also demonstrated the loss of the ability to walk among adults with cerebral palsy (which was caused at least in part by the withdrawal of physical therapy) (Bottos *et al.*, 2001).

Therefore, based on our observations as well as those of others, cerebral palsy does not appear to be a 'static' encephalopathy. From a neurologic standpoint, it has been postulated that there is erratic sprouting of new neurons as patients age, which may cause a worsening of dystonic movements (Burke *et al.*, 1980) and possibly increasing paraparesis. Based on the observation that the ability to walk decreases with time in adults with cerebral palsy, there may also be some functional deterioration in the muscles or perhaps damage to the joints which partially account for this deterioration, and this is frequently noted clinically.

Epidemiology

The prevalence of cerebral palsy in children is 1.5 to 2.5 per 1000 (Oxford Register of Early Childhood Impairment: Annual Report, 1998). From the mid-1960s to the mid-1980s, there has been an increase in the prevalence of cerebral palsy which parallels the increasing survival of low-birth-weight infants (Goldenberg & Rouse, 1998). Based on two more recent studies, there has been a decrease of 0.5 per 1000 live births from 1980 until 1989 and 1992 (Bottos *et al.*, 1999; Oxford Register of Early Childhood Impairment: Annual Report, 1998). Despite a slight decrease in incidence, the prevalence of cerebral palsy has increased significantly from the 1960s until the early 1990s. This is due to increased survival of low birthweight infants as noted previously. The incidence of neurodevelopmental sequelae (at least among the 1000 to 1500 g babies) has not changed since the late 1970s (Hack *et al.*, 2002).

Because of the lack of availability of mortality statistics and the lack of a national registry for patients with cerebral palsy (particularly adults), the exact number of adults with cerebral palsy is not known but remains a significant proportion of the population with intellectual disabilities (Murphy *et al.*, 1995). Ninety-five percent of children with diplegia and 75% of children with quadriplegia survive until age 30 (Powell *et al.*, 1988). Ninety percent of children with mild intellectual disabilities and 65% of children with severe intellectual disabilities survive until age 38 (Crichton *et al.*, 1995). Overall survival of all children with cerebral palsy until the age of 20 is 90% (Evans *et al.*, 1990). Strauss and Shavelle (1998) mention the following clinical characteristics as significant factors in determining survival to adulthood for patients with cerebral palsy:

- Location of motor dysfunction (e.g. quadriplegia, diplegia or hemiplegia), type and frequency of seizure disorder, severity of intellectual disabilities, cognitive and communications disorders and secular trends at the time survival was determined.
- Survival is related to the level of retardation as well. Survival until adulthood is 50% for those with an IQ of less than 20, whereas 92% of children with an IQ greater than 34 survive until adulthood (Blair *et al.*, 2001).

Based on the above information, the number of individuals with cerebral palsy is increasing secondary to increased survival of pre-term births, and the number surviving to adulthood is significant. Despite these demographic trends and the increasing tendency to transfer adults with cerebral palsy from institutions to the community, primary care physicians and specialists in the adult health care system have usually not had specialized training in caring for adults with cerebral palsy and other intellectual disabilities (Garrard, 1982). This has resulted in less than optimal care for adults with cerebral palsy. One study demonstrated excess mortality in adults with cerebral palsy from cancer, stroke, ischemic heart disease and cancer (Strauss *et al.*, 1999) and a second study cited a lack of periodic health examinations including breast examinations and routine gynecologic care (Murphy *et al.*, 1995).

Etiology

Cerebral palsy has multiple etiologies (Table 4.1). As more genetic, metabolic and neurologic syndromes are described, which fulfill the definition of a non-progressive encephalopathy beginning in the perinatal or prenatal period (or an encephalopathy which progresses slowly), the number of specific etiologies within the broad diagnostic category of cerebral palsy will increase.

Table 4.1   Specific etiologies of cerebral palsy (Badawi *et al.*, 1998).

(A) Syndromes sometimes (but not always) associated with a motor impairment, which historically have been included

Absent septum pellucidum: Hydranencephaly/porencephaly, migration abnormality/ heterotopia, seizures, spasticity/increased tendon reflex.

Allan-Herndon syndrome: Severe intellectual deficit, dysarthria, ataxia, athetoid movements, muscle hypoplasia, spastic paraplegia with hyperreflexia.

Arginase deficiency: Ataxia, cerebral atrophy/myelin abnormality, dementia, extrapyramidal disorder, intellectual deficit, microcephaly, seizures, spasticity/increased tendon reflex.

Behr syndrome: Intellectual deficit with optic atrophy, ataxia, spasticity and posterior column loss. Not progressive.

Congenital rubella syndrome: A consequence of maternal infection resulting in various developmental abnormalities such as cardiac and ocular lesions, deafness, microphaly, intellectual deficit.

Corpus striatum syndrome (neuronal ceroid lipofuscinosis: also Vogt's disease): Frequently associated with birth trauma, characterized by bilateral athetosis, walking difficulties, spasmodic outbursts of laughing or crying, speech disorders, excessive myelination of the nerve fibers of the corpus striatum giving it a marbled appearance.

Endemic cretinism (fetal iodine deficiency): Intellectual deficit, spastic diplegia, deafness, strabismus, nystagmus.

Fetal cytomegalovirus infection (CMV): Microcephaly, intellectual deficit, seizures, spasticity/ increased tendon reflex.

Fetal iodine deficiency (see endemic cretinism).

Continued

Table 4.1 Continued.

Fetal methyl mercury poisoning (Minamata disease): Microcephaly, aberrant muscle tone, deafness, blindness.

Fryns syndrome: Cerebral atrophy/myelin abnormality, hypotonia, joint contractures, intellectual deficit, microcephaly, seizures, spasticity/increased tendon reflex.

Lyposomal storage disorder (Salla disease): Ataxia common, cerebral atrophy/myelin abnormality, dementia, hypertonia, intellectual deficit, seizures, spasticity/increased tendon reflex.

Microcephaly-chorioretinopathy: Hypertonia, intellectual deficit, seizures, spasticity/increased tendon reflex. Autosomal recessive syndrome.

Microcephaly-intracranial calcification: Cerebral atrophy/myelin abnormality, lissencephaly, intellectual deficit, seizures, spasticity/increased tendon reflex.

Minamata disease (see fetal methyl mercury poisoning).

Neuronal ceroid lipofuscinosis (see corpus striatum syndrome).

Oculo-renal-cerebellar syndrome: Cerebellar abnormalities, intellectual deficit, spasticity/increased tendon reflex.

Rett syndrome: Neurodevelopmental disorder occurring exclusively in females. Autistic behavior, ataxia, dementia, seizures, loss of purposeful use of the hands, cerebral atrophy.

Salla disease (see lysosomal storage disorder).

Schinzel-Giedion syndrome: Profound intellectual deficit, seizures, opisthotonus, spasticity.

Smith-Lemli-Opitz syndrome: Variable altered muscle tone (may be hypotonic in early infancy with tendency to become hypertonic with time), intellectual deficit, seizures.

Sulphite oxidase deficiency: Neonatal seizures, spasticity, intellectual deficit, dislocated lenses. Motor disorder likely to be static; condition underdiagnosed.

Trisomy 4p syndrome: Hypertonia during infancy followed by hypotonia, seizures.

Troyer syndrome (familial spastic diplegia): Spinocerebellar degeneration. Ataxia with retained deep tendon reflexes.

Vogt's disease (see corpus striatum syndrome).

X-linked hydrocephalus syndrome: Intellectual deficit and spasticity, especially of the lower limbs.

X-linked microcephaly: Microcephaly, spasticity (diplegia or quadriplegia), epilepsy, sometimes intellectual deficit and deafness.

(B) Syndromes which produce secondary motor impairment due to vascular or metabolic defects are included. If the causes of such motor impairment are recurrent, the syndrome may be described as progressive, though it is not degenerative and should be included

---

Glutaryl-coenzyme A dehydrogenase deficiency: Encephalitis following normal development. 'Progressive' dystonia.

Homocystinuria syndrome: Neurological defect, especially spasticity, often asymmeteric – presumably the consequence of vascular thrombosis.

Continued

Table 4.1 Continued.

Maple syrup urine disease: A genetic aminoacidopathy due to an enzyme deficiency causing severe ketoacidosis and producing death in about 50% of newborn infants, seizures, coma, physical and intellectual disability.

Methylmaonic acidaemia: Basal ganglia hypodensity due to metabolic cause.

Moyamoya disease: Cerebral ischemia due to occlusion and small hemorrhages from rupture of an abnormal network of vessels at the base of the brain, causing neurological disability.

Partial NADH dehydrogenase deficiency: Spasticity developing athetoid movements about age 5, 'progressive' loss of motor skills, cerebral dysfunction.

Sturge-Weber syndrome: Cerebral hemangiomata with secondary cerebral cortical atrophy; seizures, paresis, intellectual deficit.

Most of the known causes of cerebral palsy can be classified as infections (e.g. cytomegalovirus), vascular (e.g. Sturge Weber syndrome), chromosomal abnormalities (e.g. X-linked microcephaly), metabolic (e.g. arginase deficiency), congenital structural neurologic problems (e.g. porencephaly) or trauma. One must remember that no etiology can be determined for a large percentage of cases.

In addition to the specific etiologies listed in Table 4.1, there are a group of patients where abnormalities related to coagulation may be important causal factors. For many cases, there is evidence that lytic lesions in the area of the ventricles (periventricular leukomalacia) are thought to be the result of hypercoagulability leading to ischemic changes. These lesions can be detected by imaging studies in the first weeks of life. Studies demonstrating a mutated Factor V Leiden (a coagulation factor) (Harum *et al.*, 1999) and increased cytokines (which cause increased coagulation) (Nelson *et al.*, 1998) have further elucidated the mechanisms by which ischemia and periventricular leukomalacia may arise. Hemorrhage, of course, may occur by the same mechanism and is a common cause of cerebral palsy.

The role of prematurity, both with regard to its possible relationship to periventricular leukomalacia via vascular immaturity (and subsequent ischemia) and its importance as an important historical criteria for the diagnosis, should be emphasized since low birthweight, particularly below 1500 g (Bhushan *et al.*, 1993; Powell *et al.*, 1988) is a risk factor for cerebral palsy. A significant percentage of adults with cerebral palsy were premature (although not all patients were premature). It is important to review the criteria (including the perinatal history) for the diagnosis of cerebral palsy in the case of an adult patient with cerebral palsy to be certain that:

■ no infections or vascular, genetic, neurological or metabolic cause of cerebral palsy was missed (see the section on diagnosis towards the end of this chapter), since the implications for the occurrence of other clinical features and possible treatment may be significant
■ the diagnosis of cerebral palsy is correct.

History

Communication issues

Eliciting a history may be difficult in the patient with cerebral palsy in view of speech and language deficits or cognitive impairment. Many patients lack the ability to give a full oral history but can achieve yes or no responses. These responses may come in the form of non-verbal responses, such as nodding the head or unintelligible verbal responses that only the carer or family member may understand. Many patients are able to comprehend speech but are non-verbal, and it is important to recognize such patients. It is important to recognize the patient's level of cognitive ability as well and the extent to which he or she can participate in health care decision-making and understand procedures and studies that must be performed (this is particularly important when the procedures are painful). If the patient has moderate or severe cognitive deficits, often informed consent must be obtained from a close relative or court-appointed guardian if surgery or a medical procedure must be performed. In these cases, it is important that the health care proxy who gives permission accompanies the patient when he/she goes for the procedure or surgery. In any case, the patient must be informed about the procedure to the extent that his or her cognitive state allows.

Antecedent features

When the history is taken, the delivery should be discussed, and this is usually done by the parent (with the help of records if they exist). A number of studies and reviews over the last 20 years have conclusively demonstrated the poor correlation of low Apgar scores and cerebral palsy (Naeye et al., 1989; Nelson & Ellenberg, 1986). As mentioned previously, however, low birthweight and prematurity, whether accompanied by a low or high Apgar, have been shown to be correlated with cerebral palsy (Bhushan et al., 1993). There is no conclusive evidence that cerebral palsy is related to injury sustained at birth or perinatal asphyxia related to delivery (Grether *et al.*, 1996).

Childhood medical history

It is important to obtain a childhood medical history in the adult with cerebral palsy. In the great majority of instances, the child with cerebral palsy develops spasticity before the age of 15 months and may be hypotonic before spasticity is noted (Ingram, 1964). During the first two years of life, seizures, which can be of any type and persist for a variable period of time, often develop (Alesu, 1990). It is not uncommon for adults with cerebral palsy to become seizure free while on anticonvulsant medications and remain seizure free even after those medications are withdrawn.

Children with cerebral palsy are often late in reaching developmental milestones so that it is wise to inquire about the eventual achievement of these milestones (Table 4.2) when one attempts to verify the diagnosis of cerebral palsy in an adult.

Table 4.2 Abbreviated history of age of attainment of developmental milestones.

Motor and language development	Age skills achieved by 90% of healthy children (Months)
Rolls over (from stomach to back)	$5\frac{1}{2}$
Sits up without support	7
Walks well	15
Says one word	15
Combines words	24

Data from Frankenburg, W, Dodds, J. (1990) *Denver II Technical Manual*, p. 71. Denver Developmental Materials Inc, Denver, CO.

Functional and social history

The functional and social history of the patient help the carer to provide advice and consultation regarding the need for aids in achieving the activities of daily living (such as a walker), or to provide information regarding the appropriateness of the patient's place of residence and social situation. Often patients lack appropriate ambulatory aids or are inappropriately placed in a large institution when a small group home would be more appropriate. Other important social skills are school, leisure or recreational activities and involvement with peers and family members.

One should inquire about the patient's ambulatory status; 20% of adults with cerebral palsy can walk, 40% are able to walk with assistance and 40% are non-ambulatory (Brown *et al.*, 1992). Many who need a wheelchair do not have one or do not have an appropriate one, so that an inquiry concerning appropriate ambulatory aids should be made.

The patient should also be questioned about his or her place of residence, which should be as non-restrictive as possible and facilitate the skills of independent living. The patient's ability to dress and eat without assistance, perform household chores and manage his or her financial affairs should be assessed. These skills should be developed to the level that the patient's physical and cognitive abilities allow increasing personal and societal independence.

Many of the parents of patients with cerebral palsy are elderly and cannot care for an adult with cerebral palsy (Lewin, 1990). Since one-third of adults with cerebral palsy live at home (Brown *et al.*, 1992), it is appropriate to ask if their carers have the physical capacity to care for them, and to ask about contingency plans for future care as well. Those patients who can use a computer, and their family members, may benefit from a website from an American cerebral palsy organization (www.ucpa.org) which includes information about recent research, computer assisted communication devices and employment opportunities.

Clinical issues

Most of the clinical features of cerebral palsy involve the neurologic and musculoskeletal systems. The patient with cerebral palsy may present with spasticity, choreoathetosis or other dystonic movement disorders, but other bodily systems may be involved as well.

Hearing and vision problems

From 25–39% of adults with cerebral palsy have visual defects (Granet *et al.*, 1997). The causes among adults with cerebral palsy have not been investigated, but in children visual deficits may result from cataracts, optic atrophy and retinitis (Ingram, 1964). From 8–18% of adults have hearing deficits (Janicki, 1989). Since both hearing and vision become worse with age, re-testing periodically is a necessity.

Gross auditory testing in the patient with severe cognitive difficulties may include the patient's response to a noise, although for a more precise measurement, studies which measure the neurophysiologic response to sound in the form of auditory evoked potentials are recommended.

Visual testing in the form of following the examiner's finger is useful when a cursory visual examination of the patient is done. The ophthalmologist is able to measure refraction by means of an autorefractor and further information about whether images which reach the retina do indeed reach the optic cortex can be obtained by means of an electroretinogram if the patient is not cooperative for standard visual testing. For further details on vision and hearing in people with intellectual disabilities, see Chapters 5 and 6.

Cardiovascular problems

Although detailed studies are not available, 9–10.5% of adults with cerebral palsy have cardiovascular problems (the majority of which are either hypertension or coronary artery disease) (Kiely *et al.*, 1984). One study demonstrated excess mortality among adults with cerebral palsy from ischemic heart disease (Strauss *et al.*, 1999). This may reflect the fact that many patients with cerebral palsy are non-verbal, and the fact that subtle clues to ischemic heart disease such as agitation, change in skin color or the emergence of moderate respiratory distress, are not recognized. Often these subtle signs are noted by carers or family members.

Decreased temperature, swelling and discoloration of the limbs may be noted by the patient's carers or a family member. Decreased temperature has been noted in the literature (MacDonald, 1985) but a precise pathophysiological explanation of these changes is lacking. (It does appear that the autonomic nervous system is behaving abnormally in these instances.) Although it has not been noted in the literature, we have noted a low incidence of deep vein thrombosis in patients with spastic quadriplegia, despite immobility, swelling and contractures in these patients which should predispose to thrombosis. It is important for patients to wear proper shoes and compression stockings to reduce swelling. Proper foot hygiene and toenail care is also important to prevent infection and ischemic ulcers.

Pulmonary system and swallowing function

Aspiration may result from impaired swallowing or regurgitation of gastric contents due to slow gastric emptying. In our experience, the latter is a more frequent cause and is often accompanied by regurgitation of food and acid into the esophagus, causing esophagitis. Patients with spastic quadriparesis are at particular risk for aspiration (Brown *et al.*, 1992). Gastrostomy tubes may alleviate the problem in some patients but aspiration may persist despite tube placement (Finucaine & Bynum, 1996) in a significant number, particularly if the feedings are given in bolus fashion rather than through continuous infusion. Nasal regurgitation, elevated temperature, slowly progressive dyspnea and lethargy are indicators of aspiration (Kuruvilla & Trenby, 1989). Our experience is that patients with aspiration may have a moderate temperature elevation (in the range of 99°–101°F) and a white blood count in the range of $13 \times 10^9/l$ 16×10^9 /l. Very often the chest X-ray is clear, and although blood cultures should certainly be done, most cases resolve without the use of antibiotics. Beta-adrenergic agonists such as albuterol followed by vigorous postural drainage are helpful, both because they help to clear secretions and possibly because they eliminate the reflex bronchospasm that accompanies aspiration.

One should inquire about the presence of coughing during or immediately after meals. A clinical swallowing evaluation accompanied by video fluoroscopy should be performed if such symptoms are elicited. A change in solid and liquid diet consistency may be necessary, and proper positioning during and after meals will decrease the occurrence of pulmonary involvement (Brin & Younger, 1988). Speech therapists and dieticians can be helpful for providing an appropriate diet.

Gastrointestinal problems

Vomiting and constipation are frequent in adults with cerebral palsy. Both are probably due to neurogenic influences related to gastric motility. Poor gastric motility results in gastroesophageal reflux which becomes worse during the adolescent period (Gustafson & Tibbling, 1994). It is important to monitor esophagitis endoscopically, since acid reflux causes intestinal metaplasia (or Barretts syndrome) of the esophagus which then predisposes the patient to carcinoma of the esophagus (Drewitz *et al.*, 1997). The preferred treatment for esophagitis is the use of protein pump inhibitors (such as omeprozole). Because of the severity of esophagitis in these patients and the predisposition to Barretts esophagus and cancer, most patients need to be on acid suppression therapy for their entire lives.

Constipation in adults with cerebral palsy is frequent. Abnormal control of gastrointestinal motility, immobilization and poor oral intake with prolonged colonic transit are factors (Giudice, 1997). Altered gastrointestinal motility, probably via abnormal activity of the autonomic nervous system, can cause full blown intestinal pseudobstruction. It is important to rule out surgical causes of intestinal obstruction in these cases (such as volvulus). Treatment involves stopping the patient from eating and drinking for a short time and administering intravenous fluid after an initial period of drainage via nasogastric tube.

For those individuals who have constipation only, the appropriate treatment is the use of a stool softener for a week, followed by a mild stimulant laxative such as senna. For those who are impacted and/or soiling, full evacuation of the rectum is advised, and in some cases this evacuation should be accompanied by lavage with propylene glycol administered by nasogastric tube. It is helpful to obtain a flat plate of the abdomen to detect dilatation of the proximal colon when constipation continues despite bowel stimulants and stool softeners. If such dilatation exists, it indicates the need not only for gastric lavage but also for careful surveillance and record keeping of bowel movements so that future episodes of impaction can be prevented. The most important principle is to keep the rectum free of stool. Propylene glycol lavage should not be performed on patients with a history of aspiration since they may aspirate even if it is given by nasogastric tube.

Speech and swallowing problems

Approximately 60% of young adults with cerebral palsy have a speech or communication problem. This problem may result from cognitive difficulties, oral motor apraxia, difficulty with management of oral secretions or dysphagia of esophageal origin in the patient with esophagitis (Gisel & Patrick, 1988; Logemann, 1988).

Feeding adults with cerebral palsy may take from 45 minutes to $1\frac{1}{2}$ hours, and if sufficient time is not allowed poor caloric intake and weight loss may result. Since total body fat and lean body mass are already deficient in many adults with cerebral palsy (see section on diet and nutrition later in this chapter), further weight loss may result in inadequate energy stores and decreased immunity, and we frequently see a significant decrease in albumin (and occasionally edema secondary to this decrease) in this population. If there is evidence of weight loss, a food intake and weight diary should be kept to monitor nutritional status, and consideration should be given to providing nutritional supplements.

Musculoskeletal system

If the patient with cerebral palsy complains of increased pain in the groin and anterior thigh while sitting and standing, this may be a sign of degenerative hip disease or acetabular dislocation. This is particularly common during the adolescent growth spurt and in individuals of all ages with athetoid cerebral palsy (Currie *et al.*, 1993). Any suggestion of either of these two problems based on the history should prompt referral to an orthopedist.

Scoliosis is more common in patients with cerebral palsy. It occurs in 25–64% of institutionalized adults (Majd *et al.*, 1997). These patients must be observed very carefully, particularly during the growth spurt (which may not be complete until the young adult years), and all patients with cerebral palsy who have scoliosis should be referred to an orthopedist for a baseline evaluation. Uncorrected scoliosis may result in spinal cord compression and even more commonly can cause pressure sores in the patient because of the added factors of decreased subcutaneous tissue, atrophic and spastic muscles and immobility (Majd *et al.* 1997).

Low bone density and osteopenia have been found in children with cerebral palsy, particularly if they are non-ambulatory. We have found a disproportionate number of adults with osteopenia as well. Low dietary intake of calcium may be a contributing factor (Ferling *et al.*, 1992). Factors such as decreased exposure to the sun, immobility, spasticity and the metabolic conversion of the precursors of vitamin D to inactive metabolites by anti-convulsants (Lee & Lyne, 1990) predispose the patients to fractures and osteoporosis. Osteoporosis becomes worse as the patient with cerebral palsy ages. Those patients with risk factors (such as family history, post-menopausal state and fractures) should undergo X-ray absorptiometry. If osteoporosis is documented, then appropriate exercises, calcium supplements and possibly biphosphonates should be prescribed. Initial evaluation by an endocrinologist is helpful, particularly since there is an increasing number of biphosphonates which have become available.

Because of evidence that adults with cerebral palsy may lose their ability to walk (Bottos *et al.*, 2001) and because declining muscular strength and increasing contractures are certainly factors, health promotion for the adult with cerebral palsy should include exercises emphasizing strength as well as flexibility. Usually the initial determination of what the exercise program should consist of should be made by a physical therapist or physiatrist.

Neurologic system

Seizures are present in 30% of patients with cerebral palsy. Every variety of seizure can be seen in cerebral palsy. Seizures may persist for the lifetime of the patient or may cease at any time. If the patient has been seizure-free for a two-year period, often anticonvulsants may be discontinued under the guidance of a neurologist. Whether withdrawal of medications is considered depends to some extent on whether there are focal spikes on the electroenchelogram and whether structural abnormalities are noted on a recent imaging study, so these studies should be obtained on patients with cerebral palsy who have seizures. See Chapter 7 for detailed information on seizures in people with intellectual disabilities.

As noted earlier, neurologic change in an adult patient with cerebral palsy does occur, but these changes are not dramatic and either occur gradually or intermittently over years in a patient who is at least 40–45 years old in our experience. Any dramatic change or any change that occurs over a short period (weeks to one to two years) should prompt referral to a neurologist. Depending on the experience of the primary physician, it may be wise to refer a patient who develops any neurologic change regardless of the time course.

Reproductive system and sexuality

Our observations and those of others are that a significant percentage of adolescents with cerebral palsy and other static encephalopathies have delayed and prolonged puberty with a poor nutritional state as the primary reason and in a few instances they may develop precocious puberty (Siddiqui et al., 1999). It is important to recognize this altered schedule for sexual maturation (and therefore for the emergence of sexual drive when maturation does begin). One must also determine if the patient is sexually active and be aware of the possibility of sexual abuse.

Urinary tract

As with any nursing home population, older institutionalized adults with cerebral palsy may experience asymptomatic bacteriuria and this need not be treated. A small percentage of children with cerebral palsy have either a small irritable bladder that results in frequent urination and possible ureteral reflux (as a result of upper motor neuron lesions) or a large hypotonic bladder (resulting from a lower motor neuron lesion) Both can result in incontinence and infection. Our experience with adults is similar, although the lack of learning capacity resulting in an inability to drain the bladder is the principal reason for incontinence in adults. Structural lesions that lead to recurrent infection are rare so there is no need for screening for these lesions unless there are signs of an infection (Brodak et al., 1994). Signs of dysuria in the patient with cerebral palsy include grimacing, incontinence and frequency. As with other illnesses, other signs such as restlessness, behavior problems or self-abuse may be indicative of a urinary tract infection.

Diet and nutrition

Studies of children with severe cerebral palsy have documented that they consume enough calories for their energy needs but not enough for their nutritional needs. Fat free mass is thus deficient in children with severe cerebral palsy (Stallings *et al.*, 1995) and remains so in adults. Feeding problems in adolescents and the resultant low caloric intake result in poor growth and decreased muscle mass at maturity, since their caloric intake cannot keep pace with the increased needs of the rapid growth phase (Bandin *et al.*, 1991), so it is not surprising that many adults have low lean body mass. Athetoid patients require special attention since their caloric requirements are high (Johnson *et al.*, 1996).

We have found that weight loss secondary to poor appetite occurs without explanation in adults on some occasions, probably as a result of neurologic factors influencing diet. If an adult with cerebral palsy loses weight, they are doing so at some jeopardy because they already have a low fat free mass as noted above. Every effort should be made to maintain body weight through dietary supplements or, in rare cases, feeding through a nasogastric tube for a short period or inserting a gastric (G tube) or jejunal (J tube) if caloric supplements are necessary for a longer period.

We have noted that a significant number of adults with cerebral palsy have high cholesterol and low density lipids levels, principally as a result of immobility in our opinion. This, of course, should prompt the institution of a low fat, low cholesterol diet and an exercise program to the extent that the patient can participate. Iron deficiency is common in women with cerebral palsy (Ferling *et al.*, 1992), and in this case iron supplementation may be needed as well as a diet high in iron. For detailed information on nutrition in people with intellectual disabilities see Chapter 10.

The physical examination

A comprehensive physical examination should be performed on patients with cerebral palsy. The physician's office should be wheelchair accessible, which includes a doorway and bathroom entrance of adequate width and an examination room where a patient may maneuver his or her wheelchair around the room.

The neuromuscular system

Cerebral palsy is frequently described as hemiplegic, diplegic, quad-riplegic or choreoathetoid. The examiner should note changes in limb strength, spasticity or involuntary movements over time. The extent and location of limb involvement should also be noted.

In cerebral palsy, there is a loss of inhibitory control of spinal reflexes which results in spasticity (Biotte *et al.*, 1988) and exaggerated reflexes, including deep tendon reflexes accompanied by clonus (Ingram, 1964) in some cases. In many adults, spasticity evolves into contractures (Thomas *et al.*, 1989). The shortened contracted muscle has fewer sarcomeres (and therefore less weight and power) than the normal muscle (Hufschmidt & Mauritz, 1985). Shortening of the muscles by contractures in cerebral palsy decreases the range of length over which tension can be actively generated (O'Dwyer *et al.*, 1989), resulting in weakness, decreased range of motion and poor coordination which become worse as the patient ages (Garrard, 1982). Therefore, the effect of the patient's contractures and spasticity on his or her mobility and coordination during activities such as reaching or walking should be noted. Spasticity and contractures vary with position and patient stress. The patient should be examined in active and passive movement and voluntary functional activities.

Range of motion of extremities should be noted. Figure 4.1 demonstrates normal range of motion for the large joints of the arms and legs. The most common contractures are flexion and pronation of the forearm, internal rotation and adduction of the shoulder, flexion of the wrist, flexion of fingers at the interphalangeal joints and adduction of the thumb or the 'thumb in palm deformity'. In the lower limbs, the most common contractures are flexion of the hip and knee, adduction of the hip, flexion of the toes and plantar flexion of the foot. The Ashworth scale (Table 4.3) is a non-quantitative scale that has been used widely as a clinical measure of spasticity and seems to have good face validity (Ashworth, 1964). Release of joint contractures has been successfully performed, and

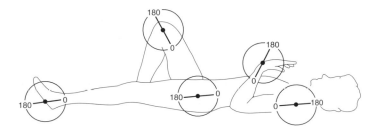

Fig. 4.1   Range of motion chart for large joints of the upper and lower limbs.

Table 4.3 Ashworth scale.

	Description
0	No increase in tone
1	Slight increase in tone, resulting in a catch when affected limb is moved in flexion or extension
2	More marked increase in tone but limb easily flexed
3	Considerable increase in tone; passive movement difficulty
4	Limb rigid in flexion or extension

orthopedic referral should be considered. Intramuscular injections of Botulinum toxin have been successfully used for spasticity (Gooch & Sandell, 1996) by blocking presynaptic release of the neurotransmitter at the neuromuscular junction (Taylor, 1996).

The patient's gait pattern should be observed. Gait analysis studies in patients with spastic hemiplegia show the following (Winters *et al.*, 1987):

■ variable involvement of the limb from mild plantar flexion of the foot during the swing phase of the gait to persistent equinus;
■ knee extension
■ dynamic hip flexion contracture with lumbar lordosis and exaggerated pelvic tilt.

These abnormalities may occur in variable combinations.

Patients with spastic diplegia most commonly show scissoring or hip adduction due to spasticity of the adductors during the swing phase (Gage *et al.*, 1984). Initial contact of the foot with the floor often does not occur in the normal heel-first manner, causing calluses in the metatarsal area along with pain and joint deformities. An abnormal ankle foot system (which may take a variety of forms) may be caused by a tight heel cord, spasticity of the anterior or posterior tibialis muscles or a spastic gastrocnemius soleus muscle. Computer assisted gait analysis will indicate which of these abnormalities is causing the problem. Computer assisted gait analysis is also essential before treatment interventions, since a dynamic change may be the result of bone and ligament malalignment, soft tissue laxity, muscle timing (activation and shut-off during the cycles of gait), spasticity or contractures. Intervention depends on the specific cause, since surgical approaches often follow gait analysis.

Examination of the genitals

The incidence of cryptorchidism in adults with cerebral palsy is higher than in the general population with an incidence of 53% at age 21 (Smith *et al.*, 1989). To do an adequate examination, the patient must be standing. In this way, it is possible to determine whether the patient has undescended testicles or whether they are simply retracted. If the testes cannot be palpated while the patient is in the standing position, then referral to an urologist is necessary. Usually the urologist will do an ultrasound examination if he determines that the testes are not descended.

Pelvic and breast examination

A pelvic examination may be a particularly difficult experience for an adult with cerebral palsy, resulting in poor cooperation, and this may cause much frustration among carers and family members. The difficulty is the result of fear, tension and spasticity of the adductors of the thighs. A history of sexual abuse may also contribute to the patient's fears. The examination may be performed in the lateral decubitus position, which may improve cooperation and allow easier insertion of the speculum and collection of the specimen for the Papanicolaou smear. Use of a small speculum may also facilitate successful completion of the examination (Table 4.4). If the patient is uncooperative despite oral sedation, general anesthesia may be required. After the initial examination under anesthesia, a pelvic ultrasound may be substituted for the pelvic examination for the following two years, assuming there are no symptoms of possible gynecologic disorders (Bradshaw *et al.*, 1996). Another examination with the patient under anesthesia need not be done for another two years (Table 4.4).

Mammography is often difficult because of poor cooperation and because the patient's dysmorphic condition does not allow her to be properly positional on the X-ray table. In these cases, a good breast examination (which should be done in any case) and referral to a specialist in breast disease and an ultrasound if a breast lesion is found, is indicated.

Dental examination

Lack of cooperation on the part of the patient with cerebral palsy and intellectual disabilities is frequently a problem in the case of the dental examination. However, our experience is that it is usually possible to perform an examination if a sequential series of steps is followed.

The primary care physician and the dentist should first discuss the situation and the behavioral problems that make the examination difficult

Table 4.4 Suggestions for performing examinations and procedures.

Examination or procedure	Frequently encountered problems in patients with cerebral palsy	Suggestions for alternative approaches
Pelvic examination	The patient is agitated and uncooperative and will not allow examination to be completed	(1) An initial pelvic examination may be done under general anesthesia (2) For the next two years, pelvic ultrasound may be substituted for the examination, in the absence of suggestive symptoms. Then the examination can be repeated under anesthesia and the same sequence starts again (3) The examination may be done in the lateral decubitus position (4) A small speculum may be used
Sigmoidoscopy	Dysmorphic habitus prevents proper positioning of the patient and insertion of the sigmoidoscope	Perform examination in the left lateral decubitus position
Dental examination	Patient is too uncooperative to allow dental procedure	(1) Attempt procedure with oral sedation (2) If (1) is ineffective, the following methods may be tried in the order listed: sedation with restraints, monitored intravenous sedation, or general anesthesia
Mammography	Dysmorphic habitus prevents proper positioning of breasts; poor cooperation	(1) Annual breast examination (2) When there are positive findings, refer to specialist or do ultrasound of breast or both (ultrasound is confirmative, not diagnostic)

for a given patient. The following sequential approach is suggested (American Dental Association 1992) (Table 4.4):

(1) oral sedation
(2) restraints and oral sedation
(3) intramuscular or intravenous sedation
(4) general anesthesia.

It is important to determine what type of sedation has been important previously (our experience has been that restraints without sedation are not effective). If general anesthesia is selected, it is often expeditious to do as much dental work as possible at one time so that repeated general anesthesia is not necessary. The procedure should be scheduled so the effects of sedation are still present when the patient is examined or undergoes treatment. Further information on dentition and oral health in people with intellectual disabilities is given in Chapter 9.

Dysmorphic findings

Dysmorphic findings that are increased in frequency in cerebral palsy are numerous. Prominence of the occiput, hyperextensibility of the digits, multiple nevi, microcephaly, a long thin upper lip, malformed ears, chorioretinitis, syndactyly and polydactyly have all been described (Ingram, 1964). Obviously some of these are abnormal features, such as microcephaly in a patient with cytomegalovirus infection and some may reflect manifestations of genetic syndromes (Badawi *et al.*, 1998). As more genetic syndromes are described and defined which qualify as cerebral palsy, more dysmorphic features will obviously be detected in patients with cerebral palsy.

Diagnosis

Cerebral palsy is a clinical diagnosis aided by imaging and laboratory evidence of the specific etiology. Many different conditions with different etiologies are included under the umbrella of cerebral palsy (Table 4.1). What these conditions share in common is that they are static encephalopathies beginning in the perinatal period with motor manifestations (most commonly dystonic movements or spasticity). As was previously discussed, patients with cerebral palsy may demonstrate progressive symptoms but the rate of progression tends to be slower than other neurological disorders with which it may be confused, and the progression usually begins at a later age – a clinical scenario which is compatible with a perinatal etiology with progression to spasticity or dystonic movement disorders such as choreoathetosis during the first 15 months of life. Other clinical characteristics such as prematurity (which is not present in all patients), delayed developmental milestones and a seizure disorder before the age of two may provide additional information which supports the diagnosis and are part of this common scenario (Table 4.5).

Table 4.5   Cerebral palsy typical scenario.

Clinical findings
Prematurity (birthweight < 1500 g) Delayed developmental milestones Spasticity or athetoid movements before 15 months Seizure disorder before 2 years

All patients should have had an imaging study at some point in their lives. It is preferable that this study should be magnetic resonance imaging (MRI). If there is a clear morphologic etiology for cerebral palsy such as microcephaly, and there is no progression, there is no need to repeat it in adulthood. If the original MRI was negative or the patient never had one, (a common situation since MRI scans did not exist when many adult patients were children), he or she should have one as an adult. Obviously, if there are symptoms which suggest progression, an MRI should be done for this reason as well. All adult patients should have had a chromosomal analysis within the last five years. A chromosomal analysis may have been done in childhood, but because of the explosive growth of genetics a more recent analysis is important. Specific DNA probes may be indicated if the clinical picture merits it. Serum amino acids, urinary organic acids and a serum ammonia level should be done if the patient does not fit the typical clinical scenario for cerebral palsy or is observed to have intermittent lethargy and evidence of hypoglycemia or ketosis.

A frequent diagnostic dilemma in adults who have been diagnosed as having cerebral palsy is that the diagnosis may be correct but the correct etiology has not been determined. For example, after examining the childhood medical history, if the developmental milestones were accomplished in a timely fashion and some time between 6 and 18 months when the patient began to regress and if the child demonstrated 'hand wringing' movements some time between 1 and 3 years, only to be followed by the development of spasticity during adolescence, the most likely diagnosis is Rett syndrome (Moeschler *et al.*, 1988). The gene was recently discovered (the MeCP2 gene) and because of its discovery, prenatal testing may soon be possible to detect Rett syndrome in families with an affected daughter and detect an asymptomatic carrier state in sisters of Rett syndrome patients. Therefore, determining the correct etiology of cerebral palsy (in this case Rett syndrome) may prevent others in the family from developing Rett syndrome since a prenatal test is being developed (Amir *et al.*, 1999). In addition, it may be possible to treat children when genetic therapy is developed with the disease since it takes a number of months to develop (Amir *et al.*, 1999).

A second dilemma is that the patient has been diagnosed as having cerebral palsy but the diagnosis is incorrect and the patient has a progressive neurologic disorder. An example is provided by a 40-year-old 'retarded spastic quadriplegic' who had been diagnosed with cerebral palsy as a child and who also was transferred from home to a long-term care facility where he was evaluated by one of the authors. He was noted to have a rash typical of adenoma sebaceum on his face and a biopsy provided histological confirmation. An MRI was done and demonstrated tubers and a large glioma, and a computerized tomography scan of the kidney revealed an angiomyolipoma. All of these features are part of tuberous sclerosis and have therapeutic implications as well as implications for future surveillance. In this case, making the correct diagnosis (which was not cerebral palsy but tuberous sclerosis) revealed other features which were part of a genetic syndrome and required periodic follow-up.

Lastly, it should be remembered that adults with cerebral palsy can develop other neurologic conditions such as brain tumors or cerebrovascular accidents, and this is another reason why progressive symptoms should always be investigated, even though they often occur during the natural course of cerebral palsy.

Conclusion

It is important to focus on aspects of cerebral palsy which are unique to adults as well as characteristics of cerebral palsy in children which may have become more severe with age. When evaluating the patient, one should be as specific as possible in determining whether the adult patient actually has cerebral palsy. If the patient has cerebral palsy, the correct etiology (if known) is important for prognosis, treatment possibilities and diagnosing other conditions which may exist as part of a syndrome. From 65–90% of children with cerebral palsy survive into adulthood, creating a large number of adults with a need for medical care. The incidence may continue to increase because of increased survival of very low-birth-weight infants and/or increased longevity of the general population.

This chapter has reviewed the important aspects of the history, review of systems, and physical examination of adults with cerebral palsy. Suggestions for performing examinations and procedures on patients with cerebral palsy were provided as well. Evans *et al.* (1990) wrote that it was their hope that cerebral palsy will become 'a condition with which one lives rather than one from which one dies'. It is suggested that this is an appropriate mission statement as we attempt to develop a medical care delivery system for adults with cerebral palsy and provide appropriate training for physicians to meet their needs.

References

Alesu, F. (1990) Nature and prognosis of seizures in patients with cerebral palsy. *Developmental Medicine and Child Neurology*, **32**, 661–68.

American Dental Association (1992) *Oral Health Care Guidelines: Patients With Physical and Mental Disabilities*. American Dental Association Council on Community Health Hospital, Institutional and Medical Affairs, Chicago, IL.

Amir, R.E., Van den Veyver, I.B., Wan, M., Tran, C.Q., Francke, U. & Zoghbi H.Y. (1999) Rett syndrome is caused by mutations in X-linked MECP2, encoding methyl-CpG-binding protein 2. *Nature Genetics*, **23**, 185–188.

Ashworth, B. (1964) Preliminary trial of carisoprodol in multiple sclerosis. *The Practitioner*, **192**, 540–542.

Badawi, N., Watson, L., Petterson, B., Blair, E., Slee, J., Haan, E. & Stanley, F. (1998) What constitutes cerebral palsy? *Developmental Medicine and Child Neurology*, **40**, 520–527.

Bandin, L.G., Schoeller, D.A., Fukagawa, N.K., Wykes, L.J. & Dietz, W.H. (1991) Body composition and energy expenditure in adolescents with cerebral palsy or myelodysplasia. *Pediatric Research*, **29**, 70–77.

Bhushan, V., Paneth, N. & Kiely, J.L. (1993) Impact of improved survival of very low birthweight infants on recent secular trends in the prevalence of cerebral palsy. *Pediatrics*, **91**, 1094–1100.

Biotte, M.J., Nidral, V.L. & Akeson, W.H. (1988) Spasticity and contracture: physiologic aspects of formation. *Clinical Orthopedics and Related Research*, **233**, 7–18.

Blair, E., Watson, L., Badawi, N. & Stanley, F.J. (2001) Life expectancy among people with cerebral palsy in Western Australia. *Developmental Medicine and Child Neurology*, **43**, 509–515.

Bottos, M., Granato, T., Guiseppa, A., Giocchia, C. & Puato, M.L. (1999) Prevalence of cerebral palsy in northeast Italy from 1965 to 1989. *Developmental Medicine and Child Neurology*, **41**, 26–39.

Bottos, M., Felklangeli, A., Gericke, C. & Vianello, A. (2001) Functional status of adults with cerebral palsy and implications for treatment. *Developmental Medicine and Child Neurology*, **43**, 516–528.

Bradshaw, D., Elkins, T.E. & Quint, E.H. (1996) *The Gynecologic Exam in the Patient with Mental Retardation: a Continuing Education Monograph*. University of Texas Medical Center at Dallas.

Brin, M.F. & Younger, D. (1988) Neurologic disorders and aspiration. *Otolaryngologic Clinics of North America*, **21**, 691–699.

Brodak, P.P., Scherz, H.C., Packer, M.G. & Kaplan, G.W. (1994) Is urinary tract screening necessary for patients with cerebral palsy? *The Journal of Urology*, **152**, 1586–1587.

Brown, M.C., Bontempo, A. & Turk, M.A. (1992) *Secondary Consequences of Cerebral Palsy: Adults With Cerebral Palsy in New York State*. Developmental Disabilities Planning Council, Albany, NY.

Burke, R.E., Fahn, S. & Gold, A.P. (1980) Delayed onset dystonia in patients with static encephalopathy. *Journal of Neurology, Neurosurgery, and Psychiatry*, **43**, 789–797.

Crichton, J., MacKinney, M. & Light, C.P. (1995) The life expectancy of persons with cerebral palsy. *Developmental Medicine and Child Neurology*, **37**, 567–576.

Currie, D.M., Gershkoft, A.M. & Cofu, D.X. (1993) Geriatric rehabilitation: mid and late life effects of early life disabilities. *Archives of Physical Medicine and Rehabilitation*, **74**, 5413–5415.

Drewitz, D.J., Sanpliner, R.E. & Gasewal, H.J. (1997) The incidence of adenocarcinoma in Barretts esophagus: a prospective study of 170 patients followed 4.8 years. *The American Journal of Gastroenterology*, **92**, 212–215.

Evans, P.M., Evans, S.J.W. & Alberman, E. (1990) Cerebral palsy: why we must plan for survival. *Archives of Disease in Childhood*, **65**, 1325–1333.

Ferling, T.M., Johnson, R.K. & Ferarra, M.S. (1992) Dietary and anthropometric assessment of adults with cerebral palsy. *Journal of the American Dietetic Association*, **92**, 1083–1086.

Finucaine, T.E. & Bynum, J.P.W. (1996) Use of tube feeding to prevent aspiration pneumonia. *Lancet*, **348**, 1421–1423.

Gage, J.R., Fabian, D., Hicks, R. & Tashman, S. (1984) Pre- and postoperative gait analysis in patients with spastic diplegia: a preliminary report. *Developmental Medicine and Child Neurology*, **4**, 715–725.

Garrard, S.D. (1982) Health services for mentally retarded people in community residences: problems and questions. *American Journal of Public Health*, **72**, 1226–1228.

Gisel, E.G. & Patrick, J. (1988) Identification of children with cerebral palsy unable to maintain a sound nutritional state. *Lancet*, **6**, 238–284.

Giudice, E.D. (1997) Cerebral palsy and gut-functions. *Journal of Pediatric Gastroenterology and Nutrition*, **24**, 522–523.

Goldenberg, R.L. & Rouse, D.J. (1998) Prevention of premature birth. *The New England Journal of Medicine*, **339**, 801–817.

Gooch, J.L. & Sandell, T.V. (1996) Botulinum toxin for spasticity and athetosis in children with cerebral palsy. *Archives of Physical Medicine and Rehabilitation*, **77**, 508–511.

Granet, K.M., Balaghi, M. & Jaeger, J. (1997) Adults with cerebral palsy. *New Jersey Medicine: The Journal of the Medical Society of New Jersey*, **94**, 51–54.

Grether, J.K., Nelson, K.B., Emory, E.S. & Cummins, S.K. (1996) Prenatal and perinatal factors in cerebral palsy in very low birthweight infants. *The Journal of Pediatrics*, **90**, 171–176.

Gustafson, P.M. & Tibbling, L. (1994) Gastroesophageal reflux and esophageal dysfunction in children and adolescents with brain damage. *Acta Paediatrica Scandinavica*, **83**, 1081–1085.

Hack, M., Flannery, D.J., Schlucter, M., Carter L., Borawski E. & Klein N. (2002) Outcomes in young adulthood for very low birthweight infants. *New England Journal of Medicine*, **346**, 149–157.

Harum, K.H., Hoon, A.H. & Casella, J.F. (1999) Factor V Leiden: a risk factor for cerebral palsy. *Developmental Medicine and Child Neurology*, **41**, 781–785.

Hufschmidt, A.& Mauritz, K.H. (1985) Chronic transformation of muscle in spasticity: a peripheral contribution to increased tone. *Journal of Neurology, Neurosurgery and Psychiatry*, **48**, 676–685.

Ingram, T.T.S. (1964) *Pediatric Aspects of Cerebral Palsy*. E & S Livingstone, Ltd, Edinburgh, Scotland.

Jahnsen R. & Holm, I. (2001) Life span development of locomotion in persons with cerebral palsy. *Developmental Medicine and Child Neurology*, **43**, Supplement No. 88, 9.

Janicki, M.P. (1989) Aging, cerebral palsy, and older persons with mental retardation. *The Australian and New Zealand Journal of Developmental Disabilities*, **15**, 311–330.

Johnson, R.K., Goran, M.I., Ferrara, M.S. & Poehlman, E.T. (1996) Athetosis increases resting metabolic rate in adults with cerebral palsy. *Journal of the American Dietetic Association*, **96**, 145–148.

Kiely, M., Lubin, R.A. & Kiely, J.L. (1984) Descriptive epidemiology of cerebral palsy. *Public Health Reviews*, **12**, 79–101.

Kuruvilla, J. & Trenby, P.N. (1989) Gastroesophageal disorders in adults with severe mental impairment. *British Medical Journal*, **98**, 95–96.

Lee, J.K. & Lyne, E.A. (1990) Pathologic fractures in severely handicapped children and young adults. *Journal of Pediatric Orthopedics*, **10**, 497–500.

Lewin, T. (1990) As the retarded live longer, anxiety grips again parents [special report]. *New York Times*, 28 October, 1 and 32.

Logemann, J.A. (1988) Swallowing physiology and pathophysiology. *Otolaryngologic Clinics of North America*, **21**, 613–623.

MacDonald, E.P. (1985) Medical needs of severely developmentally disabled persons residing in the community. *American Journal of Mental Retardation*, **90**, 171–176.

Majd, M.E., Muldowney, D.S. & Holt, R. (1997) Natural history of scoliosis in the institutionalized adult cerebral palsy population. *Spine*, **22**, 1461–1466.

Moeschler, J.B., Charman, C.E., Berg, S.Z. & Graham, J.M. (1988) Rett Syndrome: Natural History and Management. *Pediatrics*, **82**, 1–9.

Murphy, K.P., Molnar, G.E. & Lankasky, K. (1995) Medical and functional status of adults with cerebral palsy. *Developmental Medicine and Child Neurology*, **37**, 1075–1084.

Naeye, R.L., Peters, E.C., Bartholomew, M. & Landis, R. (1989) Origins of cerebral palsy. *American Journal of Diseases of Children*, **143**, 1154–1161.

Nelson, K.B. & Ellenberg, J. (1986) Antecedents of cerebral palsy: multivariate analysis of risk. *The New England Journal of Medicine*, **315**, 81–86.

Nelson, K.B., Dawbrosia, J.M., Grether, J.K. & Phillips T.M. (1998) Neonatal cytokines and coagulation factors in children with cerebral palsy. *Annals of Neurology*, **44**, 665–675.

O'Dwyer, N.J., Neilson, P.D. & Nosh, J. (1989) Mechanisms of muscle growth related to muscle contracture in cerebral palsy. *Developmental Medicine and Child Neurology*, **31**, 543–552.

Oxford Register of Early Childhood Impairment: Annual Report (1998) National Perinatal Epidemiology Unit, Oxford, England.

Powell, T.G., Pharoah, P.O.D., Cooke, R.W.I. & Rosenbloom, L. (1988) Cerebral palsy in low birthweight infants II: spastic diplegia: associations with fetal immaturity. *Developmental Medicine and Child Neurology*, **30**, 19–25.

Scoles, P. (1982) *Pediatric Orthopedics in Clinical Practice*. Yearbook Medical Publishers, Chicago, IL.

Siddiqui, S.V., Van Dyke, D.L., Donohue, P. & McBrien, D.M. (1999) Premature sexual development in individuals with neurodevelopmental disabilities. *Developmental Medicine and Child Neurology*, **41**, 392–395.

Smith, J.A., Hutson, J.M., Beasley, S.W. & Reddihough, D.S. (1989) The relationship between cerebral palsy and cryptorchidism. *Journal of Pediatric Surgery*, **24**, 1303–1306.

Stallings, V.A., Cronk, C.E., Zomel, B.S. & Charney, E.B. (1995) Body composition in children with spastic quadriplegic cerebral palsy. *The Journal of Pediatrics*, **126**, 833–839.

Strauss, D & Shavelle R. (1998) Life expectancy of adults with cerebral palsy. *Developmental Medicine and Child Neurology*, **40**, 369–75.

Strauss, D., Cable W. & Shavelle R. (1999) Causes of excess mortality in cerebral palsy. *Developmental Medicine and Child Neurology*, **41**, 580–585.

Taylor, P. (1996) Agents acting at the neuromuscular junction and autonomic ganglia. In: Goodman and Gilmans *The Pharmacological Basis of Therapeutics* (eds J.G. Hardman, L.E. Limbird, P.B. Molinott & R.W. Ruddon) 9th edn, pp. 185–186. McGraw-Hill, New York.

Thomas, A.P., Bax, M.C.O. & Smyth, D.P.L. (1989) The health and social needs of young adults with physical disabilities. In: *Clinics in Developmental Medicine*, no. 106, p. 7. Blackwell Publishing, Oxford, England.

Treves, T. & Korczyn A.D. (1986) Progressive dystonia and paraparesis in cerebral palsy. *European Neurology*, **25**, 148–153.

Winters, T.F., Gage, J.R. & Hicks, R. (1987) Gait patterns in spastic hemiplegia. *The Journal of Bone and Joint Surgery*, **69**, 437–441.

5 Visual Impairment

Mette Warburg

Introduction

Vision explains the world better than any other sensory input. Vision begins in the eye where photoreceptors and bipolar cells transfer the energy of light to the ganglion cells which transmit the messages to the brain. The eye develops from the fore part of the brain, and the biochemistry of the retina is similar to that of the brain. Conscious seeing is a cerebral function and therefore it is not surprising that people with cerebral dysfunction often have visual impairment.

Across the developed world, adults with intellectual disabilities can expect an increasing life-span. All elderly people will find that their vision changes with age and the majority will need spectacles. This is considered a normal phenomenon provided that visual acuity with spectacles is normal. Elderly people are also at risk of visual impairment due to cataracts, age-related macular dystrophy, glaucoma and other less common disorders. In glaucoma the optic nerve suffers, and high pressure in the eyes is an important risk factor. Patients with glaucoma often do not observe loss of their peripheral vision because the central vision remains intact for a long time.

Adults with intellectual disabilities have additional risks. Those adults with Down syndrome often present with cataracts and keratoconus, and they have an increased risk of developing diabetes, which may induce retinal pathology over time. Individuals with chromosomal aberrations often have malformations of the eyes; other syndromes are associated with disorders of the cornea, lens or retina. Adults with moderate, severe or profound visual impairment usually do not complain of poor vision since they do not know how well others can see, and a considerable number may have limited communication skills, hence regular monitoring of vision is important.

This chapter reviews the principal issues of visual impairment in people with intellectual disabilities. The majority of research has been undertaken on people with moderate, severe or profound intellectual disabilities and this chapter reflects this. Further, although not all the abnormalities associated with visual impairment are discussed, most of the prevalent topics are covered.

Definitions of visual impairment

Visual acuity is defined as the smallest letter recognized at a distance of 6 meters or 20 yards. If persons seated 6 meters (20 yards) from the wall chart can identify a letter which people with normal vision can just recognize 6 meters away, visual impairment is 6/6, or 1.0 or 20/20. If the person can recognize only larger letters at a distance of 6 meters, visual impairment is expressed as 6/9; 6/12; 6/18; 6/24; 6/36 or 6/60 according to the distance at which normal individuals can recognize the same letters. The fractions are often converted to decimals. The letters are constructed so that the distance between the strokes is equal to the width of the strokes. Such letters are called optotypes or Snellen letters. Picture charts are constructed in most countries in such a way that they are comparable to optotypes. It is important to notice that assessment with single letters or single pictures gives better visual acuity than assessment with optotypes in a line.

While the optotype test shows that the person can recognize the letters or pictures, the Teller acuity test (Mash & Dobson, 1998) and the Cardiff acuity test (Woodhouse & Oduwaiye, 1992) are less demanding (Fig. 5.1A). The examiner observes if the person fixates the gratings or the pictures or possibly points at them, meaning that he or she can resolve one stripe from the next. These tests are often called 'preferential looking' tests, because everybody prefers to look at objects that can be seen rather than at blank surfaces (Fig. 5.1B). Assessments of vision with the Teller acuity cards or Cardiff cards are near tests; hence the results are not comparable with optotype assessment at a distance. Moreover, grating acuity is a measure of the resolution of the visual system, but not of recognition of shapes.

The results of grating acuities have been compared with the results of optotype acuities in children; several studies have shown a reasonable agreement, but Mayer et al. (1984) showed that grating visual acuity tests overestimate visual acuity as compared to recognition tests, the greater the degree of vision loss being tested. Similarly, poor optotype acuities showed better grating than optotype acuities in ex-premature children (Dobson et al., 1995). Based on a study of 69 persons aged 8–40 years, Kushner et al. (1995, p. 491) found that 'if Teller Acuity Cards indicate normal visual acuity, there is still a high likelihood that it may be abnormal; if Teller Acuity Cards suggest abnormal vision, there is a high likelihood that it is abnormal'; and vice versa: 'If Snellen visual acuity was normal in one or both eyes, it was always normal with Teller cards'.

Even preferential looking tests are sometimes too difficult for patients with intellectual disabilities; in such cases the eyesight may be screened

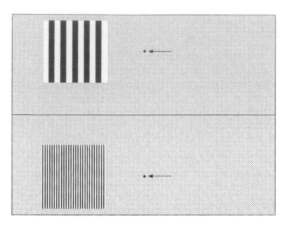

Fig. 5.1(a)   Teller acuity cards consist of a series of cards with stripes of decreasing width and separation. The stripes are on one side and there is a uniform grey at the other side. In the middle there is a peephole (arrow) through which the practitioner observes the subject.

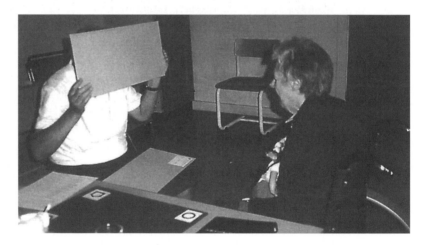

Fig. 5.1(b)   Assessment with Teller acuity card. The clinician sits 55 cm from the examinee and observes the fixation pattern through the central hole.

by observing if a person can find very small beads in front of him/her. This is a test of 'minimum visible'. If a person cannot find a bead of 1 mm ('hundreds and thousands', i.e., colorful sugar beads used as cake decorations or nonpareil sugar beads for instance) on the table in front of him when the contrast is good, vision is presumably below 0.1 (< 6/60 or < 20/200). Assessing vision with beads, however, is very imprecise (Richman & Garcia, 1983).

Visual impairment is defined by constriction of the visual fields and the degree of visual impairment in the best eye with best correction (i.e. best spectacles). In other words, it is a definition referring to vision at a distance, but unfortunately many people with intellectual disabilities can only be tested at near range, for instance with the Teller or the Cardiff technique.

For adults with intellectual disabilities, vision at near range is usually more important than distance vision because the occupational programs usually involve near work. There is no accepted definition of poor vision at near; nearsighted people have good acuity for near (Fig. 5. 2) and poor vision for distance without glasses, and elderly farsighted people have poor vision both at near range and distance without their spectacles. Poor near vision after the age of 45 years is called presbyopia and is a condition that everyone will experience.

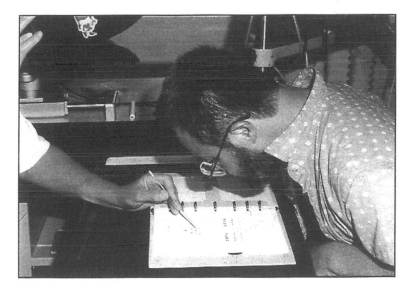

Fig. 5.2 Nearsighted person. Even with his strong minus glasses he has a very short viewing distance to the pictures.

There is more to vision than visual acuity and visual fields. Color vision, dark adaptation (i.e. adjusting the eyes to a change in illumination), seeing in reduced illumination, in twilight, and contrast sensitivity may be impaired in some disorders of the retina and the optic nerve. Understanding the message transmitted by the eyes to the brain involves recognition, perception of movement, orientation, discerning the difference between picture and background and more complex gnostic functions. Vision requires sensory integration in the brain.

If a person has one good eye and the other with poor vision, there is a visual disorder but no visual impairment; these patients often do not realize that they see with one eye only, and monocular low vision is common in persons with squint (strabismus). Strabismus is present in 25–50% of people with moderate, severe or profound intellectual disabilities (Jacobson, 1988; Woodruff *et al.*, 1980).

Lay people have difficulty recognizing visual impairment in adults; the impairment does not always give rise to handicap in well-known environments and in environments that have been adapted to visually impaired people – meaning good contrast borders around doors, good general illumination and variable acoustic or scented information. People with intellectual disabilities who have visual impairment may be mistakenly assessed as clumsy or unwilling to take part in near work; some may reject participating in walks because they have problems seeing the flagstones, or they might have difficulty seeing in too bright or too dim light.

Prevalence of visual impairment

General population

The prevalence of low vision in the general population varies both with the social and geographical environment, the age groups analyzed and the methods used, but all studies show a much lower prevalence than that found in adults with intellectual disabilities. The prevalence of best corrected visual acuity ≤ 0.3 was 3.8% and visual impairment ≤ 0.1 was observed in 1.5% of people of European heritage in the Baltimore area (Tielsch *et al.*, 1990). Hirvelä & Laatikainen (1995) found that 10% of subjects without intellectual disabilities over 70 years of age had low vision and approximately 2% were blind.

Population with intellectual disabilities

There are many studies on visual impairment in children with intellectual disabilities (Aitchison *et al.*, 1990; Kwok *et al.*, 1996; Menacker, 1993). Warburg *et al.* (1979) found that one half of Danish blind children had intellectual disabilities, and the rate of blindness (visual acuity ≤ 0.1) in children with intellectual disabilities was 200-fold that in other children. In Sweden 50% of children with visual impairment (visual acuity < 0.3) had intellectual disabilities (Blohmé & Tornqvist, 1997), and mortality during the first 19 years of life was as much as 120 times higher in children with visual impairment and intellectual disabilities than in the general population of Swedish children (Blohmé & Tornqvist, 2000). This may explain why the prevalence of visual impairment in adults with intellectual disabilities is lower than in children.

There are few surveys of visual function in adults with intellectual disabilities as compared with those performed during the last 30 years in children. The majority showed that 20–30% of adult individuals with intellectual disabilities were moderately visually impaired, and 1–5% were severely visual impaired or blind (Beange et al., 1995; Haire et al., 1991; Janicki & Dalton, 1998; Sacks et al., 1991; Van Schrojenstein Lantman-de Valk et al., 1994, 1997; Warburg, 2001b; Warburg, 1994; Woodhouse et al., 2000). In a Danish study of 837 persons with moderate, severe or profound intellectual disabilities, Warburg (2001a) found that 50% had either low visual acuity or low near vision, or both. Most studies have been concerned with a few hundred individuals, and the etiology and degree of impairment of the study population varied from one investigation to the next. Other large surveys were performed by questionnaires or notification of the affected persons by staff or medical personnel without actual assessment of acuity (Janicki & Dalton, 1998; Van Schrojenstein Lantman-de Valk et al., 1994, 1997). The prevalence of visual impairment in these studies was also 20–30%.

The largest of the series of studies of adults with intellectual disabilities comprised 45 500 individuals (Janicki & Dalton, 1998). In this study, visual impairment was reported by the staff and increased from 17% in people 35–39 years old to 34% in people aged 60–69 and 53% in 271 persons 80–89 years of age. (Van Schrojenstein Lantman-de Valk et al. (1997) found similar figures based on questionnaires to the staff of 1583 persons with intellectual disabilities. They found that the prevalence of visual impairment increased from 11% at the age of 20–29 to 17% at age 30–39. Twenty two percent in the age group 60–69 were considered to be visually impaired by the staff.

Visual impairment was noted in the case reports or observed by the staff of a large hospital in 24% of 99 adults aged 65 and above (Day, 1987). The prevalence of visual impairment increased from 18% in the 65–69 year-old people to 37% in the over 75 year-old persons, but no definition of visual impairment was given and no mention was made as to whether the staff referred to binocular or monocular visual impairment.

Down syndrome

Individuals with Down syndrome have a higher prevalence of visual impairment than do adults with other etiologies, and their risk begins earlier. Thus, in 243 persons with Down syndrome, visual impairment was observed in 23% of individuals aged 20–29, in 32% of the 40–49 year-olds and in 64% in individuals aged 60–69 (Van Schrojenstein Lantman-de Valk *et al.*, 1997). In another study, binocular vision was assessed in 96 persons with Down syndrome; visual impairment was defined as ≤ 0.3 and increased from 3% in the 30–39 year-old to 13% of people aged 50–59 (Van Buggenhout *et al.*, 1999).

Staff estimation of visual impairment

Questionnaires and notification give different information of visual impairment than actual individual assessment. Lay carers underestimate normal vision and blindness and overestimate mild and moderate visual impairment as compared to assessment of vision by professional methods (Warburg, 2001a). Screening of vision in adults with intellectual disabilities will thus give different results depending on the type of staff performing the task. Carers will find people with a visual handicap, which may respond to educational and environmental intervention. Optometrists and ophthalmologists on the other hand will disclose individuals with impairments, which may be surgically, medically or optically treatable.

Errors of refraction

Errors of refraction are very common in adults with intellectual disabilities. The largest survey (Woodruff *et al.*, 1980) demonstrated that 57% of adult residents in a large institution had ametropias comprising both spherical and astigmatic errors. Similar prevalence rates have been found by others (Haugen *et al.*, 1995; Woodhouse *et al.*, 2000). Refractive errors are treatable with glasses, contact lenses or surgery. Many studies have shown that more than one half of prescribed spectacles are in use at the time of follow-up (Bader & Woodruff, 1980; Haugen *et al.*, 1995; Jacobson, 1988; Schwartz, 1977; Warburg, 1970).

Many carers have difficulty in understanding the difference between visual acuity and refractive errors. Refraction, as a rule of thumb, is prefixed by a minus or plus sign. If a person wears correct glasses, his/her visual acuity is usually normal, even when the refractive error is high. The carer may find both the visual impairment and the power of the glasses in the letter from the optometrist or the ophthalmologist; for instance, visual impairment $1.0 - 5.0 \times -1.25(80°)$ which means that the person has normal visual acuity (i.e. 1.0) with myopic (-5.0) and astigmatic (-1.25) glasses in the 80° meridian.

Presbyopia

Correction both for near and distance is usually necessary in elderly persons, and bifocal spectacle lenses or progressive glasses are recommended (Schwartz, 1977). Patients with this condition are usually fond of their glasses, but their elderly parents, on the other hand, claim that bifocals are much too difficult to use, and persuading the parents to permit an attempt to be made can be difficult. Unfortunately the same attitude can be found in some professionals.

Some practitioners advise a gradual increase in the time that the glasses are worn, whereas others consider that adaptation to the glasses requires some time whenever the glasses are in use; therefore they recommend that the spectacles are worn all day from the very beginning. In practice, the carers individualize according to their understanding of each person.

Medical causes of visual impairment

Elderly people with intellectual disabilities have the same eye disorders as all others of the same age, but so far the life expectancy of adults with moderate, severe or profound intellectual disabilities is lower than in the remainder of the population, hence most causes of visual impairment in the elderly have been present from a younger age. The majority of ocular causes of low vision, however, are uncorrected errors of refraction (i.e. lack of appropriate spectacles). Medical disorders with visual impairment are mainly optic nerve atrophy, unoperated cataract, keratoconus, high myopia, retinitis pigmentosa, glaucoma and rare syndromes (Jacobson, 1988; McCulloch *et al.*, 1996; Warburg, 2001a; Woodhouse *et al.*, 2000). In fact, more than 345 rare syndromes, most of them genetic, present with both visual impairment and intellectual disabilities (Winter & Baraitser, 1998). Many of these syndromes are reviewed in Chapter 3.

Optic nerve atrophy

Optic nerve atrophy is seen in a large number of cerebral disorders, both congenital and acquired. It has usually run its course in adults, and the resulting visual impairment will be permanent. Optic nerve atrophy can be mild and difficult to assess in patients with spastic cerebral paresis;

however, hemianopia (loss of one half of the visual field) is common and its signs should be described to the care personnel. Optic nerve atrophy can be a sign of progression of the cerebral disorder, for instance hydrocephalus. People with optic nerve atrophy need better contrast than others, which means good illumination, contrasting borders around doors, tablecloths of one color only, contrasting plates and cutlery, etc.

Cataract

Cataracts (Fig. 5.3) are seen as a cloudy reflection behind the pupil. They are common in Down syndrome, both as congenital and acquired cataracts; moreover more than 150 syndromes present both cataracts and intellectual disabilities (Winter & Baraitser, 1998). Cataracts may also be found in adults with psychoses who beat themselves in the face. Unoperated cataracts are common findings in elderly people with intellectual disabilities (Jacobson, 1988; McCulloch *et al.*, 1996). Their vision becomes progressively blurred, and surgery with removal of the cloudy lens and implantation of an intraocular plastic lens is the standard procedure, irrespective of whether a cataract presents in people with Down syndrome or in others. A 24-hour watch is recommended for the first 48 hours after the operation to prevent the patients from rubbing their eyes (but the use of shields may draw the attention of the patients to their eyes and cause them to try to remove the occlusion). Some people with intellectual disabilities with poor vision may become agitated, aggressive, or

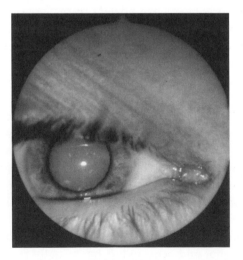

Fig. 5.3 Cataract of the right eye. The pupil has been dilated and there is a grey reflex in the pupil instead of the normal black.

bang their heads against a wall due to their vision problems, but after they have regained their eyesight their behavior usually becomes far more manageable.

Retinitis pigmentosa

Retinitis pigmentosa is the collective term for a number of progressive retinal disorders. These result in loss of peripheral vision (so-called 'tunnel vision'), and reduced or absent night vision; however, visual impairment may remain acceptable for many years while tunnel vision progresses. The ophthalmologist observes that the retina is thin and translucent, and the blood vessels are attenuated. Dark star-shaped retinal pigmentations appear later, together with pallor of the optic nerve. Physicians with little experience of retinitis pigmentosa will notice the optic nerve atrophy, but the initial attenuation of the retinal vessels is often overlooked.

Retinitis pigmentosa has a higher prevalence in people with intellectual disabilities than in the general population (Haim, 1992); it is presumably even underdiagnosed in those patients who are not subjected to regular eye examination. Although at present there is no medical treatment, the identification of retinitis pigmentosa improves the social adaptation of people with intellectual disabilities when the carers and staff have been informed of the particular difficulties encountered by these persons. Persons with retinitis pigmentosa need a high-contrast environment similar to those with optic nerve atrophy.

There are more than 1100 syndromes with intellectual disabilities, but only just over 80 where both retinitis pigmentosa and intellectual disabilities are pronounced (Winter & Baraitser, 1998); hence, the identification of retinitis pigmentosa in a person improves the establishment of a correct syndromic diagnosis.

The commonest causes of retinitis pigmentosa in adults with intellectual disabilities are Leber congenital amaurosis, a heterogeneous group of retinitis pigmentosa-like phenotypes which has been studied intensively in children, but few have been followed to old age and the prognosis as to longevity is unknown. Retinitis pigmentosa presenting in adults with intellectual disabilities also comprises Cohen syndrome, muscle-eye-brain syndrome, retinitis pigmentosa-mental retardation, and other rare syndromes. The Bardet-Biedl syndrome is variably associated with intellectual disabilities (Green et al., 1989; Riise et al., 1997).

Malformations

Malformations of the eye often lead to visual impairment. Such conditions are extremely rare in the general population, and although they are more common in persons with intellectual disabilities, they remain rare. The commonest malformations are sector-shaped defects of the iris or the retina and choroid (Fig 5.4) called colobomata, which in some patients are associated with microphthalmia. Other malformations may be observed in the interior of the eye (the vitreous), or the retina, which may be detached or folded (falciform folds). Nystagmus is a rapid oscillation of the eyes, but the environment is perceived as stationary. Congenital or infantile nystagmus is present in several eye disorders, all characterized by low vision.

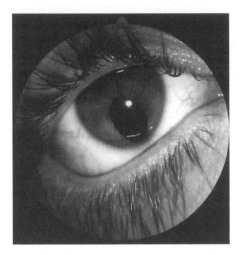

Fig. 5.4 Coloboma of the iris. Colobomas are common malformations. If they present in the iris only, there is no visual impairment, but if the retina and choroid are involved visual impairment is often present.

A number of previously undescribed or unknown syndromes have been observed in the latter years in patients with intellectual disabilities; the majority of them are genetic and thus of immense interest to the families in which they occur. Some of them give rise to serious visual impairment or blindness while others are not associated with poor vision, but all of them are important handles in the search for a precise differential diagnosis. Microphthalmia and colobomata are particularly common in persons with chromosomal aberrations, and all individuals with intellectual disabilities and colobomata or microphthalmia should be subjected to a chromosomal examination (Warburg & Friedrich, 1987).

Cerebral visual impairment

Cerebral visual impairment is a condition with poor use of vision caused by brain lesions or malformations of the brain; the eyes are normal or there is an eye disorder which does not fully explain the reduced vision. The retinal photoreceptors, bipolar and ganglion cells are but relay stations for vision, and the areas which process sight are spread over most of the cortex of the brain; hence, cerebral lesions may give rise to a variety of visual defects.

Cerebral visual impairment was not regarded as a cause of visual impairment some 20 years ago, but in the industrialized world it is now the most prominent cause of visual impairment in people with intellectual disabilities, next to uncorrected ametropia. The cause of this paradox is that people with intellectual disabilities were not subjected previously to regular eye examinations, and those who appeared to have healthy eyes without using their vision were classified as intellectually disabled and not as visually impaired. Cerebral visual impairment is becoming more prevalent, mainly because extremely premature babies now have a higher survival rate; but unfortunately a number get intracranial hemorrhage during birth, which may lead to cerebral visual impairment and to intellectual disabilities.

The most striking feature in adults with cerebral visual impairment is the indifference to objects presented at a clinical examination, as if the meaning of the object or the understanding of the task of observing it was non-existent. Some of these persons are well oriented in their usual environment and can respond to visual clues in their homes. Eyesight varies from day to day and from time to time. Patients with cerebral visual impairment may present visual field defects, and nystagmus is seen in a minority (Jacobson *et al.*, 1996).

Minor expressions of cerebral visual impairment have not yet been described in adults with intellectual disabilities, but it is well known both in children who were born prematurely and in elderly people who have suffered a stroke. Some of these individuals have problems recognizing people, while others have poor orientation so that they cannot find their way to neighbouring rooms, for instance the toilet, or the corridor with their overclothes. Examination of cooperative adults with cerebral visual impairment reveals mild to moderate visual loss not related to eye disease, and that stereoscopic vision may be impaired.

Some adults with cerebral visual impairment move about quite easily, while others have visual field loss and bump into the furniture. In some cases, the adult has difficulty in detecting moving objects (for instance, cars), while others have difficulty seeing stationary objects if they themselves are moving (for instance, sitting in a car). A very characteristic feature of these patients is that they have problems with crowding (i.e. difficulty recognizing features in a crowd such as letters in a word or intricate pictures (Dutton *et al.*, 1996; Jacobson *et al.*, 1996). Crowding may also result in expressed difficulties with finding objects placed among other things, and some adults even find eating together at a table with a number of other persons disturbing.

Cerebral visual impairment is difficult to diagnose in individuals with intellectual disabilities, and there is a risk that the affected persons are considered to have greater intellectual disabilities than they really have. The retina in cerebral visual impairment can resemble retinitis pigmentosa without abnormal pigmentations if there is mild pallor of the optic disc, and a correct diagnosis requires electroretinographic assessment.

Neuropsychological assessment is of considerable assistance in these cases in order to better understand the specific nature of the visual problems. Modern cerebral imaging and electrophysiological examination of the brain may classify the causes, so that intervention will become more precise, but only general educational strategies are available at present. When orientation is difficult, doggerels or jingles have been of help, the person reciting or singing the route as he or she goes along. It is easier for those affected to recognize other people when they speak, walk, carry recognizable jewelry or scent and carers should reintroduce themselves every day. Table 5.1 shows a series of questions that may be helpful in the diagnosis.

Table 5.1   Clinical questions relating to cerebral visual impairment.

Does the person (P) recognize the parents, the staff, other persons?
Can the P recognize shape, do picture lottery?
Does the P name and or match colors?
Does the P get lost in the house? the street? the workshop?
Can the P climb the stairs? See the curbstone?
Can the P walk in the dusk?
Can the P recognize pets? houses? cars? etc., when moving in a car or on a bus?
Can the P recognize pets? houses? cars? when the P is not moving?
Can the P find small objects on a patterned table cloth?
Can the P copy simple geometric drawings (triangle, circle, S)?
Does the P gaze at lights?
Is visual attention fleeting?

Ocular disorders in adults with Down syndrome

Down syndrome is the commonest single cause of intellectual disabilities, comprising 15–20% of people with intellectual disabilities (Partington *et al.*, 2000). The first large study of the ocular features in Down syndrome was published by Skeller and Øster (1951). Brushfield spots are seen in most persons with Down syndrome; other common features are blepharitis, strabismus (squint), keratoconus, cataract, nystagmus and high myopia.

Blepharitis is inflammation of the eyelids. It will be present in all cases unless active prevention is carried out. The inflammation presents with a sticky discharge, redness and swelling of the eyelids and the conjunctiva (the mucous membrane covering the eyeball). The eyelids may be glued together in the morning, and tears run down the cheeks. The patients have had several series of antibiotic medicine, but without permanent result. The cause of the inflammation is a sheet of dry skin cells and mucous surrounding the eyelashes where they project from the eyelids, and chronic ulceration is often present underneath this debris. The eyelashes become distorted after many recurrences, and some of them break while others turn in toward the eyeball and scratch the cornea. Most of the eyelashes are lost eventually, and the eyelids lose part of their protective property. Such eyelids without lashes are quite common in elderly persons with Down syndrome.

Prevention is simple; the lashes must be cleaned every day. This can be done by scrubbing the eyelashes with moist cotton wool while simultaneously stretching the lid slit (the rima palpebrae) with a finger on the lateral side of the eye. All traces of debris must be removed and unless the lid is stretched it is impossible to scrub sufficiently well. If an ulcer appears after scrubbing, it is not the fault of the helper; the ulcer has been present all the time. A small drop of a simple ointment without antibiotics is applied afterwards and surplus ointment removed.

The small white dots on the iris – Brushfield spots – cause no harm (Fig. 5.5). Keratoconus is a condition in adults with Down syndrome where the central part of the cornea becomes tapering, projecting, and thin (Fig 5.6). This is a rare condition in the general population where it will be treated initially with contact lenses, later with corneal transplantation. The central part of the cornea in patients with keratoconus may swell and become opaque (acute keratoconus); this is very painful but extremely rare in the general population, and when it does occur in adults with Down syndrome it gives rise to much anxiety in carers and physicians alike. However, simple treatment with drops and antibiotics over a period of one to three months will leave the cornea with a central scar which can be

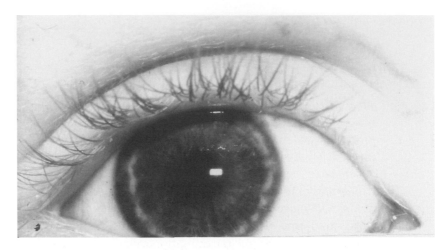

Fig. 5.5 Brushfield's spots are a concentric row of slightly elevated white nodules. They are also found in the general population and have no untoward effect.

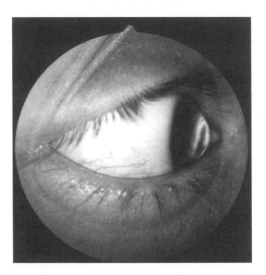

Fig. 5.6 Keratoconus. The patient looks to the left; the bright part in the corner of the eye is a protuberant clear part of the cornea – the keratoconus. Vision is severely impaired and spectacles do not improve vision. The treatment of choice is corneal transplantation.

removed by operation once the active phase is over. Steroid drops are not recommended.

Congenital or juvenile cataract may have been removed in adults with Down syndrome at a time when intraocular lenses were not available. These patients need high plus lenses, usually bifocals, unless their eyes are myopic; without their strong lenses vision will be poor. Fortunately, implantation of intraocular lenses is now routine. There is a risk that new carers may not be informed about spectacles when the individual moves from one residence to another.

In adults with Down syndrome, age-related cataracts occur at an earlier age than in the general population. Age-related cataracts may be observed from the fourth decade; therefore it is advisable for persons with Down syndrome to be systematically examined from the age of 30 years by an ophthalmologist or optometrist, so that a cataract can be removed before vision becomes seriously impaired, and before the individual develops Alzheimer's disease. Vision is usually good post-operatively, but glasses may be necessary.

A high degree of myopia is also more common in persons with Down syndrome than in the general population. Sometimes the individuals refuse to wear spectacles, presumably because their world is a near world and their ambulatory vision is sufficient without glasses. Myopia can be treated surgically with good functional results, but informed consent presents a difficult ethical question.

Accommodation is impaired earlier in adults with Down syndrome than in other adults and those who are not nearsighted will need glasses for near work (Woodhouse et al. 1993, 1996). Further, there is a higher prevalence of high ametropia (Haugen et al., 1995; Hestnes et al., 1991; van Buggenhout et al., 1999; Woodhouse et al., 2000; Woodruff et al., 1980). Among persons needing glasses, compliance for using the glasses may be poor if they are prescribed too late. It is recommended to use bifocal or progressive lenses so that the adults always wear the correct spectacles. If an adult with an intellectual disability has two pairs of glasses, one for distance and one for near-work, carers may be confused and have difficulty in distinguishing between them.

Adults with Down syndrome have a flat nasal bridge, and spectacles have a tendency to slide down the nose. If this is remedied by shortening the sidebars, it can result in wounds behind the ears and on the root of the nose. Then, of course, the patient will reject wearing them. Well-adapted spectacles should always be demanded. Contact lenses must be prescribed with caution. Constant supervision is necessary, the lenses must always be perfectly clean, the cleaning solution must be sterile, and the lenses must be perfectly adapted to the cornea. Contact lenses may slide up under the upper eyelid and give rise to irritation, when carers may believe that the lenses are in place. If the lenses are used by someone whose personal hygiene is poor, then the cornea may become infected. A carer who has been trained to remove a contact lens must be available at all times; some carers find this a challenging responsibility.

Diabetes has a higher prevalence among individuals with Down syndrome than in the general population (Anwar *et al.*, 1998). Diabetic retinopathy and glaucoma are sight-threatening complications of diabetes, particularly in individuals with poor dietary compliance. Regular monitoring of the eyes of diabetic patients is essential and cannot be ignored.

Cost of treatment

Most eye surgery is carried out under topical anesthesia on an outpatient basis, but surgical interventions and pre-operative examinations in individuals with intellectual disabilities require general anesthesia, post-anesthetic observation, and post-operative surveillance. Often, each visit to the surgery requires a driver and escort by a carer known to the adult. Further, glasses are often broken or lost and must be renewed (Haugen *et al.*, 1995; Schwartz, 1977; Warburg, 1970). Because of these factors, the cost of surgery in people with intellectual disabilities is higher than for other people. However, the humanitarian benefit of regaining good vision is evident; aggression and fear are reduced when the adult can see what is happening, and help with basic daily living skills, such as walking, eating, dressing and toileting, becomes easier for the carers.

Coping

If people have poor vision, they need predictability. Everything needs to be in its correct place. Doors must be either fully open or closed, for half-opened doors can cause serious accidents when the adult bumps into them. The preferred illumination is difficult to predict; some eye disorders are associated with reduced vision in poorly illuminated areas, other disorders give glare if the light is too strong. The solution is understanding the eye disorder and observation of the person in question. If the visual fields are restricted (for instance, below the horizontal) then the individual may tend to stumble over objects on the floor, such as low stools, toys, rolled-up carpets and doorsteps. If the visual field is reduced to one side (hemianopia), the individual may bump into objects (furniture, persons, lampposts) on the blind side. A dinner table laid with a multicolored cloth will make it difficult to find small objects, for instance the salt shaker, the (translucent) water bottle, or a piece of chocolate. Totally blind persons prefer to be told what they have on their plate and what to choose between. Visually impaired and blind persons use sound for orientation. Continuous background music or a non-stop TV noise is deleterious to their orientation. There are sports suitable for persons with visual impairment and blindness, for instance, swimming, horseback riding, running between two ropes and tandem bicycling. It is important to continue a good habit of physical exercise even if vision becomes impaired.

Carers should remember to introduce themselves each time they come and go, and explain what is happening in the room, on the TV, and when they walk in the street with someone who is visually impaired, so that anxiety may be reduced. Special aids are often useful for people with mild intellectual disabilities. They can use the white cane or a notebook in the form of a small tape recorder; similarly a tag with the blind logo of the country tells others to take care when they pass by. Compensation tech niques may vary. For example, some severely visually impaired adults keep a series of compact discs or other musical cassettes in a particular place in their room and are able to find the one they want, or the program they want to listen to.

Prevention

The prevention of visual impairment in people with intellectual disabilities is mainly concerned with cerebral visual impairment, prenatally acquired disorders and genetic syndromes. The reduced mortality of very premature babies has initiated an epidemic of cerebral visual impairment and intellectual disabilities. The results are beginning to show up now, and professionals need to be prepared for diagnosis and treatment of these individuals; prevention of intracranial hemorrhage at birth (and later) will reduce the incidence. An international consensus statement sponsored by the International Association for the Scientific Study of Intellectual Disabilities (IASSID) recommends ophthalmological assessments when adults leave school, when a person with Down syndrome is 30 years old and for everybody at age 45 and then every five years thereafter (Evenhuis & Nagtzaam, 1998).

The eye is part of numerous syndromes and an ophthalmological examination is helpful in syndrome recognition. Many rare syndromes in people with intellectual disabilities are genetic, and genetic counseling requires a precise diagnosis. Modern molecular genetics has provided an opportunity for improving the delineation of disorders which were previously difficult to separate. Simultaneously, a large number of hitherto unknown – or undiagnosed – disorders have been described in people with intellectual disabilities. Identification of syndromes in individuals with intellectual disabilities – like syndromes in any patient – requires interdisciplinary cooperation. A considerable number of the 'new disorders' or syndromes associated with intellectual disabilities have been recognized in children, but adults with intellectual disabilities have not been given the same opportunity of taking advantage of these new developments. The reason presumably is that adults with intellectual disabilities are treated only for acute diseases – for instance pneumonia, gastric ulcers and epilepsy – and the identification of specific syndromes is not perceived as the obligation of the general physician.

A precise diagnosis is not only important in genetic counseling, but can also predict specific difficulties in later life. For example, in Williams disease the patients may expect visuospatial constructive disabilities (Atkinson *et al.*, 2001), adults with Down syndrome may run the risk of developing a premature cataract or keratoconus, adults with Lowe disease may have kidney disorders, and blind individuals who lose their hearing, such as some adults with Norrie disease, may evidence later hallucinations. Because many causes of visual impairment in people with intellectual disabilities are treatable, there is a need for firmly regulated referrals to ophthalmic or optometric care (Warburg & Riise, 1994).

Conclusion

Among adult people with intellectual disabilities, almost 50% have some degree of visual impairment either at near or distance. Moderate visual impairment at distance is present in 20–30% of all, and severe visual impairment or blindness in 1–5% dependent on the casemix and the methods used to assess vision. The most important causes of visual impairment are lack of appropriate spectacles for distance and near, cerebral visual impairment, optic nerve atrophy, cataract and keratoconus. Age-related macular degeneration, and glaucoma, which are common in elderly people in the general population, are still uncommon in elderly people with intellectual disabilities. Diabetic retinopathy is a risk, particularly in persons with Down syndrome. Surgery in people with cataract, glaucoma and keratoconus has a good prognosis in cooperative patients. Some people with intellectual disabilities may be operated on for myopia. Individuals with optic nerve atrophy and retinitis pigmentosa need rooms with good illumination, good contrast and – most important – well informed staff. Prevention of visual impairment in adult people with intellectual disabilities requires referrals of everybody to ophthalmic or optometric care at regular intervals.

Acknowledgment

Work by the author was supported in part by the Ulla and Bernt Hjejle Memorial Foundation.

References

Anwar, A.J., Walker, J.D. & Frier, B.M. (1998) Type I diabetes mellitus and Down's syndrome: Prevalence, management and diabetic complications. *Diabetes Medicine*, **15**, 160–163.

Aitchison, C., Easty, D.L. & Jancar, J. (1990) Eye abnormalities in the mentally handicapped. *Journal of Mental Deficiency Research*, **34**, 41–48.

Atkinson, J., Anker, S., Braddick, O., Nokes, L., Mason, A. & Braddick, F. (2001) Visual and visuospatial development in young children with Williams syndrome. *Developmental Medicine & Child Neurology*, **43**, 330–337.

Bader, D., & Woodruff, M.E. (1980) The effects of corrective lenses on various behaviors of mentally retarded persons. *American Journal of Optometry and Physiological Optics*, **57**, 447–459.

Beange, H., McElduff., A. & Baker, W. (1995) Medical disorders of adults with mental retardation: A population study. *American Journal of Mental Retardation*, **99**, 595–604.

Blohmé, J. & Tornqvist, K. (1997) Visual impairment in Swedish children. 1. Register and prevalence data. *Acta Ophthalmologica Scandinavica*, **75**, 194–198.

Blohmé, J. & Tornqvist, K. (2000) Visually impaired Swedish children. The 1980 cohort study – aspects on mortality. *Acta Ophthalmologica Scandinavica*, **78**, 560–565.

Day, K.A. (1987) The elderly mentally handicapped in hospital: a clinical study. *Journal of Mental Deficiency Research*, **31**, 131–146.

Dobson, V., Quinn, G.E., Tung, B., Palmer, E.A. & Reynolds, J.D (1995) For the cryotherapy for retinopathy of prematurity cooperative group. Comparison of recognition and grating acuities in very-low-birthweight children with and without retinal residua of retinopathy of prematurity. *Investigative Ophthalmology & Visual Science*, **36**, 692–702.

Dutton, G., Ballentyne, J., Boyd, G., Bradnam, M., Day, R., McCulloch, D., Mackie, R., Philips, S. & Saunders, K. (1996) Cortical visual dysfunction in children: a clinical study. *Eye*, **10**, 302–309.

Evenhuis, H. & Nagtzaam, L.M.D. (eds) (1998) IASSID International Consensus Statement. *Early identification of hearing and visual impairment in children and adults with an intellectual disability*. IASSID, Special Interest Research Group on Health Issues. Available at www.iassid.org

Green, J.S., Parfrey, P.S., Harnett, J.D., Farid, I.D., Cramer, B.C., Johnson, G., McManamon, P.J., O'Leary, E. & Pryse-Philips, W. (1989) The cardinal manifestations of Bardet-Biedl syndrome, a form of Laurence-Moon-Bardet-Biedl syndrome. *New England Journal of Medicine*, **321**, 1002–1009.

Haim, M. (1992) Prevalence of retinitis pigmentosa and allied disorders in Denmark. II. Systemic involvement and age at onset. *Acta Ophthalmologica*, **70**, 417–426.

Haire, A.R., Vernon, S.A. & Rubinstein, M.P. (1991) Levels of visual impairment in a day centre for people with a mental handicap. *Journal of the Royal Society of Medicine*, **84**, 542–544.

Haugen, O.H., Aasved, H. & Bertelsen, T. (1995) Refractive state and correction of refractive errors among mentally retarded adults in a central institution. *Acta Ophthalmologica Scandinavica*, **73**, 129–132.

Hestnes, A., Sand, T. & Fostad, K. (1991) Ocular findings in Down's syndrome. *Journal of Mental Deficiency Research*, **35**, 194–203.

Hirvelä, H. & Laatikainen, L. (1995) Visual acuity in a population aged 70 years or older; prevalence and causes of visual impairment. *Acta Ophthalmologica Scandinavica*, **73**, 99–104.

Jacobson, L. (1988) Ophthalmology in mentally retarded adults. A clinical survey. *Acta Ophthalmologica*, **66**, 457–462.

Jacobson, L., Ek, U., Fernell, E., Flodmark, O. & Broberger, U. (1996) Visual impairment in preterm children with periventricular leukomalacia – visual, cognitive and neuropaediatric characteristics related to cerebral imaging. *Developmental Medicine and Child Neurology*, **38**, 724–735.

Janicki, M.P. & Dalton, A.J. (1998) Sensory impairments among older adults with disability. *Journal of Intellectual and Developmental Disabilities*, **23**, 3–11.

Kushner, B.J., Lucchese, N.J. & Morton, G.V. (1995) Grating visual acuity with Teller Cards compared with Snellen acuity in literate patients. *Archives of Ophthalmology*, **113**, 485–493.

Kwok, S.K., Ho, P.C.P., Chan, A.K.H,, Gandhi, S.R. & Lam, D.S.C. (1996) Ocular defects in children and adolescents with severe mental deficiency. *Journal of Intellectual Disability Research*, **40**, 330–335.

Mash, C. & Dobson, V. (1998) Long-term reliability and predictive validity of the Teller acuity card procedure. *Vision Research*, **38**, 619–626.

Mayer, D.L., Fulton, A.B. & Rodier, D. (1984) Grating and recognition acuities of pediatric patients. *Ophthalmology*, **91**, 947–953.

McCulloch, D.L., Sludden, P.A., McKeown, K. & Kerr, A. (1996) Vision care requirements among intellectually disabled adults: a residence-based study. *Journal of Intellectual Disability Research*, **40**, 140–150.

Menacker, S.J. (1993) Visual function in children with developmental disabilities. *Pediatric Clinics of North America*, **40**, 659–674.

Partington, M., Mowat, D., Einfeld, S., Tonge, B. & Turner, G. (2000) Genes on the X-chromosome are important in undiagnosed mental retardation. *American Journal of Medical Genetics*, **92**, 57–61.

Richman, J.E. & Garcia, R.P. (1983) The bead test: a critical appraisal. *American Journal of Optometry and Physiological Optics*, **60**, 199–203.

Riise, R., Andréasson, S., Borgström, M.K., Wright, A.F., Tommerup, N., Rosenberg, T. & Tornqvist, K. (1997) Intrafamilial variation of the phenotype in Bardet-Biedl syndrome. *British Journal of Ophthalmology*, **81**, 378–385.

Sacks, J.G., Goren, M.B., Burke, M.J. & White, S. (1991) Ophthalmologic screening of adults with mental retardation. *American Journal of Mental Retardation*, **95**, 571–574.

Schwartz, R.E. (1977) An optometric clinic in a state institute for the severely retarded. *Journal of the American Optometric Association*, **48**, 59–64.

Skeller, E., & Øster, J. (1951) Eye symptoms in mongolism. *Acta Ophthalmologica (Copenhagen)*, **29**, 149–161.

Tielsch, J.M., Sommer, A., Witt, K., Katz, J. & Royall, R.M. (1990) The Baltimore Eye Survey Research Group: Blindness and visual impairment in an American urban population. *Archives of Ophthalmology*, **108**, 286–290.

Van Buggenhout, G.J.C.M., Trommelen, J.C.M., Schenmaker, A., De Bal, C., Verbeek, J.J.M.C., Smeets, D.F.C.M., Ropers, H.H., Devriendt, K., Hamel, B.C.J. & Fryns, J.P. (1999) Down syndrome in a population of elderly mentally retarded patients: genetic – diagnostic survey and implications for medical care. *American Journal of Medical Genetics*, **85**, 376–384.

Van Schrojenstein Lantman-de Valk, H.M.J., Haveman, M.J., Maaskant, M.A., Kessels, A.G.H., Urlings, H.F.J. & Sturmans, F. (1994) The need for assessment of sensory functioning in ageing people with mental handicap. *Journal of Intellectual Disability Research*, **38**, 289–298.

Van Schrojenstein Lantman-de Valk, H.M.J., van den Akker, M., Maaskant, M.A., Haveman, M.J., Urlings, H.F.J., Kessels, A.G.H. & Crebolder, F.J.M. (1997) Prevalence and incidence of health problems in people with intellectual disability. *Journal of Intellectual Disability Research*, **41**, 42–51.

Warburg, M. (1970) Tracing and training of blind and partially sighted persons in institutions for the mentally retarded. *Danish Medical Bulletin*, **17**, 148.

Warburg, M. (1994) Visual impairment among people with developmental delay. *Journal of Intellectual Disability Research*, **38**, 423–432.

Warburg, M. (2001a) Visual impairment in adult people with moderate, severe, and profound intellectual disability. *Acta Ophthalmologica Scandinavica*, **79**, 450–454.

Warburg, M. (2001b) Visual impairment in adult people with intellectual disability. A literature survey. *Journal of Intellectual Disability Research*, **45**, 424–438.

Warburg, M. & Friedrich, U. (1987) Coloboma and microphthalmos in chromosomal aberrations. Chromosomal aberrations and neural crest cell developmental field. *Ophthalmic Paediatric Genetics*, **8**, 105–118.

Warburg, M. & Riise, R. (1994) [Ophthalmological services to mentally retarded persons. A review and recommendations.] In Danish. *Ugeskrift for Læger*, **156**, 6366–6369.

Warburg, M., Rattleff, J. & Kreiner-Moller, J. (1979) Blindness among 7700 mentally retarded children in Denmark. In: *Visual handicap in children* (eds Smith & Keen) pp. 56–67. Spastics International Medical Publications/Heinemann Medical Books, London.

Winter, R.M. & Baraitser, M. (1998) *Dysmorphology Database*, Oxford Medical Databases, version 2. Oxford University Press, Oxford, UK.

Woodhouse, J.M. & Oduwaiye, K.A. (1992) The Cardiff test: a new visual acuity test for toddlers and children with intellectual impairment. A preliminary report. *Optometry and Visual Science*, **69**, 427–432.

Woodhouse, J.M., Meades, J.S., Leat, S.J. & Saunders, K.J. (1993) Reduced accommodation in children with Down syndrome. *Investigative Ophthalmolology & Visual Science*, **34**, 2382–2387.

Woodhouse, J.M., Pakeman, V.H., Saunders, K.J., Parker, M., Fraser, W.I., Lobo, S. & Sastry, P. (1996) Visual acuity and accommodation in infants and young children with Down's syndrome. *Journal of Intellectual Disability Research*, **40**, 49–55.

Woodhouse, J.M., Griffiths, C. & Gedling, A. (2000) The prevalence of ocular defects and the provision of eye care in adults with learning disabilities living in the community. *Ophthalmic Physiolology and Optics*, **20**, 79–89.

Woodruff, M.E., Cleary, T.E. & Bader, D. (1980) The prevalence of refractive and ocular anomalies among 1242 institutionalized mentally retarded persons. *American Journal of Optometry and Physiological Optics*, **57**, 70–84.

6 Hearing Impairment

Sybil Yeates

Introduction

It is essential that hearing is normal from infancy, throughout childhood and into older adult life. If there is any abnormality this should be diagnosed and treated at the earliest possible stage. Without this stimulation all facets of development may be retarded (Marcell, 1995; Yeates, 2000). For example, if an individual's curiosity is not aroused by the interesting sounds of the surrounding environment, then that individual is less likely to try to interact with them. His or her locomotor efforts may well be developed more slowly. Comprehension of words, and increasingly of sentences, is bound up with the beginnings of education for which good hearing is essential.

An individual with an intellectual disability is very likely to have problems with communication. The addition of a hearing loss multiplies this problem rather than merely adding to the problem (Stewart, 1978). Recent work has shown that approximately 40% of people with intellectual disabilities have a hearing loss. It is therefore important that professionals dealing with persons with intellectual disabilities should be very aware of any symptoms that may indicate a hearing loss and should refer them for appropriate tests. In cases such as Down syndrome it is suggested that in adult life routine tests should be carried out at around the ages of 25 years, 40 years and 60 years.

When an infant or young child has been found to show slow development, or a specific condition involving intellectual disabilities, it is especially necessary to monitor hearing. There is now no excuse for failure to use modern methods of monitoring hearing as described later in this chapter. Early diagnosis will prevent other problems arising in adult life. It is worth mentioning that in the past, failure to diagnose a profound hearing loss has resulted in an individual spending years in a hospital for the mentally handicapped. As Williams (1982, p. 26) wrote, 'Too often deafness masquerades as mental handicap. In the mental handicapped themselves deafness is a compounding handicap.'

At the other end of life, adults showing signs that could be interpreted as features of senility should always be tested for hearing loss. The problems associated with the high frequency loss of presbyacusis can often mimic the signs and symptoms associated with senile change. When a hearing loss is diagnosed, every effort should be made to manage the loss in an optimal fashion, often persuading the individual to use an appropriate hearing aid. Efforts can be rewarded with pleasing behavior improvements.

Hearing impairment can be classified into four types:

(1) *Conductive hearing impairment* which results from abnormalities in the external or middle ear
(2) *Sensori-neural hearing impairment* which results from a dysfunction of the cochlea of the inner ear or auditory nerve
(3) *Central hearing impairment* which is caused by pathology of the cochlear nuclei or their cortical projections
(4) *Mixed hearing impairment* which is a combination of any of the above.

In this chapter hearing loss will be discussed with generally no specific reference to type and etiology.

Prevalence of hearing loss

Extensive population surveys of hearing impairment in people with intellectual disabilities have been reported (Denmark & Adams, 1982; Monley, 1994; Van Naarden *et al.*, 1999). The survey by Denmark & Adams (1982) yielded a low rate of 7.8%, including the categories of 'deaf' and also those of 'partially hearing', whereas Monley (1994) found a higher rate of 39.1%. Even higher prevalence rates (45%) in adults of sensorineural loss plus mixed loss (Nolan *et al.*, 1980), and 68% for sensorineural plus mixed loss (Keiser *et al.*, 1981) have been reported. Evenhuis (1995) reported the findings for hearing impairment in 70 people with intellectual disabilities aged between 60 and 92 years. The total prevalence of mild to severe hearing loss (33.3% in the 60-70 years age group and 70.4% in those age 70 years and over) was comparable to reported data for the population without intellectual disabilities.

Such surveys depend on observation by care staff and differing methods of measuring hearing loss and are therefore open to inaccuracies and differences in their results (Karchmer & Allen, 1999; Lavis *et al.*, 1997). In order to gain an accurate picture of the hearing status in people with intellectual disabilities, it is necessary to carry out a full audiological examination, as far as this is possible, in a reasonable sample of such people. Such a sample should then be analyzed for the types of examination used, the incidence of sensorineural loss, conductive loss and mixed loss. As far as possible the etiology of the problems shown in the sample should be noted, although this is sometimes very difficult and the cause of the disability cannot be ascertained. Such an exercise was undertaken by the author (Yeates, 1995) with a random sample of 500 people. Nearly 40% of the sample was found to have a loss sufficiently severe to require treatment with amplification. Of these, 30% showed a pure sensorineural loss, 29% showed a mixed sensorineural-conductive loss, 10% showed a conductive loss, and the remainder could not be categorized because they were diagnosed by electro-physiological tests. Every effort was made to find the etiology of each person's disability. Two factors were especially notable in the sample of 500: 23.8% of the cases were persons with Down syndrome, and 10% had known perinatal problems.

An association between hearing impairment and Down syndrome has been well established (Evenhuis *et al.*, 1992; Prasher, 1995). In the research project by Yeates (1995) when 500 people with intellectual disabilities were examined, 119 cases of Down syndrome were identified. Of these, 56 (47% of cases) were found to have a hearing loss. It was very significant to find that 36 people (64.2% of the Down cohort) had a mixed conductive sensorineural loss. The sample showed that adults frequently developed a high frequency sensorineural loss in early middle life. This loss was similar to that found in presbyacusis although it tended to occur earlier.

Tests of hearing

The following tests of hearing are available and all can be used in people with intellectual disabilities, provided the right test is chosen for the individual concerned. Also, it is essential that in the more able people the tests be given in the proper order. Severe mistakes occur when tests are not given in suitable sequence so that a person, lacking comprehension, becomes frightened and may easily revert to challenging behavior. It is greatly hoped that everyone responsible for deciding on methods of diagnosing hearing loss will see the enormous advantages of purchasing the required apparatus and training personnel in its use. Tests which are used in older children or adults with intellectual disabilities can be much more difficult, time consuming and less accurate.

The auditory response cradle (Bennett & Wade, 1980)

This apparatus has been used in a few selected centers and seeks to measure certain hearing indicators in infants. These are head turn, startle reflex, body activity and changes in respiration. There is no intrusion and the test is quick and easy and can be carried out by nursing staff.

However, there can be two problems. First, a loss of less than 45dB may not be detected. More seriously, because of recruitment, a greater hearing loss may not be identified. Although the test has many advantages (ease of application, speed and lack of any discomfort), it can only be used as a screening tool and cannot be used as a reliable method of diagnosing a hearing loss.

Oto-acoustic emissions (OAE)

The most reliable, rapid and low-cost method for ascertaining hearing loss is the oto-acoustic emission (OAE) test (Gorga *et al.*, 1995; Kemp & Ryan, 1990). There are two types of measurement which can be made. The first is that produced spontaneously by the cochlea itself without any external stimulation, while the second is that produced as a result of stimulation by broad band clicks. It would appear that a greater number of emissions are recorded after stimulation by broad band clicks (Burr *et al.*, 1996).

Distraction tests

These are known as localizing tests. The apparatus used is a high frequency rattle, producing sounds at 8 KHz (Manchester rattle or Nuffield rattle), a sibilant voice sound (ss-ss-ss) at 4 KHz, a soft humming voice sound and a conversational voice sound, not a whisper, both measured at 35–40 dB. Two examiners are needed to carry out distraction tests. One sits in front of the patient, who must be persuaded to sit as calmly as possible on a suitable chair. The first examiner's task is to hold the patient's visual attention by means of a suitable object depending on the age of the person under the test. When this has been secured satisfactorily, the visual object is removed and at this point the sound is made behind the patient at a distance of 1 meter, out of the visual field and at an angle of approximately 45°. This test depends on the satisfactory cooperation between the examiner obtaining the patient's visual interest and the second examiner standing behind ready to produce the sound immediately the visual stimulus is removed. The tests are repeated on each side and care must be taken to avoid other localizing stimuli such as squeaking shoes or strong perfume. These tests are difficult to administer satisfactorily on adults.

Five object test

This test involves the use of five common familiar objects (i.e., cup, spoon, brush, car or doll, and airplane). The person under test is seated at a suitable table on a chair of suitable size. The objects are placed in front of them, one at a time, and they are named in a firm voice. The adult is then asked to identify each object, in order to ensure that they have verbal comprehension. If this is satisfactory, they are told that the examiner is going to use a small voice and that they must listen carefully to pick out the objects. The test is then repeated using a voice metered at 35–40 dB at a distance of 1 meter. Criticism of the use of toys when testing adult patients is usually misplaced and it is more often the fault of the examiner who has failed to arouse interest by the use of intermittent conversation. However, some examiners may prefer to use the relatively new South London object test (SLOT; Moorey, 1996) which is described below.

Toy discrimination test

If the five object test has been completed satisfactorily, it is useful to attempt the toy discrimination test (McCormick, 1977). The purpose of this test is to ascertain whether the person hears high frequency sound. High frequency sounds are found in the consonants and give intelligibility to speech. High frequency loss results in the person hearing words inaccurately because one consonant is replaced by another and the sense of the sentence is lost. The person who has such a loss is often misdiagnosed and this can have disastrous results.

In this test the following pairs of objects are used and it will be seen that each pair has a common vowel but different consonants (vowels are low frequency sounds which give the speech its energy, carrying power and emotional quality):

- Cup and duck
- Plate and plane
- House and cow
- Lamb and man
- Key and tree
- Shoe and spoon
- Horse and fork

The test is administered in the same way as the simpler five object test. The objects are placed in front of the person one at a time and named in a clear voice. The person is then asked to identify the objects, once again to ascertain the verbal comprehension. If this is satisfactory, the voice is lowered to a level of 35–40 dB and the test repeated. If examiners prefer to use more adult objects, the SLOT test can be attempted. This uses the following objects:

- Key and cheese
- Ball and fork
- Bread and pen
- Soap and comb
- Jam and bag
- Cake and tape

Conditioning tests

These tests, which vary from a simple form using voice sounds to an audiogram which measures hearing in each ear separately and can measure across a wide range of frequencies (i.e. 125 Hz to 8 KHz), all depend on a modeling technique. If the best possible result is to be obtained, it is necessary to start with the simplest test and to take adequate time, and use adequate patience, over achieving a satisfactory result. It is totally useless to place a person with an intellectual disability in a soundproofed booth and tell them to press a button when they hear a sound. The result is a frightened, distraught person who may be screaming or showing other signs of difficult behavior. The way to avoid such a useless and disastrous result is to help the person to enjoy the first simple test. Many demonstrations may be needed before the person understands what is involved. He is then helped to make the first response by one examiner lightly holding his hand and helping him to drop the brick at the correct moment. The help is gradually withdrawn and if the person obviously can cooperate, the intensity of the voice sound is lowered to 35–40 dB.

Use of free field audiometer or warble tone audiometer

These use pure tones so that a more accurate result can be obtained. The free field audiometer produces sounds from 125 Hz to 4 KHz at intensities between 5 dB and 80 dB. The same method is used as for the simpler voice test described above. The person is again taught to make a simple movement every time a sound is heard. The warble tone audiometer produces narrow band sounds centered on a specific frequency. These sounds are more interesting to the person and produce more accurate results because they overcome the phenomenon of 'standing waves' which may distort the intensity of the sound used.

Use of the pure tone audiometer

If the person has been taken step by step and interest has been maintained by the examiner it should be reasonably easy to pass to the use of the pure tone audiometer. This is used to measure hearing in each ear separately, using headphones, but still using the same simple movements which have indicated that the sound was heard by the person. Most audiometers measure sound from 125 Hz to 8 KHz and from −10 dB to 120 dB.

Similar methods are used to introduce the person to the pure tone audiometer, but the initial problem is to persuade them to accept the headphones. The examiner can demonstrate by wearing the headphones himself, or the person can try using a Walkman which arouses interest. It may take time and patience before the person is happy to use the headphones. When the person has acquiesced in their use, a sound of 60 dB at 1 KHz is usually a good starting point. As with the previous tests, the person is helped to put a brick into the box, or similar movement, when the sound is heard. Many attempts may be needed before the person indicates that he fully understands the process. The sound is then lowered by 10 dB steps until the person makes no further attempts to make the movement which, by now, is very familiar. At this point the sound is raised by 5 dB steps until the movement is again made. Having obtained a result at 1 KHz my own preference is to proceed to 500 Hz and then 250 Hz although many textbooks suggest going from 1 KHz to 2 KHz and 4 KHz. It will be seen that an audiogram measuring hearing in right and left ears separately, across a wide range of frequencies and intensities, can be obtained by patient demonstration and without the use of language.

Objective tests

The tests that have been described are principally subjective tests. Several objective tests are available which are used when the person is unable to offer any cooperation (Tucker & Nolan, 1986). However a problem arises when anesthesia is required.

Post-aural myogenic response

The post-aural muscle behind the ear is well developed in those animals that rely largely on their hearing to escape from predators. In man the muscle is vestigial but there is still a well-developed electrical response to sound. Electrodes are placed behind the ears and the sound employed is a sharp-onset click. As each response is very small, about 100 clicks are needed in order for an averaging computer to produce a recorded result. The test is quick and totally non-invasive, but unfortunately it is not accurate.

Electrocochleography

This is an accurate test but is not now often used because the electrode has to be placed through the tympanic membrane and placed against the promontory of the cochlea. This, of course, requires an anesthetic. The sound stimulus is again sharp-onset clicks and the response comes from the cochlea and the adjacent part of the auditory nerve. An averaging computer records the results.

Brainstem evoked response audiometry (BSER)

This test is very reliable and detects electrical changes in the lower part of the auditory pathway in the brain, reaching as far as the inferior colliculus. An electrode is placed on the vertex and the responses to sharp-onset clicks are recorded. As each response is very small, it is necessary to produce over 1000 responses which can then be 'added' by an averaging computer which produces a visible result to be read by the audiologist. It will be seen that this test takes longer than the others so far described, for obvious reasons. However, the 30–45 minutes required are well spent as yet again the test is non-invasive and produces an accurate result. It is worth mentioning that the result obtained in very young babies is different from that seen in adults. An anesthetic must be used in adults because of the time required to complete the test.

If an individual requires a test which needs an anesthetic there may be a problem concerning the permission required. In the UK, the only adult who is legally able to give permission is the individual to be tested. However, in many cases this cannot be a meaningful permission, so the important issue of consent/assent arises. Guidelines are now usually available and involve every effort being made to explain the test procedure to the patient. If it is obviously not understood, then the following should take place. A meeting of all those who know the patient best, including their parents or any near relatives who are remaining in contact, should be called. The need for the test should be discussed and information on the test should be given. If all concerned are agreed that the test is necessary, then the senior person present, often a doctor, can sign the anesthetic form. The question that must always be answered is whether the test is in the best interests of the patient.

Impedance testing (admittance audiometry)

This is a very useful test which can be said to fall midway between a subjective and an objective procedure. It does require a probe to be placed in the external auditory canal, to obtain an airtight seal. Unfortunately some people who are touch-defensive will not allow this to be done and therefore the test cannot be used.

The probe contains three tubes. The first contains a generator producing a low-frequency sound. The second contains a very small microphone. If the middle ear is filled with catarrhal fluid as in the condition known as 'glue ear' or chronic secretory otitis media, the sound cannot be passed through the tympanic membrane and is reflected back and picked up by the microphone. If the middle ear is healthy, it is filled with air and the sound can pass through the tympanic membrane and on through the middle ear towards the inner ear. If the Eustachian tube is blocked by catarrhal material, a negative pressure is produced in the middle ear. The pump in the third tube can correct this, when the sound is able to pass through the middle ear. The apparatus produces a graph showing which condition is present in the middle ear (i.e., a normal healthy air-filled middle ear with the air coming through a patent Eustachian tube, a middle ear filled with thick 'glue-like' material preventing the further passage of sound, or a middle ear connected to a Eustachian tube filled with thick catarrhal material). This test is very useful in confirming the presence of chronic secretary otitis media which, in turn, produces a conductive hearing loss often worse in the low frequencies.

Cortical evoked response (CER)

The responses in this test are derived from the cortex, and the sound stimuli are long duration pure tones. It is the only test of this nature which uses pure tones. Its use is limited owing to the fact that the electro-encephalography (EEG) alpha rhythm may obscure the results.

Causes of hearing impairment in people with intellectual disabilities

Admiraal and Huygen (1999) recently investigated the etiology of hearing loss in the population with intellectual disabilities. The cause was acquired in 48%, inherited in 17%, chromosomal in 4% and unknown in 30%. Yeates (1995), in a study of 500 adults with intellectual disabilities,

Table 6.1 People with intellectual disabilities (sample of 500).

Etiology	Number of adults	Etiology	Number of adults
Down syndrome	119	Specific language disorder	2
Known peri-natal problem	51	Leber's congenital amaurosis	1
Rubella syndrome	21	Possible post-vaccination effect	1
Microcephaly	9	Moebius syndrome	1
Encephalitis	9	Spina bifida	1
Hydrocephalus (controlled)	9	Retts syndrome	1
Infantile convulsions	5	Friedrich's ataxia	1
Specific brain damage	4	Spinocerebella degeneration	1
Branchial arch syndrome	4	Congenital syphilis	1
Cerebrovascular accident	3	Von Recklinghausen's disease	1
Miningitis	3	De La Tourette syndrome	1
Post-trauma	3	Multiple tic disorder (variant of above)	1
Phenylketonuria	2	Lawrence Moon Bardet Biedle syndrome	1
Chromosomal abnormalities	2	Cause unknown	240
Fragile-X syndrome	2		

found a number of causes of which Down syndrome, peri-natal problems and Rubella syndrome were the commonest (see Table 6.1).

Genetic causes

Either occurring before or at conception, these include recessive causes, dominant genetic causes, X-linked genetic causes and primary chromosomal abnormalities.

Recessive genetic causes

There are two types of recessive genetic causes: clinical undifferentiated autosomal recessive deafness and syndromes that are inherited in a recessive manner. The first type is the commonest with a prevalence of 1 in 1000 of the population. As the prevalence of severe intellectual disabilities is around 4 per 1000, it seems probable that there will be individuals who are affected by both conditions, but in whom the causes are not linked (Fraser, 1976).

There are three main recessive syndromes which include hearing loss as one of the features. These are Pendreds syndrome (deafness with goiter), Ushers syndrome (deafness associated with retinitis pigmentosa), and Jervell-Lange-Nielson syndrome (deafness associated with prolongation of the Q-T interval). These syndromes are not usually associated with intellectual disabilities. But fetal hypothyroidism, if not diagnosed in early infancy, may give rise to some degree of slow development together with motor problems such as diplegia. Fortunately infants in most countries are now screened routinely for hypothyroidism.

Dominant genetic causes

Again dominant causes can be divided into two types: clinically undifferentiated and those forming part of a syndrome. Fraser (1976) found that the undifferentiated type was much less common than the recessive type. The main syndromes in this group are the auditory-pigmentary syndromes and the most important is Waardenburg's syndrome. In this syndrome there is a white forelock, heterochromia and lateral dystopia. There are some reports of intellectual disabilities associated with this syndrome (Amini-Elihou, 1970; Yeates, 1986), but other workers consider the association to be fortuitous.

Another group of conditions are those in which multiple congenital deformities are associated with deafness and sometimes intellectual disabilities. These are often the result of malformation of the branchial arches occurring in utero. The best known is probably Treacher-Collins syndrome or mandibulo-facial dysostosis. The abnormalities are seen in the outer and middle ears and intellectual difficulties are found in some of these patients (Yeates, 1986). Other problems may be found in the inner ear and, as implied by the name, deformities of the malar bone and mandible may be present. In fact there is a collection of deformities which may be present to a greater or lesser extent in different people. Other conditions which should be mentioned, although much less commonly seen, are Crouzon's disease (cranio-facial dysostosis), acrocephalo-syndactyly (Aperts syndrome), deafness-earpits syndrome, and Pierre-Robin syndrome.

X-linked genetic causes

Hunters syndrome is one of a group of mucopolysacharidoses, which is inherited in this manner. There is typical dwarfism commonly associated with both hearing loss and intellectual deficit. The latter varies widely between cases. The biochemical changes found are due to abnormal metabolism of the high molecular carbohydrates. The other mucopoly-sacharidoses are inherited in recessive fashion and intellectual deficit is severe in some (i.e. Hurlers syndrome and Sanfilippo syndrome), and very uncommon in others (i.e. Morquio's syndrome and Maroteaux-

Lamy syndrome). Hearing loss may be typical in the X-linked syndrome but can also be seen in the recessive syndromes. Also, the abnormal metabolite may be laid down in the middle ear, leading to conductive hearing loss.

Chromosomal abnormalities

The commonest of these is Down syndrome (Trisomy 21), in which the intellectual disability is often associated with a hearing problem. In childhood, upper respiratory infections are frequent, there are Eustachian tube problems and the children are mouth-breathers. As a result, middle ear problems are very frequent with consequent recurrent attacks of conductive hearing loss. Unless these are treated, the slow development of language is worsened by the frequent hearing problems. It is very wrong to ignore these hearing problems, regarding them as merely one of the symptoms found in children. It is important to treat the recurrent attacks of 'glue-ear' in the same way as for other children. A first attack may be treated with conservative methods but further attacks generally need the insertion of grommets or Good's tubes.

The diagnosis of high frequency loss is very important as when a person is unable to hear consonants (high frequency sounds) accurately, it is usual for one consonant to be replaced by another, thus altering the sense of the utterance. In this way people get wrong labels attached to them (e.g., they may be thought to be uncooperative, difficult or even senile). Thus, suitable hearing aids should be prescribed and, very often, a good deal of hard work is necessary to persuade the person to use them consistently.

There are other much rarer conditions in which chromosomal abnormalities are associated with both intellectual deficit and hearing loss. Patau's syndrome shows an extra chromosome in pairs 13–15. There are gross congenital malformations in the skull, eyes, nose and palate. There is often polydactyly, and genitalia may be abnormal, especially in males. A congenital heart lesion is often present. Severe harelip and cleft palate cause feeding difficulties. It is not surprising that this collection of problems is often fatal.

Edward's syndrome or Trisomy of 17–18 is a rare syndrome of the same group. An abnormally shaped skull has low-set ears which may also be abnormally shaped. A typical appearance of the chest is produced by a short sternum. Fingers and feet are abnormal, the fingers showing flexion deformities and the feet being rocker-bottomed in shape. Limited hip abduction is seen. Feeding difficulties are seen but in this case due to extreme micrognathia. Congenital heart lesions may be present.

The third syndrome is cri-du-chat syndrome, so called because of the infant's high-pitched mewing cry. The chromosomal abnormality is deletion of the short arm of chromosome 4–5. Some of these infants are microcephalic and have micrognathia with low-set ears. Once again a congenital heart lesion may be present. This syndrome is rather more commonly encountered in clinical practice, but although hearing loss may be seen it is not common.

Infections

Rubella

Rubella was formerly the commonest infection, which if caught by a pregnant woman during the first trimester would result in a collection of symptoms which could be extremely disabling. These included visual problems, including blindness, hearing loss which could be severe, congenital heart lesions, microcephaly associated with learning problems and cerebral palsy. At birth there is hepato-splenomegaly and sometimes a purpuric rash. The infant is infectious and serological tests are positive. The MMR vaccine (measles, mumps and rubella), which is now offered to all infants in many countries has significantly reduced the number of cases of congenital rubella seen in practice. It is unfortunate that unproven reports of the vaccine causing autism and Crohn's disease have stopped some parents from accepting the vaccine for their children. One can hope that parents will come to understand that serious problems can occur when infants are not protected. Cases of rubella are often still found in countries where the vaccine is not routinely used.

Cytomegalovirus (CMV)

CMV is a virus which, while causing very few symptoms in the mother, can cause widespread damage in the fetus, including retarded development, a hearing loss and visual problems. Many adults are already serologically positive, so a test in pregnancy is not diagnostic. However, a test in the infant can be useful and can result in a diagnosis where one would previously not have been found.

Toxoplasmosis

Toxoplasmosis is a protozoal infection which, like CMV, gives little trouble to the mother but can cause widespread trouble to the fetus. As in

CMV, the most dangerous period for infection is in the first trimester. It can cause intellectual deficit and ocular and hearing problems.

Meningitis

Meningitis is one of the commonest causes of hearing loss in childhood. The literature indicates that around 5% of children with meningitis are left with hearing loss. This is usually very severe or profound and patients must be monitored carefully so that diagnosis is made as soon as possible and treatment commenced. The type of organism causing the disease does not appear to be important and the severity of the disease does not seem to correlate with the degree of hearing loss left. Although the person should be monitored, there does not seem to be any correlation between the onset of symptoms and the onset of treatment. The usual treatment for meningitis is by the drugs chloramphenicol, penicillin and sulphonamide. Occasionally the organism causing the disease is not susceptible to this triad of drugs and gentamicin is used as a life-saving treatment. As gentamicin can be a cause of hearing loss its use should be monitored very carefully and blood levels checked. Ampicillin was once thought to be ototoxic when used in the treatment of meningitis, but further work showed this only to be the case when doses exceeded 250 mgm/kg per day (Jones & Hanson, 1977).

Other infections

Measles and mumps can cause profound unilateral deafness but, what is more important, both diseases may be complicated by encephalitis which causes both learning problems and hearing loss. This is yet another reason for encouraging parents to accept the mumps, measles and rubella (MMR) vaccine.

Peri and post-natal causes

Prematurity

Infants born prematurely may be found to have both learning problems and hearing loss. In the fragile, underdeveloped blood vessels serving the inner ear, hemorrhage is common and thus the blood supply of the organ of Corti is diminished (i.e. the oxygenation of these cells is diminished).

Also blood extravagated into this area seems to have an irreversible toxic effect on the cells. The risk of damage is increased if obstetric manipulations are required. Similar problems are found in 'dysmature' or low birthweight babies, and poor placental function giving rise to anoxia increases the problem. Careful monitoring in utero is essential in these infants.

Anoxia

Anoxia before, at or after birth can give rise to many problems in the infant, including cerebral damage and damage to the inner ear. Thus, progress around the time of birth must be carefully monitored by the obstetrician and other staff. Conditions worth special mention are very severe toxemia with infarction of the placenta, long labors with difficult presentations and possible forceps delivery. Emergency conditions such as placenta praevia and prolapsed cord can give rise to dangerous levels of anoxia. Respiratory distress syndrome or hyaline membrane disease must be carefully monitored to make sure that anoxia does not reach dangerous levels. Anoxia not only causes hemorrhage in the inner ear but may also cause damage to the cochlea nucleus in the brain stem.

Hyperbilirubinaemia

Previously the most usual cause of increased serum bilirubin levels in neonatal blood was due to Rh incompatibility. The routine use of anti-D immunoglobulin after the first pregnancy, given in the immediate post-partum period, has caused this problem to be diminished. However, AB-O incompatibility may cause the same problem and physiological jaundice in a small premature baby may also cause similar difficulties. The product of red cell breakdown (i.e. unconjugated bilirubin) may be laid down in the basal ganglia, the cochlear nuclei and the central auditory pathways. This is shown as athetoid cerebral palsy and high frequency hearing loss. It would be sensible to watch hearing levels in any infant where there has been concern over jaundice in the newborn period (e.g. when phototherapy was used, irrespective of serum bilirubin level).

Chronic secretory otitis media

The commonest cause of mild hearing loss in childhood is chronic secretory otitis media. This occurs both in children with and without intellectual disabilities. However, as has already been seen, some children with specific learning problems are especially prone to middle ear problems. Those persons with Down syndrome are the commonest, as has been discussed above. Also, those individuals with congenital multiple deformities, especially those affecting the skull bones (e.g. Treacher-Collins syndrome), often have abnormal configurations of the middle and inner ears, which can lead to both conductive and sensorineural loss.

Although the loss in chronic secretory otitis media may be small, and worse in the lower frequencies, the recurrent attacks can affect speech development. As this is already impaired in children with intellectual deficit, the addition of yet another problem can cause even slower progress. Therefore, as already stated, treatment for the condition should not be delayed. In those children where surgical intervention may possibly help (e.g. forming an artificial external auditory canal leading to a patent middle ear), the optimal time for intervention should be discussed with all concerned in monitoring the child.

Age-related hearing loss

The term 'presbyacusis' is used for hearing loss in which increasing age is the only etiological factor that can be found. However, as Willott (1991) states, the attempt to completely divorce presbyacusis from the effects of genes and the environment is counter-productive. The process of aging should be seen as encompassing the effects of endogenous factors, with biological changes in cells, tissues or systems, and exogenous factors. The latter are due to changes in the auditory system due to inevitable environmental insults (e.g. some exposure to noise, chemicals and illnesses detrimental to the auditory system).

Age-related hearing problems may begin in young adulthood or middle age, but are more widespread and worse in the elderly population. They are seen to a greater extent in males than in females. At least 25%, and perhaps more than 50%, of adults age 70 have clinically significant degrees of hearing loss (Willott, 1991). Most people are more severely affected in the high frequencies.

Because presbyacusis affects high frequency hearing, the consonants in speech are not heard or misheard. The consonants give rise to the intelligibility in speech, and problems in this area mean that words and sentences are not heard correctly. In normal speech, frequencies vary from 64 Hz to 8129 Hz. Where the higher frequencies are not heard, it can be appreciated that some words are not heard, some are partly heard, and others are misheard with one consonant being substituted for another. People with no learning problems may understand what is happening and can hopefully ask for help. But in those individuals with intellectual disabilities neither they nor those persons caring for them can appreciate the true problem and wrong 'labels' are often attached to the person with presbyacusis. They may be said to be difficult, uncooperative, exhibiting challenging behavior, and even showing the onset of senility. If the true diagnosis can be made then help can be offered, although much patience is needed in, for example, introducing a hearing aid.

Because hearing loss in old age is so widespread and so disabling, affecting people both with and without intellectual disabilities, further work on the multiple causes of the condition would be useful. Willott (1991) has produced a most useful summary of the effects of age on the ear and the auditory system, but he too agrees that more work remains to be done.

Management of hearing loss

People with intellectual disabilities have been largely moved from large, special hospitals with little privacy and few opportunities for education and leisure, to small homes where they are encouraged to live a more normal life, doing the shopping and cooking the meals for 'the family' in a home-like manner. To deal with hearing loss, protocols for early identification and diagnostic screening (Evenhuis, 1996; Evenhuis & Nagtzaam, 1998) should be developed. This particularly applies to the aging population (Van Schrojenstein Lantmen-de Valk *et al.*, 1994). Special day courses should be offered to all staff coming into contact with people having learning problems. Ways of detecting and compensating for hearing loss should be discussed. To experience hearing loss, staff may be asked to use earplugs to help them understand the effects of losing hearing. The different types of loss should be explained with their consequent effect. Even the results of having ears blocked with wax should be remembered. Above all, the notion that adults with intellectual disabilities cannot benefit from varying types of help must be firmly put to rest.

If it is intended to teach an adult to use a hearing aid, the different steps that must be used should be taught one at a time. The first step is to accustom the person to feeling an earpiece, or mould, in their ears. Initially a piece of cotton wool should be placed in the external auditory meatus. This should not be so small that it can be pushed down hard against the tympanic membrane. The person should be instructed not to push the cotton wool from where it has been placed. When this has been accepted for a short period, the length of time can be increased. Next a soft mould can be made and placed in the ear that is to be aided. Again, this is used initially for a very short time, which is gradually increased. In the same way the aid is attached to the mould, but the volume is not turned on until the person has become accustomed to the feel of the aid behind their ear.

At this stage the volume is turned on at a low level, and gradually the volume is increased to a comfortable level. It may be difficult to ascertain 'a comfortable level' in people with intellectual disabilities. The audiologist should generally err on the side of caution when choosing maximum power output of the aid. If the recipient receives a sudden burst of sound they may become worried and frightened and refuse to try a more suitable level. If, on the other hand, the level is too low, the support staff can report back that the recipient does not appear to be deriving any benefit from the aid at that level. It can then be seen that the help of the parents and/or support staff can be crucial in finding the type of aid that is optimal for each individual. It can be seen that every step takes time, and much patience is required. If any step is not accepted then the previous one should be tried again. It takes considerable time to find the appropriate aid to be used at the appropriate volume. The care staff, or the parents, should be taught in the day courses how to clean the moulds and how to re-tube them. They should be familiar with the M, T and O positions on the aid, and also with the volume positions marked on the aid. Changing the battery should also become familiar.

The above remarks refer to the small post-aural hearing aids which are now generally in use. They are small, neat and unobtrusive. However, they are easily lost and can be commonly left on a bus or thrown away with household rubbish. In our clinic, one of the adults tried flushing his aid down the lavatory! In spite of many advantages some people refuse to persevere with the post-aural aid. They may, however, be happy to use an environmental aid. A hand-held communicator held near their ear for short periods may be useful for those with mild or moderate loss. The Crystal television listening device has an appearance very similar to a Walkman and allows for personal adjustment of the television volume. A similar, but more permanent system, is the room loop.

Some cinemas and churches and other places of assembly are fitted with a loop system, which enables people with and without intellectual disabilities to enjoy meetings, films, etc. to a much greater extent. Societies providing support for people with hearing impairment often produce a range of listening devices which help in general conversation, social events, and listening to the television and radio. Other useful items are an alarm clock which has a flashing light plus a sound alarm, or one which vibrates under the pillow. Many phone amplifiers are available as are text-phones produced by local telephone companies. Special doorbells, baby, car and fire alarms are also available. These special systems are particularly important if the person with an intellectual disability is now living in a 'family home'.

Lastly, one must consider those people whose hearing loss is so great that they cannot derive any benefit from even the most powerful hearing aids. If some nerve fibers remain in the auditory system, then it may be possible to stimulate these electrically, although not acoustically. But first it is necessary to ascertain whether there are any remaining nerve fibers, and if so where they are within the system. Adults who have retained 5–10% of their auditory nerve fibers are thought to present the best cases for implantation. In this type of implant one electrode is passed through the upper opening of the Eustachian tube, while a second is placed through the round window into the basal turn of the cochlea for rather less than half of its length. However, there still remains much discussion over the optimal number of electrodes to be used and their method of insertion.

Another type of implant, suitable for patients with moderate to severe sensorineural loss, is known as the sound-bridge and it works by increasing the amplitude of natural ossicular vibration. A floating mass transducer is attached to the long process of the incus. The transducer is made up of a hermetically sealed titanium bobbin wrapped in gold wire. This contains a magnet that moves back and forth according to the frequency and amplitude of the sound signal (Richards & Gleeson, 1999).

It seems probable that further advances in implants will make them available for people of different ages and with different types of hearing loss. At the moment only people able to withstand surgery can be accepted for this type of treatment. But as a significant number of adults (some 8.7 million in the UK alone) are deaf or hard of hearing, much remains to be done for both the able and disabled population.

Conclusion

Much work is being done to improve the quality of life of persons who are deaf and hard of hearing. But a more sympathetic attitude is needed together with every effort to 'normalize' the life of people who are deaf. The idea that people with intellectual disability and hearing loss cannot be helped or even diagnosed is very wrong. In this chapter it has been shown why the two conditions frequently coexist, and why the numbers of people having both learning problems and hearing loss are much larger than previous indications. The true prevalence can only be ascertained by using suitable tests up to the limit of the adult's ability. The tests used should commence with the simplest ones that the patient can undertake. The subsequent tests should gradually require more ability until a surprising number are able to produce an audiogram. This is only possible if the examiner is patient, does not attempt short-cuts, and adopts a step-by-step approach. The introduction of a hearing aid should only be undertaken by people who have received special training and who are prepared to be patient and not give up along the way. These should be care staff or parents who believe in what they are doing and who appreciate that the end results can help a person with intellectual disability to achieve a better quality of life.

References

Admiraal, R.J. & Huygen, P.L. (1999) Causes of hearing impairment in deaf pupils with a mental handicap. *International Journal of Pediatric Otorhinolaryngology*, **51**, 101–108.

Amini-Elihou, S. (1970) A Swiss family with Klein-Waardenburg's syndrome associated with hyperkeratosis of the palms and feet and with serious oligophrenia. *Journal of Human Genetics*, **18**, 307–363.

Bennett, M.J. & Wade, H.K. (1980) Automated newborn hearing screening using the auditory response cradle. In: *Disorders of Auditory Function III* (eds I.G. Taylor & A. Markides). Academic Press, London.

Burr, S.A., Mulhera, M. & Degg, C. (1996) *Characterisation of click-synchronised spontaneous oto-acoustic emissions in humans*. Paper presented at the Annual Meeting of the British Society of Audiology, Cambridge, 22–23 September.

Denmark, J.C. & Adams, J. (1982) Questionnaire Survey into Hearing Impairment in Institutions in England, Scotland and Wales. In: *Sensory Impairment in Mentally Handicapped People* (ed. D. Ellis) pp. 35–60. Croom Helm, London.

Evenhuis, H.M. (1995) Medical aspects of ageing in a population with intellectual disability: II Hearing impairment. *Journal of Intellectual Disability Research*, **39**, 27–33.

Evenhuis, H.M (1996) Dutch consensus on diagnosis and treatment of hearing impairment in children and adults with intellectual disability. *Journal of Intellectual Disability Research*, **40**, 451–456.

Evenhuis, H.M & Nagtzaam, L.M.D (eds) (1998) IASSID International Consensus Statement. *Early identification of hearing and visual impairment in children and adults with an intellectual disability*. IASSID, Special Interest Research Group on Health Issues.

Evenhuis, H.M., van Zanten, G.A., Brocaar, M.P. & Roerdinkholder, W.H.M. (1992). Hearing loss in middle-aged persons with Down syndrome. *American Journal on Mental Retardation*, **97**, 47–56.

Fraser, G.R. (1976) *The Causes of Profound Deafness in Childhood*, Chapters 6–7. Balliere Tindall, London.

Gorga, M.P., Stover, L., Bergman, B.M., Beauchaine, K.L. & Kaminski, J.R. (1995) The application of otoacoustic emissions in the assessment of developmentally delayed patients. *Scandinavian Audiology*, **24**, (Supplement 41), 8–17.

Jones, F.E. & Hanson, D.R. (1977) H influenzae meningitis treated with ampicillin or chloramphenicol, and subsequent hearing loss. *Developmental Medicine and Child Neurology*, **19**, 593–597.

Karchmer, M.A. & Allen, T.E (1999) The functional assessment of deaf and hard of hearing students. *American Annals of the Deaf*, **144**, 68–77.

Keiser, H., Montague, J., Wold, D., Maune, S. & Pattison, D. (1981) Hearing loss of Down syndrome adults. *American Journal of Mental Deficiency*, **85**, 467–472.

Kemp, D.T. & Ryan, S. (1990) A guide to the effective use of otoacoustic emissions. *Ear Hear*, **II**, 93–105.

Lavis, D., Cullen, P. & Roy, A (1997) Identification of hearing impairment in people with a learning disability: from questioning to testing. *British Journal of Learning Disabilites*, **25**, 100–105.

Marcell, M.M. (1995) Relationships between hearing and auditory cognition in Down's syndrome youth. *Down's Syndrome: Research and Practice*, **3**, 75–91. The University of Portsmouth.

McCormick, B. (1977) The Toy Discrimination Test: an aid for screening the hearing of children above the mental age of two years. *Public Health*, **91**, 67–69.

Monley, P. (1994) Hearing impairment in the Western Australian intellectually handicapped population. *Australian Journal of Audiology*, **16**, 89–98.

Moorey, M. (1996) *South London Object Test: from Specialist Audiology Services for Adults with Learning Disabilities*. Booklet prepared for study day. Guy's Hospital, London.

Nolan, M., McCartney, E., McArthur, K. & Rowson, V.V. (1980) A study of the hearing and receptive vocabulary of the trainees of an adult training centre. *Journal of Mental Deficiency Research*, **24**, 271–286.

Prasher, V.P. (1995) Screening of hearing impairment and its associated effects on adaptive behaviour in adults with down syndrome. *The British Journal of Developmental Disabilities*, **XLI**, 126–132.

Richards, A. & Gleeson, M. (1999) Recent advances: Otolaryngology. *British Medical Journal*, **319**, 1110–1113.

Stewart, L.G. (1978) Hearing impaired/developmentally disabled persons in the United States: Definitions, causes, effects and prevalence estimates. *American Annals of the Deaf*, **123**, 488–495.

Tucker, I. & Nolan, M. (1986) Methods of objective assessment of auditory function in subjects with limited communication skills. In: *Sensory Impairments in Mentally Handicapped People* (ed. D. Ellis) pp. 218–237. Croom Helm, London.

Van Naarden, K., Decoufle, P. & Caldwell, K. (1999) Prevalence and characteristics of children with serious hearing impairment in metropolitan Atlanta. *Pediatrics*, **103**, 570–575.

Van Schrojenstein Lantman-de Valk, H.M.J., Haveman, M.J., Kessels, A.G.H., Urlings, H.F.J. & Sturmans, F. (1994) The need for assessment of sensory functioning in ageing people with mental handicap. *Journal of Intellectual Disability Research*, **38**, 289–298.

Williams, C. (1982) Deaf not daft: the deaf in mental subnormality hospitals. *Special Education: Forward Trends*, **9**, 26–28.

Willott, J.F. (1991) *Aging and the Auditory System: Anatomy, Physiology and Psychophysics*. Singular Publications Group, San Diego, California.

Yeates, S. (1986) Medical and otological aspects of hearing impairment in mentally handicapped people. In: *Sensory Impairments in Mentally Handicapped People* (ed. D. Ellis) pp. 115–148. Croom Helm, London.

Yeates, S. (1995) The incidence and importance of hearing loss in people with severe learning disability: the evolution of a service. *British Journal of Learning Disabilities*, **23**, 79–84.

Yeates, S. (2000) Audiological assessment of people with special difficulties. In: *Mental Health and Deafness* (eds P. Hindley & N. Kitson) pp. 25–41. Whurr, London and Philadelphia.

7 Epilepsy

Stephen Brown

Introduction

The epilepsies constitute a group of conditions that vary in presentation, age of onset, natural history and prognosis. The associated morbidity in some types of epilepsy is much greater than in others, and there is an associated mortality that is only partly due to seizures alone (Tomson, 2000). Epilepsy occurring in the context of intellectual disability is often complex and forms part of the category sometimes referred to as 'epilepsy plus' (Brown, 1998). Frequent seizures in which falls occur may cause repeated head injuries, with implications for neurological, including cognitive, functioning (Russell-Jones & Shorvon, 1989). Repeated seizures may have other effects on cognition (Brown, 1999).

Non-convulsive seizures and abnormal interracial EEG activity may be difficult to diagnose in people with intellectual disabilities, and yet their occurrence at critical times in life may have serious implications for learning and social development (Kasteleijn-Nolst Trenite, 1995). Anti epileptic drugs may have effects on mood and cognitive function (and in some cases endocrine function too), and people with intellectual disabilities may be especially prone to adverse effects (Harbord, 2000). Convulsive seizures are associated with an increased mortality (Nashef & Brown, 1997). Good management may require careful use of the specialist skills of the intellectual disabilities team. This chapter draws together the available information and describes the presentation and optimal management of epilepsy in adults with intellectual disabilities.

What is epilepsy?

The word epilepsy is derived from the Greek επιλαμβανειν meaning 'to be seized, taken hold of or attacked'. An epileptic seizure is a brief, usually unprovoked, stereotyped disturbance of consciousness, behavior, emotion, motor function or sensation that on clinical grounds results from cortical neuronal discharge (Brown *et al.*, 1998). Hughlings Jackson used the term 'occasional, sudden, excessive, rapid and local discharges of grey matter', a definition overembracing enough for him to also state that 'a sneeze is a sort of healthy epilepsy' (Jackson 1873, quoted in Reynolds, 1986). This was of course written before the advent of the encephalograph. Today we would also acknowledge that true epileptic seizures are accompanied by characteristic EEG phenomena. However, an EEG recording is not usually being carried out when someone has a seizure, and even if it is, the recording may not necessarily involve the precisely relevant brain area, so epilepsy remains primarily a clinical diagnosis.

Epileptic seizures are considered to result from an imbalance of the brain's excitatory and inhibitory mechanisms, and involve both excessive and synchronous firing of neurones. Such imbalance may arise for many reasons. Seizures occurring as a direct result of a known or suspected cerebral insult are referred to as acute symptomatic seizures. Where there is no acute precipitating insult the term 'unprovoked seizures' is used. Some unprovoked seizures are consequent on well-established antecedent conditions such as strokes, penetrating head injuries, and cerebral palsy or central nervous system malformation. These are referred to as remote symptomatic seizures. These antecedent conditions are associated with a substantially higher risk of developing epilepsy.

Definitions and classification

Epilepsy is defined as a condition characterized by recurrent unprovoked seizures. There are many types of epileptic seizures. The precise description of seizure types together with various other clinical features, such as age of onset and EEG findings, characterize specific epileptic syndromes. A syndrome diagnosis may give clues to causation and outcome, and carries treatment implications. The classification of seizures and syndromes is led by a commission of the International League Against Epilepsy (Commission on Classification and Terminology of the International League Against Epilepsy, 1989).

By international convention, seizures are classified into two main groups. In generalized seizures, clinical and EEG evidence points to involvement of both cerebral hemispheres from the onset. These include absence seizures, myoclonic seizures, tonic-clonic (grand mal) seizures and atonic seizures (drop attacks). Absence seizures are further subdivided into typical (not especially related to intellectual disabilities and accompanied by 3 Hz EEG spike-wave discharges) and atypical (associated with intellectual disabilities and accompanied by slower, less regular EEG spike-wave discharges at 2–2.5 Hz). Partial (focal) seizures are defined as having an onset from a restricted area of one cerebral hemisphere and tend to follow a stereotyped course in each adult. They are formally classified as simple or complex depending on whether awareness and contact with surroundings is retained or lost respectively – a definition with a degree of subjectivity in interpretation.

Where partial seizures are concerned, a part of the brain with a structural pathology that is the direct cause of seizures is called an epileptogenic lesion. Depending on its nature, it may be identified by neuroimaging or from histopathological study. The area of brain tissue from which the first clinical symptoms of seizures arise is called the symptomatogenic zone. This may be the same as the area from where the seizures are initiated, but sometimes seizures arise in a cortical area that does not give rise to symptoms, before spreading to the symptomatogenic zone. According to agreed nomenclature, this initiating area is called the ictal onset zone. The area that gives rise to epileptiform EEG changes between seizures is known as the irritative zone. A cortical area producing focal dysfunction not related to seizures is referred to as the functional deficit zone (Lüders *et al.*, 1993).

Epileptic syndromes are classified into two main types, localization-related and generalized. The classification also allows for some other special syndromes and cases that are undetermined. In localization-related syndromes the seizures begin at a specific focus. Examples include temporal lobe and frontal lobe epilepsy. Epileptogenic lesions include tumors, areas of gliosis, and hippocampal sclerosis. In generalized syndromes the seizures begin with synchronous discharges across both hemispheres. They include an idiopathic group of age-related onset mainly in childhood and adolescence and generally of genetic etiology. This group is not especially associated with intellectual disabilities. They also include a symptomatic group where epilepsy is secondary to a cerebral insult either demonstrated or assumed. These are often associated with intellectual disabilities, and include the Lennox-Gastaut syndrome, discussed below.

Types of seizures and syndromes seen in people with intellectual disabilities

Some seizure types are said to be more common in adults with intellectual disabilities, especially atonic, tonic, atypical absence and myoclonus. Other seizure types, such as complex partial and tonic-clonic seizures, are common in epilepsies with or without the presence of intellectual disabilities. These seizure types are described in Table 7.1.

The epileptic syndromes that are especially associated with intellectual disabilities are symptomatic or cryptogenic generalized epilepsies with onset in childhood. It is not always easy to apply the international classification to the general population. Manford *et al.* (1992) found that only

Table 7.1 Seizure types said to be especially common in the intellectual disabilities population.

Seizure	Description	Putative ictal onset zone	Other features
Atonic	Generalized seizures characterized by a sudden loss of muscle tone. If standing the person will fall	Pontine brain stem reticular formation may be ictal onset zone, or may be symptomatogenic zone responding to onset from motor cortex	May be difficult to distinguish from tonic seizures, or non-epileptic events without careful history taking
Tonic	Diffuse increase in muscle tone, consciousness usually impaired, no clonic phase	Brainstem, especially area around red nucleus; some may have mesial frontal cortical origin	Often occur in sleep, especially slow-wave clonic phase
Atypical absence	Clouding of consciousness and cessation of ongoing activities associated with bilaterally synchronous spike-and-wave EEG discharges (usually slower than 3 Hz, sometimes irregular) last longer and are more likely to show postural changes than typical absences	Thalamocortical circuits; these may in some cases represent the symptomatogenic zone, with ictal onset zone in thalamus or cortex	
Myoclonus	Involuntary, abrupt, arrhythmic movements affecting neck, arms or shoulder, or less commonly, legs	Some from caudal brain stem reticular formation, some have diffuse cortical origin	
Complex partial	*Mesial temporal lobe origin*: aura (typically visceral sensation) followed by impaired consciousness, fixed stare, dilated pupils, leading to oral-alimentary automatisms (lip smacking, chewing, tooth grinding, swallowing). Semi-appropriate response to environment (reactive automatism), or else fixed, stereotyped automatism, or both. Unilateral tonic or dystonic posturing may occur and is contralateral to side of onset. *Frontal lobe origin*: Sudden onset, rapid recovery, nocturnal preponderance, complex motor automatisms (e.g. bicycling, scissoring movement of legs), sexual automatisms, tendency to clustering or complex partial status epilepticus. Supplementary motor area seizures also show prominent tonic posturing of contralateral arm, contraversive head and eye deviation. Sometimes consciousness is preserved. May be mild post-ictal Todd's paresis	*Mesial temporal lobe origin*: mesial temporal cortex, epileptogenic lesion is often in hippocampus or medial temporal lobe (sclerosis, hamartoma). Occasionally ictal onset zone may be elsewhere and mesial temporal cortex is symptomatogenic	Not all seizures follow all stages; some stop with fixed stare only, length and complexity of automatism varies from person to person
Tonic-clonic	Generalized 'grand mal' seizure; tonic (stiffening) phase followed by clonic (jerking) phase. If secondarily generalized, may be preceded by a partial seizure of which the aura may be the sole manifestation	Primary generalized from brainstem and thalamocortical circuits, secondarily generalized from cortex via brain stem	Clinical distinction between primary and secondary generalized may be difficult. Primary generalized will lack obvious focal onset, but may be preceded by myoclonus, or even a brief clonic phase

34% of a sample of the general population could be so classified. There is little information about syndromes seen in the older intellectual disabilities population. In one review of differential diagnosis, Iivanainen (1999) mainly describes relevant syndromes with onset in childhood and adolescence. When discussing adulthood and old age, he lists etiological factors in older people in the general population, pointing out that from the age of 35 localization-related epilepsies are more likely to develop than generalized ones, and states, 'patients with mental retardation may also develop these disorders'. Of the symptomatic or cryptogenic epilepsies that are so important in children with developmental disabilities, probably the most relevant for subsequent adulthood is the Lennox-Gastaut syndrome (LGS). This is a serious condition characterized by multiple seizure types but especially tonic seizures, (often nocturnal), atypical absences and atonic seizures, with interictal EEG showing slow spike wave activity, and often periods of non-convulsive status epilepticus. Some cases follow on from West syndrome (infantile spasms) in infancy.

Genton and Dravet (1997) in a general review of LGS point out the unfavorable long-term outcome. They suggest that fewer than half of children maintain the full symptom profile of LGS into adulthood. The remainder fall into three groups, one in which a severe seizure disorder persists, another in which seizures become much less troublesome but psychological problems become more disabling, and a small group in which seizures and behavior both improve considerably. The EEG changes with age, and waking recordings in older adults, although often still abnormal, do not show the characteristic slow spike-wave. However, this may still be seen in sleep records. The poorest prognosis seems related to:

- cases that are clearly symptomatic, such as those following infantile spasms, or secondary to tuberous sclerosis
- age of onset before 3 years
- high seizure frequency
- repeated episodes of status epilepticus.

Oguni *et al.* (1996), reporting a follow-up of 72 adults with LGS, noted that there was often an evolution into either severe epilepsy with multifocal independent EEG spike foci, or into refractory localization-related epilepsy. They also comment on the disabling drop attacks and gait disturbances that result in some adults becoming wheelchair-bound. It is not clear whether the gait problems are a consequence of head injuries sustained in the drop attacks and other seizures. Goldsmith *et al.* (2000) did not find any clear factors predicting outcome, but they did emphasize the persistence of a severe seizure disorder in the majority of adults.

Status epilepticus

Status epilepticus refers to a fixed epileptic state lasting 30 minutes or longer. The term refers both to convulsive and non-convulsive states. Convulsive (tonic-clonic) status epilepticus is a well-recognized medical emergency and a cause of brain damage. It is commonly symptomatic of an underlying metabolic toxic or infective condition, and may therefore be seen in people without previously established epilepsy. In people with established and treated epilepsy it is relatively unusual for the seizure disorder itself to be so unstable as to cause episodes of status without other obvious provocation. Intercurrent infection may precipitate status in some adults. One of the commonest causes in people with established epilepsy is abrupt withdrawal of anticonvulsant medication. The differential diagnosis includes non-epileptic attack disorder (hysterical or pseudostatus epilepticus). Non-convulsive status epilepticus is often misdiagnosed as a behavioral or other psychiatric condition. It may present only as changes in affect and behavior, or by subtle cognitive deterioration (Staufenberg & Brown, 1994).

There is a theoretical division into absence or complex partial status, although the distinction is not always clear clinically. Both these conditions are almost certainly underdiagnosed and much more common than is usually appreciated. Careful mental state examination will usually reveal obvious organic features if the adult is accessible enough. Psychotic features may appear, and the episode may conclude with a tonic-clonic seizure if not aborted pharmacologically. In absence status the adult will show clouding of consciousness which can vary in severity over a period of hours or even days.

Clinical features vary from stupor to quite subtle changes in behavior which can only be detected by people who know the adult well. It is usually seen in young adults with a history of generalized epilepsy, but in older people overt psychotic symptoms may be more prominent. The impression is that absence status is probably more common in older people with intellectual disabilities than in older people in the general population, although as yet there have been no studies designed to give a definitive answer. Complex partial status is characterized by repeated stereotyped episodes of behavior occurring against a background confusional state. The stereotypes represent the automatism of the seizure (e.g. lip-smacking or fumbling movements). The adult may appear to be psychotic with or without clouding of consciousness and sometimes the repetitive nature of the behavior only becomes apparent with careful observation. Complex partial status may be associated with Alzheimer's disease.

Epidemiology

In Western Europe and North America the overall incidence of epilepsy is usually said to be between 50–80 per 100 000 per year, with a lifetime risk (cumulative incidence) of about 5% and a prevalence for active epilepsy of 5–10 per 1000. For example, a large study of over five years in England and Wales showed a period prevalence of 5.15/1000 with an overall incidence of 80.8/100 000. Overall prevalence per thousand was higher in older people, rising with age from 6.01 in the 65–69 age group to 7.73 in those aged 85 or over, with incidence per 100 000 also increased at 85.9 in the 65–69 age group up to 135.4 in those aged 85 or more (Wallace *et al.*, 1998). It seems that nearly one quarter of all new presentations of epilepsy occur in people aged 60 or over (Sander *et al.*, 1990). This increase is mainly due to cerebrovascular disease and to seizure disorders accompanying dementia.

Epidemiological studies relating to epilepsy in intellectual disabilities have so far tended to concentrate on children and young people. There are relatively few population-based reports of the prevalence of epilepsy in adults with intellectual disabilities. Forsgren *et al.* (1990), who surveyed all age groups with intellectual disabilities, found active epilepsy in 20% of their sample. Hand (1994) in a comprehensive survey of people with intellectual disabilities aged 50 or more living in New Zealand, found that 17% had a current diagnosis of epilepsy. These figures suggest that epilepsy occurs among people with intellectual disabilities in the order of 25–30 times more frequently than the general population, but in contrast there is not as yet evidence that the overall prevalence increases a great deal with age. This observation is unexpected and invites comment.

In contrast to adults with other etiologies of intellectual disability, older adults with Down syndrome have relatively high rates of dementia (Cooper, 1997) and, for example, late onset seizures are a well-recognized feature of this syndrome (Evenhuis, 1990; Prasher & Corbett, 1993). It is uncertain what the rate of late-onset seizures is among people with intellectual disabilities other than Down syndrome. One explanation may be that the number of studies is still small, and that a clearer picture will emerge with greater research effort. The evidence so far mainly refers to prevalence. Figures may be distorted by mortality rates. If late onset epilepsy in people with intellectual disabilities carries a high risk of early death, the higher incidence will be masked by low prevalence. This would be clarified by more explicitly reported population-based studies of incidence.

Diagnosis and differential diagnosis

Epilepsy is primarily a clinical diagnosis, which typically relies on eye-witness and subjective accounts of seizure phenomena. Investigations such as the EEG are properly used to decide which epilepsy syndrome the person has, and imaging and other tests may clarify etiology. Occasionally where there is diagnostic uncertainty, the epileptic nature of seizures may be investigated by prolonged EEG monitoring using either ambulatory or videotelemetry systems, but these are not routine investigations. It should be remembered that non-specific EEG abnormalities are common in the absence of epilepsy in the intellectual disabilities population.

It may be difficult to obtain the subjective component of the history because of communication difficulties, besides which certain non-epileptic behaviors in adults with intellectual disabilities may mimic seizures. Members of the clinical team need to have the experience to be able to make these distinctions. Aspects of the differential diagnosis that may be relevant to people with intellectual disabilities are listed in Table 7.2.

Table 7.2   Differential diagnosis of seizures in people with intellectual disabilities.

- Epilepsy
- Acute symptomatic seizures (e.g. metabolic, toxic or infectious cause, or due to acute head injury)
- Syncope
    In context of cardiac dysrrhythmia
    Other causes
- Transient ischemic attacks (TIAs)
- Migraine, especially basilar migraine
- Dyskinesias
- Falls due to perceptual difficulties

Certain of these merit further consideration. Transient ischemic attacks (TIAs) are arbitrarily defined as lasting less than 24 hours. The actual resolution time is usually much shorter, about a quarter being completed within five minutes and half within 30 minutes (Levy, 1988), which may cause some confusion with epilepsy. Paroxysmal dyskinesias may consist of any combination of dystonic posturing, chorea or athetosis. Kinesogenic dyskinesias in particular often appear later in life and the attacks may be frequent, of short duration, precipitated by startle or hyperventilation, and sometimes unilateral (Plant, 1983). Esophageal reflux may cause episodes of discomfort in which the person swallows and looks distressed. If the adult is not able to describe the experience, the phenomenon may be mistaken for a complex partial seizure. Children may show limb posturing and eye deviation in response to acid reflux, and this may be mistaken for seizure activity (Pedley, 1983). This might theoretically be observed in adults with intellectual disabilities, although it has yet to be reported.

Behavioral consequences

Behavioral changes, which vary with the severity, type and frequency of seizures, are recognised phenomena in the natural history of complex epilepsy. A sudden decrease in seizures, e.g. by change of medication, may precipitate psychotic or other behavioral change in some patients. This phenomenon is called 'paradoxical normalisation', and management may involve judicious combination of anti-psychotic medication and anti-epileptic drugs. On other occasions, treating the seizures reduces seizure frequency but prodromal mood or behavioral changes that usually precede seizures persist. This may respond to increasing the anti-epileptic drug, and should not be regarded as an anti-epileptic drug side-effect.

Sometimes a cluster of seizures, usually tonic-clonic, is followed (often after a brief lucid interval) by a brief psychotic episode. This post-ictal psychosis may indicate a predisposition to develop a chronic psychosis later in life, and this in turn may be something to which people with temporal lobe epilepsy are especially vulnerable. An account of behavioral consequences of seizures in people with intellectual disability is given by Brown (1998).

The occurrence of frequent minor seizures for many years may cause the appearance of lethargy, psychomotor retardation and feeding difficulties. Carers may regard this as part of the person's normal personality. A change of medication that successfully treats the epilepsy may therefore manifest as a personality change with overactivity and a reduced need for sleep. Family and carers may interpret this as a behavioral side effect of the new drug. In fact, it is merely a consequence of the person's personality being unleashed from the effects of the epilepsy. This sudden unleashing may present an adjustment problem and require separate management, but it does not represent a side effect of the anti-epileptic drug.

The special issue of Down syndrome

It is now accepted that epilepsy is a frequent accompaniment to Down syndrome. A study of adults aged 19 years or over found an overall prevalence of 9.4%, which increased with age, reaching 46% in those over 50 (McVicker et al., 1994). There are two main epilepsy populations with

Down syndrome. Some develop a seizure disorder in infancy or childhood, while there is a second peak of onset in older age. Pueschel et al. (1991) noted that although 40% of people with Down syndrome who had epilepsy had onset in the first year of life, another 40% had onset after age 40. The early onset group includes a large proportion with a syndrome of idiopathic type of West syndrome (infantile spasms), which has been thoroughly described by Silva et al. (1996). In these cases it seems the prognosis with appropriate management is relatively favorable, unless there is complicating hypoxic insult (Stafstrom & Konkol, 1994). Nevertheless it seems that about 1% of children with Down syndrome develop infantile spasms (Stafstrom et al., 1991), compared to a general population rate of about one in 2000 (Riikonen & Donner, 1979).

In people with Down syndrome there is a high rate of reflex seizures, especially those precipitated by noise or touch (Guerrini et al., 1990). The reason for this may be related to the finding that brains of people with Down syndrome show a defect in the mechanisms that naturally inhibit afferent stimuli, leading to an overall increased excitability (Straumanis et al., 1973). Various pathological and physiological mechanisms may be implicated. Dorsal root ganglion neuron studies from aborted fetuses with Down syndrome suggest abnormalities in the genesis of the action potential (Nieminen et al., 1988). There is a decrease in GABAergic interneurones in neocortical layers II and IV (Wisniewski et al., 1984). Dendritic spines are abnormal in shape and fewer in number than in normal brains (Becker et al., 1986). The gene that codes for the excitatory kainate receptor GluR5, involved in regulation of inhibitory synaptic transmission, is located in the part of the distal arm of chromosome 21 that is of interest in Down syndrome (Eubanks et al., 1993). The free radical scavenger enzyme copper/zinc superoxide dismutase (SOD1) is increased in the cortex of people with Down syndrome, and it has been suggested that this may be involved in hyperexcitability and possible seizure genesis by altering aspects of normal functioning in which apoptosis plays a part (Busciglio & Yanker, 1995). All these mechanisms may favor the appearance of certain generalized seizure types, such as tonic seizures.

The appearance of epilepsy in older people with Down syndrome is believed to be an accompaniment to the development of neuropathological changes of Alzheimer's disease. In older people without Down syndrome the appearance of seizures is associated with Alzheimer's disease (Romanelli et al., 1990). However, only about 10% of people with Alzheimer's disease in the general population develop epilepsy (Hauser et al., 1986) whereas in older people with Down syndrome the figure has been reported as high as 80% (Evenhuis, 1990). It is not clear to what extent this reflects a true increase in seizure propensity in this particular group, as opposed to being a consequence of people with Down syndrome developing Alzheimer's disease 30–40 years earlier in life than expected, as described by Holland *et al.* (1998). Also, studies of epilepsy in older people with Down syndrome often remark on the frequency of myoclonic seizures, whereas general population studies may specifically exclude this seizure type (Romanelli *et al.*, 1990).

Wisniewski *et al.* (1985) and Lai and Williams (1989) both found that the seizures in Down syndrome tended to appear after the onset of other features of mental deterioration, as was described by Romanelli in the non-Down syndrome population. Seizures were mainly tonic-clonic, with myoclonus and occasionally complex partial events being described. In Wisniewski *et al.*'s small series, the mean time to death after the onset of clinical features of Alzheimer's disease was between five and six years, with mean time of epilepsy appearing about four years after the other symptoms of deterioration.

The nature of the myoclonus seen in Down syndrome, especially in the group with late-onset epilepsy, has been a subject of interest and speculation. Sabers (1999) intriguingly points out the superficial resemblance of some presentations in this group to the syndrome of juvenile myoclonic epilepsy (JME). The features of interest include myoclonic seizures on awakening, generalized tonic-clonic seizures, and a characteristic EEG picture. However, in contrast to JME, as dementia progresses the myoclonus can become very resistant to treatment. There is another more serious epileptic condition, progressive myoclonic epilepsy, the gene for which has been mapped to chromosome locus 21q22 (Serratosa *et al.*, 1999). Sabers suggests that this might be more relevant in the severe myoclonus sometimes seen in older people with Down syndrome, and she coins the term 'senile myoclonic epilepsy' for the particular presentation.

Management

Investigation

Besides describing the seizure types and attempting to identify epilepsy syndromes, the investigation of epilepsy should include consideration of etiology. Among adults with intellectual disabilities, seizure disorders are associated with a number of conditions, some of which have a genetic basis, and more detailed description of these is beyond the scope of this chapter. Most become apparent in early life and should be diagnosed as part of the normal work-up of children with developmental problems.

When reviewing adults it is important to re-check that all appropriate tests have been carried out, as more modern investigations may not have been available when the person presented as a child.

Besides these special syndromes, people with intellectual disabilities are also prone to the same types of epilepsy as the rest of the population and should have the same level of investigation for these. Localization-related epilepsy in particular should be investigated by neuroimaging. Magnetic resonance imaging (MRI) may reveal underlying neoplasm or dysgenesis that may not be seen with computerized tomography. An ordinary EEG recording may provide enough information to support a diagnosis of generalized epilepsy. Localization-related syndromes may not cause much change in the interictal EEG. In cases where there is uncertainty about the nature of some paroxysmal behavior, video recording taken by carers can be shown to specialist clinicians, and where doubt persists, combined video and EEG recording can be useful.

Sometimes carrying out investigations such as these presents difficulties in the intellectual disabilities population. The person may not understand what is happening and may be apprehensive or frightened by the procedure. Good neurophysiology and radiology departments will have developed ways of engaging clients who might have such problems. This may involve preparing information leaflets or videos that are specially designed for people with special needs and which relate specifically to each department, and working with carers and intellectual disabilities team professionals with desensitization and modeling programs. There are various materials more generally available for people with intellectual disabilities and literacy or communication problems, such as the Books Without Words series (Hollins *et al.*, 1999). Nevertheless, sometimes MRI scanning is best accomplished under general anesthetic.

The aims of treating epilepsy are to stop seizures or reduce their frequency and severity as far as possible, and to minimize treatment-related health loss. The treatment plan has to be delivered in a way that is acceptable to the person with epilepsy, in an environment in which the person feels comfortable. People with epilepsy, and where appropriate their carers, are part of the team that is managing the epilepsy and should be able to play a full part in arriving at treatment decisions. The development of specialist nurse practitioners has been pivotal in developing services for this client group (Graydon, 2000). Treatments available include anti-epileptic drugs, surgery, diet, behavior therapy, environmental manipulation and complementary medicine. Seizure disorders are often also influenced by associated illnesses, the treatment for which also improves the epilepsy. For most people in the population considered here, anti-epileptic drugs will be the mainstay of management. Surgery is unlikely to be an option in this age group and will not be discussed further.

Behavioral techniques have been studied in individuals with intellectual disabilities and show some promise (Dahl, 1992). Seizure frequency can be influenced by environmental factors such as life events and by the attitudes of carers toward the adult (Brown & Jadresic, 2000). Community intellectual disabilities teams are typically concerned with the environment of the client and its impact on health, including epilepsy. Those who care for people with intellectual disabilities often incorporate elements of complementary medicine, especially aromatherapy, into their approach, and there has been interest in this as a treatment for epilepsy (Betts, 1996). However, the rest of this account will focus on the importance of treating concomitant health conditions that affect epilepsy and using anti-epileptic drugs.

Concomitant illnesses

Where there is already an established diagnosis of epilepsy, worsening seizure control associated with behavior change should alert the physician to the possibility of intercurrent infection. Infections of the ear and of the urinary tract are especially likely to go undiagnosed at first in people with communication problems. It is not always clear whether the distress, discomfort and pain are the cause of deterioration in the epilepsy, or whether there is a more direct physiological relationship. There is some evidence that seizures may often be triggered by bacterial infections even when no clinically apparent bacterial infection has been recognized (Iivanainen et al., 1983). Antibiotic treatment may also alter the effectiveness of anti-epileptic drugs by a variety of mechanisms. Anti-epileptic drugs that are not metabolized and are not protein bound, such as gabapentin or lamotrigine, may be less likely to interact (Loiseau, 1998).

Constipation is a common health problem for people with intellectual disabilities. Carers often attribute to it the cause of deterioration in seizure control. Bohmer et al. (2001) found that constipation in institutionalized people with intellectual disabilities was significantly correlated with the use of anti-epileptic drugs. Less frequently, constipation is a feature of some syndromes in which seizures also occur, although there are no accounts of how these two features interact in such cases (Romano et al., 1994).

Obstructive sleep apnea has been shown to be a factor that makes epilepsy worse, and recognition and treatment of sleep disorders may improve seizure frequency (Koh et al., 2000). Subdural hematoma may follow as a result of epileptic seizures, and may present as deterioration in someone's seizure control (Arieft & Wetzel, 1964). Clinical features of raised intracranial pressure may not be apparent. A high index of diagnostic suspicion is therefore needed.

Using anti-epileptic drugs

Anti-epileptic drugs are mainly used continuously as prophylaxis against seizures. In addition, some anti-epileptic drugs are used intermittently:

- to reduce the likelihood of seizures at certain vulnerable times
- to break up clustering of seizures
- to stop serial seizures developing into status epilepticus
- to treat status epilepticus.

The management of convulsive status is beyond the scope of this chapter; a standard text is that of Shorvon (1994). Other aspects of anti-epileptic drugs use are considered below.

Most therapeutic trials of anti-epileptic drugs have been carried out in people without intellectual disabilities (Working Group of the International Association of the Scientific Study of Intellectual Disability, 2001). The main exception is the Lennox-Gastaut syndrome (Motte *et al.*, 1997; Sachdeo *et al.*, 1999). Such other studies as exist are mainly concerned with add-on therapy using new anti-epileptic drugs in people whose epilepsy is unresponsive to previous treatment, and there is little on management of seizures in those who are newly diagnosed (Crawford *et al.*, 2001).

When to start drug treatment

All authorities are agreed that drug treatment should not be started unless there is certainty about the diagnosis, and that the recommendation to initiate drug treatment should be undertaken by a physician who is skilled in the diagnosis and management of epilepsy (e.g. SIGN, 1997). The physician's choice of a drug will be influenced mainly by the seizure type(s) that the person experiences. There are some particular issues regarding seizure disorders presenting in people with intellectual disabilities. Decisions about treatment will be made where possible by the person with the condition, but this may not be achievable. Intellectual disabilities specialists will be familiar with the need to involve relevant carers and relatives in the management process, and with the skills needed to make this work in the adult's best interests.

Whether to recommend treatment after a single tonic-clonic seizure depends on the likelihood of further seizures occurring. Acute symptomatic seizures should be managed by consideration of the provoking factor (e.g. alcohol withdrawal). Where there is no immediate provoking factor, anti-epileptic drugs may nevertheless be offered in certain circumstances. These are:

(1) previously unremarked myoclonic, absence, or partial seizures revealed by detailed history taking
(2) the presence of unequivocal epileptiform EEG discharges
(3) a structural etiology such as a tumor.

Most other seizure types tend to present after several episodes have occurred and the risk of recurrence is more obvious.

Choice of anti-epileptic drugs

Anti-epileptic drugs are chosen by seizure type. Broadly speaking, most anti-epileptic drugs fall into one of two groups. Some, such as carbamazepine, are effective mainly in partial onset seizures and may make some generalized seizures (especially absences and myoclonus) worse, while others, such as valproate, have a broader spectrum of activity. Some anti-epileptic drugs are licensed as first-line treatments, and others as adjunctive treatments. To some extent the license indications, both for seizure types and whether first-line or add-on, are reflections on the stage of a drug's development rather than statements of best use. Thus, topiramate only has a license for adjunctive treatment or treatment in otherwise therapy-resistant cases, but there is no evidence that it is not effective as a first-line agent. Likewise, levetiracetam is currently licensed as adjunctive treatment in partial and secondarily generalized seizures, yet there is evidence that it may be extremely useful in other generalized seizure types (Jain, 2000), while further reports are needed to establish a possible role as a first-line treatment. It is possible, therefore, that license indications for these drugs may change with time as more evidence becomes available. On the other hand, there is good evidence that carbamazepine, oxcarbazepine and gabapentin may precipitate or exacerbate some types of generalized seizures (Gaily et al., 1998) and so it is extremely unlikely that their current spectrum of indications will be changed.

First-line anti-epileptic drugs

Table 7.3 summarizes the indications for different anti-epileptic drugs. The IASSID working group (Working Group of the International Association of the Scientific Study of Intellectual Disability, 2001) suggest

Table 7.3   Indications for anti-epileptic drugs.

Seizure types	Partial	Secondary generalized	Primary generalized
Carbamazepine	1st line	1st line	
Valproate	1st line	1st line	1st line
Lamotrigine	1st line*	1st line	1st line
Oxcarbazepine	1st line*	1st line	
Topiramate	2nd line	2nd line	2nd line (tonic-clonic)
Gabapentin	2nd line	2nd line	
Tiagabine	2nd line	2nd line	
Levetiracetam**	2nd line	2nd line	

* probably advantageous over other 1st line treatments
** recently licensed and may have wider indications in due course

valproate, carbamazepine and lamotrigine as first-line treatments for partial and secondarily generalized seizures, pointing out that lamotrigine may have a more favorable cognitive profile than carbamazepine. The working group did not report an opinion on oxcarbazepine, although this anti-epileptic drug has been studied in a group of adults with intellectual disabilities (Gaily *et al.*, 1998).

For generalized seizures (e.g. absences, myoclonic and primary generalized tonic-clonic seizures), sodium valproate and lamotrigine are generally accepted drugs of first choice (Working Group of the International Association of the Scientific Study of Intellectual Disability, 2001).

Second-line drugs

The use of a second-line anti-epileptic drug may be indicated if seizures continue in spite of treatment with an appropriate first line agent, or if the first anti-epileptic drug is associated with an unacceptable adverse reaction. Second line drugs in common use include topiramate (for generalized and partial seizures), levetiracetam (currently licensed for partial onset seizures, but this may be broadened in time) and gabapentin and tiagabine (partial onset seizures only). Other second line agents for partial onset seizures that are used less often include vigabatrin and phenytoin. Piracetam is useful in some cases of cortical myoclonus (Fedi *et al.*, 2001). Aspects of the use of second line drugs are described in Table 7.4. There is as yet no firm evidence for difference in efficacy between most of these drugs in the population as a whole (e.g. Marson *et al.*, 1997), and very little work in the field of intellectual disabilities.

Benzodiazepines have a broad spectrum of anti-epileptic activity.

Table 7.4 Second-line anti-epileptic drugs.

	Potential disadvantages	Other practice points
Topiramate	■ Cognitive and behavioral side-effects ■ Mild hepatic enzyme inducer ■ Risk of renal calculus ■ Recent reports of raised intraocular pressure	■ Also licensed in Lennox-Gastaut syndrome ■ Potential for license indication to expand, but concern over side-effects may limit use ■ Using slow dose escalation may limit CNS-related side-effects
Gabapentin	■ Bulky capsules	■ Effective add-on in people with intellectual disabilities and partial onset seizures ■ Usually well-tolerated
Tiagabine	■ Short half-life, more doses per day than other drugs ■ Hepatic enzyme inducer ■ Peak plasma level related confusion may be misdiagnosed as absence status	■ Use slow dose escalation in people with intellectual disabilities
Levetiracetam	■ License currently restricted to add-on in partial onset seizures	■ Not an enzyme inducer, low risk of drug interaction ■ May have wider role in intellectual disabilities population than current license indications
Vigabatrin	■ Risk of psychosis and behavioral change ■ Associated with visual field defects	■ Initiation of treatment now mainly restricted to particular pediatric group with West syndrome ■ Adults should have regular visual field testing ■ Manufacturers will supply a procedure for visual field testing in patients with a developmental age of less than 9 years
Phenytoin	■ Huge range of potential side-effects, saturation kinetics and drug interactions make this no longer a popular choice among epilepsy specialists, especially for treating people with learning disabilities ■ Large doses used in clinical practice (up to 20 g daily) may be inconvenient to patients ■ Avoid abrupt withdrawal ■ Caution in the elderly	■ Sometimes effective treatment for cortical myoclonus

Those in clinical use as oral preparations include 1,4 benzodiazepines such as diazepam, lorazepam, nitrazepam and clonazepam, and the 1.5 benzodiazepine clobazam. The 1,4 group are particularly perceived to have disadvantages with development of tolerance, disinhibited behavior, sedation, dependency, and the effects of decreased muscle tone including drooling, with swallowing and aspiration difficulties in some adults (Wyllie *et al.*, 1986). In older people, lorazepam may be preferred to diazepam for intermittent oral use because it has a shorter elimination half-life, does not have an active metabolite, and is metabolized by primary glucuronidation, which is relatively unaffected by age, the latter property being shared with midazolam (Ko *et al.*, 1997).

Clobazam, being structurally different to the others, may have fewer adverse effects, although tolerance is still an issue (Remy, 1994). Before the advent of newer anti-epileptic drugs through the 1990s, benzodiazepines, especially clobazam, were often added to first-line drugs where seizure control was not optimal (Callaghan & Goggin, 1988). There has been a perception that such adjunctive therapy would be ineffective as sole treatment. Yet where this has been studied in children, the results are surprisingly positive (Canadian Study Group for Childhood Epilepsy, 1998). The main problem is the development of tolerance, and most studies report this as a relapse of seizure frequency after an initially positive response. Barcs & Halasz (1996) found that the proportion of adults seizure-free dropped from 71% to 15% over 24 months following starting clobazam. Singh *et al.* (1995) found that tolerance seemed related to longer duration of epilepsy and to epilepsy being cryptogenic. Other perceived disadvantages include behavioral disturbances. Sheth *et al.* (1997) described aggressive agitation, self-injurious behavior, insomnia and incessant motor activity in 11% of children treated with clobazam, and autism has been described as a risk factor for behavioral disturbance (Marrosu *et al.*, 1987). However, in a standard monotherapy trial in children, Bawden *et al.* (1999) found that there was no difference in behavioral or cognitive effects of clobazam compared to carbamazepine or phenytoin.

Benzodiazepines are said to occasionally produce a paradoxical increase in seizures, especially in Lennox-Gastaut syndrome (Bittencourt & Richens, 1981); yet clobazam is still recommended as a potential treatment (Schmidt & Bourgeois, 2000). Most studies have been in children but some involve adults. It is not clear to what extent potential adverse behavioral reactions are affected by age or by the presence of intellectual disabilities. In the general population of older people, there is a view that benzodiazepines should be avoided. Thomas (1997) in a review of epilepsy in older people warns against the use of various potential anti-epileptic drugs, including clobazam which is listed as undesirable along with barbiturates, primidone and calcium channel blockers. However, Calkin *et al.* (1997), in a study of older adults with dementia but without epilepsy, found clonazepam (a 1,4 benzodiazepine, and therefore theoretically more likely to cause adverse effects than clobazam) to be well-tolerated and associated with improvement in psychiatric symptoms, with only 1 out of 21 people developing sedation and confusion.

Clobazam may be especially useful as intermittent treatment, given in short courses to break up clusters of seizures (Milligan *et al.*, 1984) or to provide short-term cover against seizures at especially vulnerable times such as prolonged journeys. In females of reproductive age it may help treat premenstrual seizure clustering if given at the appropriate stage in the cycle (Feely & Gibson, 1984).

Acetazolamide is a carbonic anhydrase inhibitor that has been used to treat epilepsy for nearly 50 years. Its use has nearly always been as adjunctive treatment, and, as with the benzodiazepines, the view has been that tolerance develops quickly in many cases and that monotherapy is not recommended (Lombroso & Forsythe, 1960). Like clobazam, it has been proposed as a treatment for catamenial epilepsy (Lim *et al.*, 2001). There is a potential long-term risk of renal calculus (Paisley & Tomson, 1999), so it is probably best avoided in people who are immobile or who have a low fluid intake. There is some evidence of effectiveness as add-on to carbamazepine in partial-onset seizures (Oles *et al.*, 1989), but overall its use has probably been underinvestigated.

Other rescue medication

The use of rectal, as opposed to intravenous, diazepam to treat status epilepticus (both convulsive and non-convulsive) and to abort acute repetitive 'pre-status' clustering of seizures (to which some people with intellectual disabilities are prone), has been of great value in the community care of people with intellectual disabilities. Although general efficacy is not in doubt (Mitchell *et al.*, 1999), respiratory depression has been reported in childhood use (Norris *et al.*, 1999). Excessive use in adults with intellectual disabilities may lead to a pattern of cyclic reappearance of seizures due to a rebound effect, which requires careful management (Brodtkorb *et al.*, 1999). Because diazepam has a long half-life, its use may cause psychomotor impairment for 12 hours or more following rectal use (Jensen *et al.*, 1997). Brodtkorb *et al.*, (1993) have also described the precipitation of non-convulsive status epilepticus by over-administration of rectal diazepam. There is therefore a need to seek alternative rescue medication that can be given by a more esthetic route and has a shorter half-life. Diazepam can be given nasally (Lindhardt *et al.*, 2001), but the use of buccal or nasal midazolam seems to hold out most hope at present. Midazolam is an imidazole-substituted benzodiazepine with an extremely short half-life. Buccal administration is as effective as rectal diazepam and more socially acceptable (Scott *et al.*, 1999). Nasal administration has also been studied in adults as well as children, and found to be effective and preferred to rectal diazepam (Wassner *et al.*, 2001).

General principles of using anti-epileptic drugs in people with intellectual disabilities

There is some largely anecdotal evidence that people with intellectual disabilities are more likely than the rest of the population to experience some of the potential side-effects, especially behavioral, of antiepileptic drugs (Harbord, 2000), and there is a view that using lower starting doses than usual combined with slower dose escalation may minimize this (Kerr, 1998). The IASSID working party recommended firstly ensuring that the correct first-line treatment is chosen and used adequately, and if seizures continue, to then consider reviewing the diagnosis and treatment adherence. Where change of treatment is considered it is recommended that an alternative drug could be slowly introduced and the dose built up alongside the first drug. A good response would suggest slow withdrawal of the first drug. If reasonable options for monotherapy have been explored, and seizures continue unacceptably, long-term two-drug polytherapy could be tried (Working Group of the International Association of the Scientific Study of Intellectual Disability, 2001).

There is now some evidence that certain combinations of anti-epileptic drugs may be synergistic, such as lamotrigine and valproate (Brodie & Yuen, 1997). Care needs to be taken with this particular combination as both anti-epileptic drugs compete for the same renal excretion sites, and valproate is an inhibitor of lamotrigine metabolism (Yuen *et al.*, 1992). Consequently, much lower doses of lamotrigine are needed in the presence of valproate than without it. Introduction of lamotrigine is generally recommended to be slow, to minimize possible allergic reactions, and when added alongside valproate this needs to be even more cautious.

Conclusion

The epilepsies are a major cause of health loss in people with intellectual disabilities. Despite a paucity of specialized data, it is possible to draw some conclusions. Seizures in this population may be difficult to diagnose, and may have direct effects on mental state and cognition. Convulsive seizures may cause death. Carbamazepine, oxcarbazepine and gabapentin may precipitate or exacerbate some types of generalized seizures, and should be avoided in these seizure types. However, some people with a previous diagnosis of generalized epilepsy, such as Lennox-Gastaut syndrome, develop a seizure pattern in later life that may respond to such drugs, so precise seizure description is important. Some drugs used in generalized seizures may produce paradoxical reactions, such as the precipitation of tonic seizures by benzodiazepines and myoclonus by lamotrigine. Clinicians should be aware of presentation of non-convulsive status epilepticus in this patient group. Intermittent benzodiazepine use may be of great benefit but care should be taken that excessive use does not play a part in precipitating non-convulsive status. Epilepsy in people with Down syndrome often includes myoclonus and tonic seizures, and the seizures often have a reflex presentation. The risk of a person with both Down syndrome and Alzheimer's disease developing epilepsy may be much higher than the risk for someone without Down syndrome but who develops Alzheimer's disease.

References

Arieft, A.J. & Wetzel, N. (1964) Subdural hematoma following epileptic convulsion. *Neurology*, **14**, 731–732.

Barcs, G. & Halasz, P. (1996) Effectiveness and tolerance of clobazam in temporal lobe epilepsy. *Acta Neurologica Scandinavica*, **93**, 88–93.

Bawden, H.N., Camfield, C.S., Camfield, P.R., Cunningham, C., Darwish, H., Dooley, J.M., Gordon, K., Ronen, G., Stewart. J. & van Mastrigt R. (1999) The cognitive and behavioural effects of clobazam and standard monotherapy are comparable. Canadian Study Group for Childhood Epilepsy. *Epilepsy Research*, **33**, 133–143.

Becker, L.E., Armstrong, D.L. & Chan, F-W. (1986) Dendritic atrophy in children with Down's syndrome. *Annuals of Neurology*, **20**, 520–526.

Betts, T. (1996) Further experience of the smell memory technique in the behavioural treatment of epilepsy. *Epilepsia*, **37**, Supplement 4, 60 (abstract).

Bittencourt, P.R.M. & Richens, A. (1981) Anticonvulsant-induced status epilepticus in Lennox-Gastaut syndrome. *Epilepsia*, **22**, 129–134.

Bohmer, C.J., Taminiau, J.A., Klinkenberg-Knol, E.C. & Meuwissen, S.G. (2001) The prevalence of constipation in institutionalized people with intellectual disability. *Journal of Intellectual Disability Research*, **45**, 3–8.

Brodie, M.J. & Yuen, A.W. (1997) Lamotrigine substitution study: evidence for synergism with sodium valproate? 105 Study Group. *Epilepsy Research*, **26**, 423–432.

Brodtkorb, E., Sand, T., Kristiansen, A. & Torbergsen, T. (1993) Non-convulsive status epilepticus in the adult mentally retarded. Classification and role of benzodiazepines. *Seizure*, **2**, 115–123.

Brodtkorb, E., Aamo, T., Henriksen, O. & Lossius R. (1999) Rectal diazepam: pitfalls of excessive use in refractory epilepsy. *Epilepsy Research*, **35**, 23–33.

Brown, S.W. (1998) Managing severe epilepsy in the community. *Advances in Psychiatric Treatment*, **4**, 345–355.

Brown, S.W. (1999) Epilepsy dementia: Intellectual deterioration as a consequence of epileptic seizures (chapter). In: *Epilepsy and Mental Retardation*, (eds M. Sillanpaa, L. Gram, S.I. Johannessen & T. Tomson) pp. 115–134. Wrightson Biomedical Publishing, Petersfield.

Brown S.W. & Jadresic E. (2000) Expressed emotion in the families of young people with epilepsy. *Seizure*, **9**, 255–258.

Brown, S.W., Betts T.A, Crawford, P., Hall, W.W., Shorvon S. & Wallace S. (1998) Epilepsy needs revisited. *Seizure*, **7**, 435–446.

Busciglio, J. & Yanker, B.A. (1995) Apoptosis and increased generation of reactive oxygen species in Down's syndrome neurons in vitro. *Nature*, **378**, 21–28.

Calkin, P.A., Kunik, M.E., Orengo, C.A., Molinari, V. & Workman, R. (1997) Tolerability of clonazepam in demented and non-demented geropsychiatric patients. *International Journal of Geriatric Psychiatry*, **12**, 745–749.

Callaghan, N. & Goggin, T. (1988) Adjunctive therapy in resistant epilepsy. *Epilepsia*, **29**, Supplement 1, S29–35.

Canadian Study Group for Childhood Epilepsy (1998) Clobazam has equivalent efficacy to carbamazepine and phenytoin as monotherapy for childhood epilepsy. *Epilepsia*, **39**, 952–959.

Commission on Classification and Terminology of the International League Against Epilepsy (1989) Proposal for revised classification of epilepsies and epileptic syndromes. *Epilepsia*, **30**, 389–395.

Cooper, S.A. (1997) High prevalence of dementia among people with learning disabilities not attributable to Down's syndrome. *Psychological Medicine*, **27**, 609–616.

Crawford, P., Brown, S. & Kerr, M. (2001) The Parke Davis Clinical Trials Group. Efficacy of gabapentin in adults with intellectual disabilities and resistant epilepsy: a randomised open-label comparative study of gabapentin with lamotrigine. *Seizure*, **10**, 107–115.

Dahl, J. (1992) *Epilepsy: A behaviour medicine approach to the assessment and treatment in children*. A handbook for professionals working with epilepsy. Hogrefe and Huber, Gottingen.

Eubanks, J.H., Puranam, R.S., Kleckner, N., Bettler, B., Heinemann, B. & McNamara, J.O. (1993) The gene encoding the glutamate receptor subunit GluR5 is located on human chromosome 21q21.1–22.1 in the vicinity of the gene for familial amyotrophic lateral sclerosis. *Proceedings of the National Academy of Science USA*, **90**, 178–182.

Evenhuis, H.M. (1990) The natural history of dementia in Down's syndrome. *Archives of Neurology*, **47**, 263–267.

Fedi, M., Reutens, D., Dubeau, F., Andermann, E., D'Agostino, D. & Andermann,

F. (2001) Long-term efficacy and safety of piracetam in the treatment of progressive myoclonus epilepsy. *Archives of Neurology*, **58**, 781–786.

Feely, M. & Gibson, J. (1984) Intermittent clobazam for catamenial epilepsy: tolerance avoided. *Journal of Neurology, Neurosurgery and Psychiatry*, **47**, 1279–1282.

Forsgren, L., Edvinsson, S.O., Blomquist, H.K., Heijbel, J. & Sidenvall, R. (1990) Epilepsy in a population of mentally retarded children and adults. *Epilepsy Research*, **6**, 234–248.

Gaily, E., Granstrom, M.L. & Likkonen, E. (1998) Oxcarbazepine in the treatment of epilepsy in children and adolescents with intellectual disability. *Journal of Intellectual Disability Research*, **42**, 41–45.

Genton, P. & Dravet, C. (1997) Lennox-Gastaut Syndrome and other childhood epileptic encephalopathies. In: *Epilepsy: A Comprehensive Textbook* (eds J. Engel Jr & T.A. Pedley) pp. 2355–2366. Lippincott-Raven, Philadelphia PA.

Goldsmith, I.L., Zupanc, M.L. & Buchhalter, J.R. (2000) Long-term seizure outcome in 74 patients with Lennox-Gastaut syndrome: effects of incorporating MRI head imaging in defining the cryptogenic subgroup. *Epilepsia*, **41**, 395–399.

Graydon, M. (2000) Do learning disability services need epilepsy specialist nurses? *Seizure*, **9**, 294–296.

Guerrini, R., Genton, P., Bureau, M., Dravet, C.H. & Roger, J. (1990) Reflex seizures are frequent in patients with Down syndrome and epilepsy. *Epilepsia*, **31**, 406–417.

Hand, J.E. (1994) Report of a national survey of older people with lifelong intellectual handicap in New Zealand. *Journal of Intellectual Disability Research*, **38**, 275–287.

Harbord, M.G. (2000) Significant anticonvulsant side-effects in children and adolescents. *Journal of Clinical Neuroscience*, **7**, 213–216.

Hauser, W.A, Morris, M.L., Heston, L.L. & Anderson, V.E. (1986) Seizures and myoclonus in patients with Alzheimer's disease. *Neurology*, **36**, 1226–1230.

Holland, A.J., Hon, J., Huppert, F.A., Stevens, F. & Watson, P. (1998) Population-based study of the prevalence and presentation of dementia in adults with Down's syndrome. *British Journal of Psychiatry*, **172**, 493–498.

Hollins, S., Bernal, J. & Thacker, A. (1999) *Getting on with epilepsy*. Books Without Words. Gaskell/St George's Hospital Medical School, London.

Iivanainen, M. (1999) Diagnosing epilepsy in patients with mental retardation. In *Epilepsy and Mental Retardation* (eds M. Sillanpaa, L. Gram, S.I. Johannessen & T. Tomson) pp. 61–72. Wrightson Biomedical, Petersfield.

Iivanainen, M., Hietala, J., Malkamaki, M., Waltimo, O. & Valtonen, V.V. (1983) An association between epileptic seizures and increased serum bacterial antibody levels. *Epilepsia*, **24**, 584–587.

Jackson, J.H. (1873) On the anatomical physiological and pathological investigation of epilepsies. West Riding Lunatic Asylum Medical Reports, 3, 315–339. In John Hughlings Jackson, Selected Writings Volume One, *On Epilepsy and Epileptiform Convulsions* (eds J. Taylor, G. Holes & F.M.R. Walshe). Hodder & Stoughton Ltd, London (1931) pp. 90–111, reprinted by Arts & Boeve, Nijmegen (1996).

Jain, K.K. (2000) An assessment of levetiracetam as an anti-epileptic drug. *Expert Opinion on Investigational Drugs*, **9**, 1611–1624.

Jensen, H.H., Hansen, H.C. & Drenck, N.E. (1997) Comparison of psychomotor performance after intravenous and rectal diazepam. *Anesthesia Progress*, **44**, 5–10.

Kasteleijn-Nolst Trenite, D.G. (1995) Transient cognitive impairment during subclinical epileptiform electroencephalographic discharges. *Seminars in Pediatric Neurology*, **2**, 246–253.

Kerr, M.P. (1998) Topiramate: uses in people with an intellectual disability who have epilepsy. *Journal of Intellectual Disability Research*, **42**, Supplement 1, 74–79.

Ko, D.Y., Rho, J.M., DeGiorgio, C.M. & Sato, S. (1997) Benzodiazepines. In: *Epilepsy: A Comprehensive Texbook* (eds J. Engel Jr & T.A. Pedley) pp. 1475–1489. Lippincott-Raven, Philadelphia PA.

Koh, S., Ward, S.L., Lin, M. & Chen, L.S. (2000) Sleep apnea treatment improves seizure control in children with neurodevelopmental disorders. *Pediatric Neurology*, **22**, 36–39.

Lai, F. & Williams, R.S. (1989) A prospective study of Alzheimer disease in Down syndrome. *Archives of Neurology*, **46**, 849–853.

Levy, D.E. (1988) How transient are transient ischemic attacks? *Neurology*, **38**, 674–677.

Lim, L.L., Foldvary, N.. Mascha, E. & Lee, J. (2001) Acetazolamide in women with catamenial epilepsy. *Epilepsia*, **42**, 746–749.

Lindhardt, K., Gizurarson, S., Stefansson, S.B., Olafsson, D.R. & Bechgaard, E. (2001) Electroencephalographic effects and serum concentrations after intranasal and intravenous administration of diazepam to healthy volunteers. *British Journal of Clinical Pharmacology*, **52**, 521–527.

Loiseau, P. (1998) Treatment of concomitant illnesses in patients receiving anticonvulsants: drug interactions of clinical significance. *Drug Safety*, **19**, 495–510.

Lombroso, C.T. & Forsythe, I. (1960) A long-term follow-up of acetazolamide (Diamox) in the treatment of epilepsy. *Epilepsia*, **1**, 493–500.

Lüders, H.O., Engel, J. Jr & Munari, C. (1993) General principles. In: Surgical Treatment of the Epilepsies (ed. J. Engel Jr) pp. 137–153. Raven Press, New York.

Manford, M., Hart, Y.M., Sander, J.W. & Shorvon, S.D. (1992) The National General Practice Study of Epilepsy. The syndromic classification of the International League Against Epilepsy applied to epilepsy in a general population. *Archives of Neurology*, **49**, 801–808.

Marrosu, F., Marrosu, G., Rachel, M.G. & Biggio, G. (1987) Paradoxical reactions elicited by diazepam in children with classic autism. *Functional Neurology*, **2**, 355–361.

Marson, A.G., Kadir, Z.A., Hutton, J.L. & Chadwick, D.W. (1997) The new anti-epileptic drugs: a systematic review of their efficacy and tolerability. *Epilepsia*, **38**, 859–880.

McVicker, R.W., Shanks, O.E. & McClelland, R.J. (1994) Prevalence and associated features of epilepsy in adults with Down's syndrome. *British Journal of Psychiatry*, **164**, 528–532.

Milligan, N.M., Dhillon, S., Griffiths, A., Oxley, J. & Richens, A. (1984) A clinical trial of single dose rectal and oral administration of diazepam for the prevention of serial seizures in adult epileptic patients. *Journal of Neurology Neurosurgery and Psychiatry*, **47**, 235–240.

Mitchell, W.G., Conry, J.A., Crumrine, P.K., Kriel, R.L., Cereghino, J.J., Groves, L. & Rosenfeld, W.E. (1999) An open-label study of repeated use of diazepam rectal gel (Diastat) for episodes of acute breakthrough seizures and clusters: safety, efficacy, and tolerance. North American Diastat Group. *Epilepsia*, **40**, 1610–1617.

Motte, J., Trevathen, E., Arvidsson, J. F., Barrerra, M.N., Mullens, E.L. & Manasco, P. (1997) Lamotrigine for generalised seizures associated with the Lennox Gastaut syndrome. *New England Journal of Medicine*, **337**, 1807–1812.

Nashef, L. & Brown, S.W. (eds) (1997) Epilepsy and sudden death. *Epilepsia*, **38**, Supplement 11.

Nieminen, K., Suarez-Isla, B.A. & Rappaport, S.I. (1988) Electrical properties of cultured dorsal root ganglion neurones from normal and trisomy human fetal tissue. *Brain Research*, **474**, 246–254.

Norris, E., Marzouk, O., Nunn, A., McIntyre, J. & Choonara, I. (1999) Respiratory depression in children receiving diazepam for acute seizures: a prospective study. *Developmental Medicine and Child Neurology*, **41**, 340–343.

Oguni, H., Hayashi, K. & Osawa, M. (1996) Long-term prognosis of Lennox-Gastaut syndrome. *Epilepsia*, **37**, Supplement 3, 44–47.

Oles, K.S., Penry, J.K., Cole, D.L. & Howard, G. (1989) Use of acetazolamide as an adjunct to carbamazepine in refractory partial seizures. *Epilepsia*, **30**, 74–78.

Paisley, K.E. & Tomson, C.R. (1999) Calcium phosphate stones during long-term acetazolamide treatment for epilepsy. *Postgraduate Medical Journal*, **75**, 427–428.

Pedley, T.A. (1983) Differential diagnosis of episodic symptoms. *Epilepsia*, **24**, Supplement 1, S31–44.

Plant, G. (1983) Focal paroxysmal kinesigenic choreoathetosis. *Journal of Neurology, Neurosurgery and Psychiatry*, **46**, 345–348.

Prasher, V.P. & Corbett, J.A. (1993) Onset of seizures as a poor indicator of longevity in people with Down syndrome and dementia. *International Journal of Geriatric Psychiatry*, **8**, 923–927.

Pueschel, S.M., Louis. S. & McKnight, P. (1991) Seizure disorders in Down syndrome. *Archives of Neurology*, **84**, 318–320.

Remy, C. (1994) Clobazam in the treatment of epilepsy: a review of the literature. *Epilepsia*, **35**, (Supplement 5), S88–S91.

Reynolds, E.H. (1986) The clinical concept of epilepsy, an historical perspective. In: *What is Epilepsy? The Clinical and Scientific Basis of Epilepsy* (eds M.R. Trimble & E.H. Reynolds) pp. 1–7. Churchill Livingstone, Edinburgh.

Riikonen, R. & Donner, M. (1979) Incidence and etiology of infantile spasms from 1960 to 1976: a population study in Finland. *Developmental Medicine and Child Neurology*, **21**, 333–343.

Romanelli, M.F., Morris, J.C., Ashkin, K. & Coben, L.A. (1990) Advanced Alzheimer's disease is a risk factor for late-onset seizures. *Archives of Neurology*, **47**, 847–850.

Romano, C., Baraitser, M. & Thompson, E. (1994) A clinical follow-up of British patients with FG syndrome. *Clinical Dysmorphology*, **3**, 104–114.

Russell-Jones, D.L. & Shorvon, S.D. (1989) The frequency and consequences of head injury in epileptic seizures. *Journal of Neurology, Neurosurgery and Psychiatry*, **52**, 659–662.

Sabers, A. (1999) Epilepsy in Down Syndrome. In: *Epilepsy and Mental Retardation* (eds M. Sillanpaa, L. Gram, S.I. Johannessen & T. Tomson) pp. 41–45. Wrightson Biomedical Publishing, Petersfield.

Sachdeo, R.C., Glauser, M.D., Ritter, F., Reife, R., Lim, P. & Pledger, G. (1999) A double-blind randomised trial of topiramate in Lennox-Gastaut syndrome. *Neurology*, **52**, 1882–1887.

Sander, J.W., Hart, Y.M., Johnson, A.L. & Shorvon, S.D. (1990) National General Practice Study of Epilepsy: newly diagnosed epileptic seizures in a general population. *Lancet*, **336**, 1267–1271.

Schmidt, D. & Bourgeois, B. (2000) A risk-benefit assessment of therapies for Lennox-Gastaut syndrome. *Drug Safety*, **22**, 467–477.

Scott, R.C., Besag, F.M. & Neville, B.G. (1999) Buccal midazolam and rectal diazepam for treatment of prolonged seizures in childhood and adolescence: a randomised trial. *Lancet*, **353**, 623–626.

Serratosa, J.M., Gardiner, R.M., Lehesjoki, A.E., Pennacchio, L.A. & Myers, R.M. (1999) The molecular genetic bases of the progressive myoclonus epilepsies. *Advances in Neurology*, **79**, 383–398.

Sheth, R.D., Goulden, K.J. & Ronen, G.M. (1997) Aggression in children treated with clobazam for epilepsy. *Clinical Neuropharmacology*, **17**, 332–337.

Shorvon, S.D. (1994. *Status Epilepticus: its Clinical Features and Treatment in Children and Adults*. Cambridge University Press, Cambridge, UK.

SIGN (1997) *Diagnosis and Management of Epilepsy in Adults*. A National Clinical Guideline recommended for use in Scotland by the Scottish Intercollegiate Guidelines Network, Royal College of Physicians, Edinburgh.

Silva, M.L., Cieuta, C., Guerrini, R., Plouin, P., Livet, M.O. & Dulac. O. (1996) Early clinical and EEG features of infantile spasms in Down syndrome. *Epilepsia*, **37**, 977–982.

Singh, A., Guberman, A.H. & Boisvert, D. (1995) Clobazam in long-term epilepsy treatment: sustained responders versus those developing tolerance. *Epilepsia*, **36**, 798–803.

Stafstrom, C.E. & Konkol, R.J. (1994) Infantile spasms in children with Down syndrome. *Developmental Medicine and Child Neurology*, **36**, 576–585.

Stafstrom, C.E., Patxot, O.F., Gilmore, H.E. & Wisniewski, K.E. (1991) Seizures in children with Down syndrome: Etiology, characteristics and outcome. *Developmental Medicine and Child Neurology*, **33**, 191–200.

Staufenberg, E.F.A. & Brown, S.W. (1994) Some issues in non-convulsive status epilepticus in children and adolescents with learning difficulties. *Seizure*, **3**, 95–105.

Straumanis, J.J., Shagass, C. & Overton, D.A. (1973) Somatosensory evoked responses in Down syndrome. *Archives of General Psychiatry*, **29**, 544–549.

Thomas, R.J. (1997) Seizures and epilepsy in the elderly. *Archives of Internal Medicine*, **157**, 605–617.

Tomson, T. (2000) Mortality in epilepsy. *Journal of Neurology*, **247**, 15–21.

Wallace, H., Shorvon, S. & Tallis, R. (1998) Age-specific incidence and prevalence rates of treated epilepsy in an unselected population of 2 052 922 and age-specific fertility rates of women with epilepsy. *Lancet*, **352**, 1970–1973.

Wassner, E., Morris, B., Fernando, L., Rao, M. & Whitehouse, W.P. (2001) Intranasal midazolam for treating febrile seizures in children. Buccal midazolam for childhood seizures at home preferred to rectal diazepam. *British Medical Journal*, 322, 108 (letter).

Wisniewski, K.E., Laure-Kamionowska, M. & Wisniewski, H.M. (1984) Evidence of arrest of neurogenesis and synaptogenesis in brains of patients with Down's syndrome. *New England Journal of Medicine*, **311**, 1187–1188.

Wisniewski, K.E., Dalton, A.J., Crapper McLachlan, D.R., Wen, G.Y. & Wisniewski, H.M. (1985) Alzheimer's disease in Down syndrome. *Neurology*, **35**, 957–961.

Working Group of the International Association of the Scientific Study of Intellectual Disability (2001) Clinical guidelines for the management of epilepsy in adults with an intellectual disability. *Seizure*, **10**, 401–409.

Wyllie, E., Wyllie, R., Cruse, R.P., Rothner, A.D. & Erenberg, G. (1986) The mechanism of nitrazepam-induced drooling and aspiration. *New England Journal of Medicine*, **314**, 35–38.

Yuen, A.W. Land, G., Weatherley, B.C. & Peck, A.W. (1992) Sodium valproate acutely inhibits lamotrigine metabolism. *British Journal of Clinical Pharmacology*, **33**, 511–513.

8

Endocrinological Issues

Aidan McElduff

Introduction

Endocrinology is the study of one of the two systems which integrate function in complex organisms, including man. The other is the nervous system. The endocrine system is characterized by special chemical mediators, classically called hormones, which are involved in every facet of human well-being including reproduction, growth and development, the maintenance of the internal milieu, and the utilization and storage of energy. Coordination of the endocrine system is controlled within the brain, particularly in the hypothalamus and surrounding areas. The system is complex and easily disrupted.

In times of stress and/or illness there are adaptive mechanisms which are beneficial in the short term but detrimental if they continue in the long term. Reproductive function and growth can be affected in this way. In times of stress it could be considered that the body does not want to 'waste' resources on reproduction and/or growth but rather wants to conserve resources to deal with the immediate crises. At such times reproductive function is shut down and growth is inhibited. The relationship between life-stresses such as examinations, and amenorrhea in young, otherwise healthy women, is well known. Similarly, stress or disturbances of physical or emotional well-being have been identified as contributors to other disease states, including the insulin resistance syndrome, obesity, dyslipidemia, glucose intolerance, diabetes and hypertension (Chrousos, 2000).

With this background, it is not a great step to suggest that in people with intellectual disabilities, particularly those with dysfunctions involving the brain and/or multiple organs, it is very likely that some endocrine systems would be disturbed to a greater or lesser extent. Endocrine disorders, which can result from the failure of the normal integration of complex physiological processes, include growth failure, hypogonadism, obesity and its complications, and/or osteoporosis.

Clinical issues

Clinical endocrinology involves the study of the problems which result from disruption of the hormonal system (see Tables 8.1 and 8.2) either through deficient or excess biological activity. Endocrine disorders are common in the general population and therefore, based on the previous discussion, one would predict that they are very common in adults with

Table 8.1 Pituitary hormones.

Hormone	Function
Adrenocorticotropic hormone	Controls adrenal glands
Thyroid stimulating hormone	Controls thyroid gland
Luteinizing hormone Follicle-stimulating hormone	Act in concert to control the gonads
Growth hormone	Growth via insulin-like growth factor (predominantly produced in the liver)
Prolactin	Breast milk production
Anti-diuretic hormone	Controls fluid status by inhibiting excess water loss from the kidneys

Table 8.2 Various hormones and their function.

Gland	Hormone(s)	Function
Thyroid	Thyroxin Tri-iodothyronine	Widespread actions on multiple tissues
Adrenal	Crotisol aldoesterone	Stress responses Fluid and electrolyte balance
	Androgens	Female libido
Testis	Testosterone	Maleness
Ovary (Gonad)	Estrogens and progesterone	Femaleness
Pancreas*	Insulin and others	Energy balance
Skin	Vitamin D then activated metabolites	Calcium and bone Homeostatis

* The islets of cells in the pancreas, which are the endocrine component of the pancreas, secrete other hormones including glucagon, somatostatin, gastrin.

an intellectual disability (Beange *et al.*, 1995a). There are also other reasons for a more likely occurrence. Firstly, endocrine disease can be an integral part of the syndrome responsible for the intellectual disability (syndrome-specific), either causally (e.g. hypothyroid cretinism) or a constant association (e.g. obesity in Prader-Willi syndrome). Secondly, endocrine disease may be more common in particular syndromes (e.g. hypothyroidism and diabetes in Down syndrome).

Lifelong care and appropriate stepping (mile) stones

A premise of this chapter is the role of the endocrine system in the integration of the human body. As we grow to maturity each milestone of development is used as a stepping-stone for the next stage of development. An error or fault in this process may have long lasting consequences that can never be fully corrected. In the usual course of events, growth and development leading to peak maturity are followed by early adult life with optimal health and then gradual but inevitable decline, as one grows older. We are all aware that the decline can be accelerated by an unhealthy lifestyle.

Additional factors which compound this decline, or 'normal' healthy aging, are the effect(s) of age-related diseases. These also include the effects of disabilities in people with intellectual disabilities as such effects will compound with time, particularly if they are present from birth and thus during development. They will inevitably limit the attainment of peak potential and/or accelerate decline. Thus, every effort should be made to minimize the adverse consequences of the disability. Energy should be invested in optimizing the initial growth in an attempt to have adults reach their maximal potential even if this is restricted by the underlying developmental problems. This lifelong or lifespan approach is recommended by the World Health Organization (WHO, 2000). Recommendation 2 of the WHO report on physical health issues states:

> 'Health care providers caring for people with intellectual disabilities of all ages should adopt a lifespan approach that recognizes the progression of consequences of specific diseases and therapeutic interventions.'

Risk factors for endocrine problems

Several of the 'disease' processes affecting people with intellectual disabilities may be the same as those affecting the general population, although they may have a different spectrum of causes within a multi-factorial etiology. Some of these contributing factors could be regarded as iatrogenic. Perhaps the simplest example of this concept is obesity. Basically, obesity relates to the imbalance between our energy intake (i.e. eating) and our energy output (i.e. activity). There are individual variations in the efficiency of this relationship but overall an imbalance with more intake than output will result in weight gain. One hypothesis is that people with intellectual disabilities are more prone to habitual overeating for complex societal reasons. On the other side of the energy balance, they are also likely to be underactive simply because of problems with motor activity, or more subtly because of a cautious or neglectful approach by carers to their participation in physical activities. Thus, while the basic reasons for obesity are the same as for the general population, that is an imbalance between energy intake and energy output, the reasons for this imbalance may relate to the nature of the person's disability and/or the societal response to that disability.

Another example can be found in the use of some types of anti-convulsants. In individuals with restricted or limited access to sunlight the use of anticonvulsants can lead to vitamin D deficiency. Anti-convulsant use is common in patients with intellectual disabilities and some more severely affected, immobile sub-groups may have restricted access to sunlight. Unless this potential problem is recognised, the long-term skeletal consequences of vitamin D deficiency will occur in patients receiving some types of anticonvulsants (particularly phenytoin).

Finally, there is the difficult issue of pubertal development. In some children with intellectual disabilities pubertal development will not occur. The reasons for this are varied and include insidious under-nutrition; diffuse non-specific damage to the hypothalamus resulting in secondary hypogonadism; a generalized non-specific abnormality relating to the stress of the illness; or a syndromic association (e.g. Turner's syndrome). Whatever the reasons, when puberty fails to occur in a child already diagnosed as having an intellectual dis-ability, it is frequently not regarded as a problem but may be seen as a blessing by some parents. In the general population failure to undergo puberty is recognized as a reason to seek medical help. This does not happen in people with intellectual disabilities. For a number of reasons, this is a complex area. Some of the fears of pubertal devel-opment among adolescents with intellectual disabilities are more fanci-ful than factual. There may also be major consequences of failure of pubertal development, including lack of appropriate growth and devel-opment and lack of the normal aging process. The decision whether or not to treat the failure of normal pubertal development needs to be taken as an active process rather than allowing pubertal non-devel-

opment by default. This is an issue of some import and will be discussed more fully later.

Endocrine and related disorders

Obesity and undernutrition are not strictly speaking endocrine disorders.
Both are often seen by endocrinologists interested in metabolic disorders
to exclude unusual underlying endocrine disorders and to supervise
therapy. Both are associated with a range of endocrine complications.
They will be discussed briefly again here but will be reviewed in more
depth in Chapter 10.

Obesity

Obesity is increasingly common in developed nations. While in the general population, obesity is related to age, among adults with intellectual
disabilities there may be other reasons for its prevalence. For example,
some adults with intellectual disabilities, particularly those with Down
syndrome, appear to be more at risk for obesity for reasons discussed
above (Prasher, 1995). Obesity is best managed by prevention since successful long-term correction of obesity is rare in the general population.
People with intellectual disabilities may actually be advantaged in this
regard. Experience with a structured intervention programme involving
an experienced dietitian and an exercise physiologist suggests that people
with intellectual disabilities are best compared with men who have never
had health care advice. Relatively simple dietary advice and an attractive,
organized and supervised group exercise programme can result in significant weight loss. The loss of weight can lead to an obvious and marked
improvement in the individual's self-esteem, together with an improvement in cardiovascular risk factors and other positive health benefits
including mobility.

Undernutrition

Undernutrition commonly results from simple failure to provide nutrients to persons who cannot eat without the help of others. Adults with
cerebral palsy and those with severe intellectual and physical disabilities
have a high incidence of dysphagia, which places them in a high-risk
group for severe undernutrition. The consequences of this on their health,
including an elevated risk of osteomalacia and fragility bone fracture,

have been well documented (Beange *et al.*, 1995b). A proactive approach by health care professionals and carers alike is necessary to bring about successful nutrition interventions for those people who suffer chronic undernutrition.

Thyroid disease

Thyroid disease can occur at any age but is more common with increasing age and is particularly common in the Down syndrome population (Prasher, 1999). Thyroid disease can be difficult to diagnose in any group of patients and this is particularly so in persons with intellectual disabilities. Often the only symptom is reported by the carer, usually the mother, who observes that the patient's behavior has changed in some non-specific way. For this reason thyroid function tests should be performed on any unusual presentation and on a routine (preferably annual) basis in persons at high risk, such as those with Down syndrome. The management is usually straightforward but may also involve supervision of medication.

Hypothyroidism

Primary hypothyroidism (due to thyroid failure) is easily diagnosed. The thyroid stimulating hormone (TSH) is elevated above the normal range and the measurement of free thyroxin (T4) is low. The changes from normal are a measure of the degree of hypothyroidism. The presence of thyroid auto-antibodies suggests an auto-immune etiology. Investigation of the underlying etiology beyond measuring auto-antibodies is rarely warranted. Rarely TSH is elevated with high or high normal free T4. This requires specialist referral. Thyroid hormone resistance and TSH secreting tumors can produce these unusual findings.

Secondary hypothyroidism (due to pituitary/hypothalamic disorders) can be difficult to diagnose. The TSH can be low, normal or paradoxically slightly elevated. Free T4 is relatively low but usually only at the lower limit of normal. Other evidence of pituitary/hypothalamic disturbances should be present, particularly secondary hypogonadism. If secondary hypothyroidism is suspected it requires specialist referral and investigation, including imaging, to determine the underlying pituitary/hypothalamic disorder.

In the absence of cardiac disease, hypothyroidism can be treated with an initial dose of 1.5 ug/kg/day thyroxin. Thyroid function tests should not be repeated for at least eight weeks. Therapy is titrated to achieve a normal TSH. The most common error is to repeat thyroid function tests at too short an interval following a dose adjustment before a new equilibrium or steady state has been established. If cardiac disease is suspected or possible, thyroxin therapy should be introduced slowly. One possible regimen is to initiate therapy with thyroxin 25 micrograms per day increasing by 25 micrograms per day at 6–12 weekly intervals provided the patient remains asymptomatic from a cardiac point of view. If symptoms are induced, cardiac intervention (either surgical or medical) will be required.

Hyperthyroidism (thyrotoxicosis)

Thyrotoxicosis or hyperthyroidism is easily diagnosed in most situations. Free (tri-idothyronine) T3 and free T4 are elevated with a suppressed (low) TSH. Elevated free T4 or free T3 in the presence of a normal TSH level requires specialist investigation as mentioned previously. TSH suppression should be in proportion to the elevation in the free T3 and free T4. The underlying cause of the hyperthyroidism must be identified. This may involve performing a thyroid scan and possibly measuring anti-TSH receptor antibodies.

The long-term treatment will depend on the underlying etiology. Initial treatment of most thyrotoxicosis (i.e. Graves' disease or toxic nodular disease) consists of oral antithyroid medication (e.g. carbimazole or equivalent, or propylthiouracil). Thyrotoxicosis due to thyroiditis can be managed symptomatically with beta-blockers until the thyroiditis settles, usually spontaneously. Antithyroid medications are ineffective in this situation. The dose of antithyroid medication is adjusted as the patient responds. This can be difficult under ideal circumstances. Compliance is an important issue as non-compliance can confuse dose titration. The initial dose of antithyroid medication is in proportion to the severity of the disease. A clinical response should become apparent within a few weeks. It is recommended to repeat the thyroid function tests at four-weekly intervals with an appropriate dose adjustment until the tests are stable. Specialist referral should be considered, particularly for more severe disease. Severe symptoms can be controlled with beta-blockers until the antithyroid medication has taken effect. Definitive therapy with radio-active iodine is a reasonable long-term option for Graves' disease, recognizing that hypothyroidism is almost inevitable. Life-long follow-up to detect hypothyroidism is mandatory after radioactive iodine treatment. Recall should be automatically initiated by the physician and should not be dependent on the patient.

Thyrotoxicosis associated with multinodular thyroid disease may require investigation to exclude malignancy in one of the nodules. Surgery may be a preferable definitive treatment option in this situation. Malignancy is rare but not unknown in single toxic nodule. Thyroid biopsy should not be performed when the patient is thyrotoxic as the cytological findings in a toxic nodule cannot be distinguished from malignancy. Radioactive iodine should not be administered until the question of underlying malignancy has been settled.

Goiter

The discussion above has dealt with only functional thyroid disturbances. Structural problems can also arise and need not be associated with a disturbance in function. Thyroid enlargement can be generalized or nodular in nature. Thyroid nodules require investigation to exclude thyroid cancer. This involves a fine needle aspiration biopsy, which is frequently performed under ultrasound control and the biopsy sample is sent for cytological examination. A small (< 1 cm) nodule found on ultrasound and impalpable on physical examination does not require a biopsy. Diffuse thyroid enlargement does not require separate investigation apart from thyroid function tests and the measurement of thyroid auto-antibodies. Thyroid auto-antibodies suggest the presence of thyroid auto-immunity and indicate a small ($\sim 2\%$/year) risk of hypothyroidism.

Diabetes

Diabetes mellitus is very common in the general population. An Australia-wide population study (AusDiab; Shaw *et al.*, 2001) found a prevalence of 7.5% in the adult population (age over 25). Shaw noted that the prevalence increased dramatically with age, such that in 80-year-olds, one in four had type II diabetes. One half of the patients identified with diabetes had not been diagnosed. The prevalence is increasing in both the developed and the developing world. Lifestyle factors (such as obesity and inactivity) are believed to be responsible for this increased prevalence. Since obesity and inactivity are common in adults with intellectual disabilities, it seems reasonable to assume that diabetes will also be common and that at least a similar proportion go undiagnosed. Strategies designed to prevent obesity and increase activity should reduce the frequency of diabetes. An increased awareness of this problem and routine testing of at-risk sub-groups should lead to an increased rate of diagnosis and the introduction of appropriate management.

Since we now have strong Level 1 evidence that the micro and macrovascular complications of type II diabetes can be reduced with appropriate treatment, it is important that diabetes is diagnosed as early as possible. For type II diabetes, which can be asymptomatic, this will require screening. The best test to screen for diabetes is currently under active debate. The gold standard diagnostic test is the glucose tolerance test, but this test is inconvenient, cumbersome, unpleasant and expensive. A fasting plasma glucose (normal is equal to or less than 6 mmol/L) is less sensitive but easier to perform on a repeated basis. Favored is the measurement of glycosylated hemoglobin, but this is more expensive and not yet validated (see section on screening later in this chapter). Risk factors for diabetes include obesity, immobility, age and a positive family history.

A large component of the management of diabetes involves screening for the specific microvascular (i.e. retinopathy, nephropathy and neuropathy) and macrovascular (i.e. cardiac, cerebral and peripheral) complications. This may be difficult in adults with intellectual disabilities. Sensory neuropathy can be difficult to detect as clinical examination is subjective. Eye examination for retinopathy may require general anesthetic. Similarly, for macrovascular disease, patients may not report symptoms and a high degree of clinical suspicion may be required to detect problems. As people with intellectual disabilities live to an older age, macrovascular disease will become a more common problem.

On a more positive note, experience has shown that patients with Down syndrome do not develop retinopathy at a rate expected from their degree of glycemic control. This may be due to the fact that they almost universally have low/normal blood pressures. The recent United Kingdom Prospective Diabetes Study (Adler *et al.*, 2000; UKPDS Group, 1998) demonstrated that retinopathy was prevented by treatment directed toward lowering blood pressure. Thus, patients with Down syndrome and diabetes may be at less risk of retinopathy because of typically low blood pressure. This is an example of how, in some situations, specific features of people with intellectual disabilities may provide benefit rather than adverse effect.

The current management strategies for people with diabetes are to promote self-care and responsibility, aiming for tight glycemic control. The risk of this strategy is hypoglycemia with all its potentially devastating consequences. Major, potentially life-threatening hypoglycemia is relatively common. As a general rule patients with intellectual disabilities are not capable of assuming appropriate self-care. The treatment targets for adults with intellectual disabilities who have diabetes will almost certainly be modified from that of the general population because of the dangers of hypoglycemia. The target for glycemic control should be to make them feel well and free of symptoms, whereas in the general population the target is a tighter degree of glycemic control aiming to prevent or delay the progression of diabetic complications. My own experience differs from that reported by Anwar *et al.*, (1998), who observed that patients with Down syndrome and diabetes had similar degrees of glycemic control to the general population. However, this data may reflect poor controls from the general population. In our diabetic clinic the mean glycosylated hemoglobin in patients with type I or type II diabetes is less than 7.5%. Experience has shown that this is not the case in patients with diabetes and intellectual disabilities, most of whom have Down syndrome. In our clinic, we have accepted glycosylated hemoglobin values of 9–10% in this group (in an assay with an upper limit normal of 6%).

Patients with type I or insulin-requiring diabetes are more difficult to manage than those with type II diabetes. Assistance with insulin administration and home glucose monitoring is almost always required. Diabetes should be treated in collaboration with a diabetic clinic. One uncommon condition which is more prone to diabetes where diabetic control is also difficult is Prader-Willi syndrome. Given the difficulties in controlling diet in this disorder, treatment of diabetes is exceptionally difficult.

Several studies (DPP, 2001 and Tuomilehto *et al.*, 2001) have reported that lifestyle modification involving increased activity and diet to obtain modest weight loss ($\sim 5\%$ of body weight) significantly reduced the occurrence of type II diabetes in high-risk groups. This benefit should be extended to high-risk individuals with intellectual disabilities. This would include individuals with obesity, inactive individuals, those with a family history of type II diabetes and those with any previous abnormality in glucose tolerance, including high glucose levels during an illness.

Vitamin D deficiency

There has been controversy over the role of anticonvulsants in producing low vitamin D levels and subsequently osteoporosis (Wark *et al.*, 1979). Adequate sun exposure may provide a source of excess vitamin D that protects against the increased metabolism induced by anticonvulsant therapy. In people who receive low sun exposure, some anticonvulsant therapy increases the risk of becoming vitamin D deficient in the absence of supplementation. Vitamin D deficiency can result in either osteomalacia or osteoporosis (Compston, 1995). Vitamin D status is best reflected by the measurement of 25 hydroxy vitamin D. This should be measured annually at the end of winter.

Hypogonadism

There are various definitions of hypogonadism. The gonad (testis or ovary) has two separate but interlinked functions: gamete production and sex hormone production. In males the testis constantly produce sperm, while in females the ovary releases eggs which have been 'present' since embryological ovarian formation. Sperm production requires adequate levels of testosterone. A man may produce normal levels of testosterone but have abnormal or sub-normal sperm production. Testicular volume is an acceptable surrogate for the sperm producing function of the testis because most of the volume of the testis is made up of sperm producing cells. A small volume testis is very likely to have impaired sperm production, although the reverse is not true (i.e. there is no guarantee that a normal testis has normal sperm production). The normal adult testis is 24 +/− 4 ml in volume (mean +/− SD) (Santen, 1991). Testicular volume should be measured by comparison to an orchidometer.

The normal premenopausal ovary contains eggs and a woman is not regarded as hypogonadal unless the ovary contains no eggs. Thus a woman who does not have regular menstruation in the presence of ovaries which contain eggs is only considered hypogonadal if the circulating estradiol level is low. Hypogonadism in a premenopausal woman is usually secondary to low gonadotrophins due to a disturbance in the hypothalamic/pituitary region of the brain. This is often precipitated by undernutrition. Thus, hypogonadism can be defined in relationship to gamete production/presence, sex hormone production, or the combination of both. The broader definition of hypogonadism, including an impairment in either function, is adopted in this discussion unless otherwise stated.

Hypogonadism is particularly common in adults with intellectual disabilities and management of the condition is fraught with difficulty on a number of levels. Among some parents there is an often spoken joy at the gentle, childlike qualities of the hypogonadal (no sex hormone production) adult male because there is an underlying fear that testosterone at puberty will be associated with aggressiveness. Among parents the fear for adult women is that menstruation will be difficult to manage and the risk of pregnancy is often an unspoken concern. However, the risk of pregnancy is very low if gonadal function is impaired enough to require sex hormone replacement therapy. Hormone replacement therapy in this situation can be tailored in both men and women to provide contraception if fertility is an issue. Infertility has no direct medical consequences.

Hypogonadism (no sex hormone production) does have destructive medical consequences, not the least of which is an increased risk of osteoporosis and probably obesity. The decision not to treat is usually made passively rather than actively discussed. Any decision to provide a different standard of care than in the general population should be explicitly communicated to family and carers and clearly documented.

The possibility of hypogonadism should be considered if physical changes of puberty are not clearly evident by the age of 14–16 years. The threshold for girls should be towards the lower end of this range and for boys towards the upper end. The possibility of pubertal delay can be confirmed by a combination of physical examination and special investigations, including measuring of luteinising hormone, follicle stimulating hormone and the specific gonadal steroid, either testosterone or estradiol. This assessment should be made by a specialist. In some circumstances gonadal failure is inevitable (e.g. Turner's syndrome) and is something that should be anticipated and planned.

As noted above, the testes fulfill two functions. The majority of the volume of the testes is composed of sperm producing cells. A man with small testes will not necessarily have decreased circulating testosterone, whereas all males with small testes will have at a minimum impaired sperm production. This latter abnormality will not require treatment if fertility is not desired, and it should be thought of separately from a deficiency in androgen production.

Cryptorchidism

Cryptorchidism (or undescended testes or testes not in the scrotum) is more common in hypogonadal males. Cryptorchidism carries an increased ($\times 4$) lifetime risk of testicular cancer. This risk is further increased in certain chromosomal disorders (Cortes et al., 1999) and possibly in Down syndrome (Satge et al., 1997). In clinical practice, if two testes are not identified, a search for the undescended testes should be undertaken. Ultrasound examination is probably the first step in most patients. In adults, intra-abdominal testes are usually removed and at the very least should be brought into the scrotum to allow routine regular surveillance. Testicular examination should be part of routine physical examination in patients with intellectual disabilities as they may be at increased risk of a relatively common cancer and are unlikely to perform self-examination.

Menopause

The other aspect of hypogonadism is the natural hypogonadism which occurs in women at the time of the menopause. In the general population there is vigorous discussion about the need to treat all postmenopausal women with hormone replacement therapy (HRT). There is a general consensus that younger women with ovarian failure do require therapy. There are clear-cut benefits of HRT in the prevention or minimization of post-menopausal symptoms and in the prevention of osteoporosis. Many women have no or few symptoms and many will not develop osteoporosis, although our ability to predict who is at risk has not yet been perfected. On this basis, not all women will require treatment. There are side effects of HRT; the biggest fears are breast cancer (uterine cancer if progesterone is not included in the HRT regimen) and venous thrombosis. Is HRT warranted in postmenopausal women with intellectual disabilities? As in the general population, this decision must be individualized. Either a plethora of symptoms, which might not be spontaneously reported, or a low bone mineral density reading at the time of assessment, would tend to push the decision towards administration of HRT. If that decision is made, then careful monitoring is required.

There is increasing evidence that continuous HRT in women five years or more past the menopause is effective. In the immediate post-menopause, cyclic therapy is more appropriate. In the immediate post-menopause, therapy could be with Premarin 625 micrograms per day and cyclical medroxyprogesterone, 10 mg for the last 12 days of each month. This should result in an appropriate withdrawal bleed, although either therapy may require individual adjustment. For continuous therapy in patients who have been hypogonadal for several years, it is more reasonable to start with a smaller dose of Premarin and increase slowly to 625 micrograms per day, in an attempt to minimize the breast tenderness which many women report. Established therapy of Premarin (625 micrograms per day) and medroxyprogesterone (5 mg per day) results in appropriate hormone replacement with the absence of menstruation in the majority of women.

All women receiving HRT require annual surveillance for breast cancer and endometrial hypertrophy. Men, particularly those over 50 years of age, receiving testosterone therapy require assessment for prostatic cancer.

Osteoporosis

As outlined previously, the achievement and maintenance of normal bone mineral density is a complex integrated process which relies on normal growth and development, the normal timing of puberty, the maintenance of adult sex hormone concentrations, normal activity and nutrition and the absence of other diseases. Osteoporosis (defined as a disease characterized by low bone mass and microarchitectural deterioration in bone tissue leading to enhanced bone fragility and a consequent increase in fracture risk (Consensus Development Conference, 1993)) can result from a failure to achieve peak bone mass and/or accelerated bone loss with age. Severe or established osteoporosis is defined as osteoporosis in the presence of a fragility or minimal trauma fracture. Factors which may impair the achievement of peak bone mass and/or result in rapid bone loss are frequent in people with intellectual disabilities. Thus adults with intellectual disabilities are more likely to be osteoporotic. This has recently been confirmed in a relatively young (mean age 35 years) sample of adults with intellectual disabilities (Center et al., 1998). There may be a specific problem in people with Down syndrome disproportional to their smaller body size (Center et al., 1998; Kao et al., 1992; Sepúlveda et al., 1995).

Age and small body size are the best clinical predictors of low bone mineral density. Other predictive factors include Down syndrome and hypogonadism. In one population, low bone mineral density was associated with a history of fracture among females, although this was not the case with males (Center et al., 1998).

To minimise the possibility of low bone density, individuals with intellectual disabilities should receive adequate nutrition and be encouraged to achieve maximal mobility. Those with no regular exposure to sunlight or no routine vitamin D supplementation will need careful monitoring of their vitamin D status. Medical surveillance of people with intellectual disabilities will need to include an explicit approach to the assessment and treatment of osteoporosis.

Fractures and osteoporosis

Fractures can occur with minimal trauma. Minimal trauma is defined as the force involved in a fall from standing height or less. Factors that contribute to these minimal trauma fractures are a propensity to fall and the change in the strength of the bones, reducing their ability to withstand fracture. The latter has two components that can occur individually or together. The first is a decrease in bone density so that there is less bone per unit volume (osteoporosis). The second component is a change in the quality of the bone, but at this time this is difficult to measure (although ultrasound may address this in the future).

Some sub-groups of adults with intellectual disabilities are at increased risk of fracture compared with the general population (Tannenbaum *et al.*, 1989). This increased risk appears to be associated with an increased risk of falling (Spreat & Baker-Potts, 1983). Fractures in this population are associated with increased morbidity (Spreat & Baker-Potts, 1983).

Measurement of bone mass and fracture risk

There are several non-invasive low radiation techniques for measuring bone mass, loosely termed bone mineral density (BMD), including dual photon absorptiometry (Johnston *et al.*, 1991). These techniques have been shown to measure BMD precisely and accurately although technical artifacts can and do occur, particularly with commonly performed spinal measurements. The bone mineral density of groups with and without fracture overlap, consistent with the idea that other factors (i.e. propensity to fall) must be involved. Reduced bone mineral density is a continuous risk factor for fracture similar to hypercholesterolemia and heart disease.

Treatment

In the general population there are a number of available treatment options (Australian National Consensus Conference, 1996; Eastell *et al.*, 1998; Meunier *et al.*, 1999). These treatments have generally been validated as reducing the risk of minimal trauma fracture based on changes in vertebral shape (i.e. the so-called sub-clinical vertebral wedge fractures). Fewer of the treatments have been validated as reducing the risk of clinical peripheral fractures. Treatments which have been shown to reduce peripheral fractures, such as treatment with alendronic acid, require a large number of patients to be treated to prevent one clinically relevant fracture. Treatments are not without side-effects. Alendronic acid can result in esophageal reflux and esophagitis. If the person already had any signs of dysphagia they are already very vulnerable to esophageal reflux. Ideally before these treatments are widely used in patients with intellectual disabilities there should be specific studies demonstrating their safety and efficacy. It would be reasonable to postulate that patients with Down syndrome who may have a particular abnormality related to their poor muscle function might have a different response to these therapies than the general population. However, this remains to be seen.

The overall approach to reducing the risk of fractures should be broad-based rather than a traditional single therapy approach. It should be lifelong, aiming at prevention, and should include attention to lifestyle factors. Physicians who treat patients with intellectual disabilities will understand this approach particularly well. A multifactorial approach to falls reduction has been shown to reduce the number of falls and consequent fractures (Tinetti *et al.*, 1994). One component of this multifactorial approach not previously mentioned is a reduction in the number of drugs which aggravate falling. Many psychotropic medications fit into this category. Care should be taken in balancing this risk with the benefits obtained from such therapies.

Dyslipidemia

This is a relatively uncommon cause for endocrinological referral. Treatment for adults with intellectual disabilities is the same as in the general population. Lifestyle factors, particularly diet, should be addressed. Persistent predominant hypercholesterolemia can be treated with the 3-hydroxl-3-methylglutaryl coenzyme A (HMG CoA) reductase inhibitors (the statins). Other agents such as the acid resins and nicotinic acid are less well tolerated. Gemfibrozil or other fibric acid derivatives can be used in this hypercholesterolemia and are preferred for predominant hypertriglyceridemia.

Screening

Medical problems among adults with intellectual disabilities are significantly underdiagnosed (Beange *et al.*, 1995a). Reasons for this are discussed in Chapters 11 and 12. It seems entirely reasonable to recommend routine screening for all adults with intellectual disabilities for a range of common conditions, including those listed above. In some cases this will require only a physical examination. In the event of economic constraints, screening could be restricted to high-risk patients. It is easy to justify annual thyroid function tests in adults with Down syndrome. Similarly, as diabetes is so common in the population, routine screening could also be easily justified. For simplicity, it is recommended to use glycosylated hemoglobin. This is not a sensitive test for the detection of diabetes but it is specific (apart from those with some underlying hemoglobinopathies). Furthermore, since the goal of treatment is to normalize glycosylated hemoglobin, provided the patient has a normal glycosylated hemoglobin, no further action need be taken. This will avoid the difficult problem of interpreting plasma glucose in relation to meals or ensuring that the patient is fasting. A diagnosis of diabetes suspected on glycosylated hemoglobin screening should be confirmed by appropriate glucose measurements. Vitamin D status should certainly be assessed annually in patients on anticonvulsant therapy by measuring 25 hydroxy vitamin D concentration.

Therapeutic approaches

Efforts to optimize nutritional care and bring about healthy eating habits should be a priority. This is necessary to prevent both over and under-nutrition, both of which are significant problems in this at-risk group and both of which can have long-term, wide-spectrum consequences later in life, leading to several easily identified problems such as obesity, diabetes, osteoporosis or gonadal dysfunction. Similarly, when self-initiated activity is restricted, programs to promote maximum use of motor skills are required. This has an immediate benefit for the person involved and in the longer term will prevent or minimize limitations in future motor skills. In addition, where known interactions of drug therapy (for example, phenytoin and an environment lacking sun exposure) are known to have deleterious effects, these need to be counteracted. The identification of specific endocrine disorders is part of this approach, which is in keeping with the approach recommended by the WHO (2000) where it is proposed that:

'People with intellectual disabilities, and their carers, need to receive appropriate and ongoing education regarding healthy living practices in areas such as nutrition, exercise, oral hygiene, safety practices and the avoidance of risky behavior, such as substance abuse and unprotected or multiple partner sexual activity'

(Recommendation 6. Report 1-Physical Health Issues)

Access to health care in the usual paradigm of health care delivery

As a general principle, endocrine disease should be managed as in the general population, but the current paradigm for the delivery of health care is often not optimized to deal with this special subgroup of the population. Particular problems in accessing appropriate health care for endocrinological disorders include:

1. Many endocrine diseases present with a predominance of symptoms rather than physical signs. Adults with intellectual disabilities generally cannot verbally communicate their symptoms and so they often present

in an atypical fashion. Recommendation 9 by the WHO (2000) states: 'Functional decline in older adults with intellectual disabilities warrants careful medical evaluation; undiagnosed mental health and medical conditions can have atypical presentations in people with limited language capabilities. Regular screening for visual and hearing impairment should be implemented for people with intellectual disabilities during the childhood and late adulthood years'. Further, Recommendation 11 highlights possible deficiencies in service providers, by stating: 'Carers need training in assessing and communicating the basic health status of the adults with intellectual disabilities'.

2. Physical signs in endocrine disease are often subtle and are potentially easily masked by dysmorphic features particularly to an examiner who does not see a significant number of adults with intellectual disabilities: 'Health care providers serving older adults with intellectual disabilities should recognize that adult and older-age onset medical conditions are common in this population and may require a high index of suspicion of clinical diagnosis.' (Recommendation 8-WHO, 2000)

3. Physical examination is difficult in the uncooperative patient.

4. Endocrine test results can be influenced by medications frequently used in this population, although these problems are increasingly well recognized and newer laboratory methodologies often overcome the difficulties.

5. Current management of chronic diseases involves a significant component of self-care or self-management. The management of diabetes can be regarded as a prototype. Patients with intellectual disabilities as a group are almost always unable to assume the increased responsibility involved in self-care. This results in suboptimal management. People with intellectual disabilities require increased supervision of care including assistance to ensure compliance with medication.

Often patients with intellectual disabilities do not readily fit into our current model of health care delivery. This is exacerbated if the system is time constrained in any way. A different method of delivering health care to this subgroup is needed to deal with these problems. This has been highlighted by the WHO in recommendation 10 (WHO, 2000): 'Health care providers and policy makers need to eliminate attitudinal, architectural, and health care reimbursement barriers, that interfere with the provision of high quality health services for people with intellectual disabilities.' More general problems and deficiencies in the provision of appropriate health care to people with intellectual disabilities are discussed in Chapters 11 and 12.

Conclusion

Endocrine problems are common in people with intellectual disabilities for the same reasons as in the general population and for reasons specifically associated, directly or indirectly, with the disability itself. Some of the indirect associations may be correctable. All efforts to maximize an individual's potential will have long-term benefit. This is true for all aspects of the person's mental and physical state and is not limited to the endocrine system. Nevertheless, as the endocrine system has a widespread coordinating role, many of the failures in achieving maximal potential will occur through failure of integration via the endocrine system. Once the diagnosis of intellectual disabilities is made, the pitfalls that can lead to problems in the future need to be recognized and avoided (WHO, 2000).

Common endocrine problems occurring among adults with intellectual disabilities include obesity and diabetes with its associated coronary artery disease risk, hypogonadism, osteoporosis and hypothyroidism. These diseases can have additive, compounding, long-term effects on the individual. For an individual to achieve their maximum potential and to maintain this potential for as long as possible, these disease processes need to be anticipated and prevented if at all possible, or detected early and treated vigorously. Only in this way will the health and longevity of people with intellectual disabilities be improved.

References

Adler, A.I., Stratton, I.M., Neil, H.A., Yudkin, J.S., Matthews, D.R., Cull, C.A., Wright, A.D., Turner, R.C. & Holman, R.R. (2000) Association of systolic blood pressure with macrovascular and microvascular complications of type II diabetes (UKPDS 36): prospective observational study. *British Medical Journal*, **321**, 394–395.

Anwar, A J., Walker, J.D. & Frier, B.M. (1998) Type I diabetes mellitus and Down's syndrome: prevalence, management and diabetic complications. *Diabetic Medicine*, **15**, 160–163.

Australian National Consensus Conference (1996) Consensus statement: the prevention and management of osteoporosis. *The Medical Journal of Australia*, (1997) **167**, Supplement 7.

Beange, H., McElduff, A. & Baker, W. (1995a) Medical disorders in adults with intellectual disability: a population study. *American Journal of Mental Retardation*, **99**, 595–604.

Beange, H., Gale, L. & Stewart, L. (1995b) Project Renourish: a dietary intervention to improve nutritional status in people with multiple disabilities. *Australian and New Zealand Journal of Developmental Disabilities*, **20**, 165–174.

Center, J., Beange, H. & McElduff, A. (1998) People with mental retardation have an increased prevalence of osteoporosis: a population study. *American Journal of Mental Retardation*, **103**, 19–28.

Chrousos, G.P. (2000) Stress, chronic inflammation, and emotional and physical well-being: concurrent effects and chronic sequelae. *Journal of Allergy and Clinical Immunology*, **106** (Supplement 5), S275–291.

Compston, J.E. (1995) The role of vitamin D and calcium supplementation in the prevention of osteoporotic fracture in elderly. *Clinical Endocrinology*, **43**, 393–405.

Consensus Development Conference (1993) Diagnosis, prophylaxis and treatment of osteoporosis. *American Journal of Medicine*, **94**, 646–650.

Corteo, D., Visfeldt, J., Mullei, H. & Thorup, J. (1999) Testicular neoplasia in cryptorchid boys at primary surgery: case series. *British Medical Journal*, **319**, 888–889.

DPP (2001) Diabetes Prevention Program www.nih.gov/news/pr/aug2001/niddk-08.htm

Eastell, R., Boyle, I.T., Compston, J., Cooper, C., Fogelman, I., Francis, R.M., Hosking, D.J., Purdie, D.W., Ralston, S., Reeve, J., Reid, D.M., Russell, R.G.G. & Stevenson, J.C. (1998) Management of male osteoporosis: report of the UK Consensus Group. *Quarterly Journal of Medicine*, **91**, 71–92.

Johnston, C.C., Slemenda, C.W. & Melton, L.J. (1991) Clinical use of bone densitometry. *New England Journal of Medicine*, **324**, 1105–1109.

Kao, C.H., Chen, C.C., Wang, S.J. & Yeh, S.H. (1992) Bone mineral density in children with Down syndrome detected by dual photon absorptiometry. *Nuclear Medicine Communications*, **13**, 773–775.

Meunier, P.J., Delmas, P.D., Eastell, M.R., Papapoulos, S., Rizzoli, R., Seeman, E. & Wasnick, R.D. (1999) Diagnosis and management of osteoporosis in postmenopausal women: clinical guidelines. *Clinical Therapeutics*, **21**, 1025–1039.

Prasher, V.P. (1995) Overweight and obesity amongst Down syndrome adults. *Journal of Intellectual Disability Research*, **39**, 437–441.

Prasher, V.P. (1999) Down syndrome and thyroid disorders: A review. *Down Syndrome Research and Practice*, **6**, 105–110.

Santen, F.J. (1991) Male hypogonadism. In *Reproductive Endocrinology* (eds S.S.C. Yen & R.B. Jaffe) 3rd edn, p. 745. W.B. Saunders Co, Philadelphia.

Satge, D., Sasco, A.J., Cure, H., Leduc, B., Sommelet, D. & Vekemans, M.J. (1997) An excess of testicular germ cell tumors in Down's syndrome: three case reports and a review of the literature. *Cancer*, **80**, 929–935.

Sepúlveda, D., Allison, D.B., Gomez, J.E., Kreibich, K., Brown, R.A., Pierson, R.N. & Heymsfield, S.B. (1995) Low spinal and pelvic bone mineral density among individuals with Down syndrome. *American Journal of Mental Retardation*, **100**, 109–114.

Shaw, J.E., Dunstan, D.W., Zimmet, P.Z., Cameron, A.J., de Courten, M.P. & Welborn, T.A. (2001) Epidemic glucose intolerance in Australia. *Proceedings of the 37th Annual Meeting of the European Association for the Study of Diabetes*. Abstract 9.

Spreat, S. & Baker-Potts, J.C. (1983) Patterns of injury in institutionalized mentally retarded residents. *Mental Retardation*, **21**, 23–29.

Tannenbaum, T.N., Lipworth, L. & Baker, S. (1989) Risk of fractures in an intermediate care facility for persons with mental retardation. *American Journal of Mental Retardation,* **95**, 444–451.

Tinetti, M.E., Baker, D.I., McAvay, G., Claus, E.G., Garrett, P., Gottschalk, M., Koch, M.L., Trainor, K. & Horwitz, R.I. (1994) A multifactorial intervention to reduce the risk of falling among elderly people living in the community. *New England Journal of Medicine,* **331**, 821–827.

Tuomilehto, J., Lindstrom, J., Eriksson, J.G., Valle, T.T., Hamalainen, H., Ilanne-Parikka, P., Keinanen-Kiukaanniemi, S., Laakso, M., Louheranta, A., Rastas, M., Salminen, V., Aunola, S., Cepaitis, Z., Moltchanov, V., Hakumaki, M., Mannelin, M., Martikkala, V., Sundvall, J. & Uusitupa, M. (2001) The Finnish Diabetes Prevention Study Group. Prevention of Type II diabetes mellitus by changes in lifestyle among subjects with impaired glucose tolerance. *New England Journal of Medicine,* **344**, 1343–1350.

UKPDS Group (1998) UK Prospective Diabetes Study Group. Efficacy of atenolol and captopril in reducing risk of macrovascular and microvascular complications in type 2 diabetes: UKPDS 39. *British Medical Journal,* **317**, 713–720.

Wark, J.D., Larkins, R.G., Perry-Keene, D., Peter, C.T., Ross, D.L. & Sloman, J.G. (1979) Chronic diphenylhydantoin therapy does not reduce plasma 25-hydroxy-vitamin D. *Clinical Endocrinology,* **11**, 267–274.

WHO (2000) *Healthy Ageing – Adults with Intellectual Disabilities.* Background Reports on Physical and Mental Health, Women's Health and Ageing and Social Policy – Physical Health Issues. World Health Organization, Geneva, Switzerland.

9 Dentition and Oral Health

Hans Malmstrom, Rosemeire Santos-Teachout and Yang-Fang Ren

Introduction

With the dramatic increase in life expectancy during the twentieth century, there has been a great need for availability of health services. As oral health influences psychological well-being and satisfaction in the general population, consideration must be given for individuals with intellectual disabilities. One of the most stressful transitions in life for any individual is coping with illness. It is common in later life to experience a variety of chronic illnesses, which may be more severe in persons with special needs such as those with intellectual disabilities. Identifying and meeting the health care needs of the population with intellectual disabilities needs to be addressed. The changes in our society in the twenty-first century challenge the health practitioners from all disciplines to be knowledgeable of special problems presented by this segment of the population. This chapter discusses common oral disease, which can start in early age and without intervention may complicate the well-being of the individual with intellectual disabilities for his/her entire life. Many oral diseases may have systemic implications; therefore, early diagnosis and treatment may prevent the progression of the medical problem.

Epidemiology

The epidemiology of dental diseases in this population is still not clear, although the oral health status of individuals with intellectual disabilities has generally been reported to be poorer than that of the general population. The dental treatment needs of persons with disabilities are usually greater than those of the population at large. Studies have reported that persons with intellectual disabilities present with poorer state of oral hygiene, various levels of periodontal disease, untreated dental caries and greater need for extraction than the general population (Shapira *et al.*, 1998).

Numerous studies have reported that de-institutionalization of individuals with intellectual disabilities has had a variable impact on their oral health status. Lower caries prevalence has been reported among institutionalized individuals with intellectual disabilities as compared with the non-institutionalized and healthy controls (Shapira *et al.*, 1998). Caries rates in the de-institutionalized population may become more similar to those of general populations, yet non-institutionalized individuals with intellectual disabilities may have also received more extractions and fewer restorations, and exhibit more periodontal disease (Nowak, 1984; Pieper *et al.*, 1986). Data is limited on the prevalence of oral disease in the growing population of aging adults with disabilities who live in the community. Several surveys provide general, rather than disability-specific, data.

In the US, a study of 2218 non-institutionalized individuals with intellectual disabilities aged 16 years and older reported that the missing (M) rates were higher than either the decayed (D) or filled (F) rates from the teeth (DMF-T). Individuals with various handicapping conditions were more likely to have teeth extracted than to have teeth restored (Nowak, 1984). Pieper *et al.* (1986) examined a group of 199 non-institutionalized German individuals aged 17–64 years that were diagnosed as 'mentally sub-normal'. The DMF-T values ranged from 17.4 in the 17–24 year-old age group to 26.9 in the 55–64 year-old age group. In all age groups, the F-T component was less than 20% as tooth loss increased rapidly with age, possibly due to high prevalence of periodontal disease. In another study assessing the dental needs of 194 institutionalized Irish individuals, age range 21–50, the DMF-T indicated the greatest treatment need as extractions (Holland & O'Mullane, 1986).

At present, an increasing number of persons with disabilities still have several oral needs unmet due to lack of access to trained professionals providing dental care to this segment of the population. Holland and O'Mullane (1986) pointed out that providing dental care for persons with disabling conditions can be very difficult. Proper diagnosis and treatment of oral disease may be prevented by incomplete clinical and radiographic information due to uncooperative behavior. In many cases, dental treatment must be provided under general anesthesia. With the use of general anesthesia, it is possible to provide the necessary preventive, restorative and surgical treatment in one appointment.

Intellectual disabilities and edentulism

The prevalence of edentulism (absent teeth) in the healthy population is declining in most industrialized countries (Ainamo & Osterberg, 1992; Chembara, 1993). It has been documented that loss of teeth is closely associated with an individual's socioeconomic status. Patients with low economic status have significantly fewer teeth in an older age. Adults with intellectual disabilities generally belong to a lower socioeconomic status, which may affect the treatment decision in regard to keeping or extracting their teeth. For example, in the US during the 1990s, about half (51%) of the less educated were dentate, compared to a little more than a quarter (29%) of the more highly educated population.

The residual alveolar ridge continues to resorb for several decades following the extraction of teeth, yet elders rarely seek treatment for their denture problems possibly because many have been dissatisfied with previous treatment. When they do complain, they usually mention an uncomfortable or loose denture and flat residual ridges, and consequently they frequently experience difficulty in chewing hard food. Elderly individuals usually adapt poorly to new dentures, and this probably can explain why patients seldom return to have an old but familiar denture replaced.

Several factors may influence denture comfort. The problems most often encountered in an elderly edentulous mouth are stomatitis and other inflammatory responses to defective or unhygienic dentures. This can obviously make dentures very uncomfortable to wear. As many adults with intellectual disabilities have a problem communicating to their doctor, it is important to have frequent evaluations even though they have no teeth remaining. This is to evaluate the edentulous area in the oral mucosa and the denture fit to ensure the comfort level for the patient. Saliva flow is important for removing plaque; it also acts as a lubricant and a chemical buffer for the comfort and function of the mouth.

Disturbance to the quality or quantity of saliva is especially difficult for complete denture wearers because of the central role of saliva in retaining and stabilizing dentures. When the flow of saliva is disturbed, food may have a metallic or salty taste and sensitivity to bitter and sour food can increase, but a reduced sensitivity to sweet taste can generate an unhealthy craving for sugar. As we age we have a tendency to chew slowly, and this could possibly be explained by the decrease in muscle tone by as much as 20 to 25% in old age.

Nutrition and dentures

The role of dentition and mastication in food selection is complex, but it seems that poorly fitting dentures predispose patients to a soft diet, high in fermented carbohydrates.

Prevention and treatment

Prosthodontic treatment of an edentulous patient requires an accurate diagnosis of systemic and local problems before any attention is paid to the fabrication of the prosthesis. Systemic problems, including psychological distress, as well as physiological disturbances are complicated and very frequently accompanied by an inappropriate use of prescribed medications. Local inflammation of the alveolar mucosa caused by unhygienic and structurally defective dentures is corrected relatively easily by relining and repairing the dentures. Subsequently, the mucosal inflammation can be resolved by improving oral and denture hygiene. New dentures are not accepted easily by older patients and whenever possible it is recommended to modify the existing dentures. It is important that the carer of the individual is well educated in denture hygiene to properly assist with the care.

Common oral diseases in adults with intellectual disabilities

Presently, there are a limited number of publications available regarding specific oral diseases in adults with intellectual disabilities. In particular, there is a scarcity of published reports regarding elderly persons with intellectual disabilities, although it is expected that this population may have even higher treatment needs and prevalence of oral diseases compared to a general geriatric population. In this section, we will present a short etiology and discuss prevention and management of the common oral diseases in patients with intellectual disabilities.

Dental caries

Dental caries can be categorized as two types: coronal caries (caries of the crown part of the tooth) and root caries (caries of the root part below the crown). Coronal caries is prevalent in younger individuals but seems to decline in older adults. Virtually all cross-sectional surveys have demonstrated an increased prevalence of root caries in advanced age. The prevalence rates for root caries, including fillings, range from 3 to 14% for people of 20–29 years of age, but from 38 to 70% for those 60 years of age and older (Katz *et al.*, 1982).

Etiology

It has been conclusively demonstrated that microorganisms are required for the initiation and progression of coronal dental caries. The bacteria most commonly implicated are *streptococcus mutans* (Nikiforuk, 1985). In regard to root caries, it has been proposed that another microflora may be involved (Jordan & Hammond, 1972). It has been suggested that the root lesion's microflora probably changes with the state of the lesion or the state of the development of the lesion (Bowden, 1990). For instance, *streptococcus mutans* has been recovered predominantly from initial lesions (similar to enamel caries), while *lactobacillus* microorganisms are associated with advanced lesions. It is presently accepted that dental caries is a chronic disease. It progresses from the surface of the tooth toward the pulp and destruction is caused primarily through the decalcification of mineralized tissues.

The caries process depends on three essential factors: the tooth and its environment, microorganisms and diet. Many secondary factors associated with a host (age, sex, saliva, immune response and oral hygiene), the agent (type, number and variance of the micro-organism), or substrate (cariogenic potential of foods and beverages), may affect the rate of progression of dental caries. Dietary factors consume an important component of developing caries lesions through decalcification. Root caries in humans appears to be enhanced by dietary sugars. The prevalence of both coronal and root caries coincide with the daily intake of sugar, especially when taken frequently between meals (Gustafsson *et al.*, 1953).

The rate of formation of caries lesion or cavity is the function of:

(1) The frequency of eating sugar or carbohydrate snacks between meals and the resulting lowering of the pH.
(2) The availability of fluoride ion to counteract the process through remineralization.
(3) The quality and frequency of oral hygiene of the individual, especially in relation to the use of fluoride toothpaste and mouth rinses.
(4) The flow and quality of saliva to remove and neutralize acids.

Saliva production can be reduced by salivary gland disease or the use of certain medications (see the section later in this chapter on the interrelationship between oral disease and systemic disease). The lack of saliva can increase the number of bacteria and the formation of plaque on teeth and can prolong the damaging effect of a low pH (Nikiforuk, 1985).

Prevention and treatment

The dentist should evaluate the patient and see if they are at high risk for development of coronal or root caries. The patient and carer should be advised regarding diet, especially the between-meals diet, and the effects that diet can have on caries development. Tooth brushing and flossing should obviously be advocated but the preventive effect is limited as the plaque is only temporarily removed. In adults with intellectual disabilities, these procedures are often performed by the carer. With regard to chemical plaque control, the most commonly recommended means is chlorhexidine gluconate rinse. It has been reported that, in an institutionalized elderly population, rinsing with 0.2% chlorhexidine resulted in a significant reduction of plaque (Yanover *et al.*, 1988).

The beneficial effect of fluoride in reducing root caries progress has been clearly demonstrated for life-long residents of a fluoridated community (Burt *et al.*, 1986). In addition, a topical fluoride preparation can be used in caries treatment for adults. The degree of remineralization, however, depends on the severity of the lesion and its location (Schupbach *et al.*, 1990). These fluoride therapies include daily topical fluoride at home, rinsing with 0.05% of sodium fluoride solution, or applying 1.1% sodium fluoride gel. With regard to patients with medication-induced reduction of salivary flow, the dental professional should discuss possible alternatives or adjustments to the responsible medications with the physician and others in the health care team to improve the patient's saliva flow. The health care team should address the significance of diet and reduced salivary flow in the caries process and the impact that these factors can have. In cases where the dental diseases cannot be reversed or prevented, the dentist must place a restoration in the cavity developed by the caries progression.

Periodontal disease

Periodontal disease (disease of the gums and supporting bone) is any disease of the periodontium (the tissue around and supporting the teeth). The most common type of periodontal disease is chronic gingivitis (inflammation of the gums) and periodontitis (inflammation of the membranes around the teeth and loss of the bone holding the teeth) (Youngson, 1992). The reasons for the progression from gingivitis to periodontitis remain unclear but may reflect aberrations of host cells responsive to plaque infection, or may represent colonization or infection by highly pathogenic plaque bacteria (Suzuki *et al.*, 1991).

Etiology

Chronic adult periodontitis usually occurs in adults over 35 years of age. This form of periodontitis is directly related to the accumulation of the tooth-associated materials plaque and calculus. The rate of pathogenesis of chronic adult periodontitis commonly takes years or even decades to progress (Suzuki *et al.*, 1991). Periodontal disease in adults does not appear to be a specific disease but instead is the result of a chronic adult periodontitis. Although age-related changes in the periodontium of older adults have been documented, these changes do not appear to be the cause of periodontal disease in this population (Page & Schroder, 1982). The association of systemic diseases with periodontal disease and relative risks is discussed in a separate section. These systemic problems include cardiovascular and cerebrovascular disease, respiratory problems and diabetes. Generally, periodontal disease in adults is not a quickly progressive disease. The onset of adult periodontal disease often occurs in young to middle adulthood, and by older adulthood periodontal disease represents a long-standing disease. Studies indicate that advanced periodontal disease is less prevalent in the elderly than moderate periodontal disease (Hunt *et al.*, 1990).

Prevention and treatment

The approach of periodontal disease treatment in older adults differs from that of younger adults. Several factors must be considered during treatment planning for adult patients.

Depending on the nature of the periodontal defects, surgical periodontal therapy may be indicated in patients. The patients responding best to surgical intervention are those who are able to maintain the surgical results through meticulous oral hygiene practice. Those individuals who are frail or medically compromised can often be managed by aggressive, non-surgical therapy including meticulous oral hygiene, scaling and root planning, and closed curettage. Recall appointments may be scheduled more frequently: every two to three months rather than the standard procedure of every six months. For successful outcomes of periodontal disease treatment, daily oral hygiene is important.

Adults with intellectual disabilities commonly need the assistance of a carer when performing daily oral hygiene. Electric toothbrushes are available to assist those adults having difficulty in performing the mechanical cleaning with a regular brush. These devices can also assist the carer in providing more appropriate oral hygiene. If the adults reside in a congregate care setting, it is important to make sure that the staff receive proper training to assist with oral hygiene.

There are anti-plaque agents such as chlorhexidine gluconate that can assist with improving oral hygiene and gingival health. In trials that use the experimental gingivitis model, 0.2% chlorhexidine gluconate used twice daily prevented the accumulation of plaque and calculus (Loe & Schiott, 1970). Side effects of chlorhexidine include increased calculus build-up, staining of teeth and bitter taste.

Oral infectious diseases

Herpes zoster

Etiology

Herpes zoster (shingles) is an extremely painful and incapacitating disease. Evidence indicates that the signs and symptoms are caused by a reactivation of the latent varicella-zoster (chicken pox) virus acquired during a previous attack of chicken pox. The disease is most common in older adults (over 45 years of age), causing fever, general malaise, and pain and tenderness along the course of involved sensory nerves. Within a few days there is a linear papular eruption of the skin or mucosa that is supplied by the infected nerves. The triggering factors in the onset of herpes zoster include trauma and immunosuppressive therapy. When neither of the above factors is evident, it is often the result of the loss of immune vigor because of advanced age. It has been proposed that a severe insult to the localized vascular supply directly affected by herpes zoster infection can result in necrosis of the alveolar bone (Wright *et al.*, 1983).

Prevention and treatment

At present we can only provide palliative care for this problem while the disease is running its course. Mouth rinses with a 2% lidocaine viscous solution are beneficial and facilitate eating of soft foods, drinking and oral hygiene. The antiviral agent acyclovir may also be of some benefit.

Candiadiasis

Candiadiasis is also known as thrush. Candiadiasis is caused by the fungus of the genus Candida. This infection affects the warm, moist areas of the body such as the mouth. It is the most common oral mycotic infection. Estimates indicate a disease frequency of 10% of older adults who are debilitated and live in institutions. In individuals with dentures, this condition can be present in deep folds of the mucosa of the lips secondary to overclosure. In addition, it may be present in the hard palatal mucosa, predominately under maxillary dentures (Eyre & Nally (1971); Pindborg 1985).

The incidence of candidiasis has increased remarkably since the widespread use of antibiotics, which upset the normal oral environment and destroy bacteria that apparently inhibit the growth of Candida albicans. The disease is also common in patients who use immuno-suppressant drugs or large doses of corticosteroids. Acute pseudo-membranous candidiasis is the most common form of the disease and may occur at any age, although the debilitated, chronically ill and elderly are especially at risk. Oral lesions are characterized by the appearance of soft, white, slightly raised plaques on the buccal mucosa and tongue. The palate, gingiva or floor of the mouth may also be involved. Chronic atrophic candidiasis is considered synonymous with denture sore mouth. Although there is no absolute age correlation with atrophic candidiasis, most persons affected are over the age of 55 (Budtz-Jorgensen, 1970).

Etiology

In addition to age, contributing factors include denture trauma, continuing denture wear, poor oral hygiene habits, poor denture cleaning and possibly diet.

Prevention and treatment

This condition can be treated simply with topical applications of nystatin. In denture-related disease, nystatin cream can be used on the affected tissue and in the denture itself to provide prolonged contact and to eliminate the organism from the denture material. It is recommended that patients with removable dentures should be on regular recalls, approximately every six months, to evaluate the denture's cleanliness and remind both the patient and carer of the importance of a daily thorough cleaning and that the denture should be removed at night.

Oral facial tumors

No orofacial tumors are particular to adults with intellectual disabilities, but many tumors can be more often missed in this population as compared to the general population.

Benign tumors

Keratodontoma

Keratodontoma is a benign epithelial (skin) lesion that closely resembles epidermoid carcinoma. It occurs twice as frequently in men than in women, the majority of cases occurring between 50 and 70 years of age. About 90% of these tumors occur on the exposed skin, most often on the cheeks, nose and dorsum of the head.

Prevention and treatment

Most of the lesions disappear or regress by themselves, although some have persisted for as long as two years. Since spontaneous regression does not occur in every case, surgical incision is the usual treatment.

Fibrous hyperplasia

Fibrous hyperplasia (inflammatory fibrous hyperplasia epulis fissuratum, redundant tissue), although not a tumor in the usual sense of the word, is one of the most common tissue reactions to ill-fitting dentures. It usually occurs along the denture border, but it may be seen on the gingival buccal mucosa, on the angle of the mouth or wherever chronic irritation of any type exists.

Prevention and treatment

Most commonly, the denture may be relined and a surgical procedure performed to remove the excess tissue.

Premalignant lesions

Leukoplakia

Leukoplakia is a white patch on the mucosa that cannot be identified as a diagnosable entity such as lichen planus, white sponge nevus, candidiasis or chemical burns. What is important here is the fact that oral leukoplakia is a disease occurring primarily in the 50–80 year-old age group. Although the site as well as the incidence varies throughout the world, Waldron and Shaffer (1975) found that the greatest number (25%) of cases of leukoplakia occurred on the mandibular alveolar ridge, gingiva or muccobuccal fold. The next most common site was the buccal mucosa at 22%. Clinically, patches of leukoplakia vary from a thick, non-palpable, faintly translucent white area to thick, fissured, pappillomatous, indurated lesions. Some leukoplakia lesions undergo malignant transformations to epidermoid carcinoma; biopsy is required for definitive diagnosis.

Malignant lesions

The incidence of oral cancer in the US is about 20 per 100 000 for men and 5 per 100 000 for women; 32% were in the 70 year-old group, with 90% ranging from 40 to 99 years of age. All oral primary malignancies account for 4% of new cancers identified. Each year oral cancer is responsible for 2% of all cancer-related deaths in males and 1% of cancer-related deaths in females. The male to female ratio has changed from it being predominantly a male disease to a male to female ratio of 2:1 (Silverberg & Lubera, 1987). The five-year survival rate recorded for adults of European heritage was 53% during the years 1977 to 1983.

Basal cell and epidermoid carcinoma

Basal cell carcinoma is probably the most common type of carcinoma in humans; 85% of the cases of basal cell carcinoma occur in the head and neck. In a study of 9000 cases, Colton (1961) found the incidence for metastasis to be only 0.1%, indicating the benign character of this tumor. Epidermoid carcinoma (squamous cell carcinoma) is the most common malignant neoplasm in the oral cavity. Although it may occur anywhere in the mouth, some sites are more frequent than others. Clinically, it may be indistinguishable from simple hyperkeratosis, epithelial dysplasia or carcinoma in-situ. It can appear white as a result of hyperkatosis or epithelial thickening, red as a result of decreased maturation of the squamous cells, or both red and white. The use of alcohol and both combustible and smokeless tobacco products has been linked to an increased risk of developing squamous cell carcinoma (Winn *et al.*, 1981).

Prevention and treatment

During their recall appointments it is very important that all patients receive a complete head, neck and soft tissue examination to rule out the possibility of any mucosal changes. If there is any doubt regarding any lesions, a biopsy should be performed. The management of epidermiod carcinoma includes radical excision, radiation and chemotherapy. Prevention includes educating patients and carers about the risks involved with smoking, smokeless tobacco and alcohol consumption, and encouraging enrollment in smoking cessation programs.

Other oral problems

Aphthous ulcer

Recurrent aphthous ulcer (canker sore) is a non-traumatic ulcer that affects the mucus membranes. The incidence has been reported to be 20–60% depending on the population studied (Axell & Henricsson, 1985). The most common form of recurrent aphthous ulcer is the minor aphthous ulcer, which appears on the vestibular mucosa, buccal mucosa, tongue, soft palate, fauces and floor of the mouth.

Etiology

Although the causes of aphthous ulcer are unknown, factors such as alteration of the immune system, microbial balance, nutrition, hormonal alteration, stress, trauma and food allergies have been reported. An aphthous ulcer can be a single, painful, oval ulcer covered with yellow fibrinase membrane and surrounded by an erythematous hollow. When the lateral and ventral surface of the tongue are affected, the pain tends to be out of proportion to the size of the lesion and it can last for seven to ten days. Tingling or burning occurs before the appearance of the lesion; when the lesions are present there may be pain, especially when eating or drinking.

Prevention and treatment

Corticosteroids offer the best chance of disease containment. In severely affected patients systemic steroids may be used, but in patients with mild to moderate disease topical therapy is justified. Dietary changes have been suggested to avoid reoccurrence of aphthous ulcer. The use of elimination diet in the treatment of recurrent aphthous ulcerations of the oral cavity has been advocated (Hay & Reade, 1984; Wilson, 1980).

Xerostomia (salivary gland dysfunction)

Salivary gland dysfunction results in xerostomia, which is often found in older adults. This condition consists of dryness of the mouth as a result of decreased salivary flow.

Etiology

Xerostomia can result from medication use (at least 400 prescribed medications can cause xerostomia as a side effect, especially when multiple medications are used). Other causes include:

- Radiation therapy for head or neck tumors.
- Chemotheraputic agents used for cancer and immune suppressant therapy.
- Physiological disorder (such as fibrosis of the parotid gland subsequent to mumps; blockage of the salivary duct).
- Primary or secondary Sjögren's syndrome – an autoimmune process that causes xerostomia as a result of lymphocytic replacement of salivary glands.

Prevention and treatment

If the xerostomia is medication induced, the older adult's physician should be consulted regarding the possibility of changing the medication or dosage. In cases of burning sensation, lidocaine provides temporary relief from pain. In addition to xerostomia, possible causes of burning mouth syndrome include fungi, bacterial infections, nutritional deficiencies, hormonal imbalances and mechanical trauma. Empirical treatment is frequently the approach that most clinicians use for patients with this problem. Anti-fungal agents, solutions containing tetracycline-nystatin-diphenhydramine hydrochloride (Benadryl) or topical steroids are some of the most commonly used medications. Frequent rinsing with water or artificial saliva should be encouraged in these patients.

Gingival hyperplasia

Etiology

Some therapeutic agents and medicaments may lead to pathological changes in the periodontal tissue, especially the gingiva, causing gingival overgrowth. Such agents are classified as:

- Topically applied compounds with direct, local, adverse affects to periodontal tissue.
- Heavy metals.
- Systemic medications with periodontal side effects.

Particular drugs which can cause significant problems are:

Phenytoin. Phenytoin has been the drug of choice for grand mal epilepsy for more than 50 years. This is marketed under the trade name Dilantin and is used by a large number of adults with intellectual disabilities. Overgrowth of the gingiva is one of the most common and troublesome side effects of phenytoin. Gingival overgrowth occurs in about half of all individuals who ingest phenytoin on a chronic regimen as their sole anti-epileptic medication. However, the prevalence of gingival overgrowth is much higher when phenytoin is taken in combination with other epileptic agents and when the oral hygiene is poor. It should be noted that teenagers and young adults up to about 30 years of age are affected more frequently than elderly individuals. Gingival overgrowth often becomes clinically apparent during the first six to nine months of therapy as the interdental papilla overgrow and extrude, forming firm, mobile, triangular tissue masses (Hassell *et al.*, 1978).

Cyclosporine. Cyclosporine has been used in the US since 1984 for prevention of rejection phenomena following organ or bone marrow transplantation. Accumulation of excess connective tissue, including gingival overgrowth, is a major adverse effect of long-term cyclosporine therapy (Rateitschak-Pluss *et al.*, 1983). The gingival lesions are often clinically indistinguishable from those developed by phenytoin. With increased life expectancy of adults with intellectual disabilities, we may also see an increase of cyclosporine use in this population due to organ transplantation.

Nifedipine. Nifedipine has been used widely since 1978 for the treatment of angina pectoris and post-myocardial syndrome. It has been reported that nifedipine induces gingival overgrowth in persons with heart disease (Lucas *et al.*, 1985). Gingival lesions that are elicited by nifedipine in humans are clinically similar to those elicited by phenytoin and cyclosporine (Hassell, 1990).

Prevention and treatment

Treatment of gingival enlargement is often necessary if it results in gingival inflammation, dental caries, esthetic and speech effects, impaired function or discomfort. Esthetically objectionable gingival overgrowth may be effectively treated by one or more of the following strategies (Hutchens, 1981):

(1) Replacing the medication with an alternative drug. Not uncommonly, spontaneous regression of excess tissue may occur within 12 months after such replacement if the patient's oral hygiene is good.
(2) Conservative periodontal therapy, including frequent professional prophylaxis and a rigorous home care regimen. This will reduce the inflammatory components of the enlargement and may reduce the need for surgical treatment. Effective oral hygiene will also delay or prevent the lesion's reoccurrence. Daily rinsing of chlorhexidine can also be helpful.
(3) Surgical elimination of redundant tissue by means of a scalpel or electrosurgery. This is a relatively straightforward gingivectomy procedure and can be performed at dental premises with local anesthesia. Reoccurrence of overgrowth should be expected in one to two years. If oral hygiene is inadequate, regrowth can occur extremely quickly.

Interrelationships between oral diseases and systemic diseases

With the rapid advancement of medical science, the life expectancy of individuals with intellectual disabilities has increased dramatically over the last century. With increased longevity, the oral health problems existing in the aging population present an increasing challenge to professionals in providing both oral and general health care. Common oral diseases, especially chronic periodontal infections and dental caries, are more prevalent in adults with intellectual disabilities than in the general population. The higher prevalence of oral diseases is due to underlying congenital anomalies, the inability to perform personal prevention practices, and the high cost of professional care. Because this population usually presents with multiple and complex medical problems, oral diseases have not been considered conditions of priority. However, oral diseases have complex interrelationships with many systemic diseases commonly seen in aging individuals with intellectual disabilities. Chronic oral infections, usually in the form of periodontitis (gum disease), have been associated with cardiovascular disease, cerebrovascular disease, diabetes and other systemic disorders; accordingly, health care professionals are becoming increasingly aware of the importance of oral health as an integral component of general health. It is therefore imperative for health care professionals to have adequate knowledge about the interrelationships between common oral diseases and systemic diseases.

Periodontal infection and cardiovascular and cerebrovascular diseases

Periodontitis is a chronic bacterial infection of tooth-supporting (periodontal) tissues, as described previously. It is especially common in adults with Down syndrome. Periodontal pathogens are also thought to affect cardiovascular and cerebrovascular diseases through several mechanisms (Beck *et al.*, 1999). Bacteria from infected periodontal tissue may directly infect arterial vessel walls and cause local vascular inflammation and injury, and they may be important factors in the development of athrosclerosis, especially in the coronary artery and the carotid artery. A recent study found that *Porphyromonas gingivalis*, a potent periodontal pathogen, existed in 42% of athrosclerotic plaques removed from carotid arteries (Chiu, 1999). *P. gingivalis* can actively invade human endothelial cells and activate latent host metalloproteinases which may contribute to plaque rupture and in turn cause ischemic heart disease and stroke. *Streptococcus sanguis*, another common oral bacteria, was also found in 12% of carotid plaques. The presence of *P. gingivalis* and *S. sanguis* in athrosclerotic plaques suggests that these bacteria may have entered the bloodstream from infected oral tissues.

Both *P. gingivalis* and *S. sanguis* have the potential to induce platelet aggregation (Herzberg *et al.*, 1994). A protein structure on the surface of common strains of these bacteria resembles the platelet-interactive regions of collagen molecules. Exposure of this collagen-like structure to flowing blood may trigger platelet clotting and contribute to microthrombosis during the development of athrosclerotic plaques. Advanced periodontal infection, like chronic infections in other parts of the body, may also cause a hypercoagulable state by increased concentrations of plasma fibrinogen, Factor VIII complex, betathromboglobin and decreased concentrations of antithrombin III (Valtonen, 1999). Changes in the coagulation system may be an important factor in the development of thrombosis and subsequent ischemic heart disease and stroke.

The association between periodontal disease and cardiovascular and cerebrovascular diseases is more than theoretical and has been confirmed in many prospective clinical studies. After adjusting for age, smoking and blood pressure, it was found that males with periodontal disease were 1.5 times more likely to develop coronary heart disease over a 25-year period and were 1.9 times more likely to develop fatal coronary heart disease than control subjects (Beck *et al.*, 1996). In the 14 year follow-up of 9670 people from the first National Health and Nutrition Examination Survey, it was found that there was a 25% increased risk of cardiovascular disease in individuals with periodontitis as compared with those with minimal periodontal disease (DeStefano *et al.*, 1993). In the 21 year follow-up of the same group of people, periodontitis was found to be a significant risk factor for ischemic cerebrovascular disease. Compared with no periodontal disease, the relative risks for incident non-hemorrhagic stroke were 1.24 for gingivitis and 2.11 for periodontitis (Wu *et al.*, 2000).

Periodontal infection and diabetes

Both Type I and Type II diabetes are associated with increased occurrence and progression of periodontitis. Numerous studies have consistently reported increased prevalence, extent and severity of periodontal disease in patients with either type of diabetes. Population-based studies provided epidemiologic estimates of the association of diabetes and signs of periodontitis with odds ratios between 1.9 and 2.3 (Grossi *et al.*, 1994). There are several possible mechanisms to explain why adults with diabetes are more susceptible to periodontal infection (Oliver & Tervonen, 1994). These include vascular changes in periodontal tissue, diminished host immune response, and altered microflora in periodontal pockets. There is also evidence to show that a two-way connection exists between diabetes and periodontitis: adults with diabetes are more susceptible to periodontitis, and periodontal disease decreases the efficiency of glycemic control through interference with the action of insulin (Grossi & Genco, 1998).

Periodontal infection and respiratory disease

Respiratory infection has recently been associated with poor oral health, especially periodontal disease (Hayes *et al.*, 1998; Scannapieco *et al.*, 1998). Respiratory pathogens are present in dental plaques of patients with very poor oral hygiene. Respiratory infection in these patients is likely to be caused by aspiration of oropharyngeal fluids containing these pathogenic microorganisms, which colonize the lower respiratory tract and predispose the patients to the development of pneumonia. Various anaerobic bacteria, most of which are known pathogens for periodontitis, have been cultured from infected lung fluids, including *P. gingivalis*, *Bacteroids oralis*, *Eikenella corrodens*, *Fusobacterium nucleatum*, *Actinobacillus actinomycetemcomitans*, *Clostridum* and *Actinomyces* (Scannapieco, 1999). Laboratory animal studies also showed that P. *gingivalis* could cause marked inflammation when seeded into the lungs. Other than direct infection, oral bacteria may alter the host defense mechanism and render the patient more susceptible to bacterial infection (Scannapieco *et al.*, 1998). Periodontal disease-associated enzymes in saliva may alter the mucosal surface of the respiratory tract to promote adhesion and colonization by pathogenic microorganisms. Cytokines originated from periodontal tissue may also alter the respiratory epithelium to facilitate the infection by respiratory pathogens (Scannapieco, 1999).

Periodontal bone loss and osteoporosis

One of the prominent signs of periodontitis is the gradual loss of alveolar bone support of tooth with the progression of disease. Such progressive bone loss will lead to increased mobility of teeth and may result in eventual loss of teeth. Osteoporosis has long been suspected as a risk factor for periodontal bone loss. Periodontal disease, as indicated by alveolar bone loss, was found to be significantly related to the skeletal bone mineral density in the femur (Wactawski-Wende *et al.*, 1996). After adjusting for age, smoking, body mass index, estrogen use and years after menopause, it was concluded that osteopenia is related to alveolar bone height and tooth loss in post-menopausal women. Periodontal attachment loss, a pivotal sign of periodontitis, was also related with osteoporosis in older female patients (von Wowern *et al.*, 1994). It is clear that osteoporosis is also a factor influencing oral health, especially in women.

Coordination of oral care

Adults with intellectual disabilities may view the dental premises as a threatening environment (harboring needles and possible painful treatment) and react initially with agitation and restlessness. Conversely, they may withdraw and refuse to cooperate. Such patients may become more cooperative if they are allowed to be accompanied by a family member or staff member from a group home or other residential setting. Should such behavioral interventions fail, premedication with a benzodazepine, such as lorazepam 0.5 mg orally 1 hour prior to a dental visit, is reasonable (Messinger-Rapport & Rapport, 1997). It is helpful to have the adult accompanied at each visit by a carer who knows the patient well and brings a list of current medications, previous dental records, or a written summary of the adult's past medical, surgical and developmental history (Santos-Teachout *et al.*, 2000).

Preventive care and coordination of services

As in the general population, middle-aged and elderly persons with intellectual disabilities are more likely than younger persons to have chronic health problems such as arthritis, high blood pressure and heart disease. In addition to these health care problems, at times a greater number of these adults experience depression and other mental disorders than seen in the general population (Jenkins et al., 1993). Preventive interventions should play an important role in the health plan for this population, as routine dental care is difficult in many patients because of poor cooperation, especially for invasive procedures. It may be possible to accomplish yearly dental examinations, but proper prophylaxis and restoration may only be possible with conscious sedation or under general anesthesia. Adults who have Down syndrome may require appropriate antimicrobial prophylaxis when receiving dental care due to a higher incidence of heart murmurs in that population (Dajani et al., 1997). Echocardiogram should be considered as part of the routine physical examination for this population.

Coordination with other specialties may be accomplished when patients are scheduled for dental treatment under general anesthesia, as well as other procedures such as pelvic examinations with Pap tests and endometrial biopsy, endoscopic procedures in patient with dyspepsia, or cytoscopy in patients with hematuria or recurrent urinary tract infections. Coordinating the rotation of disciplines such as dentistry, gynecology and others through the operating room is time-consuming and best accomplished when planned in advance.

Conclusion

At present limited research is available regarding the prevalence, prevention and treatment of oral disease in elderly persons with intellectual disabilities. Frequent (minimally biannual) dental visits for intra and extra oral examinations and prophylaxis are strongly advised. More frequent dental visits may be necessary as determined by the patients' oral health status and other risk factors. Adults who are edentulous still need to be evaluated on a regular basis to assure a healthy oral mucosa and well-fitting and comfortable dentures. Oral diseases should not be looked on as problems limited to the oral cavity. Many oral diseases have complex interrelationships with systemic diseases commonly seen in aging individuals with intellectual disabilities. Oral diseases, especially chronic infections, are gradually being recognized as risk factors for many life-threatening disorders. Therefore, eradication of oral diseases and improvement of oral health should be considered as important strategies to improve the overall health of aging individuals with intellectual disabilities. Persons with intellectual disabilities and complicated medical or behavioral needs require a coordinated multidisciplinary team approach.

Acknowledgment

The authors would like to acknowledge the contributions and assistance of Terence Roach.

References

Ainamo, A. & Osterberg, T. (1992) Changing demographics in oral diseases and treatment needs in the Scandinavian population of old people. *International Dental Journal*, **42**, 311–312.

Axell, T. & Henricsson, V. (1985) The occurrence of recurrent aphthous ulcers in an adult Swedish population. *Acta Odontologica Scandinavica*, **43**, 121–125.

Beck, J., Garcia, R., Heiss, G., Vokonas, P.S. & Offenbacher, S. (1996) Periodontal disease and cardiovascular disease. *Journal of Periodontol Research*, **67**, 1123–1137.

Beck, J.D., Pankow, J., Tyroler, H.A. & Offenbacher, S. (1999) Dental infections and atherosclerosis. *American Heart Journal*, **138**, S528–533.

Bowden, G.H. (1990) Microbiology of root surface caries in humans. *Journal of Dental Research*, **69**, 1205–1210.

Budtz-Jorgensen, E. (1970) Denture stomatitis. 3. Histopathology of trauma- and candida-induced inflammatory lesions of the palatal mucosa. *Acta Odontologica Scandinavica*, **28**, 551–579.

Burt, B.A., Ismail, A.I. & Eklund, S.A. (1986) Root caries in an optimally fluoridated and a high-fluoride community. *Journal of Dental Research*, **65**, 1154–1158.

Chembara (1993) *National Oral Health Survey Australia 1987–1988*. Australian Department of Health, Housing, Local Government and Community Services.

Chiu, B. (1999) Multiple infections in carotid atherosclerotic plaques. *American Heart Journal*, **138**, S534–536.

Colton, R.S. (1961) Metastasizing basal cell carcinoma. *Cancer*, **14**, 1036.

Dajani, A.S., Taubert, K.A., Wilson, W., Bolger, A.F., Bayer, A., Ferrieri, P., Gewitz, M.H., Shulman, S.T., Nouri, S., Newburger, J.W., Hutto, C., Pallasch, T.J., Gage, T.W., Levison, M.E., Peter, G. & Zuccaro, G., Jr. (1997) Prevention of bacterial endocarditis: recommendations by the American Heart Association. *Journal of The American Dental Association*, **128**, 1142–1151.

DeStefano, F., Anda, R.F., Kahn, H.S., Williamson, D.F. & Russell, C.M. (1993) Dental disease and risk of coronary heart disease and mortality. *British Medical Journal*, **30**, 688–691.

Eyre, J. & Nally, F.F. (1971) Oral candidosis and carcinoma. *British Journal of Dermatology*, **85**, 73–75.

Grossi, S.G. & Genco, R.J. (1998) Periodontal disease and diabetes mellitus: a two-way relationship. *Annals of Periodontology*, **3**, 51–61.

Grossi, S.G., Zambon, J.J., Ho, A.W., Koch, G., Dunford, R.G., Machtei, E.E., Norderyd, O.M. & Genco, R.J. (1994) Assessment of risk for periodontal disease. I. Risk indicators for attachment loss. *Journal of Periodontology*, **65**, 260–267.

Gustafsson, B.E., Quensel, C.E., Lanke, L.S., Lundqvist, C., Grahnén, H., Bonow, B.E. & Krasse, B. (1953) Vipeholm dental caries study: the effect of different levels of carbohydrate intake on caries activity in 436 individuals observed for five years. *Acta Odontologica Scandinavica*, **11**, 232–364.

Hassell, T.M. (1990) Local and systemic action of drugs and other chemical agents on periodontal tissues. In: *Contemporary Periodontics* (eds R. Genco, H.M. Goldman & W. Cohen). Mosby, St. Louis.

Hassell, T.M., Page, R.C. & Lindhe, J. (1978) Histologic evidence for impaired growth control in diphenylhydantoin gingival overgrowth in man. *Archives of Oral Biology*, **23**, 381–384.

Hay, K.D. & Reade, P.C. (1984) The use of an elimination diet in the treatment of recurrent aphthous ulceration of the oral cavity. *Oral Surgery, Oral Medicine, Oral Pathology*, **57**, 504–507.

Hayes, C., Sparrow, D., Cohen, M., Vokonas, P.S. & Garcia, R.I. (1998) The association between alveolar bone loss and pulmonary function: the VA Dental Longitudinal Study. *Annals of Periodontology*, **3**, 257–261.

Herzberg, M.C., MacFarland, G.D., Liu, P. & Erikson, P.R. (1994) The platelet as an inflammatory cell in periodontal diseases: interaction with Porphyromonans gingivalis. In: *Molecular Pathogenesis of Periodontal Disease* (eds R. Genco, S. Hamada, T. Lehner, J. McGee & S. Mergenhagen) pp. 247–255. American Society for Microbiology, Washington DC.

Holland, T.J. & O'Mullane, D.M. (1986) Dental treatment needs in three institutions for the handicapped. *Community Dentistry and Oral Epidemiology*, **14**, 73–75.

Hunt, R.J., Levy, S.M. & Beck, J.D. (1990) The prevalence of periodontal attachment loss in an Iowa population aged 70 and older. *Journal of Public Health Dentistry*, **50**, 251–256.

Hutchens, L.H., Jr. (1981) Phenytoin gingival overgrowth: treatment. In: *Epilepsy and Oral Manifestation of Phenytoin Therapy* (ed. T Hassel). S. Karger, Basel, Switzerland.

Jenkins, E.L., Hildreth, B.L. & Hildreth, G. (1993) Elderly persons with mental retardation: an exceptional population with special needs. *International Journal of Aging and Human Development*, **37**, 69–80.

Jordan, H.V. & Hammond, B.F. (1972) Filamentous bacteria isolated from human root surface caries. *Archives of Oral Biology*, **17**, 1333–1342.

Katz, R.V., Hazen, S.P., Chilton, N.W. & Mumma, R.D., Jr. (1982) Prevalence and intraoral distribution of root caries in an adult population. *Caries Research*, **16**, 265–271.

Loe, H. & Schiott, C.R. (1970) The effect of mouth rinses and topical application of chlorexidine on the development of dental plaque and gingivitis in man. *Journal of Periodontal Research*, **5**, 79–83.

Lucas, R.M., Howell, L.P. & Wall, B.A. (1985) Nifedipine-induced gingival hyperplasia. A histochemical and ultrastructural study. *Journal of Periodontology*, **56**, 211–215.

Messinger-Rapport, B.J. & Rapport, D.J. (1997) Primary care for the developmentally disabled adult. *Journal of General Internal Medicine*, **12**, 629–636.

Nikiforuk, G. (1985) *Understanding Dental Caries*. S. Karger, Basel, Switzerland.

Nowak, A.J. (1984) Dental disease in handicapped persons. *Specialist Care In Dentistry*, **4**, 66–69.

Oliver, R.C. & Tervonen, T. (1994) Diabetes – a risk factor for periodontitis in adults? *Journal of Periodontology*, **65**, 530–538.

Page, R.C. & Schroder, H. (1982) *Periodontitis in Man and Other Animals*. S. Karger, Basel, Switzerland.

Pieper, K., Dirks, B. & Kessler, P. (1986) Caries, oral hygiene and periodontal disease in handicapped adults. *Community Dentistry and Oral Epidemiology*, **14**, 28–30.

Pindborg, J.J. (1985) *Atlas of Diseases of the Oral Mucosa*. W.B. Saunders, Philadelphia.

Rateitschak-Pluss, E.M., Hefti, A., Lortscher, R. & Thiel, G. (1983) Initial observation that cyclosporin-A induces gingival enlargement in man. *Journal of Clinical Periodontology*, **10**, 237–246.

Santos-Teachout, R.R., Malmstrom, H., Moss, M.E. & Handelman, S.L. (2000) Oral health care. In: *Community Supports for Aging Adults with Lifelong Disabilities* (eds M.P. Janicki & E.F. Ansello) pp. 341–357. Brookes, Baltimore, MD.

Scannapieco, F.A. (1999) Role of oral bacteria in respiratory infection. *Journal of Periodontology*, **70**, 793–802.

Scannapieco, F.A., Papandonatos, G.D. & Dunford, R.G. (1998) Associations between oral conditions and respiratory disease in a national sample survey population. *Annals of Periodontology*, **3**, 251–256.

Schupbach, P., Guggenheim, B. & Lutz, F. (1990) Histopathology of root surface caries. *Journal of Dental Research*, **69**, 1195–1204.

Shapira, J., Efrat, J., Berkey, D. & Mann, J. (1998) Dental health profile of a population with mental retardation in Israel. *Specialist Care In Dentistry*, **18**, 149–155.

Silverberg, E. & Lubera, J. (1987) Cancer statistics, 1987. *A Cancer Journal for Clinicians*, **37**, 2–19.

Suzuki, J.B., Niessen, L.C. & Fedele, J.D. (1991) Periodontal disease in older adults. In: *Geriatric Dentistry: Aging and Oral Health* (eds A.S. Papas, L.C. Niessen & H.H. Chauncey), pp. 189–201. Mosby, St. Louis, MI.

Valtonen, V.V. (1999) Role of infections in atherosclerosis. *American Heart Journal*, **138**, S431–433.

von Wowern, N., Klausen, B. & Kollerup, G. (1994) Osteoporosis: a risk factor in periodontal disease. *Journal of Periodontology*, **65**, 1134–1138.

Wactawski-Wende, J., Grossi, S.G., Trevisan, M., Genco, R.J., Tezal, M., Dunford, R.G., Ho, A.W., Hausmann, E. & Hreshchyshyn, M.M. (1996) The role of osteopenia in oral bone loss and periodontal disease. *Journal of Periodontology*, **67**, 1076–1084.

Waldron, C.A. & Shafer, W.G. (1975) Leukoplakia revisited. A clinicopathologic study 3256 oral leukoplakias. *Cancer*, **36**, 1386–1392.

Wilson, C.W. (1980) Food sensitivities, taste changes, aphthous ulcers and atopic symptoms in allergic disease. *Annals of Allergy*, **44**, 302–307.

Winn, D.M., Blot, W.J., Shy, C.M., Pickle, L.W., Toledo, A. & Fraumeni, J.F., Jr. (1981) Snuff dipping and oral cancer among women in the southern United States. *New England Journal of Medicine*, **304**, 745–749.

Wright, W.E., Davis, M.L., Geffen, D.B., Martin, S.E., Nelson, M.J. & Straus, S.E. (1983) Alveolar bone necrosis and tooth loss. a rare complication associated with herpes zoster infection of the fifth cranial nerve. *Oral Surgery, Oral Medicine, Oral Pathology*, **56**, 39–46.

Wu, T., Trevisan, M., Genco, R.J., Dorn, J.P., Falkner, K.L. & Sempos, C.T. (2000) Periodontal disease and risk of cerebrovascular disease: the first national health and nutrition examination survey and its follow-up study. *Archives of Internal Medicine*, **160**, 2749–2755.

Yanover, L., Banting, D., Grainger, R. & Sandhu, H. (1988) Effect of a daily 0.2% chlorhexidine rinse on the oral health of an institutionalized elderly population. *Journal of the Canadian Dental Association*, **54**, 595–598.

Youngson, R. (1992) *Dictionary of Medicine*. Harper Collins, Glasgow.

10 Nutrition and Physical Health

Dawna Torres Mughal

Introduction

Food and nutrition are fundamental determinants of health. As such, they are an important part of health promotion, disease prevention and service provision for all, including individuals with intellectual disabilities. Good nutritional status can help maintain health and prolong productive lives. Health promotion should include regular nutrition screening to identify individuals who are at risk for malnutrition or who are malnourished, and refer them to appropriate services for assessment and intervention. Prevention and intervention strategies should include effective nutrition education that enables individuals and their carers to adopt healthful dietary practices. This education should be linked to food because people better understand nutrition and health messages communicated through food rather than through nutrients. Because culture determines people's food choices, the application of nutrition principles to dietary guidance should take into consideration the cultural context of the individuals' environment.

As there are no specific dietary guidelines for adults with intellectual disabilities, the concepts and principles in the guidelines for the general population and their relevance to the nutritional needs of individuals with intellectual disabilities in certain conditions will be discussed. This chapter focuses on the dietary guidelines and food guides, the macronutrients (protein, carbohydrate and lipids), energy, selected micronutrients (fat-soluble vitamins A, D, E and K; water-soluble vitamins ascorbate/vitamin C, folate and vitamin B_{12}; and the minerals calcium, iron and iodine), and fluid. The exclusion of the other nutrients and substances in food does not imply that they are less important to health. It should be emphasized that the guidelines are for almost all healthy people and that people with special health needs should be referred to qualified health professionals for individualized assessment and intervention.

Role of nutrition in health

Health throughout the life span is widely recognized as an important determinant of the quality of life. Health promotion and disease prevention strategies should begin with maternal and child health, minimize the risk factors for non-communicable diseases through the life course, and provide service for older adults. Food and nutrition are an important part of these strategies. This concept recognizes that other factors (genetics, cultural patterns, the status of women and social stability) also profoundly affect health (Davies, 1999) and that physical activity works with nutrition for better health outcomes.

Individuals with intellectual disabilities are a nutritionally vulnerable group. Feeding problems, poor oral health, drug-nutrient interactions, metabolic disorders, decreased mobility and altered growth patterns affect food intake and put these individuals at risk for malnutrition (ADA, 1997). Table 10.1 shows the nutrition problems that are often associated with select conditions often coincident with intellectual disabilities and that contribute to nutritional risk. As more people with intellectual disabilities live longer (Patja et al., 2000), they are likely to develop the same disabling chronic diseases which are prevalent in the general aging population. Superimposing the syndrome-specific morbidity and other concurrent illnesses on the age-related physiologic and physical changes magnifies the risk for malnutrition. Achieving and maintaining good nutritional health poses a challenge because people with intellectual disabilities have conditions that can interfere with eating a balanced diet and maintaining proper nutrition.

Food, health and culture

The adage that 'health is wealth' conveys the value of health as an individual and social goal. Another adage that 'you are what you eat' reflects recognition of the relationship between food and health. However, culture determines how a person defines health, recognizes illness and seeks treatment. It influences food and health beliefs and practices and the definition of 'good food' and 'bad food'. The cultural context, therefore, and the complex interaction of the individuals with their environment should be taken into consideration in translating nutrition science and dietary guidelines into what people should do or eat. They have implications for nutrition education that aims to facilitate desirable changes in dietary and other lifestyle behaviors. As Solomons has stated, 'although the *principles* of nutrition are universal, its *prescription* may need regional

Table 10.1 Selected developmental disabilities: frequently reported nutrition problems and factors contributing to high nutritional risk. (ADA, 1997) © American Dietetic Association. Used with permission.

Syndrome or disability	Altered growth, underweight, obesity	Altered energy need	Altered nutrient needs, nutrient deficient	Constipation/ diarrhea	Feeding problems	Drug-nutrient interactions	Others
Cerebral palsy	✓	✓	✓	✓	✓	✓	Orthopedic problems
Epilepsy			✓	✓		✓	Gum hypertrophy
Muscular dystrophy		✓		✓	✓		
Myelomeningocele	✓	✓	✓	✓	✓		
Down syndrome	✓	✓	✓	✓	✓	✓	Gum disease
Prader-Willi syndrome	✓	✓			✓		
Intellectual disability, unknown etiology	✓			✓	✓	✓	Pica
Autism					✓	✓	Pica

distinctions' (Solomons, 1999, p. 1770). 'Cultural distinctions' in their broad sense should be added to this.

This chapter's limited scope cannot address adequately the numerous variations in food practices and customs and available food supply (quality and quantity) that can affect dietary intake and nutrition. In any given place where sufficient good quality and safe food is available, a wide variety of local foods can be combined to create a healthful diet. Many factors, however, affect food availability and access to it. Poverty is one of these and it is the single biggest cause of ill-health (Davies, 1999). In general, in developing countries, the priority is often survival – meeting the basic need for food and shelter. However, a double burden is evident (Gopalan, 1994). The old burden (incidence of low birthweight infants and growth retardation, vitamin A deficiency, iodine deficiency disorder, anemia and protein-energy malnutrition) remains, as the new burden of increased prevalence of chronic degenerative diseases (cancer, obesity, diabetes and coronary heart disease) has emerged. This double burden further strains the already thin and fragile resources. The strain affects the allocation of resources to meet people's urgent needs for survival and can further marginalize the vulnerable groups – the old and individuals with intellectual disabilities.

Dietary guidelines for healthful diets

This section provides an overview of the qualitative and quantitative dietary guidelines. As Schneeman (1997) has pointed out, dietary guidelines are advisory statements about diet for the population with regard to diet-related diseases. Wherever these guidelines are used as a basis for nutrition policy, they will affect the dietary and lifestyle recommendations as well as the efforts of various sectors to promote the health of the population. The sets of advisory statements vary among countries, depending on a country's major diet-related concerns (prevention of deficiency and/or prevention of overnutrition-induced chronic diseases and health promotion). Socioeconomic conditions, cultural traditions and food habits also contribute to the variations. However, in general the guidelines share similar concepts and good intentions for public health. The nutrition principles in the dietary guidelines for the general population are relevant to the nutritional health of people with disabilities. However, the translation of these principles to a diet plan for a specific person requires individualization.

The qualitative dietary guidelines

The World Health Organization (WHO) has recommended that dietary recommendations be related to food choices because people better understand educational messages communicated through food rather than through nutrients. In contrast, the quantitative nutrient-based guidelines, such as the recommended dietary allowances (RDAs) and the dietary reference intakes (DRIs), are estimates of the requirements for essential nutrients in humans and focus on the components of foods. They relate to nutrition and agricultural policies, nutrition targets or goals, and population needs, and are intended for use by government agencies, policy developers and health care professionals (Schneeman, 1997). The national and international recommended dietary reference values for nutrients and energy, including the dietary recommendations in industrialized and developing countries, have been comprehensively summarized elsewhere (Block & Shils, 1999). As of 1999, 40% of the countries had national dietary goals or guidelines (WHO, 1999). WHO (1999) emphasizes that the new food-based dietary guidelines, which are country-specific, address not only foods but also ways of food production, preparation, and food processing and development. As such, they are more practical for the consumer and can therefore improve nutrition education for the public.

This chapter does not intend to compare the sets of guidelines but rather to relate their general common themes to nutrition and food. The themes stress the importance of eating a wide variety of foods within each major food group, and sufficient calories to maintain appropriate body weight. They also stress the importance of food safety and cleanliness, the appeal of food to the senses (food should look, smell and taste good), personal preferences as a determinant of food acceptance, and the sharing of food in a pleasant and caring community of individuals or social environment. The emphasis on food conveys the central and powerful role of food in life; food meets not only the biological need for survival but also people's social, psychological and emotional needs.

Many factors affect food choices. These include taste, nutrition, cost, convenience and weight control concerns, but taste is the most important of these (Glanz et al., 1998). In addition to taste, health, familiarity and family preference also determine food choices (Lian, 1997). Nutrition education programs should consider these factors in designing and communicating nutrition and health messages. This education can focus on individuals and their carers as in dietary or nutrition counseling, or on the population for public health. However, as Clay (1997) pointed out, it takes more than isolated efforts to achieve and sustain good nutrition. It requires year-round availability of a variety of good quality, safe and affordable foods, adequate economic resources, education of individuals about their nutritional needs and ways to meet these needs through food, and adoption of healthful eating and lifestyle behaviors.

The Dietary Guidelines for Americans (USDA & USDHHS, 2000) aim to provide sound, current advice to the public regarding healthful eating to promote health and reduce risk for chronic diseases (see Figure 10.1). As the basis of the US federal nutrition policy, they affect federal nutrition programs. Their principles are incorporated into the USDA food guide pyramid, the nutrition facts on the food label and other nutrition education tools for consumers. Intended for healthy children and adults, the guidelines emphasize these three basic messages: 'Aim for fitness', Build a healthy base' and 'Choose sensibly for good health' or 'ABC' (Johnson & Kennedy, 2000).

Principles for good health

Aim for fitness
▲ Aim for a healthy weight.
▲ Be physically active each day.

Build a healthy base
■ Let the Pyramid guide your food choices.
■ Choose a variety of grains daily, especially whole grains.
■ Choose a variety of fruits and vegetables daily.
■ Keep food safe to eat.

Choose sensibly
● Choose a diet that is low in saturated fat and cholesterol and moderate in total fat.
● Choose beverages and foods to moderate your intake of sugars.
● Choose and prepare foods with less salt.
● If you drink alcoholic beverages, do so in moderation.

Fig. 10.1 Dietary guidelines for Americans. Source: USDA & USDHHS (2000)

The first message advises people to aim for healthy weight and suggests specific strategies for engaging in physical activity to balance calorie intake with food, and for controlling calorie intake. Healthy weight should be encouraged in children (2 years old and older) but weight loss is not recommended for them unless it is guided by a health care provider (USDA & USDHHS, 2000).

The second message advises people to build a healthy base by letting the pyramid guide their food choices (recognizing that there are many healthful eating patterns), by building the eating pattern on a wide variety of plant foods (grains, especially whole grains, fruits and vegetables), and by keeping foods safe to eat. The message emphasizes that certain groups have higher needs for some nutrients. For example, adolescents and older adults need more calcium for bone health; children, teenage girls and childbearing women need adequate sources of iron; women who could become pregnant need extra folic acid; and older adults need extra vitamin D. Foods should be handled, prepared, stored and served safely to prevent foodborne illnesses (USDA & USDHHS, 2000).

The third message advises people to choose a diet that is low in saturated fat and cholesterol and moderate in total fat, to choose beverages and foods to moderate intake of sugars, to choose and prepare foods with less salt, and for those who drink alcoholic beverages to do so in moderation. Sugars should be limited because they can contribute to unwanted weight gain and tooth decay if proper oral hygiene is not practiced, and they may replace nutritious foods in the diet. A diet that contains less salt/sodium can help reduce the risk of hypertension. Because alcoholic beverages provide calories with few nutrients and are harmful when consumed in excessive amounts, they should be consumed in moderation (no more than two drinks per day for men and no more than one drink for women). One drink is 12 ounces of regular beer (150 calories), or 5 ounces of wine (100 calories), or 1.5 ounces of 80-proof distilled spirits (100 calories) (USDA & USDHHS, 2000).

Wherever individuals with intellectual disabilities live, the quality of their diet and nutritional health can be affected by the dietary guidelines and the food-based recommendations that their countries have established to promote public health and to address prevalent diet-related health problems. Translating the advisory statements and food-based guidelines to specific behaviors of choosing and eating healthful foods to meet individual nutritional needs is a goal and a challenge.

Food guides

This section discusses some of the ways of translating the advisory statements into food guidance that can help adults and their carers choose a variety of healthful foods. As in the case of dietary guidelines, many countries and groups have developed their food guides. Some of these are quantitative (they specify the amount and/or the number of servings from each food group), while others are qualitative. For detailed information, the dietary guidelines and food guides of various countries and cultural groups can be accessed at several websites such as the Asian Food Information Center (www.afic.org), the Oldways Preservation and Exchange Trust (www.oldwayspt.org), and the Food and Nutrition Information Center of the USDA (www.nal.usda.gov/fnic).

Like the country-specific sets of dietary guidelines, the various graphic representations of food-based recommendations have many conceptual similarities. These include the emphasis on a wide variety of plant foods (whole grains and grain products, fruits, and vegetables); the inclusion of some protein-rich foods (meat and/or alternatives) and calcium-rich foods (milk products or alternatives based on cultural preferences); moderation of fats, sweets and alcoholic beverages; plenty of fluids; the role of physical activity; preservation of cultural heritage; and the message that it is the total diet and combination of foods that provide the nutrients. Individuals and their carers can use the principles for meal planning, taking into consideration individual preference and tolerance, necessary dietary modifications, cultural food patterns and available food supply. It is emphasized again that qualified professionals should be consulted in assessing special health needs and in planning and implementing therapeutic interventions.

The USDA Food Guide Pyramid (USDA, 1992) is shown in Figure 10.2. Table 10.2 and Figure 10.3 give details regarding the recommended number of servings and the definition of a serving. As the official food guidance system in the US, the Food Guide Pyramid is the most widely distributed nutrition education tool. It is a dietary pattern for healthy

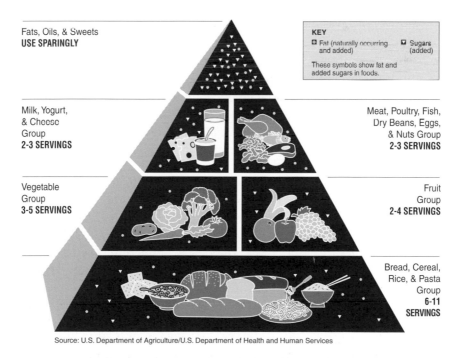

Source: U.S. Department of Agriculture/U.S. Department of Health and Human Services

Fig. 10.2   Food Guide Pyramid – a guide to daily food choices.

Table 10.2 The recommended number of servings per day for different groups of people. Source: USDA & USDHHS (2000).

Food group	Children aged 2–6 years, women, some older adults (about 1600 calories)	Older children, teen girls, active women, most men (about 2200 calories)	Teen boys, active men (about 2800 calories)
Bread, cereal, rice and pasta group (grains group)	6	9	11
Vegetable group	3	4	5
Fruit group	2	3	4
Milk, yogurt and cheese group (milk group) preferably fat-free or low-fat	2 or 3*	2 or 3*	2 or 3*
Meat, poultry, fish, dry beans, eggs and nuts group (meat and beans group) – preferably lean or low-fat	2, for a total of 5 ounces	2, for a total of 6 ounces	3, for a total of 7 ounces

* The number of servings depends on age. Older children and teenagers (aged 9–18 years) and adults over the age of 50 need 3 servings daily. Others need 2 servings daily. During pregnancy and lactation, the recommended number of servings from the milk group is the same as for non-pregnant women.

people that provides a balance and quantity of nutrients to meet the RDAs and reduce the intake of fat, saturated fat, cholesterol and sugar to reduce risk for diet-related chronic diseases (Nestle, 1998). It helps consumers apply the dietary guidelines into food choices. Its three major concepts of variety, moderation and proportionality guide food selection. Variety means eating a wide selection of foods within each and among major food groups. Moderation means eating foods, especially those high in fat and added sugar, in recommended portions, and eating fats, oils and sweets sparingly. Proportionality means eating relatively more from the larger food groups and less from the smaller food groups (Achterberg *et al.*, 1994). The ranges in the number of servings for each of the five food groups indicate flexibility to meet different energy needs. Although the numeric recommendations are met, the types of foods chosen within each food group affect the nutrient composition of the day's meals. For example, oranges contain much more vitamin C than apples. However, it should be emphasized that the quality of an individual's food intake should be evaluated over time and that the nutritional quality of a food should be judged in the context of the total diet quality.

What counts as a serving?

Bread, cereal, rice and pasta group (grains group) – preferably whole grain and enriched

- Slice of bread
- About 1 cup of ready-to-eat cereal
- $\frac{1}{2}$ cup of cooked cereal, rice or pasta

Milk, yogurt and cheese group (milk group) (includes lactose-free and lactose-reduced milk products)

- 1 cup of milk* or yoghurt*
- $1\frac{1}{2}$ ounces of natural cheese*
- 2 ounces of processed cheese*
- 1 cup of soy-based beverage with added calcium

Vegetable group

- 1 cup of raw leafy vegetables
- $\frac{1}{2}$ cup of other vegetables – cooked or raw
- $\frac{3}{4}$ cup of juice

Fruit group

- 1 medium fresh fruit (apple, banana, orange)
- $\frac{1}{2}$ cup of chopped, cooked or canned fruit
- $\frac{3}{4}$ cup of juice counts as 1 ounce of meat

Meat, poultry, fish, dry beans, eggs and nuts group (meat and beans group)

- 2–3 ounces of cooked lean meat, poultry or fish
- $\frac{1}{2}$ cup of cooked dry beans† or $\frac{1}{2}$ cup of tofu counts as 1 ounce of lean meat
- $2\frac{1}{2}$ ounces of soyburger or 1 egg counts as 1 ounce of lean meat
- 2 tablespoons of peanut butter or $\frac{1}{3}$ cup of nuts counts as 1 ounce of meat

*Fat-free or reduced fat dairy products should be chosen often to control fat and cholesterol intake. Example of natural cheese: cheddar; Example of processed cheese: American.

†Dry beans, peas and lentils can be counted as servings in either the meat and beans group or the vegetable group. As a vegetable, $\frac{1}{2}$ cup of cooked dry beans counts as 1 serving (2 ounces of meat).

Fig. 10.3 Definition of one serving of food in each food group. Source: USDA & USDHHS (2000)

Nutritional needs

This section leads the general guidelines discussed previously into some specific nutritional considerations for individuals with intellectual disabilities. The nutrient needs of these individuals are the same as those of the general population. Nutrition-related problems frequently observed in certain disabilities (see Table 10.1) require individualization of dietary modifications. Food supplies the nutrients and other substances that, together, produce better health outcomes than any one of the components alone. The discussion of selected nutrients, energy and fluid in the following section should be viewed in this context.

Macronutrients

The macronutrients (carbohydrate, protein and lipids) not only yield energy but also perform other vital functions.

Proteins

Proteins are essential to life. They function as enzymes, hormones, parts of muscles and bones, antibodies for warding off infection, transporters of fats and other nutrients and medications in circulation, and as a fluid balance regulator. As an alternate energy source, they provide 4 kcal/g (Groff & Gropper, 2000). The RDAs for protein vary among countries, and it has been conceded that harmonizing these RDAs is a challenge. It should also be noted that the RDAs are for almost all healthy people in a given population and that the RDA is not the same as an individual's protein requirement (Nandi, 1998). In the US, the RDA for protein is 0.8 g per kg bodyweight for male and female, aged 19–51+ years (FNB, 1989); the recommendation for older adults is 1.0 gm per kg bodyweight (Young, 2001). Inadequate energy intake, inferior protein quality and digestibility, hypermetabolic conditions (e.g. injury, burns, fever, infection and cancer), and physiological status associated with growth, increase protein needs (Matthews, 1999).

Sufficient caloric intake from carbohydrate and fat is important in sparing protein from being used as an alternative fuel source (Matthews, 1999). In general, individuals can meet their protein needs by consuming the recommended portions of meats and other high-protein foods (two to three servings) and milk products (two to three servings) in the USDA Food Guide Pyramid (USDA 1992). If meat is expensive, or it may not be available, or religious beliefs prohibit its consumption, combining proper kinds of plant proteins such as rice or corn and legumes can improve plant protein quality. Unlike other plant foods, soybeans provide high-quality protein (Messina, 1999) and are, therefore, good meat substitute for individuals who like them.

Carbohydrates

The food guides of various countries illustrate that carbohydrates, which yield 4 kcal/g, are the most important single energy source in the world; the extent of their use varies widely among cultures and within a culture. No RDA has been set for carbohydrates. The recommendation, however, is that carbohydrates from a wide variety of sources should supply 55% of the total calorie intake, although a wide range of intakes appears to be compatible with health (Mann, 2001). Foods high in carbohydrates (starches and fiber) provide not only energy but also dietary fiber, vitamins and minerals. In some countries, grains and starchy vegetables constitute the bulk of the day's meals. The brain, red blood cells and the renal medulla depend on glucose for energy. Carbohydrates promote complete fat oxidation, thereby preventing the development of ketosis which may impair cognitive function (Mann, 2001). Sugar in moderation can be a part of a healthful diet (USDA & USDHHS, 2000). Good oral hygiene will help prevent dental caries which are associated with sugar consumption.

Plant foods are the major carbohydrate sources, although milk contains a substantial amount of lactose, a naturally occurring simple sugar. The Food Guide Pyramid (Figure 10.2) (USDA 1992) recommends per day five to eleven servings from the bread, rice, cereal and pasta group (grains), two to four servings of fruits, three to five servings of vegetables, and two to three servings from the milk, cheese and yogurt group (milk). This combination provides ample carbohydrate for energy.

Fiber

Dietary fiber provides several health benefits. The insoluble type in wheat bran is a good natural laxative for constipation. Soluble or viscous fiber, such as pectin in apples, strawberries and citrus fruits, help lower blood cholesterol. A study of adults with intellectual disabilities who lived in group homes reported that the residents' food intake from the fruit, vegetable and milk groups was most often deficient (Mercer & Ekvall, 1992). Adequate fiber and fluid intake can help alleviate constipation, a prevalent gastrointestinal disorder among individuals with intellectual disabilities. Eating two to three servings of whole grains as part of the daily six to eleven servings of grains, five servings of fruits (whole fruits, rather than juice) and vegetables daily, and legumes at least once or twice a week will provide adequate fiber to meet the recommended amount of 20–35 g daily (ADA, 1997).

Lipids

A concentrated source of calories (9 kcal/g), lipids, like carbohydrates, spare protein from being used for energy production. They are part of the structure of cellular membrane, transport fat-soluble vitamins, cushion vital organs, and contribute to the desirable flavor and texture of certain foods. There is no RDA for lipids. Consumers are advised to moderate their fat intake, especially saturated fat. Because excessive fat intake contributes to obesity and obesity is associated with diabetes, hypertension and heart disease, the National Cholesterol Education Program (NCEP, 2001) recommends reduction of fat intake to 25–35% of the day's total calorie intake.

Because many factors contribute to the etiology of heart disease, the better way of prevention and treatment is a multifaceted lifestyle approach, designated as therapeutic lifestyle changes (TLC) (NCEP, 2001). The target is lowering low density lipoprotein (LDL), the major carrier of cholesterol in the blood. Elevated LDL level is a strong risk factor for coronary heart disease. TLC's essential features are reduced intakes of saturated fats (< 7% of total calories) and cholesterol (< 200 mg per day), therapeutic options for enhancing LDL lowering such as plant stanols/sterols (2 g per day) and increased viscous or soluble fiber (10–25 g per day), weight reduction and increased physical activity. Control of other risk factors (hypertension, obesity and diabetes mellitus) and cigarette-smoking cessation are an important part of the treatment plan (NCEP, 2001). As Wells and colleagues (1997) pointed out, most of the risk factors (obesity, hypertension and hypercholesterolemia) for cardiovascular diseases are at least as prevalent among people with intellectual disabilities as they are among people in the general population.

Because the main sources of fat, saturated fat and cholesterol are the animal-derived foods (meat and milk groups) and the fats and oils of various forms, the advice focuses on the selection and preparation of these foods. For example, choosing vegetable oils rather than solid fat, and lean meats, dry beans, peas or lentils from the high-protein group, and low-fat milk products; limiting intake of high-fat processed meats; and checking the food label for the cholesterol and fat content of prepared foods, can all help control fat and cholesterol intake. Using low-fat cooking methods, controlling portion sizes and selecting healthful foods when eating out are likewise beneficial (USDA & USDHHS, 2000). Fat, however, as a food palatability enhancer and concentrated calorie source can boost the calorie intake of individuals who have poor food intake and need to increase their weight.

Energy

Consuming adequate calories to maintain proper body weight is important to health. Both underweight and overweight conditions are risk factors for malnutrition. For the reference man (79 kg) the average energy allowance is 2900 kcal (37 kcal per kg) and for the woman (63 kg), aged 25 to 50 years, it is 2200 kcal (35 kcal per kg). A coefficient of variation of +/ − 20% is used for the range of light to moderate activity (FNB, 1989). Various factors (physical activity, growth, physiological states, fever, infection, trauma or injury) affect calorie requirement. As Table 10.1 shows, individuals with certain disabilities have altered energy needs. For example, individuals with Down syndrome and Prader-Willi syndrome need fewer calories than those with athetoid cerebral palsy. Behaviors such as head movements, jerking and rocking, which some individuals display, can increase calorie needs. With aging, people in general require less energy as a result of decreased basal metabolic rate and physical activity. Review of cohort and cross-sectional data revealed that energy intake decreased with age; between individuals aged in their twenties and those in their eighties, mean energy intake declined by 1000 to 1200 kcal in men and 600 to 800 kcal in women (Wakimoto & Block, 2001). Morley (2001) has described the anorexia of aging and its consequent decreased food intake. As pointed out earlier, many more people with intellectual disabilities now live longer, just as in the general population. Given their multiple medical problems and concurrent medications, they, especially the older ones, will likely have poor food intake, which can contribute to weight loss and malnutrition. Providing calorie-dense and nutrient-dense foods is necessary to boost depleted body stores.

Unintentional weight gain (or loss) can serve as a practical guide for judging the adequacy of calorie intake. It is generally a sign of an imbalance between energy intake and expenditure. Positive energy balance leads to obesity, a risk factor for chronic degenerative diseases, and negative energy balance predisposes an individual to malnutrition.

Underweight condition results from chronic insufficient energy intake. It increases risks for diseases and mortality, adversely affects functional status and predisposes individuals to hip fractures (Meisler & St. Jeor, 1996). Older people in the lowest 15th percentile range of the weight-for-height distribution have a higher mortality rate than do people of normal weight. Those with the best functional status are in the 15th to 85th percentile range (Gray-Donaldson, 1995).

Energy content of the dinner menu for adults with intellectual disabilities who lived in group homes was found to be significantly below one-third of the RDA (Mercer & Ekvall, 1992). In general, calorie intake is a practical correlate of the nutritional adequacy of the diet; i.e. when energy intake is inadequate, the intake of several essential nutrients is likely low (Mercer & Ekvall, 1992; Wakimoto & Block, 2001). The sparing effect of adequate calorie intake on protein has been mentioned previously. Factors that contribute to poor food intake and unwanted weight loss should be corrected to prevent decline in health. Providing calorie-dense and nutrient-dense foods that appeal to the senses, adequate time for meals, socialization, and encouragement and social support can increase calorie and nutrient intake.

Micronutrients needs

Although hidden hunger or micronutrient deficiency is not confined solely to developing countries, these countries suffer the greater burden of higher prevalence and consequences of vitamin A deficiency, iodine deficiency disorder and anemia. Because these micronutrient deficiencies (which are preventable and treatable) cause growth retardation, physical and learning impairment and morbidity, their inclusion in this chapter is relevant to the health of individuals with intellectual disabilities.

Fat-soluble vitamins

The digestion, absorption and transport of fat-soluble vitamins are related to those of lipids. Diseases that impair lipid absorption can, therefore, induce fat-soluble vitamin deficiency.

Vitamin A

Perhaps the best long-known function of vitamin A is its role in maintaining normal vision and in preventing blindness. Vitamin A is also required for cellular differentiation, growth, reproduction, bone development and the integrity of the immune system. Vitamin A deficiency affects up to 500 000 children worldwide (Russell, 2001). In Western countries, at least 70% of dietary vitamin A is preformed (all-trans-retinol), most of which is from animal origin (meat and milk products), and some of it is added to foods. The provitamin A carotenoids are the main sources of vitamin A in most tropical countries where the consumption of meat products is relatively low. The body converts the provitamin to vitamin A.

The new RDA for vitamin A, expressed as retinol activity equivalent (RAE), is 900 mcg per day for men, and 700 mcg per day for women respectively, aged 14 to > 70 years (Russell, 2001). Vitamin A supplement users should be aware that excessive intake of preformed vitamin A is toxic and can cause fetal malformation (or teratogenic effect). The teratogenic effect is more serious with synthetic vitamin A analogues. The richest sources of preformed vitamin A are fish oils, liver and other organ meats. Additional sources are fortified products. The richest sources of provitamin A carotenoids are palm fruits and red palm oil. Dark green and deep orange vegetables and fruits are rich in provitamin A (Solomons, 2001); but new evidence indicates that it takes twice as much provitamin carotene to make a unit of vitamin A than originally thought. This means that people who rely on deeply colored green and yellow plants for their vitamin A need to eat more of these plants in order to meet their vitamin A requirement (Russell, 2001).

Vitamin D

Vitamin D is essential to bone health. Because vitamin D affects calcium absorption and utilization, vitamin D deficiency can cause secondary calcium deficiency and, therefore, defective bone mineralization. Bone mineral disorders are prevalent among individuals with intellectual disabilities (Center *et al.*, 1998). Various factors adversely affect vitamin D status and bone health. These include anticonvulsant therapy, which increases risk for vitamin D and calcium deficiency because the drug interferes with vitamin D metabolism, prolonged immobilization, lack of exposure to the sun resulting in reduced vitamin D production on the skin (Ryan *et al.*, 1995), and insufficient consumption of vitamin D-fortified milk (Ryan *et al.*, 1995). These are controllable. Other factors include dark skin pigmentation which partially inhibits the conversion of vitamin D precursor on the skin (Harris & Dawson-Hughes, 1998), and age-related changes in the skin, the liver and the kidney, organs which play an important role in vitamin D synthesis and activation (Ryan *et al.*, 1995). Hormonal factors (hyperparathyroidism and estrogen loss in women) also contribute to bone loss.

Only a few foods, primarily animal foods, contain a significant but varying amount of naturally occurring vitamin D. These include fish (fish liver oil, herring, salmon and sardine), and liver. In the US milk is fortified with vitamin D (400 IU per quart). Some plant foods (some breads and cereals, soy milk) are fortified with vitamin D. The adequate intake (AI)/ DRI, expressed as cholecalciferol, for people with inadequate sunlight exposure, is 10 mcg per day for the 50 to 70-year-old and 15 mcg per day for the >70-year-old (Russell, 2001). Because many people with intellectual disabilities may not be able to get sufficient vitamin D from foods alone, they should be exposed to sunlight for a major source of additional vitamin D. Based on their assessed need, they may benefit from vitamin D supplementation, alone or with calcium. Long-term megadoses of vitamin D, however, can be toxic. Individuals should strive to eat vitamin D fortified and calcium-rich foods, have some sun exposure, engage in regular physical activity (as tolerated), and have regular medication review to assess drug-nutrient interactions that can adversely affect bone health.

Vitamin E

Vitamin E is an antioxidant and a free radical scavenger. It is a group of chemically related substances that have the biological activity of alpha-tocopherol. Vitamin E (RRR-alpha-tocopherol) is the most biologically active of the eight forms or stereoisomers. The different forms have different antioxidant activities and physiologic effects (Traber, 1999). Research has focused on vitamin E's protective role in cardiovascular diseases, cancer and cataract.

The RDA for vitamin E is 15 mg per day, expressed as alpha-tocopherol, for men and women aged 19 to >70 years (Russell, 2001). This can be easily obtained from foods, primarily edible vegetable oils and also whole grain cereals, nuts and seeds. Wheatgerm, safflower and sunflower oils are particularly rich in the most biologically active form of vitamin E (Traber, 1999). The contemporary concern over fat consumption and the medical prescription for low-fat diets can reduce the intake of fat-soluble vitamins. Conditions that impair fat absorption, such as cystic fibrosis, celiac disease and chronic pancreatitis, can impair the absorption of vitamin E and cause a deficiency (Traber, 1999). Excess intake, however, such as pharmacologic doses of vitamin E (and A) counteract the blood-clotting function of vitamin K and can increase the efficacy of anti-coagulants such as aspirin and coumarin (Olson, 1999; Rimm, 1999). This can prolong bleeding during injury and surgery.

Vitamin K

Vitamin K is sometimes called an antihemorrhagic factor because it functions in the synthesis of blood-clotting proteins. It is given to newborns as a prophylaxis for the hemorrhagic disease of the newborn. Because it also functions in the synthesis of certain bone proteins, it may also have a role in bone formation. While deficiency is rare in healthy adults, certain medications and diseases that interfere with vitamin K absorption, synthesis by microflora or metabolism can induce it. Diphenylhandantoin (phenytoin) anticonvulsant, coumadin anticoagulant, salicylates, broad spectrum antibiotics and, as mentioned previously, pharmacological doses of vitamins A and E, all inhibit vitamin K's functions. Individuals who are on long-term phenytoin therapy for seizure control, can be at risk for vitamin K deficiency. Vitamin K is obtained not only from foods (green vegetables are notable for their vitamin K content) but also from intestinal microflora synthesis (Olson, 1999); these sources can easily meet the recommended amount. The AI for vitamin K is 120 mcg and 90 mcg per day for men and women respectively, aged 19 to >70 years (Russell, 2001).

Water-soluble vitamins

Although they do not directly yield energy, the water-soluble vitamins (vitamin C/ascorbic acid, thiamin, riboflavin, niacin, vitamin B_6/

pyridoxine, folate, vitamin B_{12}, pantothenic acid and biotin) work together in energy metabolism and cellular processes that promote growth
and support life. The new DRIs have set RDAs or AIs for these vitamins
and also for choline, a substance with vitaminlike activity (Russell, 2001).
Deficiency diseases caused by primary or secondary deficiencies of certain vitamins have been well established; for example, deficiencies of
vitamin C, thiamin and folate (also vitamin B_{12}) cause respectively,
scurvy, beri-beri and anemia.

Vitamin C

Historical accounts of deaths from scurvy, a classic vitamin C-deficiency
disease, demonstrate the vital role of vitamin C to health. Vitamin C has
various essential functions. As an antioxidant it protects the lipid components of the cells from oxidative damage. It also helps in the synthesis
of collagen, an important protein matrix of the bone, and of nor-
epinephrine and serotonin which are neurotransmitters in the brain that
affect nerve function and behavior, and it enhances iron absorption.
Vitamin C deficiency is rare in developed countries. If it occurs, signs
include bleeding gums, petechia (skin discoloration due to rupture of the
blood vessels), impaired wound and fracture healing, anemia (because it
enhances iron absorption) and psychological manifestations (depression)
(Groff & Gropper, 2000). As a group, fresh fruits and vegetables are rich
sources of vitamin C. These include citrus fruits, strawberries, kiwi,
papayas, broccoli, hot and sweet peppers and mustard spinach. Adults
should strive for at least one serving of vitamin C-rich fruits or vegetables
daily. One to two servings daily can meet the RDA of 75 mg for women
and 90 mg for men, aged 19 to >70 years (Russell, 2001). Exposure to light,
heat (long cooking time), air and alkali destroy vitamin C. Processing and
preparation of vitamin C-rich foods should aim for maximum vitamin
retention.

Folate

Folate, together with vitamin B_{12}, functions in DNA synthesis and
therefore in protein or tissue synthesis, including growth and red blood
cell production. Clinical manifestations of severe folate deficiency are
well established. These include megaloblastic, macrocytic anemia characterized by abnormally large red blood cells. Megaloblastic or immature
cells are produced in all dividing cells in the body, particularly in the bone
marrow and gastrointestinal tract (Herbert, 1999). The abnormality in the
cells lining the intestinal tract induces diarrhea (Herbert, 1999), which can

cause dehydration and malnutrition. The more recent interest in folate centers on its association with depression, Alzheimer dementia, certain types of cancer and cardiovascular disease risk. Review of various studies on these topics concluded that current evidence does not support a causal relationship between folate status and these disorders and that additional and well-controlled studies should be done to clarify the medical application of folate to these conditions. However, evidence indicates that folate helps prevent neural tube defect, such as spina bifida. Consequently, as a public health measure, the US Food and Drug Administration requires fortification of uncooked and cereal grain products (140 mcg per 100 g) (Kim, 1999).

The RDA for folate is 400 mcg per day, expressed in dietary folate equivalent (Russell, 2001). Folate is widely distributed in foods, and green leafy vegetables are its richest source. Other important sources include enriched and whole grains and grain products. Because oxidation during cooking and storage can destroy as much as 50–95% of folate in foods (Herbert, 1999), vegetables should not be overcooked or held in steam tables for a long time. Certain medications interfere with folate utilization and may increase folate requirement; for example, methothrexate, a chemotherapeutic agent for cancer, is a folate antagonist. Pertinent to individuals with intellectual disabilities are the phenytoin and primidone anticonvulsants (Herbert, 1999).

Deficiencies of either folate or vitamin B_{12} or of both cause the same type of red blood cell abnormalities or megaloblastic anemia. Unlike folate deficiency, however, vitamin B_{12} deficiency causes neurological impairments. The cause should be identified correctly because folate supplementation superimposed on vitamin B_{12} deficiency can 'mask' vitamin B_{12} deficiency; i.e. folate can correct the megaloblastic anemia but not the vitamin B_{12} deficiency-induced neurological damage (Herbert, 1999). To prevent this 'masking effect' it is recommended that total folate intake be limited to 1 mg per day (FDA, 1996). It is also important to assess the person's vitamin B_{12} status when therapy or supplementation folic acid are being considered.

Vitamin B_{12}

The function and clinical deficiencies of vitamin B_{12} were discussed in the section on folate above. It should be emphasized that treatment with folate can partially correct the vitamin B_{12} deficiency symptoms and can lead to misdiagnosis. The vitamin B_{12} deficiency-induced neurological impairments can go undetected with serious consequences (Stabler, 2001). The new AI of 2.4 mcg of vitamin B_{12} per day for men and women aged 19 to >70 years, considers the needs of older persons who have reduced absorption of the food-bound vitamin. Naturally occurring vitamin B_{12} is found only in animal foods. Certain vegetarians and older persons generally consume limited amounts of these foods and may be able to meet the AI for vitamin B_{12} mainly by consuming vitamin B_{12}-fortified foods (e.g. breakfast cereals) or a supplement containing vitamin B_{12} (Russell, 2001). Dietary deficiency of vitamin B_{12} is rare, but factors that cause malabsorption can cause deficiency (Stabler, 2001).

Minerals

Calcium

Calcium is required for bone mineralization and strength through the life course. Calcium deficiency – caused by inadequate intake or secondary to vitamin D deficiency, medication use, or conditions that reduce absorption – is a risk factor for osteoporosis, a disabling chronic disease. Osteoporosis is a worldwide problem affecting not only individuals with intellectual disabilities but also other high-risk groups (McBean et al., 1993).

The interrelated functions of calcium and vitamin D in bone health have already been discussed in the section on vitamin D. The multifactorial etiology of osteoporosis requires a multifaceted prevention and treatment approach. This should address from a life course perspective the long-term use of anticonvulsants and other medications that interfere with vitamin D and calcium utilization, physical inactivity, estrogen loss in women, inadequate sun exposure, appropriate body weight, age-related changes and their overall nutritional implications, as well as poor calcium and/or poor vitamin D status caused by primary or secondary deficiencies.

The recommended calcium intake changes with age. For example, the AI for men and women aged 19–50 years is 1000 mg per day, and aged 51–>70 years is 1200 mg per day (Russell, 2001). The preferred source of calcium is calcium-rich foods, particularly milk products. Persons who do not consume these products or are lactose intolerant may use calcium-fortified products and calcium supplements, and ways for circumventing lactose intolerance. If eaten frequently or in sufficient amounts, certain green leafy vegetables (beet greens, kale, Swiss chard, turnip greens, collard and Chinese cabbage) provide some calcium. Meat alternatives, such as legumes (soybeans, black-eyed peas and Navy beans), contain significant amounts. Spinach, greens, beets, celery, some nuts and beverages contain oxalate, which binds calcium and reduces its absorption.

Other barriers to calcium absorption are excessive dietary fiber and phosphorus intake (Groff & Gropper, 2000).

Iodine

Iodine is a component of the thyroid hormone that regulates cell activity and growth (Stanbury & Dunn, 2001). Iodine deficiency disorder (IDD), manifested as goiter and a range of physical and mental impairment, is the world's greatest single cause of preventable brain damage. Cretinism in children caused by intrauterine iodine deficiency is marked by intellectual deficiency and is the most severe form of damage from IDD. Environmental deficiency of iodine in the soil and in locally grown plants and goitrogenic factors in food cause IDD (Stanbury & Dunn, 2001). The WHO (1993) Micronutrient Disorder Information Systems database shows the enormity of IDD as a worldwide problem. Globally, the prevalence of goiter is 12%; the highest prevalence is in the Eastern Mediterranean region (22.9%), while over 42.5% of the population are considered to be at risk of IDD. Southeast Asia (including India, Bangladesh and Indonesia) and the Western Pacific (including China) account for more than 50% of the world's total population at risk for IDD. Most countries in Europe are also affected. The use of iodized salt (or iodate salt in most tropical and developing countries) has been part of the prevention program (Stanbury & Dunn, 2001). The RDA for iodine ranges from 90 mcg per day for children aged 1–3 years, to 150 mcg per day for people aged > 70 years. It is higher for pregnancy and lactation (220 and 290 mcg per day, respectively) (Russell, 2001).

Iron

Iron is required for growth, oxygenation of tissues, iron-containing enzymes that catalyze various cellular reactions, and for the electron transport chain that is critical to respiration and energy metabolism. Clinical manifestations of severe iron deficiency include anemia, which is characterized by small and pale red blood cells, and the symptoms associated with it. Some of these symptoms are reduction in work performance and behavioral and cognitive abnormalities in children (Yip, 2001). Given the important functions of iron, its deficiency can exacerbate the functional and cognitive problems associated with certain disabilities.

Estimates indicate that in developing countries, the prevalence of anemia in pregnancy ranges from 35% to 75% and averages at 56%, and that anemia also affects 43% of non-pregnant women in those countries and 12% in developed countries (Allen, 1997). The RDA for iron varies with age, gender and physiological status. It ranges from 18 mg per day for non-pregnant women, aged 19–50 years, to 27 mg per day during pregnancy (Russell, 2001). Pregnant women may not meet the RDA from food alone; therefore iron supplementation is recommended (Yip, 2001). Because the absorption of iron is relatively small (5–10% of dietary iron in healthy individuals) (Fairbanks, 1999), individuals should strive to eat iron-rich foods and should be alert to conditions that favor or hinder iron absorption. Meat is the best source of iron. The heme iron from animal foods is better absorbed than the non-heme iron in plant foods. Besides the form of iron, conditions in the gastrointestinal tract can affect iron absorption; for example, low hydrochloric acid secretion in the stomach, malabsorption syndrome, phosphates and phytates (from cereals and certain plant foods), tea and coffee, and antacid medications, all reduce iron absorption. Consuming the meal with vitamin C-rich food and meat or poultry increases iron absorption (Fairbanks, 1999).

Fluids

People who are deprived of food live longer than those who are deprived of water. This illustrates the critical importance of water to life. And yet it is an often-neglected nutrient, i.e. people do not consume enough of it. Extra care must be taken to ensure that individuals, especially those who are dependent for all or most of their activities of daily living, consume sufficient fluid to prevent life-threatening dehydration. Although in clinical practice different formulas are used to calculate fluid needs depending on the medical conditions which cause fluid retention or losses, the general advice is to drink at least six to eight glasses of water per day. If this is not possible, alternative fluid sources such as fruit juices and watery food are palatable and provide needed nutrients and calories. Caffeine and alcoholic beverages have a diuretic effect and can increase fluid loss (Kleiner, 1999). Ensure that water and fluids are clean and safe to drink.

Conclusion

What explicit or implicit lessons can we learn from these various dietary guidelines and food-related recommendations that are relevant to the nutritional needs of individuals with intellectual disabilities? The first lesson is that there are no specific guidelines for this vulnerable group and that the guidelines for this population are those for most healthy people. Given that the nutrition principles are the same, it is the implementation of the guidelines into dietary plans that meet the complex health needs of the individual person, that poses the greatest challenge. Secondly, to facilitate health-promotive behavior changes, effective, culturally competent, nutrition education is needed to communicate the messages to the individuals and their carers. Thirdly, the improvement of nutritional status of vulnerable groups cannot be achieved through isolated efforts.

As Gopalan (1994) emphasized, nutrition should be viewed as just one component of an integrated primary health care package. An integrated approach will involve the individual and the 'microenvironment of families, neighborhood and communities, as well as the macroenvironment of societal institutions' (Sidorenko, 1999, p.12). Education should also target the components of these micro and macroenvironments. This integrated approach should include at least a systematic way of identifying the extent of the nutrition-related problems and needs, screening the individuals to detect risk factors or early signs of malnutrition, and linking them to appropriate services for further assessment and appropriate intervention. In the meantime, assuming that adequate, safe and good quality food is available, the old advice regarding proper amounts of a wide variety of foods; plenty of fluids; regular physical activity; medications review for food/nutrient and drug interactions; moderation in fat, salt, sugar and alcohol intake; food safety; and enjoyment of delicious meals with friends and other social support in a pleasant environment, remains a sensible and practical approach to nutritional health. Where adequate food is not available, efforts of all sectors should focus on the provision of food to supply the needed energy and nutrients for survival.

References

Achterberg, C., McDonnell, E. & Bagby, R. (1994) How to put the Food Guide Pyramid into practice. *Journal of the American Dietetic Association*, **94**, 1030–1035.

ADA (1997) Position of the American Dietetic Association: Nutrition in comprehensive program planning for persons with developmental disabilities. *Journal of the American Dietetic Association*, **97**, 189–193.

Allen, L.H. (1997) Pregnancy and iron deficiency: Unresolved issues. *Nutrition Reviews*, **55**, 91–101.

Block, A.S. & Shils, M.E. (1999) National and international recommended dietary reference values. In: *Modern Nutrition in Health and Disease* (eds. M.E. Shils, J.E. Olson, M. Shike &. C.A. Ross) 9th edn, pp. A19-A54-58. Williams and Wilkins, Baltimore.

Center, J., Beange, H. & McElduff, A. (1998) People with mental retardation have an increased risk of osteoporosis: a population study. *American Journal of Mental Retardation*, **103**, 19–28.

Clay, W.D. (1997) Food supplies and nutrition: The agricultural and economic implications of dietary guidelines. In: *Dietary Guidelines in Asian Countries: Towards a Food-Based Approach* (ed. R.E. Tolentino), pp. 24–27. International Life Sciences Institute (ILSI), Washington DC, USA.

Davies, A.M. (1999) Ageing and health in the 21st century: An overview. In: *World Health Organization, Ageing and Health – A Global Challenge for the Twenty-first Century*. Proceedings of a WHO Symposium, Kobe, 10–13 November 1998, pp. 20–35. World Health Organization, Geneva.

Fairbanks, V.F. (1999) Iron in medicine and nutrition. In: *Modern Nutrition in Health and Disease* (eds. M.E. Shils, J.E. Olson, M. Shike &. C.A. Ross) 9th edn, pp. 193–221. Williams and Wilkins, Baltimore, USA.

FDA (1996) *Folic acid fortification*. Office of Public Affairs Fact Sheet, 29 February, US Food and Drug Administration.
Available at http//vm.cfsan.fda.gov/dms/wh-folic/html

FNB (1989) Food and Nutrition Board, National Research Council/National Academy of Sciences. *Recommended Dietary Allowances*, 10th edn. National Academy Press, Washington DC, USA.

Glanz, K., Basil, M., Maiback, E., Goldberg, J. & Snyder, D. (1998) Why Americans eat what they do: Taste, nutrition, cost, convenience, and weight concerns as influences on food consumption. *Journal of the American Dietetic Association*, **98**, 1118–1126.

Gopalan, C. (1994) The changing nutrition scene in South-East Asia. In: *Nutrition Research in South-East Asia* (ed. C. Gopalan) pp. 1–11. World Health Organization, Geneva.

Gray-Donaldson, K. (1995) The frail elderly: Meeting the nutritional challenge. *Journal of the American Dietetic Association*, **95**, 538–540.

Groff, J.L. & Gropper, S.S. (2000) *Advanced Nutrition and Metabolism*, 3rd edn. Wadsworth/Thompson Learning, Belmont, CA, USA.

Harris, S.S. & Dawson-Hughes, N. (1998) Seasonal changes in plasma 25-hydro-xyvitamin D concentrations of young American black and white women. *American Journal of Clinical Nutrition*, **67**, 1232–1236.

Herbert, V. (1999) Folic acid. In: *Modern Nutrition in Health and Disease* (eds. M.E. Shils, J.E. Olson, M. Shike &. C.A. Ross), 9th edn, pp. 433–446. Williams and Wilkins, Baltimore, USA.

Johnson, R.K. & Kennedy, E. (2000) The 2000 dietary guidelines for Americans: What are the changes and why were they made? *Journal of the American Dietetic Association*, **100**, 769–773.

Kim, Y. (1999) Folate and cancer prevention: A new medical application of folate beyond hyperhomocysteinemia and neural tube defects. *Nutrition Reviews*, **57**, 314–320.

Kleiner, S.M. (1999) Water: An essential but overlooked nutrient. *Journal of the American Dietetic Association*, **99**, 200–206.

Lian, L.S. (1997) Opening address. In: *Dietary guidelines in Asian countries: Towards a food-based approach* (ed. R.E. Tolentino), pp. 1–2. International Life Sciences Institute (ILSI), Washington DC, USA.

Mann, J. (2001) Carbohydrates. In: *Present Knowledge in Nutrition*, 8th edn (eds. B.A. Bowman & R.M. Russell), pp. 59–71. ILSI Press, Washington DC, USA.

Matthews, D.E. (1999) Proteins and amino acids. In: *Modern Nutrition in Health and Disease* (eds. M.E. Shils, J.E. Olson, M. Shike & C.A. Ross), 9th edn, pp. 11–48. Williams and Wilkins, Baltimore, USA.

McBean, L.D., Forgac, T. & Finn, S.C. (1993) Osteoporosis: visions for care and prevention B a conference report. *Journal of the American Dietetic Association*, **94**, 668–671.

Meisler, J.G. & St. Jeor, S. (1996) Summary and recommendations from the American Health Foundation's Expert Panel on Healthy Weight. *American Journal of Clinical Nutrition*, **63**, 474S–477S.

Mercer, K.C. & Ekvall, S.W. (1992) Comparing the diets of adults with mental retardation who live in intermediate care facilities and group homes. *Journal of the American Dietetic Association*, **92**, 356–358.

Messina, M. (1999) *Soybean and health*. Presented at the Soy Connection Dietitian Seminar, 18, 1999, Cleveland, OH, USA.

Morley, J.E. (2001) Decreased food intake with aging. *Journals of Gerontology*, **56A**, 81–88.

Nandi, B.K. (1998) Harmonization of Recommended Dietary Allowances: Implications and approach. *Nutrition Reviews*, **56**, S53–S56.

NCEP (2001) *Third report of the National Cholesterol Education Program (NCEP) Expert Panel on Detection, Evaluation, and Treatment of High Blood Cholesterol in Adults (Adult Treatment Panel III)*. US Department of Health and Human Services, National Institutes of Health, NIH Publication No. 01-3670, Washington DC, USA.

Nestle, M. (1998) Toward more healthful dietary patterns – a matter of policy. *Public Health Reports*, **113**, 420–423.

Olson, R.E. (1999) Vitamin K. In: *Modern Nutrition in Health and Disease* (eds. M.E. Shils, J.E. Olson, M. Shike &. C.A. Ross) 9th edn, pp. 363–380. Williams and Wilkins, Baltimore, USA.

Patja, K., Livanainen, M., Vesala, H., Oksanen, H. & Ruopilla, I. (2000) Life expectancy of people with intellectual disability: A 35-year follow up study. *Journal of Intellectual Disability Research*, **44**, 591–599.

Rimm, E.B. (1999) *Vitamin E and cardiovascular disease*. Back-Grounder 7, 5pp. The Vitamin Nutrition Information Service, Roche Vitamins Inc, NJ, USA.

Russell, R.M. (2001) New micro nutrient Dietary Reference Intakes from the National Academy of Sciences. *Nutrition Today*, **36**, 163–171.

Ryan, C., Eleazer, P. & Egbert, J. (1995) Vitamin D in the elderly, an overlooked nutrient. *Nutrition Today*, **30**, 228–233.

Schneeman, B.O. (1997) Food-based dietary guidelines. In: *Dietary guidelines in Asian countries: Towards a food-based approach* (ed. R.E. Tolentino), pp. 9–12. International Life Sciences Institute (ILSI), Washington, DC, USA.

Sidorenko, A. (1999) From an ageing society to a society for all ages. In: *World Health Organization, ageing and health – A global challenge for the twenty-first century*. Proceedings of a WHO Symposium, Kobe, 10–13 November 1998, pp. 7–12. World Health Organization, Geneva.

Solomons, N.W. (1999) International priorities for clinical and therapeutic nutrition in the context of public health realities. In: *Modern Nutrition in Health and*

Disease, (eds M.E. Shils, J.E. Olson, M. Shike, &. C.A. Ross) 9th edn, pp. 1769–1781. Williams and Wilkins. Baltimore. USA.

Solomons, N.W. (2001) Vitamin A and carotenoids. In: *Present Knowledge in Nutriton* (eds B.A. Bowman & R.M. Russell) 8th edn, pp. 127–145. ILSI Press, Washington DC, USA.

Stabler, S.P. (2001) Vitamin B_{12}. In: *Present knowledge in Nutriton* (eds B.A. Bowman & R.M. Russell) 8th edn, pp. 230–240, ILSI Press, Washington DC, USA.

Stanbury, J.B. & Dunn, J.T. (2001) Iodine and iodine deficiency disorders. In: *Present Knowledge in Nutrition* (eds B.A. Bowman & R.M. Russell) 8th edn, pp. 344–351. ILSI Press, Washington DC, USA.

Traber, M.G. (1999) Vitamin E. In: *Modern Nutrition in Health and Disease* (eds M.E. Shils, J.E. Olson, M. Shike & C.A. Ross) 9th edn, pp. 347–362. Williams and Wilkins, Baltimore, USA.

USDA (1992) *The Food Guide Pyramid*. Human Nutrition Information Service, Home and Garden Bulletin Number 252, US Department of Agriculture, Washington, DC.

USDA & USDHHS (2000) *Nutrition and Your Health: Dietary Guidelines for Americans*, 5th edn. Home and Garden Bulletin No. 232. US Department of Agriculture and US Department of Health and Human Services, Washington DC.

Wakimoto, P. & Block, G. (2001) Dietary intake: Dietary patterns, and changes with age: An epidemiological perspective. *Journals of Gerontology*, **56A**, 65–80.

Wells, M.B., Turner, S., Martin, D.M. & Roy, A. (1997) Health gain through screening-coronary heart disease and stroke: Developing primary health services for people with intellectual disability. *Journal of Intellectual and Developmental Disability*, **22**, 251–263.

WHO (1993) *Global prevalence of iodine deficiency disorders*. Micronutrient Deficiency Information Systems Working Paper No. 1. World Health Organization, Geneva.

WHO (1999) Development of the food-based dietary guidelines for the Western Pacific Region, World Health Organization. Regional Office for the Western Pacific, Manila, pp. 1–67.

Yip, R. (2001) Iron. In: *Present Knowledge in Nutrition* (eds B.A. Bowman & R.M. Russell) 8th edn, pp. 311–328. ILSI Press, Washington DC, USA.

Young, V.R. (2001) Proteins and amino acids. In: *Present Knowledge in Nutrition* (eds B.A. Bowman & R.M. Russell) 8th edn, pp. 43–58. ILSI Press, Washington DC, USA.

11 Health Promotion and Disease Prevention

Nicholas Lennox

Introduction

People with intellectual disabilities experience premature death and high levels of unrecognized and poorly managed disease. Much of this could be addressed by improved health promotion and disease prevention activities; however, these activities are inadequately addressed in people with intellectual disabilities. Various strategies to improve the provision of health promotion/disease prevention have been developed and instituted based on this understanding and on the literature describing health promotion/disease prevention in older people from the general population and other vulnerable groups. Some of these strategies have been evaluated with encouraging, but as yet inconclusive, results. This chapter presents the evidence and reasons for the current situation and possible initiatives to redress these shortcomings in the health status of people with intellectual disabilities.

What is health promotion and disease prevention?

Health promotion has been defined by Green and Anderson as 'Any combination of health education and organizational, economic and environmental supports for behavior of individuals, groups or communities conducive to health' (Hawe *et al.*, 2000, p. 3). The Ottawa Charter defines health promotion as the process of enabling people to increase control over, and to improve, their health. To reach a state of complete physical, mental and social well-being, an individual or group must be able to identify and realize aspirations, to satisfy needs and to change or cope with environments (WHO, 1986).

It can be seen from these definitions that the scope of health promotion is extremely broad. It includes global factors (such as environmental degradation), societal factors (such as community connectedness) and individual factors, which are all interrelated and are important in health promotion. The Ottawa Charter emphasizes that effective health promotion incorporates all of the following: development of personal skills; the creation of environments that support health; the development of health policy; the refocusing of health and related services; and the engagement of the community (O'Connor & Parker, 1995; Silargy, 1998; Wass, 2000).

This approach reflects the shift in the orientation of public health thinking from the old to the new. The old public health focused on factors within the individual or factors within the social or physical environment and adopted strategies that tended to interrupt the chain of causation. It used traditional tools such as education, service provision and legislation (O'Connor & Parker, 1995). The new public health tries to address a more general set of human goals with a focus on policy and enhanced life skills. It has been argued that the public health approach should incorporate all effective strategies and knowledge, whether they arise from the old or the new conceptualization. From the perspective of the disability field, one can see a parallel shift in conceptualization over the last 30 or so years.

The commonality in language, principles and goals shared by the health promotion and disability fields is striking. The list of common principles and goals that are central in both fields includes inclusion, participation, empowerment, skills development, engagement in the community, the refocusing of health services and the promotion of environments that enhance health and quality of life. The implementation of these principles and goals has not been anywhere nearly fully achieved for people with intellectual disabilities. However, even the partial implementation has resulted in improved health and well-being, as well as enhancing the quality of life of people with intellectual disabilities. This achievement seems evident in increasing life expectancies and quality of life. However, this evidence is largely drawn from descriptive studies that lack the ability to prove causality.

The continuum of health promotion

There is a continuum of health promotion extending from optimal health to minimal disease, as illustrated in Figure 11.1. This model, where 'health field' includes health promotion at a primary, secondary and tertiary level, emphasizes the social context of the person and how policy, service provision and practice can improve health. Changes in the disability field in the last 30 years have seen service provision and policy framework moving in this direction, de-emphasizing the 'disease oriented/medical field' model. This continuum also illustrates the extent of all the possible influences on health, an understanding often not given due recognition by those who advocate strongly from either the 'health' or 'disease' focus.

Health prevention strategies ('Secondary disease prevention' in Figure 11.1), usually within the domain of the medical profession, have reaped

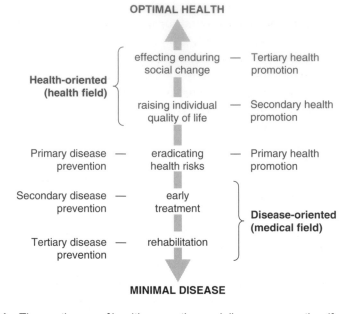

Fig. 11.1   The continuum of health promotion and disease prevention (from Wass, 2000, developed from Brown 1985, pp. 332–333).

great rewards. Successful strategies include Pap smear screening, mammography and blood pressure screening, which have resulted in early diagnosis and treatment of cervical cancer, breast cancer and hypertension respectively. Community-based, health-orientated initiatives ('Primary disease prevention' in Fig. 11.1) have also made a major contribution to health and well-being both in the developed and developing world. Important examples have been the compulsory introduction of seat belts in many countries, literacy programs for women in some developing countries, antismoking campaigns and HIV/AIDS prevention strategies. One example of the success of these programs has been a significant decline in deaths from lung cancer and coronary heart disease in the developed world as a consequence of decreased smoking in men (United States Preventive Services Task Force, 1996). Unfortunately the reverse is true of many developing countries, as smoking has increased. There is however evidence of greater health gains in per-person wealth in some developed countries, such as Sri Lanka, Costa Rica, Kerala State (in southwest India) and China. This has been attributed to better integration of tradition and modern health care, progressive social reform and a deliberate strengthening of the primary care sector (McMichael & Leon, 1998).

In the general population, many other strategies have been used to alter people's behavior to avoid or minimize morbidity, disability and mortality. The messages of health promotion have largely been heard and acted on by those in high socioeconomic groups; however, many people of lower socioeconomic groups do not experience these health gains (Turrell et al., 1999). There is ample evidence that an important determinant of health is socioeconomic status (Oldenburg et al., 2000). Factors such as literacy skills, access and the ability to implement health behaviors all influence whether a person or a group of people benefit from health promotion and disease prevention messages or interventions (such as Pap smears) (Turrell et al., 1999).

People with intellectual disabilities, like other marginalized groups, are often excluded from health promoting information or interventions despite their higher rates of premature death, high levels of unrecognized or poorly managed morbidity and adverse lifestyle risk factors. The theme of Tudor Hart's inverse care law succinctly describes this phenomenon – that those in most need of health promotion are least likely to receive it (Aspray et al., 1999). Some within the health promotion field, and many who have an appreciation of the neglect experienced by people with intellectual disabilities, strongly advocate inclusion of people with intellectual disabilities in generic health promotion strategies and the adoption of specific strategies for people with intellectual disabilities. Indeed, some models of health promotion advocate that health promotion strategies target the subpopulations who need them most (Galbally, 1992). It would seem difficult to sustain a reasonable argument not to take both approaches given the health status of people with intellectual disabilities.

Over the last 20 years there has been an increased focus on primary prevention and health promotion for the whole population. Governments have developed strategies to promote health with the goal of decreasing the disease burden and consequent impairment and premature death. It is estimated that, despite these shifts, only somewhere between 2% and 10% of health and welfare funding is directed toward disease prevention. This despite many disorders, such as stroke and sudden cardiac death and brain injury from trauma, being preventable by health promotion strategies while not being amenable to medical or surgical interventions (Leeder, 1998). Hence, even in the provision of generic disease prevention strategies, the budget provided to prevent disease is still a fraction of that directed toward treatment. Also, these preventive strategies often ignore the most disadvantaged populations, such as people with intellectual disabilities.

Why is the health promotion of people with intellectual disabilities important?

Mortality

People with intellectual disabilities often die young, with a mean age of death in the mid fifties for people with Down syndrome (Eyman *et al.*, 1991) and the mid sixties for people with other intellectual disabilities. Studies in the US and the UK have consistently found that people with intellectual disabilities experience premature death, with Hollins finding a 58 times increase in mortality for those under 50 years of age (Hollins *et al.*, 1998). Although people with intellectual disabilities generally die younger than the age peers in the general population, the gap between the two groups' life expectancy appears to be diminishing (Janicki *et al.*, 1999). A recent study by Patja *et al.* (2000) found, from a 35-year follow up of a large population sample, that people with mild intellectual disabilities had similar life expectancy as people in the general population.

In California, Eyman *et al.* (1991) found associations among early death, immobility and inability to eat without assistance. When compared to the general population a Scandinavian population study found a 1.6 times increased mortality in all people with intellectual disabilities and a five times increased mortality for those who also had epilepsy (Forsgen *et al.*, 1996). The causes of death, however, could not be directly attributable to epilepsy. Patja *et al.* (2000) found that a lower level of intelligence, epilepsy in the younger population (<20), hearing impairment lasting between one and nine years, visual impairment in people between 40 and 49 years and the within age group increase in age were all associated with increased mortality.

The life expectancy of individuals with intellectual disabilities varies according to the level of mental and physical impairment. Those with low support needs and minimal impairments have either the same or fairly close to the same life expectancy as the general population. In contrast, individuals with a great number of impairments experience premature death.

Morbidity in middle or older age adults with intellectual disabilities

A number of studies suggest that levels of morbidity among older age adults with intellectual disabilities are as high, if not higher, than the general population (Evenhuis, 1995; Hand & Reid, 1996; Kapell *et al.*,

1998) (see Chapter 1). Many studies identified previously unrecognized or poorly managed medical conditions experienced by this group (Howells, 1986; Wilson & Haire, 1990). Beange *et al.* (1995), for example, studied a group of 20–50-year-old adults with intellectual disabilities living in Sydney, Australia, in the early 1990s, and were able to compare their health assessment results with survey results from the general population. Beange *et al.* (1995) found that there were 5.4 medical conditions per person (among individuals with intellectual disabilities), half of which were unrecognized or poorly managed. Significant differences were found in the prevalence of hypertension, obesity, vision and hearing deficits, medication use, hospitalization and mortality rates, when compared to age peers in the general population. Conditions identified in the literature, which may be unrecognized or inadequately managed in adults with intellectual disabilities, are summarized in Table 11.1.

What affects health for people with intellectual disabilities?

All people, including those with intellectual disabilities, need healthy lifestyles, environments and ways to minimize the impact of any disabilities, diseases or risk of disease and to maximize health and enjoyment of life. Genetic make up also influences the health of individuals in ways that are increasingly understood. All these factors can impact on each other, although they are presented here separately.

Inherited characteristics

Inherited characteristics can place people at risk of disease. Examples of this include a family history of non-insulin dependent diabetes mellitus, breast cancer and early death from heart disease. In some cases, such as hemochromatosis and breast cancer, there is a clear genetic cause (Heisey *et al.*, 1999). In addition, for 40–60% of adults with intellectual disabilities there is an identifiable etiological cause of their disability which may have associated medical conditions (Battaglia *et al.*, 1999; Majnemer & Shevell, 1995). An identifiable etiology is more likely where the intellectual disability is more profound, as is the prevalence of physical comorbidity (Gustavson *et al.*, 1977).

There have been major criticisms of the narrow biomedical focus that conceptualizes disability in a disease or medical model framework, and some critics have taken this further and questioned the utility of syndrome diagnosis. However, to ignore the *cause* of the person's disability when addressing their health or health care can be ill-conceived. The

Table 11.1 Frequently unrecognized or poorly managed medical conditions of people with intellectual disabilities, and relevant references (prevalence, where stated).

Condition	Study
Vision impairments (10–44%)	Ellis, 1979 Tupparainen, 1983 Beange et al., 1995 Warburg, 1994 Van Schrojenstein Lantman-de Valk et al., 1997 Evenhuis, 1995
Hearing impairments (10–28%)	Wilson & Haire, 1990 Reynolds & Reynolds, 1979 Yeates, 1989 Beange et al., 1995 Evenhuis, 1995
Obesity (9.8–40%)	Rimmer et al., 1993 Wells et al., 1997 Wilson & Haire, 1990 Simila, 1991 Burkart et al., 1985 Beange et al., 1995
Dental pathology (29%)	Beange, 1991 Cathels & Reddihough, 1993
Inadequate review of medications, polypharmacy	Wilson & Haire, 1990 Beange, 1991 Parker, 1991 Gowdey et al., 1987 Van Schrojenstein Lantman-de Valk et al., 1997
Epilepsy	Wilson & Haire, 1990 Forsgren et al., 1996
Osteoporosis	Centre & Beange, 1994
Reflux esophagitis	Bohmer et al., 1997
Helicobacter pylori	Bohmer et al., 1997
Constipation and bowel obstruction	Jancar, 1994
Atherosclerotic heart disease	Beange et al., 1995
Infectious diseases (e.g. hepatitis B)	Stehr Green et al., 1991 Cunningham et al., 1994

etiology may have major consequences; for example, 47.5% of babies with Down syndrome have structural heart abnormalities which may need special investigation to be detected and which can be life threatening if missed (Frid et al., 1999). For many others, the etiology of their disability has important health implications – for example, for people with such syndromes and conditions as Down, fragile-X, Prader-Willi, Williams, Retts, Anglemans, tuberous sclerosis and cerebral palsy, among others. A limited list of syndrome-specific medical conditions is provided in Table 11.2 (see also Chapter 3). Recognition of the syndrome and the associated medical conditions can be crucial to minimize the impact on the person's quality of life.

Healthy lifestyles and healthy environments

Various lifestyle 'choices' throughout life put people at risk. Inactivity, obesity, poor nutrition, inadequate immunizations, excessive alcohol intake and smoking tobacco are all well known to increase the risk of disease in the general population (United States Preventive Services Task Force, 1996). This is equally true for people with intellectual disabilities. Inactivity, obesity and inadequate nutrition are more prevalent in adults with intellectual disabilities (Beange et al., 1995; Wells et al., 1997). Most studies suggest that the prevalence of smoked tobacco use among adults with intellectual disabilities appears to be no greater than that found in the general population. However, in one study, Tracey and Hosken reported a prevalence of 36% of adults with intellectual disabilities compared to 26% of the general population who used smoking tobacco (Rimmer et al., 1995; Tracy & Hosken, 1997). Alcohol consumption appears to be less than in the general population (Rimmer et al., 1995). All these studies, however, contain biases which make their relevance uncertain as applied to all people with intellectual disabilities. Anecdotal experience suggests that consumption of alcohol and smoking tobacco becomes less common as the adult's level of support needs increases.

Healthy lifestyle 'choices' occur for a complex set of psychosocial/environmental reasons, and can only be adequately addressed if the context of the person's life is understood (Fujiura et al., 1997). Adults with intellectual disabilities are often living in environments where healthy choices, by them or their carers, are difficult (if not impossible). Too often staff numbers and/or resources may be inadequate to allow regular exercise, or service providers use a visit to a fast food outlet as a reward. Service provider staff may need to model health enhancing behaviors, such as a healthy diet or exercise, to increase the chance that their clients will adopt these behaviors. Health promotion strategies will need to minimize or remove these barriers to be effective. Tracy & Hosken (1997) found that when health promoting strategies are made accessible to adults with intellectual disabilities, this can result in a decrease in tobacco smoking. However, studies to assess increased physical activity and decrease in weight in the obese have had variable outcomes (Burkart et al., 1985; Pitetti et al., 1993).

Table 11.2(a) Syndrome specific list for general practitioners.

	Cerebral palsy 1:500	Down syndrome 1:700	Prader-Willi 1:10 000–25 000	Fragile-X 1:6000	Phenyl/ketonuria 1:10 000–1:20 000
Audiovisual	Visual impairment Hearing impairment	Visual impairment (multifactorial), cataracts Hearing impairment (multifactorial) (Annual assessments recommended)	Strabismus Myopia	Visual impairment (multifactorial) Hearing impairment Recurrent ear infections	
Endocrine		Hypothyroidism (Annual TFT recommended)	NIDDM (secondary to obesity) Hypogonadism Delayed puberty		
Psychiatric/ psychological	Depression Variable intellectual capacity	Depression Alzheimer's type dementia (clinical onset uncommon before 40 years)	Hyperphagia Impulse control difficulties Self-injury	Attention deficit/hyperactivity Variable intellectual capacity Disabled in social functioning	Variable intellectual capacity Phobic anxiety Disabled in social functioning
CNS	Epilepsy	Epilepsy Usually clonic/tonic		Epilepsy Usually clonic/tonic, complex partial	Epilepsy Hyperactivity Tremor and pyramidal tract signs Extrapyramidal syndromes
Cardiovascular		Congenital heart defects (common in 40–50%)		Aortic dilatation, mitral valve prolapse (related to connective tissue dysplasia)	

Table 11.2(a) Continued.

	Cerebral palsy 1:500	Down syndrome 1:700	Prader-Willi 1:10 000–25 000	Fragile-X 1:6000	Phenylketonuria 1:10 000–1:20 000
Muscular/skeletal and skin	Orthopedic problems Neuromuscular problems	Atlantoaxial instability Skin disorders, alopecia, eczema	Scoliosis, kyphosis Hypotonia Skin picking	Connective tissue dysplasia Scoliosis Congenital hip dislocation	
Other	Genito-urinary problems Incontinence Constipation Dental problems Recurrent aspiration Esophagitis, gastroesophageal reflux +/− bleeding/anemia Swallowing/eating difficulties	Blood dyscrasias Childhood leukemia Sleep apnea Increased susceptibility to infections Coeliac disease	Infantile failure to thrive, then hyperphagia and severe obesity High tolerance to pain Decreased ability to vomit Sleep apnea Osteoporosis Undescended testes Dental abnormalities	Herniae (CT related) Abnormalities of speech and language	Eczema
Inheritance		Most cases are sporadic; 4% due to translocation involving chromosome 21 or rarely parental mosaicism	Atypical. Most cases are sporadic	X-linked	Autosomal recessive

Table 11.2(b) Syndrome specific list for general practitioners.

	Angelmann syndrome <1:10 000	Williams ?< 1:20 000	Rett 1:14 000 Females	Noonan <1:10 000	Tuberous sclerosis 1:6 000–17 000	Neurofibro matosis 1:3000
Audiovisual	Glaucoma	Hyperacusis strabismus	Refractory errors	Strabismus, refractive errors Vision/hearing impairments	Retinal tumors Eye rhabdomyomatas	Hearing impairment (Glioma affecting auditory nerve)
Endocrine						Various endocrine abnormalities
Psychiatric/ psychological	Easily excitable Hyperactive	Variable intellectual capacity Attention deficit problems in childhood	Severe intellectual disability	Mild intellectual disability	Variable intellectual capacity Behavioral difficulties Sleep problems	Variable intellectual capacity
CNS	Severe developmental delay Epilepsy	Perceptual and motor function reduced	Epilepsy Vasomotor instability	Epilepsy	Cerebral astrocytomas Epilepsy	Variable clinical phenomena depending on site of the tumors Epilepsy
Cardiovascular		Cardiac abnormalities Hypertension, CVAs Chronic hemiparesis	Prolonged QT interval	Pulmonary valvular stenosis ASD, VSD, PDA	Rhabdomyomatas Hypertension	

Table 11.2(b) Continued.

	Angelmann syndrome <1:10 000	Williams ?<1:20 000	Rett 1:14 000 Females	Noonan <1:10 000	Tuberous sclerosis 1:6 000–17 000	Neurofibromatosis 1:3000
Muscular/skeletal	Joint contractures and scoliosis (in adults)	Joint contractures Scoliosis Hypotonia	Osteopenia Fractures Scoliosis	Scoliosis Talipes equinovarus Pectus carinatum/excavatum	Bone Rhabdomyomata	Skeletal abnormalities especially kyphoscoliosis
Other	Speech impairment Movement and balance disorder Characteristic EEG changes	Renal abnormalities	Hyperventilation Apnea Reflux Feeding difficulties Growth failure	Abnormal clotting factors, platelet dysfunction Undescended testes, deficient spermatogenesis Lymphoedenoma Hepatosplenomegaly Cubitus valgus, hand abnormalities	Kidney and lung hamartomata Polycystic kidneys Liver Rhabdomyomata Dental abnormalities Skin lesions	Variable clinical phenomena depending on the location of the neurofibroma Tumors are susceptible to malignant change Other varieties of tumors may be associated
Inheritance	Variety of genetic mechanisms on chromosome 15	Microdeletion on chromosome 7	Usually sporadic X-linked	Autosomal dominant may be sporadic	Autosomal dominant	Autosomal dominant

Adapted from an original unpublished version by Michael Kew and Glyn Jones. Reprinted by kind permission of the University of Queensland

Social capital

Putnam (2001) has described the decrease in social capital in the developed world, which he defines as how social connectedness adds value to a society. This change has had negative impacts on the health and well-being of the society and its individuals. There is a known association between diminished social capital and increased depression, crime rates and even premature mortality. Maximizing the connectedness between people with intellectual disabilities and society has been one of the key goals of normalization as represented by deinstitutionalization and integration into mainstream services. Although deinstitutionalization has resulted in a trend toward increased choice-making and improved quality of life (Young *et al.*, 1999), community integration has thus far been limited (Donnelly *et al.*, 1996; Lord, 1991). However, despite this partial success the impact of the enduring social change, called normalization, and the impact on improving health promotion, should not be underestimated (see Figure 11.1).

There are many examples where initiatives are established to increase social connectedness. One example is Etmanski's work, where he lays out a detailed plan of action for families to assist them to 'create a safe and secure future for their relatives with a disability'. At the center of what he has seen work and recommends is the development of a planned lifetime advocacy network which at least in part seeks to provide and enhance connectedness. It also provides advocacy and recommends specific health strategies, such as the development of a lifetime book on the person, his or her life and his or her medical records (Etmanski, 2000). Etmanski's approach is consistent with those found in the generic health promotion literature which recommends that interventions be made in partnership with individuals or groups within the community. It is generally recognized that participation is important at all stages of the evolution, planning and implementation of health promotion strategies (Wass, 2000).

'The occults' or systemwide ignoring of comorbidity

A more subtle yet pervasive factor that affects the health of people with intellectual disabilities is the inability of society to develop strategies that identify and then act to correct the known high prevalence of unrecognized or poorly managed disease or implementation of health screening practices (Lennox *et al.*, 2000, 2001). Given the often extremely poor health status of this population one would usually expect governments to set up strategies to address this neglect; however, such initiatives are rare. Although difficult to substantiate, the central cause undoubtedly relates to the pervasive devaluing of this population, such that they appear as a hidden population that are often not considered by health policy-makers. The exception to this situation seems to be in the UK, where the Welsh (and more recently the English) governments have been proactive in recognizing the poor health status of this population (Welsh Health Planning Forum, 1992).

Adults with intellectual disabilities are also at particular risk of a range of morbidities, including seizures, polypharmacy and gastrointestinal disorders, that can limit their quality of life and longevity. Optimizing management of these conditions is crucial in minimizing secondary disabilities and associated impairments that can ensue.

How do we engage in health promotion for people with intellectual disabilities?

Healthy aging requires that individuals reach the 'third age', and then enter it and continue on in the best health possible for themselves. For all people, including people with intellectual disabilities, this requires a lifespan approach and then, with aging, being included and valued as a senior member of their community. Health promotion in people with intellectual disabilities through the various stages of the life cycle is discussed below.

Preconception to adolescence

There are a number of primary preventive strategies which diminish the risk of developing a disability or ameliorate the effects on people's lives. These are summarized in Table 11.3. Identification of the cause of the disability can greatly improve the health of the child or adult and decrease consequent morbidity and mortality as the person ages. Associated conditions are discussed further in Chapter 3.

Adulthood to elderly

Apart from syndrome-specific associated morbidity, there is a range of health promotion and disease prevention activities which are necessary in adults. These are summarized in Table 11.4. Screening tests should be performed according to the same indications and contraindications as for the general population. However, some tests and activities, such as cervical smears and injections, may be traumatic for some people with

Table 11.3   Preventive strategies which diminish the risk of developing a disability.

Time	Intervention
Preconception	Rubella immunization Folic acid supplementation to decrease the risk of spina bifida
Intra partum	High quality obstetric care
Neonatal period	PKU, hypothyroidism and galactasemia screening of neonates
Infancy and childhood	Measles, mumps and Hemophilus influenzae b immunization Hearing and vision screening Identification and management of associated morbidity, such as epilepsy Identification of syndromal diagnosis and management of the consequences

intellectual disabilities. An assessment of the relative risks and benefits must be made for each individual case.

Systematic interventions to improve the health of adults with intellectual disabilities

Many researchers have developed health promotion/disease prevention strategies and/or have measured their relative success at improving the health of individuals with intellectual disabilities. For example, Jones and Kerr (1996) randomly inserted a prompt in GP notes and compared the completion of the prompt to matched controls in the same practice. They found no increase in health screening activities. The notion of the annual health examination in the general population, while popular in the early 1970s, has not been demonstrated to be effective and is now not recommended (United States Preventive Services Task Force, 1996). In contrast some evidence exists to support health screening in all people over 75 years of age (Brown *et al.*, 1997; Pathy *et al.*, 1992; Perkins, 1991). The UK and Australian primary health care systems are providing incentives to encourage family practitioners to perform yearly health assessment in all people over 75 years of age (Harris, 1992).

Health care issues for people aged over 75 years have many similarities to those of people with intellectual disabilities. Both are seemingly devalued groups in our society and their medical issues are often conceptualized in terms of loss and impairments. Both groups underreport symptoms and may present illness in atypical ways (Beange, 1996), while being at high risk of sensory impairments, polypharmacy, medication side effects, limits to mobility and, at times, difficulty learning new

Table 11.4   Health screening for adults with intellectual disabilities.

Health issues	Screening frequency
Blood pressure check	Every 1 or 2 years
Dental check	Yearly (6-monthly in people with cerebral palsy)
Hearing assessment	Every 5 years by an audiologist
Medication review	Regular review of indications and side effects
Thyroid function test	Annual or biannual, depending on age
Vision assessment	Every 5 years by an optometrist/ophthalmologist
Lifestyle	
Alcohol intake review	Yearly
Diet review	Yearly
Examination for skin tumors	Yearly
Exercise review	Yearly
Sleep pattern review	Yearly
Tobacco intake review	Yearly
Weight review	Yearly
Women's health	
Breast examination by GP	Regularly if breast self-examination is not reliable
Mammography	If indicated – 50 to 69 years 2 yearly
Papanicolou smear	If indicated – in last 2 years
Immunisations	
Hepatitis A	If indicated
Hepatitis B	If indicated
Influenza	If indicated – yearly
Streptococcus pneumoniae	If indicated – 5-yearly
Diphtheria/tetanus	According to national recommendations
Other	
Epilepsy	Continual awareness of risk
Incontinence	Elucidate and treat cause of changes
Mobility	Continual monitoring and address changes
Problem behavior/s	If indicated – consider physical/psychological/social issues
Psychiatric disorder	Continual awareness of risk
Sexual activity	If indicated – contraception and safe sex advice

information (MacLennan, 1990). Given these similarities to the general population over 75 years of age, researchers have begun to look at health screening in adults with intellectual disabilities. This process is either being examined or has been reported on in New Zealand (Webb & Rogers, 1999), Australia (Lennox et al., 2001) and the UK (Kerr et al., 1996; Martin, 1997; Martin & Wells, 1997).

Kerr et al. (1996) have performed a multiple baseline trial of the Cardiff Health Check on adults with intellectual disabilities in Wales. The study identified significant improvements in some health promotion/disease prevention activities, in particular tetanus immunization rates. In New Zealand, Webb & Rogers (1999) involved all adults with intellectual disabilities under the care of the major service provider. Each individual had a comprehensive medical and development history taken as well as the completion of a health review by a family practitioner using the Cardiff Health Check. This intervention, which was a change in process rather than a controlled trial, also involved the cooperation and education of families, carers and other staff, and included the provision of an ongoing monitoring system. Of the 1311 adults screened, 1798 health actions resulted (i.e. 73% of the people screened were judged by their family practitioner to need at least one action). Most actions were related to health screening/promotion activities, although a number of significant life-threatening medical disorders were identified by this process.

Lennox *et al.* (2001) performed a pilot study in Australia and found similar results. This then led to the Comprehensive Health Assessment Programme (CHAP) which is a large randomized controlled trial involving 462 adults with intellectual disabilities in Queensland. In progress at the time of writing, this trial involves adults and their carers/families completing a detailed current and past history before their family practitioner assesses the adult with an intellectual disability. The family practitioner is given key information about the health of the adult with an intellectual disability and is asked to conduct a full review of the person's history and a full physical review. As a helpful aid, the CHAP booklet directs the people with intellectual disabilities, and their carers, family and the family practitioner, to areas of health that are commonly neglected.

The CHAP, Cardiff Health Check and other tools all attempt to minimize the barriers to good health care and serve a number of other purposes. These include improving communication and gathering health information, while providing the people with intellectual disabilities and carers with a valid and credible 'ticket of entry' to doctors (Lennox *et al.*, 1997, 2001). These strategies also provide information to the family practitioner (and the people with intellectual disabilities and carers) in the context of their environment, a strategy known to improve the chances of behavioral change (Davis *et al.*, 1995). Finally, information about medical conditions associated with specific syndromes allows the assessment to be informed and identification, management and prevention of these morbidities to be addressed.

While there are logical benefits to this process, there continues to be a lack of high quality supportive evidence. Many morbidities increase with age and it may be ideal that a process is adopted for some specific syndromes. One example is Down syndrome, where numerous health comorbidities occur which increase in prevalence with age, and where various health information sources and screening tools have been developed (Cohen, 1997). A variety of locally-based initiatives and teaching aids, such as videos, have been developed in different parts of the world. These are often highly valued by service providers, but these interventions are usually neither scientifically evaluated nor, perhaps as a consequence, implemented in other countries.

Any strategies developed need to be relevant to the psychosocial context of the person. The major issues are:

- education of people with intellectual disabilities and their families, as well as the staff and health professionals (including family practitioners) who support them
- improved access to generic and specialist services
- access to generic health promotion.

Conclusion

The substantial deficits in health, health care and health promotion/disease prevention for adults with intellectual disabilities need to be recognized. There is a pressing need for the positive message of health promotion to be tailored to this population, so that it is person-centered, accessible and able to be implemented at both individual and organizational levels. Benefits from these actions could be expected to accrue throughout life, assisting adults with intellectual disabilities to enjoy healthy aging.

References

Aspray, T.J., Francis, R.M., Tyrer, S.P. & Quilliam, S.J (1999) Patients with learning disability in the community (editorials). *British Medical Journal*, **318**, 476–477.

Battaglia, A., Bianchini, E. & Carey, J. (1999) Diagnostic yield of the comprehensive assessment of developmental delay/mental retardation in an institute of child neuropsychiatry. *American Journal of Medical Genetics*, **82**, 60–66.

Beange, H. (1991) The neglected health of the intellectually disabled. In: *Proceedings of National Conference of the Australian Society for the Study of Intellectual Disability*, Geelong, Victoria.

Beange, H. (1996) Caring for a vulnerable population. *Medical Journal of Australia*, **164**, 159–160.

Beange, H., McElduff, A. & Baker, W. (1995) Medical disorders of adults with mental retardation. *American Journal of Mental Retardation*, **99**, 595–604.

Bohmer, C.J., Klinkenberg Knol, E.C., Kuipers, E.J., Niezen de Boer, M.C., Schreuder, H., Schuckink Kool, F. & Meuwissen, S.G. (1997) The prevalence of Helicobacter pylori infection among inhabitants and healthy employees of institutes for the intellectually disabled. *American Journal of Gastroenterology*, **92**, 1000–1004.

Brown, V. (1985) Towards an epidemiology of health: a basis for planning community health programs. *Health Policy*, **4**, 331–40.

Brown, K., Boot, D., Groom, L. & Williams, E. (1997) Problems found in the over-75s by the annual health check. *British Journal of General Practice*, **47**, 31–35.

Burkart, J., Fox, R. & Rotatori, A. (1985) Obesity of mentally retarded individuals: prevalence, characteristics, and intervention. *American Journal of Mental Deficiency*, **90**, 303–312.

Cathels, B.A. & Reddihough, D.S. (1993) The health care of young adults with cerebral palsy. *The Medical Journal of Australia*, **159**, 444–446.

Centre, J.M. & Beange H. (1994) Osteoporosis in groups with intellectual disability. *Australia and New Zealand Journal of Developmental Disabilities*, **19**, 251–258.

Cohen W.I.P.B. (1997) News from the Down syndrome medical interest group (DSMIG). *Down Syndrome Quarterly*, **2**, 9–10.

Cunningham, S.J., Cunningham, R., Izmeth, M.G., Baker, B. & Hart, C.A. (1994) Seroprevalence of hepatitis B and C in a Merseyside hospital for the mentally handicapped. *Epidemiology and Infection*, **112**, 195–200.

Davis, D.A.T.M., Oxman, A.D. & Haynes, B. (1995) Changing physician performance – a systematic review of the effect of continuing medical education strategies. *Journal of the American Medical Association*, **274**, 700–705.

Donnelly, M., McGilloway, S., Mays, N., Knapp, M., Kavanagh, S., Beecham, J. & Fenyo, A. (1996) One and two year outcomes for adults with learning disabilities discharged to the community. *British Journal of Psychiatry*, **168**, 598–606.

Ellis, D. (1979) Visual handicap of mental retarded people. *American Journal of Mental Deficiency*, **83**, 497–511.

Etmanski, A. (2000) *A good life: for you and your relative with a disability*. Orwell Cove and Planned Lifetime Advocacy Network, British Columbia, Canada.

Evenhuis, H. (1995) Medical aspects of ageing in a population with intellectual disability: I. Visual impairment. *Journal of Intellectual Disability Research*, **39**, 19–25.

Eyman, R.K., Call, T.L. & White, J.F. (1991) Life expectancy of persons with Down syndrome. *American Journal on Mental Retardation*, **95**, 603–612.

Forsgren, L., Edvinsson, S., Nystrom, L. & Blomquist, H. (1996) Influence of epilepsy on mortality in mental retardation: an epidemiologic study. *Epilepsia*, **37**, 956–963.

Frid, C., Drott, P., Lundell, B., Rasmussen, F. & Anneren, G. (1999) Mortality in Down's syndrome in relation to congenital malformations. *Journal of Intellectual Disability Research*, **43**, 234–241.

Fujiura, G.T., Fitzsimons, N., Marks, B. & Chicoine, B. (1997) Predictors of BMI among adults with Down syndrome: the social context of health promotion. *Research in Developmental Disabilities*, **18**, 261–274.

Galbally, R. (1992) Planning health promotion: equity as intrinsic. In: *Public Health Association of Australia 24th Annual Conference*, selected papers.

Gowdey, C.W., Zarfas, Donald E. & Phipps, S. (1987) Audit psychoactive drug prescriptions in group homes. *Mental Retardation*, **25**, 331–334.

Gustavson, K.H., Hagberg, B., Hagberg, G. & Sars, K. (1977) Severe mental retardation in a Swedish county: I. Epidemiology, gestational age, birth weight and associated CNS handicaps in children born 1959–70. *Acta Paediatrica Scandinavica*, **66**, 373–379.

Hand, J.E., & Reid, P.M. (1996) Older adults with lifelong intellectual handicap in New Zealand: prevalence, disabilities and implications for regional health authorities. *New Zealand Medical Journal*, **109**, 118–121.

Harris, A. (1992) Health checks for patients over 75. *British Medical Journal*, **305**, 599–600.

Hawe, P., Degeling, D. & Hall, J. (2000) *Evaluating Health Promotion – a health worker's guide*. MacLennan & Petty Pty Ltd, Sydney.

Heisey, R., Carroll, J., Warner, E., McCready, D. & Goel, V. (1999) Hereditary breast cancer. Identifying and managing BRCA1 and BRCA2 carriers. *Canadian Family Physician*, **45**, 114–124.

Hollins, S., Attard, M., Fraunhofer, N., McGuigan, S. & Sedgwick, P. (1998) Mortality in people with learning disability: risks, causes, and death certification findings in London. *Developmental Medicine & Child Neurology*, **40**, 50–56.

Howells, G. (1986) Are the medical needs of mentally handicapped adults being met? *Journal of the Royal College of General Practitioners*, **36**, 449–453.

Jancar, J.S. (1994) Fatal intestinal obstruction in the mentally handicapped. *Journal of Intellectual Disability Research*, **38**, 413–422.

Janicki, M., Dalton, A., Henderson, C. & Davidson, P. (1999) Mortality and morbidity among older adults with intellectual disability: health services considerations. *Disability and Rehabilitation*, **21**, 284–294.

Jones, G. & Kerr, M. (1996) A randomised controlled trial of opportunistic health screening in primary care for people with learning disability – preliminary results. In: *Proceedings of 10th World Congress of the International Association for the Scientific Study of Intellectual Disabilities*, ISBN 951-580-173-7 Helsinki, pp. 264.

Kapell, D., Nightingale, B., Rodriguez, A., Lee, J.H., Zigman, W.B. & Schupf, N. (1998) Prevalence of chronic medical conditions in adults with mental retardation: comparison with the general population. *Mental Retardation*, **36**, 269–279.

Kerr, M., Fraser, W., Felch, D. & Hewitt, R. (1996) A randomised controlled trial of general practice based yearly health check for people with a learning disability – preliminary results. In: *Proceedings of 10th World Congress of the International Association for the Scientific Study off Intellectual Disabilities*, Helsinki, pp. 265.

Leeder, S (1998) Better health. The tasks of medicine – an ideology of care. The health needs of people with intellectual disability. In: *The Tasks of Medicine – an Ideology of Care* (ed. P. Baume) pp. 238–249. MacLennan & Petty Pty Ltd, Sydney.

Lennox, N., Diggens, J. & Ugoni, A. (1997) The general practice care of people with intellectual disability: barriers and solutions. *Journal of Intellectual Disability Research*, **41**, 380–390.

Lennox, N., Beange, H. & Edwards, N. (2000) The health needs of people with intellectual disability. *Medical Journal of Australia*, **173**, 328–330.

Lennox, N., Green, M., Diggens, J. & Ugoni, A. (2001) Audit and comprehensive health assessment programme in the primary healthcare of adults with intellectual disability: a pilot study. *Journal of Intellectual Disability Research*, **45**, 226–232.

Lord, J.P.A. (1991) Life in the community: four years after the closure of an institution. *Mental Retardation*, **29**, 213–221.

MacLennan, W. (1990) Screening elderly patients – a task well suited to health visitors? *British Medical Journal*, **300**, 694–695.

Majnemer, A. & Shevell, M. (1995) Diagnostic yield of the neurologic assessment of the developmentally delayed child. *Journal of Pediatrics*, **127**, 193–199.

Martin, B.A. (1997) Health gain through health checks: improving access to primary health care for people with intellectual disability. *American Family Physician*, **56**, 485–494.

Martin, D.M.R. & Wells, M.B. (1997) Health gain through health checks: Improving access to primary healthcare for people with intellectual disability. *Journal of Intellectual Disability Research*, **41**, 401–408.

McMichael, A. & Leon, D. (1998) Beyond medicine: The wider determinants of population and global health. In *The Tasks of Medicine – an Ideology of Care* (ed. P. Baume) pp. 183–193. MacLennan & Petty Pty Ltd, Sydney.

O'Connor, M.L. & Parker, E. (1995) *Health Promotion Principles and Practice in The Australian Context*. Allen & Unwin, Sydney.

Oldenburg, B., McGuffog, I. & Turrell, G. (2000) Socioeconomic determinants of health in Australia: policy responses and intervention options. *Medical Journal of Australia*, **172**, 489–492.

Parker, G. (1991) Developmentally disabled, doubly disadvantaged. *The Medical Journal of Australia*, **155**, 68–71.

Pathy, M.S., Bayer, A., Harding, K. & Dibble, A. (1992) Randomised trial of case finding and surveillance of elderly people at home. *Lancet*, **10**, 890–893.

Patja, K.I.M., Vesala, H., Oksanen, H. & Ruoppila, I. (2000) Life expectancy of people with intellectual disability: a 35-year follow-up study. *Journal of Intellectual Disability Research*, **44**, 591–599.

Perkins, E.R. (1991) Screening elderly people: a review of the literature in the light of the new general practitioner contract. *British Journal of General Practice*, **41**, 382–385.

Pitetti, K.H., Rimmer, H.J. & Fernhall, B. (1993) Physical fitness and adults with mental retardation. *Sports Medicine*, **16**, 23–56.

Putnam, R. (2001) *Bowling Alone: The Collapse and Revival of American Community*. Simon and Schuster, New York.

Reynolds, W. & Reynolds, S. (1979) Prevalence of speech and hearing impairment of non-institutionalized mentally retarded adults. *American Journal of Mental Deficiency*, **84**, 62–86.

Rimmer, J.H., Braddock, D. & Fujiura, G. (1993) Health characteristics and behaviors of adults with mental retardation residing in three living arrangements. *Mental Retardation*, **31**, 105–110.

Rimmer, J., Braddock, D. & Marks, B. (1995) Prevalence of obesity in adults with mental retardation: implications for health promotion and disease prevention. *Research in Developmental Disabilities*, **16**, 489–499.

Silargy, C. (1998) *The Tasks of Medicine – An Ideology of Care* (ed. P. Baume) pp. 14–25. MacLennan & Petty Pty Limited, Sydney, Australia.

Simila, S.N.P. (1991) Underweight and overweight cases among the mentally retarded. *Journal of Mental Defiency Research*, **35**, 160–164.

Stehr Green, P., Wilson, N., Miller, J. & Lawther, A. (1991) Risk factors for hepatitis

B at a residential institution for intellectually handicapped persons. *New Zealand Medical Journal*, **104**, 514–516.

Tracy, J. & Hosken, R. (1997) The importance of smoking education and preventative health strategies for people with intellectual disability. *Journal of Intellectual Disability Research*, **41**, 416–421.

Tupparainen, K. (1983) Ocular findings among children with mental retardation in Finland. *Acta Opthalmologica*, **61**, 634–644.

Turrell, G., Oldenburg, B., McGuffog, I. & Dent, R. (1999) *Socioeconomic determinants of health: towards a national research program and a policy and intervention agenda*. Report to the Commonwealth Department of Health and Aged Care, Canberra, Australia.

United States Preventive Services Task Force (1996) *Guide to Clinical Prevention Services*, 2nd edn. Agency for Healthcare Research and Quality, Washington, DC.

Van Schrojenstein Lantman-de Valk, H.M.J., Akker, M. van den., Maaskant, M.A., Haveman, M.J., Urlings, H.F.J., Kessels, A.G.H. & Crebolder, H.F.J.M. (1997) Prevalence and incidence of health problems in people with intellectual disability. *Journal of Intellectual Disability Research*, **41**, 42–51.

Warburg, M. (1994) Visual impairment among people with developmental delay. *Journal of Intellectual Disability Research*, **38**, 423–432.

Wass, A. (2000) *Promoting Health – The primary health care approach*. Harcourt, Saunders, NSW, Australia.

Webb, O. & Rogers, L. (1999) Health screening for people with intellectual disability: the New Zealand experience. *Journal of Intellectual Disability Research*, **43**, 497–503.

Wells, M.B., Turner. S., Martin, D.M. & Roy, A. (1997) Health gain through screening – a coronary heart disease and stroke: Developing primary health care services for people with intellectual disability. *Journal of Intellectual & Developmental Disability*, **22**, 251–263.

Welsh Health Planning Forum (1992) Health Document. Welsh Office NHS Directorate, Cardiff, UK.

WHO (1986) *Ottawa Charter on Health Promotion*. World Health Organisation, Ottawa.

Wilson, D.N. & Haire, A. (1990) Health care screening for people with mental handicap living in the community. *British Medical Journal*, **301**, 1379–1381.

Yeates, S. (1989) Hearing in people with mental handicaps: A review of 100 cases. *Mental Handicap*, **17**, 33–37.

Young, L, Ashman, A., Sigafoos, J. & Grevell, P. (1999) Deinstitutionalization and change in life circumstances of adults with an intellectual disability. In: *'Quality Lifestyles' – Australian Society for the Study of Intellectual Disability National Conference*. Sydney, NSW, Australia.

12 Barriers to Health Care Services and the Role of the Physician

Helen Baxter and Michael Kerr

Introduction

Research has indicated that, although people with intellectual disabilities often require more attention to their health, in practice they receive a similar amount to that experienced by the general population (Whitfield *et al.*, 1996; Wilson & Haire, 1990). Furthermore, a body of data has appeared pointing to deficits in the quality of health care received by this population. Studies world-wide have found, when compared to the general population:

- a high number of untreated common conditions among patients with intellectual disabilities (Beange & Bauman, 1990; Howells, 1986; Webb & Rogers, 1999; Wilson & Haire, 1990)
- a low level of health promotion and preventative care (Beange *et al.*, 1995; Kerr *et al.*, 1996; Whitfield *et al.*, 1996).

The gap between need and outcome is further widened by the specialist conditions and additional health care needs that individuals often have as a result of the etiology of their disability.

A number of barriers have been identified that may be preventing people with intellectual disabilities from accessing health services appropriate to their needs. Patient-based issues include physical difficulties (Minihan *et al.*, 1993), behavior problems (Lennox & Kerr, 1997) and communication difficulties (Lennox *et al.*, 1997; Wilson & Haire, 1990). Physician-based issues include a lack of specialist knowledge about health issues (Aspray *et al.*, 1999; Lennox *et al.*, 1997) and the need for additional service time and resources by many patients with intellectual disabilities (Chambers *et al*, 1998; Kerr *et al.*, 1996).

Physicians have a pivotal role in overcoming these barriers and maintaining patient access to health care, through their knowledge of the patient's health and their understanding of their country's health care system. This chapter addresses the barriers to the delivery of health care to individuals with intellectual disabilities through an analysis of five issues:

- Accessibility, mobility and sensory impairment
- Behavioral problems
- Communication
- Knowledge, attitudes and accessing specialist services.
- Time and resources.

Accessibility, mobility and sensory impairment

Accessibility

Globally, people with intellectual disabilities are usually poorer and are often dependent on social systems of care for their finances (Beange, 1996). They are unlikely to have a personal means of transport and will often need to be taken to visits for health care. Such lack of transportation can present difficulties in physically accessing health services, particularly in countries where a high proportion of people with intellectual disabilities live in rural areas where services are more scarce (Piachaud, 1994; Sonnander & Claesson, 1997). Thus, accessibility may encompass not only awkwardly sited health care resources but difficulties encountered in attempting to get to them.

For the more developing countries the urban drift of people into the towns and cities may reduce the ability of the extended family to care for an individual, thus removing a valuable source of support. Nevertheless, Piachaud (1994), in discussing this phenomenon, describes the possibility of families having a network of relations across the country in which they live. This may in turn have other advantages for individuals living in rural areas who, by utilizing this family network, may be able to access services previously inaccessible in the towns by staying with relations. A family discussion with the physician on options and opportunities for obtaining services can ensure continuous access to care and a reduction in anxiety for family members.

In developed countries individuals may be able to use social systems of care for transportation and assistance during appointments or treatment. This may require an increase in organizational support and redeployment of personnel. Chambers et al. (1998), in a study on the care of adults with intellectual disabilities moving into the community, found that doctors believed that additional home visits for these patients were due to the unavailability of staff to assist individuals in attending the practitioner's office or surgery. Awareness that patients and their carers may need more planning time to arrange consultations, and the option of different appointment times, could make the process easier to manage. It may also be beneficial for staff teams and family members to have a discussion with the physician regarding possible arrangements when the individual is unable to attend alone.

Mobility

Maintenance of acquired skills through the use of assistive devices such as sensory aids and wheelchairs (Maaskant & Haveman, 1989) can enable adults to be more independent. However, for these devices to help an adult, health service buildings and accommodation also need to be physically accessible and barrier free. In a study of 614 physicians it was reported that 12% of the physician's offices were inaccessible to their patients with mobility problems (Minihan *et al.*, 1993). In addition, early intervention or treatment of mobility impairment can be preventative by reducing the risk of secondary illness and mortality for individuals suffering from chronic constipation, incontinence, gastroesophageal reflux, deterioration of pulmonary function and coronary heart disease (Evenhuis, 1997). Evenhuis (1997) has included physical activity, control of dietary calcium, adequate treatment and control of childhood mobility impairment, surgical treatment of hip fractures and active mobilization, as well as appropriate design and adequate walking devices, in her recommendations for prevention of mobility impairment.

Sensory impairment

Sensory impairment may also reduce the ability of the patient to attend appointments alone and may increase patient distress during consultations and physical examinations as communication and comprehension are reduced. Assistive devices such as glasses and hearing aids can help to reduce the impairment and have been used successfully by people with intellectual disabilities once they are diagnosed (Evenhuis, 1995a,b). Early detection and treatment for sensory impairment has also been advocated to reduce further handicap and increase an individual's acceptance and use of sensory aids (Evenhuis, 1995a).

Behavioral problems

The prevalence of behavioral problems that obstruct physicians in examining or treating a patient is difficult to judge. There are various methods for measuring challenging (problematic) behavior (e.g. Lowe &

Felce, 1995; Qureshi & Alborz, 1992) which take account of behaviors that are difficult for others to tolerate (e.g. stereotypic behavior, sexually inappropriate behavior) or that cause harm to the individual, others or property. Behaviors classed as 'challenging' by carers or community teams, because they impinge on the individual's activities (e.g. severe stereotypic behavior), may not prove an obstacle for physical examination. Likewise, an usually compliant individual may be extremely distressed by a visit to a physician and express this inappropriately, making an examination virtually impossible. Minihan and Dean (1990) found 20% of adults with intellectual disabilities could only be examined or treated after supportive measures such as premedication or previsits for desensitization. Rates of challenging behavior in populations of people with intellectual disabilities have been found at around 17% in the UK (Qureshi & Alborz, 1992). Although levels of challenging behavior in general have been found to reduce with increasing age (Moss, 1991), other studies have shown aggressive behavior to be persistent throughout the lifespan (Day, 1987; Davidson et al.,1999). Thus, challenging behavior could still prove to be a barrier to care as individuals age into their later years.

In addition, patients with a psychiatric illness may demonstrate problem behavior that could obstruct care. Moss et al. (2000) discovered an association between patients exhibiting challenging behavior and prevalence of psychiatric symptoms, particularly depression. Rates of psychiatric disorder have been found at 47.9% (Cooper, 1997) in a population of adults with intellectual disabilities. In the same study, Cooper also discovered high rates among older people of dementia (21.6% v. 2.7%) and depression (6% v. 4.1%), although other studies (e.g. Janicki & Dalton, 2000) report a more normative rate for dementia among adults with intellectual disabilities (other than Down syndrome).

Behavioral problems may hinder diagnosis of conditions and be difficult to interpret in themselves. This is emphasized by Aylward et al. (1997) who discussed the problems of diagnosing dementia in individuals with a history of abnormal behaviors. The authors noted that the behaviors could mask the symptoms of dementia and for this reason recommended an evaluation of adults with Down syndrome around the age of 25 years to give a baseline for behavior and functioning from which to measure change. Also, in diagnosing epilepsy, challenging behavior may mimic some forms of seizure and hamper the process (Paul, 1997). Problems in interpreting a person's behavior due to unusual response patterns (Lennox et al., 1997), and distinguishing fear of a medical procedure and a patient's legal right to refuse treatment (Minihan et al., 1993), have also been highlighted as causing difficulties for diagnosis and treatment. Only one in five primary care physicians reported that they felt well prepared to handle a patient refusing to cooperate with an examination or treatment (Minihan *et al.*, 1993). The potential benefits of early evaluation in measuring some of the difficulties in diagnosis are highlighted by the findings of Lennox *et al.* (1997) who found that three quarters of physicians were unsure of their patient's baseline health and behavior.

It seems from the studies looking at the views of physicians (Aylward *et al.*, 1997; Lennox *et al.*, 1997; Minihan *et al.*, 1993) that barriers due to behavior arise from concerns with giving accurate diagnosis and issues around consent. Indeed, in these studies only 19% of physicians rated the maladaptive behaviors of patients in the office setting as a major obstacle to health care (Minihan *et al.*, 1993) and in the study by Lennox *et al.* (1997) maladaptive behavior in the surgery was not mentioned at all. Kerr (1998) suggested that an individual's difficult behavior may be more of a problem for parents or staff, who may be embarrassed and therefore reduce visits to the doctor. In a study of physicians who were not psychiatrists, 58% reported that they had been asked by a carer to treat a patient's behavioral problem (Minihan *et al.*, 1993). Physicians can do much to alleviate the worries of the family or carers by reassurance, arranging visits at quiet times so that others are not disturbed and also through treatment. Diagnosis of an underlying psychiatric illness that can be treated medically will obviously be of benefit; however, contacting psychologists and specialists in behavioral problems could also be a step forward in reducing the incidence of difficult behavior.

Communication

People with intellectual disabilities are often reliant on their family or carers to communicate their health needs on their behalf. Even when a carer knows the person very well, it may still be difficult to detect a health problem when the individual's communication skills are limited. The reliance on carers to communicate health needs has been cited as a major barrier to care. Beange *et al.* (1995) studied a population of adults with intellectual disabilities and found that despite a mean of 5.4 medical problems per patient, 65% of patients and 24% of the carers reported no symptoms. In their study of adults with intellectual disabilities attending a day center, Wilson & Haire (1990) noted that health problems had been overlooked in instances when carers believed the person to be in good health. In the same study, the authors found that carers failed to predict sensory impairment in 50% of patients who had difficulties in hearing or vision. This was happening even in adults who had been given hearing aids and who did not receive check-ups for any further problems.

Physicians also need to ensure that checks are done for medical conditions that have a high prevalence in people with intellectual disabilities, even in the absence of obvious symptoms. Evenhuis (1997) found that people with intellectual disabilities tended to tolerate symptoms or express them atypically as irritability, inactivity, loss of appetite and sleep problems, particularly for conditions such as visual impairment, hearing loss, chest pain, dyspnea, dyspepsia and micturition.

Adults with mild intellectual disabilities are able to locate pain in the same way as controls, according to Bromley *et al.* (1998) who found that adults with intellectual disabilities could indicate pain using a body map and photographs. Some adults may be able to inform the physician of their symptoms but may need some basic aids and additional time to express themselves. Kinnell (1987) has suggested that adults who cannot communicate well may have learnt to suppress mention of bodily functions, may have limited vocabulary and speech or may not have been given the opportunity to express themselves, especially if the family is under stress. It is difficult in this situation for the physician to obtain the relevant information, as the adult may well not have expressed his or her discomfort to others. Adults with intellectual disabilities may also benefit from advice and explanations on procedures from either the physician or their carer. This, unfortunately, may be placing unrealistic additional demands on the time of the physician. Duckworth *et al.* (1993), in investigating the skills involved in interviewing people with intellectual disabilities, highlighted the difficulty of time constraints when a physician may be forced to ignore the patient in order to elicit information quickly from the carer.

Kerr (1998) highlighted the problem of history taking if people cannot speak for themselves or are slow at getting information across, while Lennox *et al.* (1997) found that difficulties with history taking and communication were most prominent in primary care physicians' responses to an open-ended question on barriers to care. This problem can also be exacerbated for adults in residential services if, due to staff turnover, there is no one with adequate knowledge of the adult with whom to communicate (Crocker & Yankauer, 1987; Lennox *et al.*, 1997). Numerous authors have highlighted the need for the patient to be accompanied by someone who knows them well. This may be difficult for the physician to influence unless there is an existing relationship with the staff group. Accurate medical records, however, can reduce many of the difficulties for the physician in having to base a diagnosis on information that may be unreliable (Crocker & Yankauer, 1987).

Knowledge, attitudes and accessing specialist services

The physician's role in caring for people with intellectual disabilities can vary according to the health care system of the country and the specialism adopted. In some countries de-institutionalization has increased the primary care physician's role as the first contact with health services for people with intellectual disabilities. This has raised some concern as to whether the providers of services in the community have the concentration of specialist knowledge previously found in the institutions. Lennox *et al.* (1997) found that primary care physicians listed lack of knowledge of conditions or illnesses as among the top five barriers to care. Also in the UK, Stanley (1993), in a study of 88 general practitioners (GPs), found that over one third felt that they had no confidence in treating people with intellectual disabilities, but this reduced to less than 5% for those who had some previous specialist training. In another study, Stein (2000) found that over 50% of GPs were confident in treating people with intellectual disabilities most of the time.

Beange *et al.* (1995) found 74% of 202 individuals with intellectual disabilities had conditions for which specialist care was needed. This specialist care had, however, not always been received, and half of the identified conditions were found to be inadequately managed. Minihan and Dean (1990) found that, although physicians were managing 84% of chronic health conditions, specialist care was needed at least once a year in 54% of cases. Strauss and Kastner (1996), in a comparison of mortality rates in institutions and the community, emphasized the need for contact and good referral paths to other health professionals, and for services with expertise in intellectual disabilities.

Despite this, Minihan *et al.* (1993) found that, although half the physicians expressed a need for specialist back-up, less than 50% knew of a neurologist and only 35% knew of an orthopedist who had special experience with people with intellectual disabilities and only 45% knew of an occupational therapist. Stanley (1993) reported that 40% of primary care physicians acknowledged a difficulty in accessing an intellectual disability psychiatrist and community support teams, but that only 34% had ever actually tried. Similarly Bernard and Bates (1994) found, in their survey of primary care physicians in London, England, that these physicians were confused as to the role of the psychiatrist in intellectual disabilities. In addition, 77% had not heard of the community team for intellectual disabilities in their area, and of these, 10% wanted no further information. Although an attitude survey by Kerr *et al.* (1996) showed that physicians valued the specialist teams, in a study by Stein (2000) low levels of contact between the primary care physicians and the specialist teams was reported.

Aspray *et al.* (1999) expressed a concern that specialist knowledge in intellectual disabilities is not accessible to all the health professionals who need it. The authors suggested that research done in intellectual disabilities needs to broaden into other areas of medicine and be accessible to a range of health professionals, including primary care physicians, gynecologists, dentists and geriatricians. Dissemination of knowledge, particularly through practical resources such as handbooks, resource guides (Lennox *et al.*, 1997), lists of specialist physicians, referral guides and policy documents on informed consent (Minihan *et al.*, 1993) have all been highlighted as useful by primary care physicians.

Of particular concern is a physician's lack of information on informed consent. Minihan *et al.* (1993) noted that 53% of physicians reported that they did not know who was authorized to give consent for medical treatment of their patients with intellectual disabilities, and 65% did not know where to obtain any further information. Similarly, in a study in the UK, 64% of physicians were unaware of the correct procedures for consent to treatment for people with intellectual disabilities, according to English law (Turner *et al.*, 1999). Information on informed consent for people with intellectual disabilities is of particular importance for health professionals in areas such as dentistry and gynecology.

Time and resources

Minihan and Dean (1990) found that financial considerations were the most commonly cited barrier to health care for adults with intellectual disabilities. For example, in the US, of those adults receiving Medicaid (a federal payment for health care) almost a quarter had reported instances when a health provider had refused or had shown reluctance to serve them because of the source of payment (because the Medicaid payment rate for health services is highly regulated and below equivalent payment rates for private care). In a later study, the authors suggested that accessibility to services seemed, in part, to be a function of the willingness of some physicians to provide uncompensated or undercompensated care (Minihan *et al.*, 1993). Lennox *et al.* (1997) noted that Australian GPs stated that they would be willing to see more patients with intellectual disabilities if this brought greater remuneration. As patients with intellectual disabilities are often dependent on the social system of care for their finances (Beange, 1996) or in less developed countries are reliant on other family members (Piachaud, 1994), this is likely to continue to be a significant barrier to care unless governments intervene.

Chambers *et al.* (1998) investigated consultation rates for 136 adults with intellectual disabilities being discharged from a long stay hospital and found that the workload exceeded by 3.9 times that for age and nondisabled controls matched by age and sex. Similarly, Kerr *et al.* (1996), in a single general practice-based study, found that patients with intellectual disabilities had significantly higher outpatient attendances and contact with specialist services than age and sex-matched controls from the same practice. Walsh *et al.* (1997) demonstrated that people with intellectual disabilities had a higher number of hospital admissions and a greater average length of stay than the general population. However, the mean length of hospital stay reduced to levels comparable with that for the general population when care was coordinated (Criscione *et al.*, 1993). This study found that care coordination (e.g. organizing referrals, maintaining and communicating medical record information and assisting and supporting patients to access health care services appropriately) was associated not just with reductions in length of hospital stay, but also in readmission rates and hospital charges.

Adults with intellectual disabilities, due to mobility, sensory and communication difficulties mentioned previously, may well need longer or even additional consultations to address certain medical problems. Although this may increase workload initially, early diagnosis and treatment of conditions could reduce the need for more complicated medical procedures later on, as well as giving obvious benefits for the adult. The benefits of early detection and treatment in a population which has been shown to have a high rate of unmet health needs, has been one of the strong arguments for the use of health checks with adults with intellectual disabilities (Jones & Kerr, 1997; Kerr, 1998; Martin & Roy, 1999; Webb & Rogers, 1999). Evenhuis (1997) noted that, although adults with disabilities may fail to report symptoms, conditions can be diagnosed as accurately as for adults in the general population as long as health professionals use routine diagnostic screenings employing their knowledge of risk factors and atypical presentations, and take account of carer observations.

Conclusion

The barriers to accessing health care services facing people with intellectual disabilities can be reduced through support and awareness from health professionals. Where there are problems with mobility, assistive devices can be used to foster and maintain independence, and buildings housing both health care services and residential accommodation can be made more accessible. With a high prevalence of psychiatric disorder in populations of people with intellectual disabilities there may be additional behavioural issues due to underlying mental illness. As problem behaviors can mask some morbidities (e.g. dementia and epilepsy) and hinder diagnosis, this could be of particular concern for physicians. Early behaviour evaluation at a younger age may benefit health professionals by providing a historical baseline level of behaviour from which to judge any future changes. Although physicians have expressed concerns that behaviour can be difficult to interpret, especially in considering the adult's right to refuse to consent to treatment, disruptive or embarrassing behaviors in medical offices seem to be of more concern to carers than to physicians.

Research has highlighted the reliance of many people with intellectual disabilities on carers to communicate their health needs. Patients with mild intellectual disabilities who have some communication assets were shown to tolerate rather than report symptoms (Evenhuis, 1997). For individuals living in staffed homes this could be of particular concern as residents are often accompanied by different members of staff who may or may not be familiar with the medical history of the person brought for examination or service. There may be an increased need, therefore, for particular attention to be paid in obtaining the past medical notes for individuals with intellectual disabilities and for ensuring access to these notes for any specialists involved with their care.

Primary care physicians have expressed a concern over their lack of knowledge of the illnesses and conditions found to be more prevalent among adults with intellectual disabilities. This lack of confidence was found to reduce, however, when physicians had received some specialist training. In addition, physicians in the UK have requested that knowledge about intellectual disabilities become available to professionals in other health disciplines. In light of the lack of knowledge shown by physicians in many countries about specialist care available for adults with intellectual disabilities, broader dissemination of research about intellectual disabilities may be of benefit. Of particular benefit would be information about the correct procedures for consent to treatment for patients with intellectual disabilities, which has clear importance for physicians across various medical disciplines.

Finally, the issues of finance and resources are obvious problems in treating people with intellectual disabilities. People with intellectual disabilities have a higher use of medical resources than the general population due to additional health needs. Care coordination is one method, which has been found to make more efficient use of resources and therefore wherever possible should be maximised. In addition, successful diagnosis of conditions and early intervention could allow treatment at a younger age, which can be preventative to secondary illness and thus reduce use of resources. Similarly, the use of preventative medicine such as health checks and routine diagnostic screening is likely to benefit persons of all ages with intellectual disabilities.

The physician stands as the cornerstone of health care delivery, yet is dependent on others to ensure that individuals with intellectual disabilities can achieve health gain. The barriers will only be removed by individuals, carers and professionals alike working together. In this context apparent 'deficits' in care can be formulated as problems with health systems recognising need, rather than professional or other failure.

References

Aspray T., Francis, R.M., Tyler, S.P. & Quilliam, S.J. (1999) Patients with learning disability in the community. *British Medical Journal*, **318**, 476–477.

Aylward, E.H., Burt, D.B., Thorpe, L.U., Lai, F. & Dalton A. (1997) Diagnosis of dementia in individuals with intellectual disability. *Journal of Intellectual Disability Research*, **41**, 152–164.

Beange, H. (1996) Caring for a vulnerable population. *Medical Journal of Australia*, **164**, 159–160.

Beange, H. & Bauman, A. (1990) Caring for the developmentally disabled in the community. *Australian Family Physician*, **19**, 1558–1563.

Beange, H., McElduff, A. & Baker, W. (1995) Medical disorders of adults with mental retardation: A population study. *American Journal of Mental Retardation*, **99**, 595–604.

Bernard, S.H. & Bates, R.E. (1994) The role of the psychiatrist in learning disability: How it is perceived by the general practitioner. *Psychiatric Bulletin*, **18**, 205–206.

Bromley, J., Emerson, E. & Caine, A. (1998) The development of a self report measure to assess the location and intensity of pain in people with intellectual disabilities. *Journal of Intellectual Disability Research*, **42**, 72–80.

Chambers, R., Milsom, G., Evans, N., Lucking, A. & Campbell, I. (1998) The primary care workload and prescribing costs associated with patients with learning disability discharged from long-stay care to the community. *British Journal of Learning Disabilities*, **26**, 9–12.

Cooper, S.A. (1997) Epidemiology of psychiatric disorders in the elderly compared with younger adults with learning disabilities. *British Journal of Psychiatry*, **170**, 375–380.

Criscione, T., Kastner, T.A., Walsh, K.K. & Nathanson, R. (1993) Managed health care services for people with mental retardation: impact on inpatient utilization. *Mental Retardation*, **31**, 297–306.

Crocker A.C. & Yankauer, A. (1987) Basic Issues. *Mental Retardation*, **25**, 227–232.

Davidson, P.W., Houser, K.D., Cain, N.N., Sloane-Reeves, J., Quijano, L., Matons, L., Giesow, V. & Ladringan, P.M. (1999) Characteristics of older adults with intellectual disabilities referred for crisis intervention. *Journal of Intellectual Disability Research*, **43**, 38–46.

Day, K.A. (1987) The elderly mentally handicapped in hospital: a clinical study. *Journal of Mental Deficiency Research*, **31**, 131–146.

Duckworth, M.S., Radhakrishnan, G., Nolan, M.E. & Fraser, W.I.. (1993) Initial encounters between people with a mild handicap and psychiatrists: an investigation of a method of evaluating interview skills. *Journal of Intellectual Disability Research*, **37**, 263–276.

Evenhuis, H. (1995a) Medical aspects of ageing in a population with intellectual disability: I. Visual impairment. *Journal of Intellectual Disability Research*, **39**, 19–25.

Evenhuis, H. (1995b) Medical aspects of ageing in a population with intellectual disability: II. Hearing impairment. *Journal of Intellectual Disability Research*, **39**, 27–33.

Evenhuis, H. (1997) Medical aspects of ageing in a population with intellectual disability: Mobility, internal conditions and cancer. *Journal of Intellectual Disability Research*, **41**, 8–18.

Howells, G. (1986) Are the medical needs of mentally handicapped adults being met? *Journal of the Royal College of General Practitioners*, **36**, 449–453.

Janicki, M.P. & Dalton, A.J. (2000) Prevalence of dementia and impact on intellectual disability services. *Mental Retardation*, **38**, 277–289.

Jones, R.G. & Kerr, M.P. (1997) A randomised control trial of an opportunistic health screening tool in primary care for people with intellectual disability. *Journal of Intellectual Disability Research*, **41**, 409–415.

Kerr, M.P. (1998) Primary health care and health gain for people with a learning disability. *Tizard Learning Disability Review*, **3**, 6–14.

Kerr, M.P., Richards, D. & Glover, G. (1996) Primary care for people with a learning disability – a Group Practice survey. *Journal of Applied Research in Intellectual Disability*, **9**, 347–352.

Kinnell, H.G. (1987) Community medical care of people with mental handicaps: room for improvement. *Mental Handicap*, **15**, 146–150.

Lennox, N.G. & Kerr, M.P. (1997) Primary health care and people with an intellectual disability: the evidence base. *Journal of Intellectual Disability Research*, **41**, 365–372.

Lennox, N.G., Diggens, J.N. & Ugoni, A.M. (1997) The general practice care of people with intellectual disability: barriers and solutions. *Journal of Intellectual Disability Research*, **41**, 380–390.

Lowe, K & Felce, D. (1995) How do carers assess the severity of challenging behaviour? A total population study. *Journal of Intellectual Disability Research*, **39**, 117–127.

Maaskant, M. & Haveman, M. (1989) Ageing residents in sheltered homes for persons with mental handicap in the Netherlands. *Australian and New Zealand Journal of Developmental Disabilities*, **15**, 219–230.

Martin, D.M. & Roy, A. (1999) A comparative review of primary health care models for people with learning disabilities: towards the provision of seamless health care. *British Journal of Learning Disabilities*, **27**, 58–63.

Minihan, P.M. & Dean, D.H. (1990) Meeting the needs for health services of persons with mental retardation living in the community. *American Journal of Public Health*, **80**, 1043–1048.

Minihan, P.M., Dean. D.H. & Lyons, C.M. (1993) Managing the care of patients with mental retardation: a survey of physicians. *Mental Retardation*, **31**, 239–246.

Moss, S.C. (1991) Age and functional abilities of people with a mental handicap: evidence for the Wessex Mental Handicap Register. *Journal of Mental Deficiency Research*, **35**, 430–445.

Moss, S., Emerson, E., Kiernan, C., Turner, S., Hatton, C. & Alborz, A. (2000)

Psychiatric symptoms in adults with learning disability and challenging behaviour. *British Journal of Psychiatry*, **177**, 452–456.

Paul, A. (1997) Epilepsy or stereotypy? Diagnostic issues in learning disabilities. *Seizure*, **6**, 111–120.

Piachaud, J. (1994) Strengths and difficulties in developing countries: the case of Zimbabwe. In: *Mental Health in Mental Retardation Recent Advances and Practices* (ed. N. Bouras) pp. 383–392. Cambridge University Press, New York.

Qureshi, H. & Alborz, A. (1992) Epidemiology of challenging behaviour. *Mental Handicap Research*, **5** (2), 130–147.

Sonnander, K. & Claesson, M. (1997) Classification, prevalence, prevention and rehabilitation of intellectual disability: an overview of research in the People's Republic of China. *Journal of Intellectual Disability Research*, **41**, 180–192.

Stanley, R. (1993) Primary health care provision for people with learning disabilities: a survey of general practitioners. *Journal of Learning Disabilities for Nursing and Social Care*, **2** (1), 23–30.

Stein, K. (2000) Caring for people with learning disability: a survey of general practitioners' attitudes in Southampton and South-West Hampshire. *British Journal of Learning Disabilities*, **28**, 9–15.

Strauss, D. & Kastner, T.A. (1996) Comparative mortality of people with mental retardation in institutions and the community. *American Journal on Mental Retardation*, **101**, 26–40.

Turner, N.J., Brown, A.R. & Baxter, K.F. (1999) Consent to treatment and the mentally incapacitated adult. *Journal of the Royal Society of Medicine*, **92**, 290–292.

Walsh, K.K., Kastner, T. & Criscione, T. (1997) Characteristics of hospitalisations for people with developmental disabilities: utilization, costs and impact of care coordination. *American Journal on Mental Retardation*, **101**, 505–520.

Webb, O. & Rogers, L. (1999) Health screening for people with intellectual disability: the New Zealand experience. *Journal of Intellectual Disability Research*, **43**, 497–503.

Whitfield, M., Langan, J. & Russell, O. (1996) Assessing general practitioners' care of adult patients with learning disability: case-control study. *Quality in Health Care*, **5**, 31–35.

Wilson, D.N. & Haire, A. (1990) Health care screening for people with mental handicap living in the community. *British Medical Journal*, **301**, 1379–1381.

13 Future Prospects: A Challenge to Promote Wellness

Vee Prasher and Matthew Janicki

This book has highlighted a number of clinical and practical aspects of physical health affecting adults with intellectual disabilities, with a focus on their maturation, aging and lifestyle practices associated with wellness. A number of particular conditions were discussed, which significantly affect a majority of adults with intellectual disabilities; however, particular phenotypic physical problems (for example, septal heart defects in individuals with Down syndrome) were excluded and readers are referred to more specific books on such issues. Further, psychiatric and psychological concerns and extensive pondering of women's health issues were also excluded as these are extensively discussed in two companion books issued as part of this series. For these, readers are referred to Davidson *et al.* (2003) and Walsh & Heller (2002).

Much of our knowledge regarding physical health issues in adults with intellectual disabilities is based primarily on generalizations from clinical and research findings on the general population, and secondarily from the limited research base on adults and children with intellectual disabilities. US Surgeon General David Satcher (2002), when speaking on the problem of accessibility, stated, 'Too many doctors and dentists either refuse to treat people with developmental disabilities or they give them inferior care'. Using the venue of the Surgeon General's Conference on Health Disparities and Intellectual Disabilities (held December 2001 in the US), Satcher noted that more studies are needed to document the extent and causes of the health problems that adults with developmental disabilities face, as testimony from doctors, people with developmental disabilities and their families has shown that attending to such problems is a major weakness in many health systems. From his perspective, little has been done to synthesis the extant literature on health and adults and little more has been done to apply what is known to medical education.

These disparities in health knowledge and health care can stem from a number of sources, among them the vagaries of national health delivery systems; lack of sufficient research and information about the confluence of age, health and lifelong disability; the inadequate knowledge base of health practitioners; and the behavior of people with disabilities when they come into contact with the health system. Although the US Surgeon General's remarks were prepared for an American audience, they can apply to any place in the world. Given the expanded participation of people with disabilities within the fabric of local communities, it is important to better understand to what degree each of these factors contributes to the deficiencies that Satcher described, and from this knowledge to develop strategies that will lead to a better understanding of the interaction of aging and health and to the mitigation of problems associated with access to and financing of health care.

A framework for understanding research on physical health

In the near future, we expect that with the growing interest in the health of adults with intellectual disabilities, there will be more specific and accurate information made available regarding the diagnosis, assessment, management and prevention of physical disease and secondary conditions in this population. However, our clinical and research knowledge is scarce with respect to the implementation of social health policies, routine screening, health prevention and user involvement. Behavioral and the non-medical management of health conditions may in the future prove to be of greater relevance to people with intellectual disabilities than to the general population. In many countries de-institutionalization programs have now been completed or are well under way. Research and clinical experience would suggest that the transfer of focus from institutional-based services to community-based services needs to be placed in context with regard to our understanding of the nature of the health of people with intellectual disabilities. This has to be done for two reasons: the response (and adherence) to published studies which examined and reported on the health status of persons who have been institutionalized and then deinstitutionalized, and the shift of referent group from institutionalized adults to those whose lives have always been spent in their community.

The first factor (reliance on institution-based research) has particular relevance to us as studies based on institutional populations have always been somewhat suspect as to their natural application to adults with intellectual disabilities who have never experienced institutionalization. One suspects that these institutional populations may have been subject to a cohort effect given that families and local authorities generally institutionalized those children or adults for whom they could not suffi-ciently care (and who were perceived as sufficiently deviant) – either due to behavioral management issues, their physical condition or simply a lack of alternative community supports extended to families in general. For the past 40 years an extensive body of clinical knowledge has been built on institutional populations, most likely since they were 'captive' and therefore easily served as a convenience sample. Thus, the extent to which these reports explain the optimal or true nature of health conditions among all persons with intellectual disabilities is questionable. Yet, not to minimize their import, since institutional cohorts historically have represented a broad spectrum of functional abilities, these studies do have value and have provided us with a great deal of useful information. However, the question is to what extent would enriched and quality experiences in the community have changed patterns of health problems and decline that were observed in these institutionalized adults, and more truly been reflective of the optimal health status of adults with intellectual disabilities?

Thus, this brings us to the second factor. Clearly, in those nations with aggressive de-institutionalization policies coupled with well thought-out and financed community supports, there has been a sea change in the debate around health status and health services provision. One aspect of this is the debate regarding whether people with intellectual disabilities should assess generic services for physical health issues, or whether a specific service focusing on all health issues for people with intellectual disabilities should be developed. Another is to what extend can and actually do adults with intellectual disabilities access and receive needed health services as they become more like any other member of their community. Studies have shown that the more distance between formalized care and the adults, the less frequent are physician visits, routine medical care provision and specialized surveillance for health conditions. Disability provider organizations generally do a very good job of looking after the health care needs of adults on their case rolls, particularly if the adults are residents of formal group living programs (such as group homes). When left on their own, as Edgerton (1994) and others have reported, these adults tend not to see physicians or easily access formal health services. However, notwithstanding all of the difficulties reported with regard to health care provision in community settings, it is now clear that community-dwelling adults with intellectual disabilities are the contemporary referent group of choice (with the exception of special subgroups such as adults hospitalized for certain conditions, and so on). Certainly, it is our expectation that with appropriate planning and adequate financial support, adults with intellectual disabilities should be able to live comfortably in their communities and have the appropriate advocacy to allow them to live their lives to the best of their abilities.

A framework for health promotion and wellness

Given the above, we were pleased to see that contemporary studies are tackling diverse epidemiological issues and framing the status of epidemiological knowledge about the health status of adults with intellectual disabilities. To begin any effort at health promotion one must have a solid grounding in the epidemiology of conditions and knowledge of the factors that influence disease occurrence. When individuals have a lifelong condition and may be at significant risk of occurring secondary conditions, then epidemiological knowledge is even more important for it lays the groundwork to our understanding of the prevalence and nature of any condition.

Among the contributors to this book many note the importance of this first step. Beange, in particular, took the opportunity to synthesize what knowledge we have on how common are physical disorders in adults with intellectual disabilities. She pointed out that even with the number of studies investigating the prevalence of physical health that have now been reported, there remains a major absence of reported studies regarding the incidence, long term management and prognosis of a number of illnesses in adults with intellectual disabilities. This, in turn, raises the question of how best can the above-norm morbidity and mortality rates (compared to the general population) be reduced? Beange and a number of others have suggested a number of measures, including well-person checklists, improved screening and better collaboration between health and accommodation service providers, realizing that many of these issues are influenced by how well physical disorders can be reliably detected and to what extent the data is valid.

Following a solid grounding in epidemiological knowledge, we see the need for well-reasoned and tested approaches designed to provide accurate and prognostic assessment. With this in mind, Kerins and our other contributors have given us a roadmap for something that we should all keep in mind: that although the assessment procedure is much the same irrespective of the underlying level of disability, there are important and highly significant differences when applied to people with lifelong disabilities. Many adults with intellectual disabilities are unable to communicate and as such rely considerably on surrogates to speak on their behalf. Means of improving health communication and health symptomatology need to be developed. Absent reliable self-informants, carers and advocates need better ways of being able to observe, detect and report problems in the people for whom they care. Cooperation and compliance among adults with intellectual disabilities when confronted by physical examinations and investigatory tests can be at times quite limited. We certainly agree with Kerins' position that alternative means need to be developed to improve health assessments. For example, pin-prick tests or saliva examinations may be ways of assessing bodily fluids for routine screening (e.g. for thyroid disease in individuals with Down syndrome, as well as for DNA studies).

Following assessment, we enter the specialized area of cataloguing syndromes, conditions and diseases most prevalent among adults with intellectual disabilities. Historically, interest in the field of intellectual disability has been focused on the 'medical aspects' of syndromes, with articles and textbooks reporting on clinical features which now appear to have limited clinical significance (e.g. dermatoglyphs of Down syndrome, as noted by Smith & Berg, 1976). Since the 1980s, the social and human rights of people with intellectual disabilities have gained greater importance. However, with the recent completion of the human genome project, 'medical issues' affecting different syndromes, as described by O'Brien *et al.*, Rapp and Torres and select others, will once again become the focus of future research interest. This also raises some obvious questions, such as 'are there particular genes that predispose to, for example, premature cataracts or a particular form of epilepsy?'. In addition, considerable progress has been made in the management of particular conditions which affect adults with intellectual disabilities. These include hearing impairment, visual impairment, epilepsy, oral health, endocrine disorders and nutritional-related problems.

Adding to this is the work that has been developed in terms of international guidelines (e.g. Evenhuis & Nagtzaam, 1998; Janicki *et al.*, 1996; USDA & USDHHS, 2000; Working Group of the International Association of the Scientific Study of Intellectual Disability, 2001) with ongoing support from the International Association for the Scientific Study of Intellectual Disabilities (IASSID). However, implementation of widespread social surveillance and prevention policies requires continual research into the cost-analysis of such policies and their health status impact. Good health promotion and the difficulties people with intellectual disabilities face in assessing services are fundamental areas for future development.

In this book, Lennox and Baxter & Kerr have delved into some of the main issues. We also recognize outside contributions, like those of the series of reports emanating from the World Health Organization (Evenhuis *et al.*, 2001; Hogg *et al.*, 2001; Thorpe *et al.*, 2001; Walsh *et al.*, 2001; WHO, 2001) and the invitational research symposium on healthy aging and intellectual disabilities that was sponsored by the University of Illinois at Chicago (Heller *et al.*, 2002). Further, as advances in areas such as molecular genetics and drug therapy are rapidly leading to changes in the accepted management of disorders in individuals with intellectual disabilities, it is likely that 'biological markers' will soon be developed for particular disorders. It is important that such 'breakthroughs' are appropriately applied to people with intellectual disabilities; however, capacity and consent issues and ethical considerations must be involved in all of these medical advances. We are convinced that both research and the efforts of such consensus meetings need to continue to play a major part in the development of good quality health care and the development of appropriate services for people with intellectual disabilities.

A few other thoughts warrant our consideration. As noted in the report of the Chicago Invitational Research Symposium on Healthy Aging and Intellectual Disabilities (Heller *et al.*, 2002), physical health issues are significantly influenced by a number of factors. Three main life domains dominated this symposium and we see these as a good means of expanding our discussion of health and aging.

First is the consideration of the interaction of mental and physical health; second is the consideration of nutrition and health; and third is the consideration of physical conditioning and health. With regard to the first, clinical experience and the research literature support our belief that there is an interaction between mental and physical health and that it is important to identify key risk factors for disease that may bear on this interaction. With this in mind, a number of specific concerns should be raised, including considering the adverse effects of a number of exogenous factors affecting this interaction, such as the effects of physical and mental abuse on health – both short and long term – and predispositions for being affected by stress. While we recognize that there is an important link between the psyche and the body, we also recognize that there is a continuing need for more reliable, valid and standardized screening tools for assessing health status and personal condition.

Given the above, a research agenda needs to include an examination of competence and consent aspects for participants in research, an assessment of the interaction of general life satisfaction and health status, and the impact of confident relationships and friends of substance, as well as a daily routine of meaningful activities, as a contributor to health and wellness. Other areas that warrant attention include the effects of staff knowledge and competence on identifying and maintaining health status, identifying effective means of promoting healthy lifestyles, the relationship of poverty and health status using cross-cultural studies to tease out culturally beneficial health practices, and identifying the key factors that make for 'healthy agers' (as to who are the people who survive the longest and why do they survive in good health for as long as they do).

With regard to the second area, nutrition and wellness, we see a need to better understand some of the metabolic and dietary challenges facing older adults with intellectual and developmental disabilities as they age, including on the plus side the trend toward healthier nutrient intake, and on the minus side the fact that many adults with intellectual disabilities are overweight and are at risk for significant health problems due to obesity. Interestingly, although one would imagine that nutrition and caloric intake would be a fairly simple matter, even here there are definitional difficulties – beginning with a significant problem with data collection standardization on nutritional status and diet. In addition, genetics play a role in metabolism and related factors, such that there are notable differences in exercise and weight conditions among syndromes (for example, among adults with Down syndrome in contrast to most other etiologies of intellectual disability).

In the area of nutrition and wellness, there are a number of research areas of importance, including examining nutritional issues through comparative studies of Down syndrome versus other etiologies of intellectual disability, identifying factors that significantly contribute to obesity and weight difficulties, examining the meaning of food and its implications on mental health, and the effects of staff and carer role models on eating habits and weight status. As noted by Heller *et al.* (2002), other relevant research areas include the use of longitudinal designs that 'track' populations to look at weight and physical status over a lifetime, as well as ones that can identify factors contributing to obesity, examine medication effects and dietary outcomes, and assess the relationship of eating habits and stress.

The third area of consideration revolves around physical activity. Here ideas about promoting wellness are often more diffuse since little research provides a basis for hypothesis framing. However, one area of concern revolves around how to motivate people with intellectual and developmental disabilities to exercise. Heller *et al.* (2002) have suggested that eliminating barriers to exercise and introducing both passive and active exercise modalities should be an important feature in promoting exercise. With this in mind, some areas for potential research include examining the effects of exercise differences among various etiologies of intellectual disability, identifying barriers to exercise and the effects of stress from 'involuntary' exercise, and assessing how to best promote coordination and balance (and thus decrease the rate of falls) through exercise. As Heller *et al.* (2002) have noted, other research endeavors might consider examining the effects of aerobic exercise on cardiovascular functioning, assessing the efficacy of non-traditional exercise methods (for example, Tai Chi), and conducting an in-depth analysis of nutrition and exercise – in terms of assessing which contributes more to physical wellness. Lastly, on a more social level, we would suggest examining means of tying into 'aging friendly communities' initiatives and their health promotion and exercise programs.

'Aging friendly communities' initiatives are when a community recognizes that it is composed of a significant number of older citizens and consequently develops and carries out a plan to make its physical and social amenities and other aspects completely accessible and available to its older citizens. This may involve physical barrier removal in public and private facilities, transportation resources and streets and sidewalks;

social resource investment to develop and maintain programs and facilities for the well elderly; and putting more control in the hands of its older citizens over the physical and social fabric of their community.

Some closing thoughts

As the US Surgeon General has remarked, more studies are needed to document the extent and causes of health problems and the disparities in accessing health care for people with intellectual and developmental disabilities. Thus, the future needs to be aimed at specifically addressing this challenge. There continues to be a need for more effective education and training in the assessment, diagnosis, management and care provision of physical health in people with intellectual disabilities. There remains a need for all professionals involved in care provision, such as community physicians, community care workers and specialist and generic services, to be more aware of the important health issues facing people with intellectual disabilities. Postgraduate training organizations, such as universities, must incorporate the need for better education. Further scientific research is required to determine how best to inform and educate a wide range of individuals who are involved in the care of persons with intellectual disabilities (such as families, paid carers, general practitioners, paramedical professionals, specialists and researchers). With the growth in the world wide web and better communication and initial access to information, resources are now widely available to disseminate appropriate knowledge to families, students, professionals and organizational agencies who are involved in the care of people with intellectual disabilities.

Physical health care for people with intellectual disabilities remains an important area of concern and there will always be a need for better education, assessment and management, and greater multidisciplinary and multiagency service development. This book aims to, in part, rectify some of these disparities and deficiencies.

References

Davidson, P., Prasher, V.P. & Janicki, M. (2003) *Mental Health, Intellectual Disabilities, and the Aging Process*. Blackwell Publishing, Oxford, UK.

Edgerton, R. (1994) Quality of life issues: Some people know how to be old. In: *Life Course Perspectives on Adulthood and Old Age* (eds M.M. Seltzer, M.W. Krauss & M.P. Janicki) pp. 53–66. American Association on Mental Retardation, Washington.

Evenhuis, H. & Nagtzaam, L.M.D. (eds) (1998) IASSID International Consensus Statement. *Early identification of hearing and visual impairment in children and adults with an intellectual disability.* IASSID, Special Interest Research Group on Health Issues. Available on www.iassid.org

Evenhuis, H., Henderson, C.M., Beange, H., Lennox, N. & Chicoine, B. (2001) Healthy ageing – adults with intellectual disabilities: physical health issues. *Journal of Applied Research in Intellectual Disabilities,* **14**, 175–194.

Heller, T., Janicki, M.P., Gill, C. & Factor, A. (2002) *Health disparities and a paradigm for health promotion: Report of the invitational symposium on health, aging, and developmental disabilities.* Department of Human Development and Disability, University of Illinois at Chicago.

Hogg, J., Lucchino, R., Wang, K.Y. & Janicki, M. (2001) Healthy ageing – adults with intellectual disabilities: ageing and social policy. *Journal of Applied Research in Intellectual Disabilities,* **14**, 229–255.

Janicki, M.P., Heller, T., Seltzer, G. & Hogg, J. (1996) Practice guidelines for the clinical assessment and care management of Alzheimer's disease and other dementias among adults with intellectual disability. *Journal of Intellectual Disability Research,* **40**, 374–382.

Satcher, D. (2002) Health disparities and mental retardation. US Public Health Service. *Closing the Gap: a National Blueprint for Improving the Health of Individuals with Mental Retardation.* Report of the Surgeon General's Conference on Health Disparities and Mental Retardation. Washington, DC, USA.

Smith, G.F. & Berg, J.M. (1976) Down's anomaly. In: *Dermatoglyphs* (eds G.F. Smith & J.M. Berg) pp. 76–99. Churchill Livingstone, New York.

Thorpe, L., Davidson, P. & Janicki, M.P. (2001) Healthy ageing – adults with intellectual disabilities: behavioural issues. *Journal of Applied Research in Intellectual Disabilities,* **14**, 218–228.

USDA & USDHHS (2000) *Nutrition and Your Health: Dietary Guidelines for Americans,* 5th edn. Home and Garden Bulletin No. 232. US Department of Agriculture and US Department of Health and Human Services, Washington DC.

Walsh, P. & Heller, T. (2002) *Health of Women with Intellectual Disabilities.* Blackwell Publishing, Oxford, UK.

Walsh, P.N., Heller, T., Schupf, N. & van Schronjenstein Lantman-de Valk, H. (2001) Healthy ageing – adults with intellectual disabilities: women's health and related issues. *Journal of Applied Research in Intellectual Disabilities,* **14**, 195–217.

WHO (2001) World Health Organization. Healthy ageing – adults with intellectual disabilities: summative report. *Journal of Applied Research in Intellectual Disabilities,* **14**, 256–275.

Working Group of the International Association of the Scientific Study of Intellectual Disability (2001) Clinical guidelines for the management of epilepsy in adults with an intellectual disability. *Seizure,* **10**, 401–409.

Appendix
IASSID Physical Health Recommendations for Adults with an Intellectual Disability (ID)

This has been modified from Beange, H., Lennox, N.G. & Parmenter, T. (1999) Targets for people with intellectual disability. *Journal of Intellectual and Developmental Disability*, **24**, 283–297.

Dental health

Education and behavioral interventions, which ensure that appropriate dietary habits are established and oral hygiene practices are made a part of the daily life of persons with ID, should be directed toward individuals with ID, and their caregivers, to the maximum extent possible.

Schedule dental visits for oral examinations and prophylaxis at three-month intervals for those with active disease and those at high risk for oral disease (most ID patients) and every six months for persons judged to be at low risk by the dental care team. This should be part of the overall health maintenance program for persons with ID.

Preventive therapies such as fluoride or anti-microbial agents should be implemented where indicated.

Multidisciplinary team approaches incorporating input from medical professionals and mental health providers, as well as dentists and dental hygienists, need to be adopted in many patients to ensure optimal oral health.

Vision

For adults with intellectual disabilities, routine screening for age-related visual loss at 45 years and every five years thereafter has been recommended. If possible this should be done by an ophthalmologist. An extra vision check at age 30 years has been recommended for adults with Down syndrome.

Hearing

Routine screening for age-related hearing loss of all adults at age 45 years and every five years thereafter has been recommended. If possible this should be done by an audiologist. Screening of the hearing function of adults with Down syndrome is recommended every three years throughout life.

Nutrition

Nutrition risk screening provides a systematic approach to improving recognition and management of nutrition problems that should also benefit adults with intellectual disabilities. Screening for nutrition-related problems could be performed by anyone working with people with disabilities provided a simplified screening tool is developed. The tool should use indicators of weight and weight change, eating abilities, general appearance and a simple assessment of their food and fluid intake. Some basic knowledge of nutrition and knowledge of and access to a referral system is also required. The criteria for referral should be clear and as specific as possible. Simple and safe nutrition interventions should be applicable with the use of basic nutrition educational materials.

Individuals at high risk should be referred for a more systematic assessment of nutritional status by an experienced dietitian. People with persistent underweight or overweight, eating and drinking problems, chronic constipation or specific medical conditions requiring more complex nutrition interventions (such as Celiac disease) would be among those needing systematic assessment. A dietitian, preferably working with an interdisciplinary health care team, should review the screening form and conduct assessment of nutritional status. To be comprehensive, the process involves using medical, nutritional and medication histories; physical examination and anthropometric measurements; and biochemical data.

Epilepsy

Ensure all individuals with epilepsy:

- have a plan for the acute management of seizures
- have a yearly assessment for medication side effects
- are assessed for accuracy of epilepsy diagnosis, appropriateness of current therapy and potential for improvement with further treatment

- are not restricted in terms of social, educational or employment access as a result of their epilepsy.

Provide education on epilepsy to all individuals and their carers.

Ensure all individuals and their carers have appropriate education on hazard, especially safe bathing and water hazard.

Ensure respite services are available which can support the management of seizures, in particular the administration of rectal diazepam.

Thyroid disease

Thyroid disease should be considered at any new presentation. Thyroid function tests should be performed on any unusual presentation and annually in high risk subgroups (patients with Down syndrome and patients with a previous history of thyroid disease). Thyroid function tests should be performed every three to five years in other patients with development disabilities. The management is usually straightforward but may involve supervision of medication.

Gastroesophageal reflux disease and Helicobacter pylori

Identify and treat gastroesophageal reflux disease and illness from Helicobacter pylori infection. Treatment should be undertaken with the same indications as for the general population.

Osteoporosis

Osteoporosis is common and would be best prevented. This requires a global approach, with the lifelong goal of optimizing activity and nutrition, particularly calcium intake. People with intellectual disabilities should be screened by osteodensitometry at least once in early adulthood; further decisions regarding progress screening should be based on that result. Individuals who have low sunlight exposure either due to management practices or to local climatic conditions, or who are receiving anticonvulsant therapy, should have vitamin D status assessed, and a vitamin D supplement if identified as deficient. All women should have bone mineral density assessed at the time of cessation of menstruation regardless of the reason for menopause, and all hypogonadal men require assessment. The local recommendations for treatment of osteoporosis in the general population should be followed and any decision to provide a different standard of care from that of the general population should be explicit.

Medication review

Medication should be regularly reviewed, ideally every three months and particularly when polypharmacy exists. Prescribers need to acknowledge the inherent difficulties with monitoring and ensure that the patient and carers safely and reliably administer medication, are able to recognize adverse effects, monitor the efficacy of the medication and are aware of the review process. Systems for prepackaging doses for community-based patients to maximize compliance and safety should be considered. Structured mechanisms for monitoring efficacy are valuable. Consumer and carer education on the use of medication is important in ensuring compliance, recognizing side effects and maximizing efficacy. Continuing re-evaluation should ensure the least effective dose. Side effects should be monitored and ineffective drugs discontinued.

Immunization status

Immunization schedules for adults with intellectual disabilities should follow national guidelines. At a minimum we should ensure that immunization rates for adults with intellectual disabilities are the same as for the general community. Hepatitis A and B immunizations are indicated for people who live in institutions, and hepatitis B is indicated for contacts of persons who are hepatitis B carriers. Immunization against influenza and the pneumococcus is recommended for the medically vulnerable.

The physical activity and exercise

The American College of Sports Medicine and the Centers for Disease Control and Prevention recommend 30 minutes or more of moderate intensity physical activity on most, preferably all, days of the week for the general population. It should be possible to ensure this amount of moderate activity for most people with disabilities. Two cardiovascular training programs have been developed for people with intellectual disabilities. Some active or passive movement should be provided daily for those with limited mobility due to physical impairment. Some special services will be necessary for those who cannot access services for the general population.

Comprehensive health assessments

Organize regular comprehensive physical assessment and review by a medical practitioner.

Index